Germaine

Elizabeth Kleinhenz

Germaine

the life of Germaine Greer

SCRIBE

Melbourne • London

Scribe Publications
2 John St, Clerkenwell, London, WC1N 2ES, United Kingdom
3754 Pleasant Ave, Suite 100, Minneapolis, Minnesota 55409, USA
18–20 Edward St, Brunswick, Victoria 3056, Australia

Published by Scribe 2018

Typeset in 11.5/16 pt Sabon by Midland Typesetters, Australia
Printed and bound in the UK by CPI Group (UK) Ltd, Croydon CR0 4YY

Scribe Publications is committed to the sustainable use of natural resources
and the use of paper products made responsibly from those resources.

9781911617914 (UK edition)
9781947534780 (US edition)
9781925693560 (e-book)

A CiP entry for this title is available from the British Library.

scribepublications.co.uk
scribepublications.com

For Emily, Isobel, Jake, Ava and Dan

Contents

Introduction

'Brave woman!'

How often have I heard those words spoken by people who have discovered that I am writing a biography of Germaine Greer. They are speaking not of her, but of me.

I am not especially brave, but nor am I afraid of Germaine Greer. Well, maybe just a little bit. In 2015, when I embarked on the project, my knowledge of her personal life was sketchy. I did not know how opposed she was to the idea of anyone writing a biography of her. She had sold her archive to the University of Melbourne by that time, and it seemed reasonable – even obvious – to me that the archive should be used as a biographical source. I had read and enjoyed Christine Wallace's 1997 biography *Untamed Shrew*, but it was not until I was well advanced into my research that I discovered the full extent of Greer's opposition to that book, and was shocked by her venomous attacks on its author. By then I had found a publisher and it was too late to go back. Not that I would have anyway, for Germaine's life was proving much too interesting.

Before I started work on the biography I wrote politely to Greer, telling her that I was planning to study her archive and asking her if she had any preferences as to how it might be explored by researchers such as myself. I addressed her as 'Dr Greer'. She responded coldly – rudely, actually – that it was not up to her but to the university, who now owned the archive, to decide how it should be used. She would not interfere, she wrote, but nor would she assist me in any way. Finally, she admonished me for failing to get her title right. She was 'Professor', not 'Dr'.

In February 2018, she wrote to me again, addressing me as 'Mrs Kleinhenz', knowing full well that my title is 'Dr'. 'Oh Ger*maine*,' I sighed.

I first heard the name 'Germaine' in 1959, when I was a student at the Toorak Teachers' College in Melbourne. I had become friends with a group of girls who had been at school with Germaine Greer at the Star of the Sea convent in nearby Gardenvale. They, like me, were two or three years younger than she was and they spoke of her often with a kind of reverence that annoyed me. It was: 'Germaine would have something to say about this' or 'Germaine would never agree with that', or simply, with eyes raised adoringly to the heavens, 'Oh Ger*maine*!' We were all still into our religion at that time, and some of those 'Star' girls had concerns about this Germaine person's soul. 'She could be such a force for good', 'Oh, I'm sure she would never give up her faith . . .' So the conversations went. I was bored and began to conceive a mild dislike for this distant, unknown figure. Why should she be any different from the rest of us?

It would be another ten years before I found out just how different she was. I had gone on from teachers' college to Melbourne University, started on a career as an English teacher at Melbourne's top government girls' secondary school, got married, had a baby, stopped work, was living in a raw new house in a raw new suburb and was getting used to being called 'Missus' or 'Mum' by the men who delivered the bread and groceries, or tried to sell me a vacuum cleaner. All should have been well – I was doing exactly what I was expected to do – but something, something major, was wrong. In 1971 I read *The Female Eunuch* and I began to understand. Urged on by my mother, who turned out to be an unlikely feminist of the first wave, I went back to work and bought a car. 'I think you've become a women's libber,' my brother-in-law accused. 'And you,' I replied tartly, igniting a family feud that did not heal for years, 'are a male chauvinist pig.'

Who was this Germaine Greer, who changed my life and the lives of millions across the world in the middle years of the twentieth century?[1] She was born on a hot Melbourne day, 29 January 1939, as some of the bushfires of Black Friday on 13 January – the worst in Victoria's history – were still burning around the city. Her mother, Peg, was a housewife; her father, Reg, sold advertising space in a newspaper. Her parents' marriage was not happy and the situation in the Greer household worsened after Reg came back from the Second World War. Over the years, the family's economic situation improved somewhat, two more children were born and the Greers moved into larger houses, but there were few books and little conversation. Ultimately, the levels of dullness and cultural deprivation, together with a jumble of unresolved family tensions, drove Germaine to furious rebellion.

School was her great escape. An obviously gifted pupil, she won a series of scholarships that allowed her to receive the best education a financially strapped Catholic education system could provide. At Star of the Sea, the convent of the Presentation Order of nuns where she completed the final four years of her education, she shone as the brightest pupil, soaking up knowledge, and was popular with the nuns and the other girls. She stopped believing in the nuns' God, but she never lost the sense of spirituality they had instilled in her.

Her contemporaries' memories of the tall figure of Germaine Greer striding around the campuses of her two Australian universities have become the stuff of legend. At the University of Melbourne, she completed an honours degree in English and French, and at the University of Sydney she wrote her master's thesis on Byron. She excelled in university theatre productions and gravitated to bohemian circles, namely the Drift in Melbourne and the Push in Sydney. The influence of the libertarian, anarchist philosophies and principles so fiercely argued by her Push friends and her lover of that time, Roelof Smilde, never left her.

From Sydney she won a Commonwealth Scholarship to Cambridge, where she wrote her doctoral thesis on love and marriage in Shakespeare's comedies. Once again she was a star in university theatre, becoming one of the first women to be elected to the elite Footlights dramatic club. She worked furiously on her thesis, aiming to gain a post at an English university. This turned out to be Warwick, one of the newer universities that were starting to appear in England at that period, where she was appointed as an assistant lecturer in 1967.

No family or friends were present to support her when she proceeded to the dais of the ancient Cambridge Senate House to receive her PhD from the Vice-Chancellor in March 1968. She was also alone, in a different sense, in her three-week marriage to Paul du Feu, scholar turned labourer, which took place in May of the same year. She did not marry again and she has never sustained any long-term partnerships. She has many good friends but true intimacy has eluded her. 'I am unusually insecure in relationships,' she told psychologist and television presenter Anthony Clare in 1989. 'I'm a bolter, when things get difficult, I bolt . . .'[2]

For the first few years after she left Cambridge, Germaine Greer had three identities. Mostly, she was Dr Greer, brilliant teacher and serious scholar at the University of Warwick, but each week, she travelled to the Granada studios in Manchester to perform in the national TV comedy *Nice Time*. At weekends, she caught up with friends in the emerging London underground, rock music and hippie scenes, to become a self-proclaimed, flamboyantly attired groupie. She wrote provocative articles for the London *Oz* magazine and was a founding editor of the Amsterdam-based pornographic publication *Suck*.

Her life, and the lives of millions of women across the world, changed in 1970 with the publication of her first book, *The Female Eunuch*. This book's central argument – that 'castrated' women should look to their own minds and bodies to recover and assert their female power before trying to change the world around them – was received more enthusiastically by ordinary women than by the established feminists of the second wave. She had never been a paid-up member of any feminist group, and many in the sisterhood were irked when she became, overnight, an icon of feminism. Nevertheless, *The Female Eunuch* became a – perhaps the – classic text of their movement. It brought Germaine wealth and fame. It made her an international celebrity.

In the 1970s, she bought and decorated beautiful houses in London and Tuscany, she created magnificent gardens, and entertained and was entertained by some of the most famous literary and artistic figures in the world. But always she remained a committed professional with an extraordinary work ethic. After her resignation from Warwick University in 1972 she became a working journalist, travelling extensively to report on the lives of ordinary people, especially women, who were suffering in countries like Vietnam, India, Bangladesh and famine-torn Ethiopia. Her archive houses many of the remarkable photographs she took in those communities.

In 1979, she accepted a position at the University of Tulsa, Oklahoma, as Professor of Modern Letters. On taking up the appointment she became founder and director of the Tulsa Center for the Study of Women's Literature. By that time she was beginning to realise, with great sadness, that her efforts to become pregnant, which included expensive Harley Street surgery, had failed and that she would never bear a child.

In 1985, after returning to England, she sold her home in London and moved to Mill Farm, later The Mills, a house on a small acreage at Stump Cross, near the town of Saffron Walden in Essex. Her years at The Mills, which Greer put on the market in 2018, have probably been the most contented of her life. She has been incredibly busy – away from home for long periods on lecture and promotional tours, regularly appearing on television and radio, writing books, articles and newspaper columns, attending to a huge volume of correspondence and carrying out literary research on her special interests: Shakespeare, and women artists and writers. She has done most of her work in her workshop, a large building separate from the main house at The Mills, with the aid of an assistant. This building housed her archive before it was sold to the University of Melbourne in 2013. It was also the home of Stump Cross Books, a self-financed venture dedicated to publishing the works of women writers.

No long-term lovers or friends ever lived with Greer on a permanent basis at The Mills; instead, she shared her house with a moving feast of individuals she called 'Other Peoples' Children' (OPCs) and 'Non-Paying Guests' (NPGs), many of whom were university students who were expected to work in the house, workshop and garden in exchange for their keep. Most of all she loved her standard poodles, her parrot and her cats.

From The Mills, which is only a short drive to Cambridge,

Greer was able to resume her connections with Newnham College and its library. In 1989 she was appointed as a special lecturer and unofficial fellow of Newnham, posts she held until 1998, when she resigned because of her opposition to a transgender woman becoming a fellow of the college.

In 1989, Greer wrote her most personal book, *Daddy, We Hardly Knew You.* It tells of her lonely journey across several continents to find out the truth about her father's life, only to discover, finally, that he was a liar and a fraud.

Between 1979 and 1999, in addition to scholarly works (notably *Shakespeare*, for the Oxford University Press Past Masters series), and *Daddy . . .*, Germaine Greer wrote three major books about women: *Sex and Destiny: The politics of human fertility* in 1984; *The Change: Women, ageing and the menopause* in 1991; and *The Whole Woman* in 1999. In each, she set down her thoughts about women's lives at particular life stages – each stage matching the one she herself was experiencing at that period.

Germaine Greer has lived most of her life in England, but for the past twenty years or so she has spent at least four months of each year in Australia. In 2013 she published *White Beech: The rainforest years*, which tells of her discovery and purchase of Cave Creek, a former farm in Southern Queensland, where she decided to live and work for part of every year as the director of a major rainforest rehabilitation project.

She has donated most of the three million dollars she was paid for her archive to Friends of Gondwana Rainforest, a charity she founded, whose flagship project is the Cave Creek Rainforest Rehabilitation Scheme (CCRRS).

On 29 January 2019, she will turn eighty. She continues to appear regularly on radio and television programs and to perform on public platforms in England and Australia.

The main source of information for this biography has been Germaine Greer herself – her writing, her theatre and media performances and interviews, her lectures, her academic research, her journalism. She does not hold back. For a person who insists that her personal life is not interesting, she has told us all we need to know about herself and more.

Another major source for the biography was the large volume of writing *about* Germaine from authors like David Plante, James Hughes-Onslow, Barry Humphries, Clive James, Ian Britain and Richard Neville.

Some of her old friends and acquaintances, most notably Richard Walsh, Phillip Frazer, Professor Stephen Knight, Fay Weldon and Carmen Callil, were happy to share their memories of Germaine Greer with me, but others I approached chose to remain silent. Some asked to be anonymous and I have respected their wishes while noting their comments.

In 2016, I was fortunate to meet and make friends with a group of former Star of the Sea nuns and students who were Germaine's contemporaries at school and had known her well. They and various other people who remembered her at university were more than happy to reminisce about their association with her.

The Germaine Greer Archive is another rich source of information about Greer's life and work. To say that it is massive would be an understatement. Currently, it occupies eighty-two metres of shelf space at the University of Melbourne Archives repository in Brunswick. There are about five hundred boxes that include personal, professional and other correspondence; notes and drafts relating to all of her academic studies; copies of all of her major works, with drafts, research materials, proofs, clippings and publicity; files on her print, radio and television journalism and appearances, with contracts and commissions; photographs; records relating to university appointments; research files on women and literature and women artists; the records of Stump Cross Books; honours and awards; and an extensive collection of audiovisual material.

Between March 2017 and February 2018 I spent many hours going through the boxes and listening to the audio tapes in the Germaine Greer Collection, searching for material that would inform the kind of biographical study I wanted to write. Greer has claimed that the archive is more of a representation of the times she has lived in than of herself, but in saying this she is only partly right, for what emerges from those five hundred boxes is a portrait of an extraordinary woman whose influence on the culture and mores of her time has been immense.

When deciding to write Germaine's story, I wanted to discover 'the truth' about her life, but one of the first lessons she taught me was how hard this was likely to be. 'None of us,' she wrote in 1989, 'grasps more than a little splinter of the truth.' I have endeavoured to gather some of those splinters and piece them together to create a 'truthful' coherent narrative about her life and work, but splinters they are and must remain.

In shaping the narrative, the first task I set myself was to consider her contribution to second-wave feminism. I had no wish to embark on an academic study of the many facets of this subject – better to leave that to the professional scholars in the burgeoning field of women's studies. My conclusions have been drawn from extensive study of Greer's work in light of the professional literature, but they are also based on a series of more personal impressions about a movement from which I and my contemporaries benefited and in which we participated. Only two things are certain: first, women's lives today are very different from how they were when Germaine Greer and I left school, and second, much of the change that has occurred over the past half century can be directly attributed to her influence.

My next task appeared to be more straightforward. I wanted to find out who she was – really. At first, I thought this would be a matter of exploring behind what I perceived to be the mask of her public appearances. My original working title for the book was, in fact, 'Behind the Mask', but this had to change when I realised that there is no mask. In public, as in private, as in her writing and performances, she is complex, engaging, amusing, often puzzling and frustrating, occasionally downright nasty, but if she is hiding anything of significance about herself, I have not been able to find it.

In other words, what you see with Germaine Greer is what you get. When she says, 'I don't know why I am the way I am', and 'Bugger me if I know why I'm famous', she is telling the simple truth. Rare talent like hers is never contrived. Her gifts were apparent in her earliest years and it has been natural though not easy for her to hone and cultivate those gifts through a lifetime of intense scholarship and unremitting hard work.

Some people of her own generation, especially old white males and illiberal women, still tend to dismiss her as a ratbag and, to be fair, she often acts like one. Others, however, including feminist publisher Carmen Callil and writer Fay Weldon, consider her to be a genius. I have come to believe that history will prove them right, that new generations will acknowledge the genius of Germaine Greer, and that she will ultimately be recognised as one of the most influential and significant women in the Australian diaspora.

1

Who does she think she is?

Happy families are all alike; every unhappy family is unhappy in its own way.

Leo Tolstoy, *Anna Karenina*

Germaine Greer was five years old when she and her mother went to Spencer Street station in Melbourne to pick up her father from the troop train. She had only the haziest memories of him, but she knew from the photograph on the maple sideboard at home that he would be handsome and smiling. She was sure she would recognise him.

Spencer Street station in 1944 smelled of stale urine.[1] Twenty-seven-year-old Peggy Greer was searching for her husband, at first eagerly, then anxiously, then frantically, dragging her little daughter behind her along the platform. Several times Germaine was almost knocked over in the crush of the returning servicemen's greatcoats. She began to daydream, convinced that her father was not there as, gradually, the crowds of men and their welcoming families grew thinner.

Suddenly, Peggy stopped and let go of her daughter's arm. An old man was standing by a pylon, staring mindlessly. 'His neck stuck scrawnily out of the collar of his grey-blue greatcoat. His eyes were sunken, grey and loose.'[2] Surely, thought the little girl, her mother could not be intending to bring this unfortunate person home. Much better for her to stick with one of those generous American soldiers who had been so kind to her family while her father was away.

'I had a good time with the Yanks,' Peggy told journalist Christine Wallace, who wrote the first biography of Germaine Greer in the late 1990s. 'They were nice to Germaine, too. They'd go into her nursery with cigars and tell her bedtime stories . . . Perhaps I shouldn't have done that . . .'

Perhaps she shouldn't have.

The Americans on rest and recreation leave produced a deep, competitive anger among Australian men fighting overseas who had left wives and girlfriends behind at home . . . Peggy felt threatened because she thought her daughter might have witnessed an infidelity . . . 'And she's right,' Germaine reflected more than forty years later . . . 'I was a witness . . . I can remember one episode . . . which was nearly fatal . . . I was given a knockout drop . . . People don't forget, you know . . . Mum thought she'd got away with it, and she still thinks she got away with it, I guess.'[3]

Peggy Lafrank first met Reg Greer on a fine day on Melbourne's elegant Collins Street in 1935. She was eighteen, an apprentice milliner, clicking along in high heels, the little hat she had made herself perched on her head. Reg was lounging in the sunshine with a group of his work cronies. Peg noticed him, stopped, turned and walked past the group again. He moved across to her and invited her for a cup of coffee. She suggested the cafe in the basement of the Manchester Unity Building. He was thirty years old.

The Depression was hardly over when Peggy first brought

Reg home. A couple of months earlier, her mother, Alida 'Liddy' Lafrank, had finally seen off her abusive salesman husband and was now a single mother, struggling to provide for her family of three teenagers. This new young man of Peg's, with his good looks and delightful manners, seemed very promising. Suave, beautifully dressed and well-spoken, he had a good job as the Melbourne advertising representative for an Adelaide newspaper. Peggy would be safe with him and he would provide the family with the male protection it had lost.

Reg told them a few things about himself, but the Lafranks inferred most of what they thought they knew about him from his dapper appearance and bearing. His fine, almost English accent supported his claim to have been born in Durban in about 1905, of parents who, he hinted, were of superior colonial stock, and who had been passing through Natal from England to Australia at the time of his birth. Reg also managed to give them the impression that he had gone jackerooing after he left school and had wanted to go on the land, but that because his wealthy family had refused to support him, he had severed relations with them.

Australia is a country of immigrants. Everyone but the Indigenous inhabitants ultimately comes from somewhere else, and it is perhaps because their experiences or the experiences of their ancestors in those other places were mostly unpleasant that many families have been left without memories or records of their history. For several generations, a kind of collective amnesia prevailed. Better not to ask where your great-grandmother came from, or what she did there. It would be impolite to probe the secrets of the convict ship or the hungry hovels of slum and countryside. Mind your own business.

This prevailing reserve goes some way towards explaining why Mrs Alida Lafrank did not bother to find out more about the young man who courted and married her daughter in 1937. The Lafranks knew that Reg Greer, like Alida's departed husband, was a professional salesman but they thought of this as a recommendation rather than a cause for suspicion. They were naive. Or maybe they just believed what they wanted to believe. Times were hard.

Germaine Greer's parents, Margaret May (Peggy) Lafrank and Eric Reginald Greer, married in March 1937 at St Columba's Church, Elwood. The details recorded in the parish register show his year and place of birth as 1905 in Durban, South Africa. His father's name is recorded as Robert Greer, journalist, and his mother's as Emma Wise. This information would confuse as well as assist Germaine's efforts to trace her ancestry more than half a century later. Reg was not Catholic, but because the Lafranks were, he was ready to 'turn'[4] and to promise that any children of the marriage would be brought up Catholic. Religion meant nothing to him. 'I don't know why I'm doing this,' he told his secretary, Joyce, when he described the lessons he was required to take from the parish priest, who, he said, had opened the door of the presbytery to him and Peggy dressed in a singlet, smelling strongly of alcohol.[5]

He completed his religious instruction with typical good humour, never revealing his true convictions, if any. Some would have described his behaviour as dishonest, but Reg Greer had obviously learned somewhere that it can pay to be economical with the truth.

Many years later, when Germaine was writing her book about her father, she recalled how one would-be Greer biographer had cast Reg Greer as a brave soldier who was living in an army barracks when his first child was born. The truth was more prosaic: on that hot day in Melbourne, 29 January 1939, as Peggy laboured and the deadly bushfires of Black Friday still burned around the city, Reg was enjoying a few cool beers with his mate Wally Worboys in a flat in the bayside suburb of St Kilda.[6]

Peggy said she had chosen her baby's name from that of a minor British actress she had found in an English magazine that Reg had brought home from work. Germaine's more romantic version was that she had been named for the Comte de Saint-Germain, a character in George Sand's *The Countess of Rudolstadt*, which Peggy had been reading during her pregnancy, 'because she liked the sound of it, I reckon'.[7]

As Peggy would have known, the tradition in the Catholic Church was and is that a new baby's baptismal name should be Christian in nature: something like 'Grace' or 'Charity', or the name of a saint. Parish priests were reluctant to baptise children whose parents departed from this principle. There is a Saint Germaine – a physically deformed French peasant girl, who was beaten and abused by her wicked stepmother and forced to live outside the family house in a barn. Overcoming the many vicissitudes of her miserable life, however, she cared for the homeless and was recognised in her village for her piety. Later she was believed to have had supernatural powers of healing and was canonised by Pope Pius IX in 1869. Pilgrims still visit her shrine in the village of Pibrac, near Toulouse, and it is likely that Germaine Greer has been among those visitors.

When Germaine was a toddler, the Greers lived in a small flat in Elwood, which was then a lower-middle-class bayside suburb of Melbourne. During the day, after Reg had gone off on the tram to his office at Newspaper House in Collins Street, Peg liked to walk on the beach with her small daughter, 'a good baby'. Her husband was the breadwinner and, at least on the surface, a cheerful one.

Nearly fifty years after her parents' courtship and marriage, Germaine set out to find the truth about her father and to write about it in a book. She interviewed his former secretary, Joyce, who remembered Reg Greer as 'one of the boys', always full of jokes and stories, with a long, distinguished face that made him look like the film actor Basil Rathbone. She recalled Reg's pleasant working life at Newspaper House: at noon, after having coffee with his fellow reps at 11 am, he would enjoy an expense-account lunch with one of his various contacts, and at the end of the day he would adjourn to the Australia Hotel or the St Kilda Cricket Club to drink beers and cocktails with colleagues and clients. Although he seldom worked in the afternoons, said Joyce, Germaine's father was no slouch. He was a gun salesman, ever mindful of the need to schmooze important clients and to be in the office when his chief, Sir Lloyd Dumas, called from Adelaide.[8]

Joyce also recalled Peggy's visits to the office. 'Your mother was always very smartly dressed, wonderful little hats, you know. A milliner, wasn't she? Very striking, tall. Wearing a lot of lipstick.'[9]

On 3 September 1939, seven months after Germaine's birth, the Greers, like most Australians, gathered around their bakelite radio to hear the Prime Minister Robert Menzies perform his 'melancholy duty' of informing them that because Great Britain had declared war on Germany, Australia was also at war. Blackout curtains may have gone up in a few homes, but nothing in the Greer household changed immediately. Reg continued to go to the office each day and come home each night to his pretty young wife and baby.

In the first three months of the war, the Australian Government managed to enlist only twenty thousand men in the Second Australian Imperial Forces. But this initial reluctance to fight turned around dramatically after Germany overran France in the northern hemisphere spring of 1940. Following the evacuation of Allied troops from Dunkirk in May–June 1940, shocked Australians were brought to realise that Britain, already under attack from the air, really was standing alone against the enemy and that German victory, previously unthinkable, would have serious consequences for their own country. By June 1940, AIF enlistments had increased to the point where enough men were available to fill not only the 7th and 8th Divisions, but two more as well.[10]

It was not until November 1941 that Reg Greer turned up at a recruiting centre to volunteer for officer training under the Empire Air Training Scheme.[11] Fourteen months earlier, on 27 September 1940, the Japanese had entered into a tripartite pact with Italy and Germany. One month later, on 7 December 1941, just before 8 am, Japan attacked Pearl Harbor and America entered the war. Australia now seemed under direct threat of invasion, and the volunteer enlistment rate went up, and increased again after Singapore fell in 1942. By the time conscription was introduced early in 1943, there were few to argue against it as they had done in 1916, when the war was far away.

Only Reg could know what motivated him to enlist, and maybe he was not sure either. Germaine later suspected he was running away from home and her two-year-old self, but it is likely that he, like other volunteers, felt a genuine, atavistic urge to defend his family and country from the invader. He would have been susceptible to the prevailing propaganda and peer pressure, and the idea of becoming a smartly attired officer in the air force would have appealed to him, as would the idea of training as a pilot.

He was able to satisfy the recruiting panel that he had been born in South Africa of English parents, had attended senior public secondary school until the age of fifteen, had participated in acceptable sports – cricket, rowing – and had done officer cadet training. Apparently, no checks were made. He was less successful in the medical examination. Without his fine clothes he was exposed as a tall but skinny, narrow-chested individual with some serious health problems that included chronic rhinitis and a healed but still troublesome perforated right eardrum. These defects, plus his age, 37, meant that he could not be selected for pilot training. But there were other jobs.

The broken warrior Peggy Greer and her daughter brought home from Spencer Street station in 1944 was secretive when it came to talking about his war experiences. He told his family that, after leaving Australia, he had been selected for cipher training in Cairo and that his job was called 'Secret and Confidential Publications officer'. He had very few war stories to tell, but one captured Germaine's imagination and supported some of her later theories about what he was really up to. He had been scheduled to carry a machine, which she understood to be some kind of decoding machine, 'from somewhere to somewhere' by aeroplane. At the last minute, as he was waiting by the airstrip in a jeep, someone ran up to tell him that he must give the machine to a superior officer, who would take his place on the plane. He did as he was told and remained in the jeep to watch the plane take off, only to see it attacked by a German fighter and burst into flames, killing all on board.[12]

Reg Greer was invalided out of the army early in 1944, after the examining medical panel found that he suffered from an acute anxiety neurosis that made him unfit for war duty. Family life in the Greer household resumed but it was haunted by the events of the past two years. Reg went back to his old job. He was still a very successful advertising man, but his illness had stripped away much of the bravado that had first attracted Peggy to him. On the surface, little seemed to have changed, but the tension at home was unremitting: the dynamics had shifted so that, in their own ways, each member of the little family was disturbed. Being Catholics, there was no question of divorce. Reg would sit by the window, silently smoking, while Peggy got on with her housework or applied and reapplied her make-up in another room. Often, somewhat bizarrely dressed in a leotard, she would escape to the beach to develop her tan and exercise with a medicine ball. 'Reg and I weren't really good friends,' said Peggy in 1998. 'He was always polite.'[13]

Germaine longed for her father to love her, but when she tried to hug him or climb onto his knee he would push her away, time after time, until she finally gave up. One episode recounted by her mother (if it is true, which Germaine later denied) points to some deep, pathological basis for his lack of feeling for his daughter and, probably, his wife. One afternoon, said Peggy, she was becoming anxious because Germaine, then aged about ten, was late home from school. Reg was sitting at the kitchen window as usual when he saw his daughter walking up the footpath, hand in hand with a man who was carrying her books. 'My God, what'll I do?' said Reg. 'I'm going to call the cops.'

By this time the ten-year-old and the man had disappeared into the bushes. When a policeman arrived on a bicycle he told the Greers that the fellow was known to them as 'a simple chap, always around'. He and Reg went down to the bushes and brought Germaine home. Peggy was furious. She pulled the toaster cord out of its socket and hit her daughter repeatedly as Reg looked on. But his main reaction was extraordinary.

Reg said to the cop: 'You should've let him get on with it. You shouldn't have stopped him. Then he could've been charged.' I wondered about what Reg had turned into that he took that attitude.[14]

Had Reg Greer really 'turned into' something other than what he had always been? Had the war brutalised him to the extent that he was prepared to recommend the rape of his ten-year-old daughter for no other reason than to punish the offender? Or was he always like that? Was the man behind the salesman's mask a person who was incapable of natural feeling and affection because he had little or no experience of those qualities in other important people in his life? Guiltless in one way, abominably culpable in another?

Childhood friends of Germaine recall 'Mr Greer' as a 'distant, unfriendly man – tall, with a moustache'. He did not seem to like children and they did not feel comfortable when he was around.

What was Peggy turning into in those years after her husband returned from the war? It was she who, as her grown-up daughter still insists on telling the world, was the violent parent who beat her daughter, always with an instrument like a stick or the toaster cord, always suddenly and unexpectedly for reasons the child did not understand. Somewhere inside this furious woman was the pretty, still very young, vivacious girl who might have been a model and whose only experience of freedom and happiness had been the fun she had with the Americans while her husband was away. Memories of that time may have brought guilt, but that was nothing compared with the misery of being trapped for life in a loveless marriage with a war-damaged husband. The child Germaine could understand none of this. She was angry with her mother, she told BBC interviewer Anthony Clare in 1989, not because of the adultery but because Peggy had told her that if it had not been for her, Germaine, she would have left her husband.[15]

The Greers had two more children after Germaine. Jane was born on 5 February 1945, when her older sister was six. 'I did it for [Reg], really,' said Peg, 'and for Germaine. [We] needed something to settle us down.'[16] In 1950, a son, Barry, was born. Neither of her siblings ever censured their parents to the extent that Germaine did, or felt that their childhood home was more dysfunctional than most. Many years later, Jane, who married into a wealthy and prominent Catholic family, told Germaine that her father's superior airs had always made her feel good about herself. 'When I went to Kilbreda,' she said, referring to the Catholic girls' secondary school in Mentone, 'I used to think of myself as a real toff. I reckon the old boy knew what he was doing.'[17]

Barry, who became a primary school teacher and 'a committed socialist and a gut democrat', always defended his father: '. . . he made a stable family; he brought us all up well. Three out of three's not bad going . . .'[18]

Germaine's perceptions were different. She believed that the reasons for the family's problems were never likely to surface in the strained, semi-polite milieu of the Greer household. To her repeated questions about his parents, Reg would sometimes reply that they were in England, at other times that they were dead. The child always carried with her the memory of witnessing her mother's adultery with at least one American soldier while her father was away. She knew, and her mother knew that she knew. Could the explanation for her father's coldness towards her be that he suspected what she knew and pushed her away lest she reveal the truth to him? Or was he afraid that this clever child would one day find out more about his past than he had ever confessed to anyone? Secrets, lies and deceptions were the stuff of daily life; to a young girl they were bewildering and ultimately the root of psychological damage.

Yet Germaine's parents were not so very different from many Australian people of their time and class – under-educated, not especially bright, suffering the lasting effects of war-damage. Their home held none of what Germaine later discovered to be the good things in life: there were few books, no paintings, no flowers, no music, no wine, no conversation. At mealtimes no one was permitted to speak. As Germaine grew into an intelligent, funny, curious girl, desperately eager to know about everything, she simply could not stand it. School was her one escape. Learning came as a blessed relief, and she could never get enough of it.

She started school at the age of four at St Columba's parish school, just around the corner from the Greer flat. She had not, like many similarly gifted children, taught herself to read before she started school, nor had she been encouraged to experience books at home. The maple bookcase in her family's living room, she recalled later, held only about twenty books: most of them belonged to her father. Some, like *The Way of a Transgressor*, by Negley Farson, in which she was later interested to read that whores make the best wives, bordered on being pornographic. There was a family Shakespeare and a dictionary and encyclopaedia that Reg had acquired at work. Nothing there to foster a love of literature in a child, but as an adult, she realised that she had become fascinated with words at an early age. Her grandmother gave her *Alice's Adventures in Wonderland*, which she loved, and *The Water Babies*, which she disliked. Then, inevitably, came *Six O'Clock Saints* and other sickly 'spiritual' texts. She discovered Milly-Molly-Mandy but, unlike many children of that era, she did not enter into the magic worlds of Enid Blyton or Beatrix Potter. She read as voraciously as she could up to the age of ten, but she did not read for pleasure. Reading, at home at least, was mainly a way of escape, something to do when she could find no common ground for interacting with anyone in her family.

This began to change in 1949, when her mother gave her a copy of *David Copperfield*. Emotionally engaged for the first time in a work of literature, she fell in love with her first Byronic hero, Steerforth. 'The mixture of feelings that welled up in my nearly 11-year-old bosom when Steerforth seduced Emily while Byronically hating himself for it, to end drowned at Yarmouth . . . was my introduction to grown up passion . . . that book sent me off on a life-long search for Mr Wrong, including two years post graduate work on Byron and a longer infatuation with Rochester.'[19]

From then on, she was hooked. She borrowed as much Dickens as she could find in the school library. 'Dickens had rescued me from both the aversion therapy of the schoolroom and my own perverse nature. I read for pleasure at last.'[20]

Germaine was musically gifted – she even claimed to have perfect pitch – but as a child she did not have the opportunity to learn a musical instrument. Unlike many middle- and lower-middle-class houses of that time, the Greer home did not have a piano. But both Reg and Peg liked to sing. Reg had a fine tenor voice and a large repertoire of light operatic songs like his favourite, 'Oh for the weengs, the weengs of a derve', which he loved to sing in the bath. Peg would wander around the house crooning 'Smoke gets in your eyes' and other pop songs of the time in a passable American accent.

When Germaine was twelve, her mother took her into town on the tram to see a film of *Il Trovatore*. That was the start of her life-long love affair with opera. 'When the unknown and unseen soprano swung into "Tacea la notte" I thought my soul would burst. That night I woke myself up singing a wordless version of "Gli accordi d'un luito".'[21] But her musical education, like her literary advancement, would depend not on the influences of home but of school. The nuns of the Irish Presentation Order, who were Germaine Greer's only schoolteachers, can take most of the credit for the successful early development of her talents. She was aware of this, and she later thanked them for it.

As a war baby, Germaine escaped the worst of the strains that were to bring the Australian Catholic education system to its knees during the postwar population boom: her classes, though large by today's standards, were unremarkable then. Her teachers, the unpaid, idealistic, reasonably well-qualified nuns, were at once inspired and shackled by the vows of obedience that tied them to ancient orthodoxies. At this period, before European migrants arrived with their sunnier versions of Catholicism, the Australian church still followed the florid, superstition-laden traditions of the mother Church in Ireland, and it was those traditions that Germaine's teachers did their best to transmit to their students. 'Give me a child until he is seven and I will show you the man,' once famously said Saint Francis Xavier, founder of the male teaching order of Jesuits. Germaine and many of the thousands of her contemporaries who were educated under this principle in the 1940s and 1950s proved him right. Most managed, eventually, to cast off the trappings of their indoctrination, but at some deep psychological level the old programming never went away.

In Catholic as in government schools, money was tight in the first half of the twentieth century. The prevailing view was that while a primary school education was the right of every child, and necessary for the development of a modern industrial society, secondary education should be reserved for those who could afford to pay for it – and for the very bright children of the working and lower middle classes.

Germaine Greer was firmly in the second category. In Year 7 she won a diocesan scholarship that allowed her to continue to one of the Catholic girls' central schools where nuns, for one concentrated year, deliberately and systematically 'crammed' their students to succeed in the examination for a Junior Government Scholarship that would fund their secondary education. Subjects included French, German, Latin, and, unbelievably, 'Intelligence Tests'.[22] At this school, Holy Redeemer, in Hotham Street, Ripponlea, Germaine relished the demanding curriculum and the company of other bright scholarship winners. The contrast between school and her culturally bleak home life became ever more apparent.

At the end of Year 8 and their one year at Holy Redeemer, Germaine and most of her similarly bright and well-prepared friends easily won scholarships and continued to the Star of the Sea convent in Gardenvale for the final four years of their education. The nuns loved these clever girls, but had difficulty coping with the wide differences in ability between them and the other students. In future years, whole books would be written for teachers on how to handle such 'diversity' in their classrooms, but the enterprising nuns had long before developed their own methods: 'Girls from Holy Redeemer keep your hands down,' they would demand, when posing a question for the class. 'That was the Star of the Sea version of how to manage a mixed-ability classroom,' commented one bored scholarship girl, who recalled missing the challenges of her high-pressure central school. 'I didn't learn much at all after I left Holy Redeemer,' she said years later.[23]

'If it hadn't been for the nuns,' said Greer in 1985, 'I might have gone to secretarial college, had streaks put in my hair and married a stockbroker. The nuns [at Holy Redeemer] groomed me, crammed me to bursting so that I won a scholarship . . .'[24]

The 1950s were the years of McCarthyism in America and the rising influence of the anti-communist Democratic Labor Party in Australia. Anti-communist sentiment among Catholics was high. At mass every Sunday Germaine listened, part intrigued, part bored, part puzzled while the priest droned on, citing examples of the Australian Labor Party's failure to oppose communist infiltration of the unions and reminding the flock of their duty to do something about it. Outside the church, groups of men gathered around tables where Catholic newspapers like the *Catholic Worker* and B.A. Santamaria's *News Weekly* were being sold. Some of the men seemed agitated.[25] The curious child wondered what that was all about.

Catholic schools were powerhouses of anti-communism. In their history classes and daily Christian doctrine classes, students were carefully inducted into Church dogma: 'good' was defined by Rome, 'evil' emanated from Moscow. Often, the nuns and brothers, inspired by their determination to combat the evils of the world, i.e. sex and communism, would put their own spin on the situation. Germaine has recalled Sister Cyril, her history teacher, displaying charts of Soviet missiles aimed squarely at her country and school. She and her classmates knew that sooner or later they would be called to do battle against those communist forces of darkness. The only problem was that the external examiners who would decide their fate at the Leaving and Matriculation examinations might not be Catholic. During one lesson, in which Sister Cyril was teaching the class about the incursions of the communists into Eastern Europe, Germaine raised her hand. 'Sister, wouldn't it be more useful to discuss communism as a political movement rather than a work of the devil?'

Sister Cyril's face became pink.

'What other explanation can there be but the devil's treachery?'

'But, Sister, in the exams we can't describe communism as a supernatural phenomenon.'

'I cannot talk to you in these terms, Germaine Greer,' said Sister Cyril, returning to her chart. 'Leave the room.'[26]

The Star of the Sea convent school, as Germaine has pointed out, was a self-contained female society. The world of heterosexual relations lay beyond the walls, and nobody gave it too much thought. Girls had crushes on each other and on the nuns, but most of them had never heard of lesbianism and would not have known how to practise it if they had. 'The love that dare not speak its name' was exactly that in convent life.

At Holy Redeemer, Germaine had become friends with another bright scholarship girl called Jennifer Midgley (later Dabbs). At 'Star', the relationship developed into what both girls later described as a love affair. Apparently, the nuns did not openly discourage their friendship, perhaps because they were unaware of its potentially homosexual character, more likely because both girls were so exceptionally attractive and gifted that their teachers could not conceive of anything 'unsavoury' happening between them. And they were right. Nothing did.

Jennifer excelled at singing and the piano: the two girls would seize every opportunity to be alone in an instrumental practice room, where Germaine would assume the role of George Sand to Jennifer's Chopin, scribbling poetry into an exercise book while Jennifer played nocturnes. They would hold hands surreptitiously when singing in the school choir, and together they performed the leading roles in school plays. After her acclaimed performance as the Duke of Plaza-Toro in *The Gondoliers* Germaine autographed Jennifer's program, 'Germaine Greer who belongs to JM'.[27]

The affair lived on in the memories of both women long after they left school. In her novel *Beyond Redemption*, a roman à clef written thirty years later, Jennifer described the passionate relationship between Katie Mitchell (herself) and Michaela, easily recognisable as Germaine, at their school, 'Stella Maris'.

> She wasn't what was considered to be 'pretty'; there was far too much character in her face, and a vivacious intelligence shone out of her clear green eyes. Her hair was tawny and curlier than mine. It stood out around her head like a nimbus, complementing her clear creamy skin and contrasting with those startling eyes.[28]

Was it a lesbian relationship? According to Jennifer it was 'passionate, spiritual and romantic rather than genital'. Germaine, she thought, was, like herself, 'sexually naive'.

> Germaine was the first person outside my family who loved me, and I realized: I love you. It was unconditional, heady, unlike parental love, which was conditional. The sexual thing came later. It seemed very natural, the limited amount of sexual contact we had.[29]

Germaine's view is more complex. In *The Female Eunuch*, she recalls her mother's horrified reaction at discovering a romantic letter she had written to Jennifer. To stop Peggy's hysterics, she attempted to placate her by explaining that homosexual relationships were only part of a growing-up phase, common in teenage girls, and that she was already over it. But she knew, even then, that this was a cheap denial of something fine and true. She was ashamed, not of the affair, but of her betrayal of her first love.[30]

On matters of heterosexual sex, the Church's teaching was crystal clear and the nuns neglected no opportunity to inculcate that teaching into their girls. No sex at all, 'in thought, word or deed', until marriage. A Catholic girl who was tainted by any suggestion of 'impurity' could expect that no man would want to marry her. Worse, however – much worse – was that even the smallest stirring of a sexual thought or feeling – by accidentally picking up a *Pix* magazine in the hairdressers, for example – would, if she did not instantly repress it, plunge her straight into a state of mortal sin, so that if she should die on the way home she would go straight to Hell. The only way to be purged of her sin was to confess it to a priest, and the nuns made sure that Confession was a regular event in the lives of their charges. Convent girls were taught the formula at the age of six, and the order of the ritual did not vary. Typically, it went something like this:

'Bless me, Father, for I have sinned. It has been two weeks since my last confession, Father, and I accuse myself of telling lies, swearing and thinking impure thoughts.'

Priest: 'Now, these impure thoughts, child – how often did they occur?'

Girl: 'Five times, Father.'

Priest: 'And were you alone?'

Girl: 'Yes, Father.'

Priest: 'And were the thoughts accompanied by any actions?'

Girl (not having the faintest idea what he was driving at): 'No, Father.'

Priest: 'When these thoughts come again, my child, you should picture in your mind the beautiful face of Our Blessed Lady in all her purity. Do you think you could do that?'

Girl: 'Yes, Father.'

Priest: 'Say two Our Fathers and ten Hail Marys.' Then something in Latin which meant 'Go, your sins are forgiven,' and it was all over. Oh, the blessed relief!

In 2000, in an interview with a mature-age student of English, Germaine remembered a long-ago episode in the confessional. 'When I was at school I was a clown, always could be relied upon to put myself into totally disastrous situations if I thought there was a laugh in it . . . We had this priest . . . And there I was confessing my usual impure thoughts.

'"I'm troubled with impure thoughts, Father . . ."

'"When you have these impure thoughts, are you thinking of anyone in particular?"

'And I just wanted to say "Yes Father. YOU!!!" And I thought, no, that's a sin against the Holy Ghost. You can't lie in the Confessional. But it would have been such a laugh! What would he have done? Listen, you know what men are like, he would have believed me . . . that would have been the next joke . . . "Well, actually, Father, I was kidding."'[31]

In the intervals between the many instances of religious observance, convent life would proceed as tranquilly as the daily battles with Satan and communism would allow. The main weapon against sex was denial: for much of the time the girls did not think too much about boys because theirs was a female world. But when their charges grew to about sixteen, the nuns recognised that if they were to become good Catholic wives and mothers, there would sooner or later need to be some mingling of the sexes. So they and the priests and brothers from the boys' schools managed to organise mixed-sex dances and dancing classes.

United as they were in their struggles against global inequalities, the clerical Catholic school-dance organisers of 1950s Melbourne accepted and even fostered the rigid social class divisions among their flocks. 'Marry your own' did not only mean marrying another Catholic, it also meant marrying within the economic and social circle in which God had decided to place your family. Girls from convents that charged high fees and thought themselves superior, like Loreto and Sacre Coeur, were partnered with boys from the Jesuits' Xavier College at dancing classes like those taught by the Misses Brennan at St Peters Church hall in Toorak. Girls from Star of the Sea, which belonged to a lower, though not the lowest, fee-paying tier of Catholic girls' schools, danced with boys from similarly lower-tiered boys' schools staffed by orders like the Christian Brothers.

For these petty but very real snobberies and for the artificial bonhomie of the suddenly acceptable coming together of male and female, the young Germaine Greer had nothing but scarcely comprehending scorn, but scorn could not save her from embarrassment; the dances had to be endured, and for an adolescent girl who had grown to nearly six feet tall, they were agonising affairs. 'I was a freak. At six feet I was too tall for normal sexual relationships . . . It was just agony for me to go to a dance because I couldn't get around the floor. No one could steer me and I didn't know how to succumb,' she told journalist Claudia Dreifus in 1975.[32]

She also recalled her mortification when the nuns, who, as she remarked, could hardly be expected to have any idea of the banality of sex, tried to prepare and protect their girls from the dancing boys' uncontrollable urges.

The silliness of the nuns is amazing in retrospect. Before school dances we had to be inspected to make sure our dresses did not bare any inflammatory zones of bosom or under arms. Into the boat-neck of my home-made yellow organza they thrust paper tissues, just in case I should dance with an eight-foot giant who would be the only person capable of glimpsing the top of my empty blue brassiere.[33]

Such were the influences on Germaine Greer in matters of sex, a subject upon which she would have much to say in the years that followed. There was also the spiritual side of her education, remnants of which would also remain with her for life. Christian doctrine was a core subject in all Catholic schools, taught daily like English and Maths. Much of it was about the 'proofs' of the existence of God. Germaine thought that the nuns were not particularly good at this: the strength of their simple faith was not matched by their ability to sustain a logical argument. Had she been taught by clever Jesuits, she thought later, she may never have abandoned Catholicism, but as it was, by the time she reached sixth form, 'not one of the arguments was good enough. The ghost had left the machine forever.'[34]

So she believed; but more deeply penetrating of her psyche were the Church's mystical traditions of self-denial and contemplation, as expressed in the spiritual practices of saints like Teresa of Ávila.

> I began to practise self-denial, eating things I didn't want, not eating things I did want, mortifying my flesh by sitting in uncomfortable positions or standing when I could sit or putting a stone in my shoe, uttering what were known as 'pious ejaculations' the while . . .
>
> I would slip through the convent garden after school and into the Presence of the Blessed Sacrament, kneel directly

on the cold stone floor, raise my arms and meditate on the Passion. The method was concentration; the aim was the direct apprehension of the ubiquity of Christ . . .[35]

She wondered if she had a vocation to become a nun: '"Do you really want me Lord?" I would ask. "Is this what you have in mind for me?"'

It has never left her, that unfulfilled yearning for the spiritual:

Compared to the anguish of scepticism the yoke of my religion was easy and its burden light. I love to go to the Easter ceremonies in the darkened church, and join in with the congregation in begging the light of Christ to return, as the candles are lit from the Paschal fire, and the bells are rung and the Gloria flames out. I love Mother Church as the nuns love me, when all I can do for them is get myself nominated as Australia's foremost female ratbag.[36]

Before the advent of the contraceptive pill in the 1960s, and before Germaine Greer wrote *The Female Eunuch*, Catholic mothers had one crucial piece of advice for their daughters: 'Make sure you marry a *good* man,' they would say. Behind that sentence lay a multitude of expectations and fears. If a girl did not marry, who would 'keep' her? Life for a poorly educated, single woman meant either eking out a living in a low-paid job, probably living a lonely life in a boarding house, or remaining at home as an unpaid housemaid, 'kept' by her father or brothers. Some chose the convent. Marriage was the usual way out, but the girls did not understand what their mothers were trying to tell them: marriage to a *not-good* man, or even a *poor provider*, would mean a lifetime of drudgery and abuse, weary bodies pumping out babies to satisfy the egos and sexual demands of often brutal partners.

The Catholic Church was not into male brutality in marriage. Rather, it conveniently advocated for the 'good man' theory: in the Catholic boys' schools, priests and brothers taught the boys to respect and love women as Jesus Christ loved his virgin mother, and most of them probably did. But the young girls only half understood what their mothers had learned – that, as wives and mothers themselves, they would be forced to submit. While they could hardly fail to see that all real power in marriage resided with men, gentle or otherwise, they did not understand that the consequences of their own powerlessness could be dire. Once they were married it was too late. The system was stacked against them. Divorce was a mortal sin, contraception was a mortal sin, and the many women who confided their pain to the local priest in confession were told to go home and behave themselves.

Of the fifty-plus girls in Germaine's matriculation class at Star, most chose marriage. In 1998, four of her old friends, who had also been her classmates at St Columba's Primary School – Joan O'Callaghan (nee Corboy), Theo Kinnaird (nee Molan), Jan Coleman (nee Parker) and Marian Shanahan (nee Titheredge) – reminisced about their 'class of 1954'. Their life choices and attitudes, so typical of the time, but so different from Germaine's, give some indication of the magnitude of Germaine's rebellion against the expectations of her family, Church and society.[37]

Joan won a nursing bursary, but she was only seventeen and her family did not want her to live in a nurses' home.

Dad said he didn't want me living in the nurses' home and would drive me there every morning. I knew then that I couldn't leave home, and I wasn't really keen to anyway.

She decided against a nursing career and got a job as a drafts-woman in the titles office ('Dad knew someone.'). She continued to study music, in which she excelled, and was building a small teaching practice.

> But all I really wanted to do was get married and have children. I met my husband Michael when I was 18. It was love at first sight. Michael was 26, one of eight in an Irish family, a land surveyor who was finishing off his studies. Ten days after our first date, he proposed.

Theo Kinnaird's husband, Patrick, remarked benignly that she was 'getting on a bit' when she married him at the age of 27. She had finished her nursing training by then, and worked for some years as a nurse in the St Vincent's home care program. Patrick was a veterinarian. Theo helped him in the practice they established in Black Rock, a bayside suburb of Melbourne, and they had five daughters.

Jan Coleman went to Melbourne University after leaving Star and became a librarian. She married her husband, John, in 1964 and had five children, 'one after the other'.

> Luckily I didn't have to go back to work because John, who is a barrister, was earning madly to try and keep up the pace.

Marian Shanahan's life took a different course that is indicative of the changes that were starting to occur in the 1960s. When she left Star in 1957, she became a nun with the Daughters of Charity in Sydney. She stayed for eight years. After leaving the convent she taught until 1969, leaving about a year later when she married and became pregnant. Later, she went back to teaching, got divorced, and continued with her career.

Perhaps strangely, given her later reputation for being difficult, most of Germaine's contemporaries from Star speak well of her and are proud of her success. They remember her for the fearless way she would stand up for herself and others, her academic brilliance, her acting performances in school productions, and, especially, her humour. One recalls how, when reprimanded by a nun for sniffing in class, Germaine responded by stuffing a whole bedsheet into her desk and making loud and liberal use of it as a handkerchief. A girl who sat behind her in class remembered that Germaine kept a photograph of Robert Helpmann under the lid of her desk, and when the nuns were not looking, she would kiss it, whispering 'Oh Bobby Darling!'

Even then, however, some of her friends believed that she had a mean streak. She was big and powerful and it was not wise to offend her.

> Germaine and I got on very well . . . but there was always the proviso, always the condition, that if you were going to be a friend you were also vulnerable to anything she might do with you: being very good and friendly and protective from the awful things the nuns might have done as punishment and the next day just wiping the floor with you – or running you down, or saying something terribly sarcastic, embarrassing things about you in front of everybody. She was really quite mean.[38]

Writing to Germaine in 1975, however, another old school friend, who had become a nun upon leaving school, but who later gave up her vocation to marry and have children, made the interesting observation that her friend's disconcerting habit of turning on people was not driven by 'malice'.

> I was always quite proud of you . . . but would also know better than to rely on you. Your interests were so quick-silver and without a trace of malice you could switch on and off a person to an alarming, to the person, degree.[39]

But some other students were wary. Margaret O'Keeffe, who was the leader of a drama group in which Germaine and Jennifer Midgley were talented performers, told her family that, as well as being more than a little afraid of Germaine Greer at school, she actively disliked her. She recounted how Germaine would make fun of Jennifer in the group, mimicking her friend's beautiful singing voice in an ugly, mocking falsetto. Margaret could not understand why a girl could behave so hurtfully to such a close friend. She decided to keep well clear of Germaine Greer, believing her, perhaps mistakenly, to be a 'cruel' person.[40]

Most of the other girls viewed this aspect of Germaine's character as part of her general eccentricity. 'Oh Ger*maine*!' they would exclaim, until it became a kind of catchcry.

Germaine loved the nuns. 'I am still a nun. I am still made in their likeness,' she told writer Duncan Fallowell in 1994.

> . . . the childishness of nuns, the girlishness of them. They show you there's another way of living. You don't have to be a wife and mother. It was very interesting to be with those crazy women who laughed all the time.[41]

In her chapter in *There's Something about a Convent Girl*, a collection of several prominent Australian women's memories of their convent schooling, Germaine recalled Sister Eymard, who tried to teach her the proofs of the existence of God, but failed because she didn't know them herself – or because they weren't valid. There was Sister Raymond, who had never seen a great work of art in her life, but who taught her that art was beautiful, and of whom she would always think when she later visited the great galleries of Europe.

> I sometimes wonder what it would be like if I took her with me round Europe and said 'You remember what you taught me about Chartres? Well this is Chartres and this is what it looks like.'[42]

And Sister Attracta, the choirmistress, 'a tiny Irishwoman with rose petal skin'.

'Sing, child,' Attracta demanded loudly of new-girl Germaine.

Germaine sang.

'Can ye read music?

'No, Sister.'

'Well, we should be thankful ye can hold a tewn.'

She played a melody. 'Can ye sing that?'

Germaine had a go.

'Yew can sing the discant.'

So Germaine learned to sing the descant, 'one of the greatest earthly joys, the one that will take me to heaven. Singing in harmony.' She sang at lunchtimes, after school, and even at weekends, rejoicing as much in escaping from home as in the music.[43]

But her love of the Catholic nuns who had taught her certainly did not extend to the Pope: 'The Pope! The Pope is an abominable, publicity seeking, sanctimonious shit!'[44]

The nuns' reactions to *The Female Eunuch* when it was published in 1971 say much for their levels of tolerance, erudition and compassion, especially considering their aversion to and likely ignorance about all matters of sex. The first I heard of the book was from a Presentation nun, Sister Magdalen O'Neill, my aunt, who lived at Star. 'One of our girls has written a book,' she said, as my mother and I sipped our tea in the spotless reception parlour. (Auntie Rose was not allowed to take afternoon tea with us. I used to think the nuns probably didn't eat or drink at all.) 'Her old teachers are all talking about it. They are very excited and proud of her, although I've heard it's a bit . . .' Her eyebrows went up and the sentence was left hanging in the air as Auntie Rose sat back, flicking her rosary beads and exuding her own pride in the former Star girl's achievement.

Claudia Wright, an Australian feminist radio personality and a friend of Germaine, interviewed Sister Raymond in 1971 in her cosy office at Avila College in Mount Waverley, where she had become principal. Sister Raymond said that she had found *The Female Eunuch* 'a delight to read, a work of deep scholarship'. She remembered Germaine with great fondness.

> A delightful girl, big in form and mind, [she had] a generous heart . . . She was very uninhibited and would come out with some very blunt remarks – but that was in discussion and that didn't matter in an art class because she was terribly creative and the more a person is like that the better it is.[45]

In the late 1970s, Sister Eymard wrote to her former pupil, who had contacted her upon hearing she had been ill.

So much water has passed under the bridge since the days when you challenged your teachers . . . I am proud of your courage in stating your convictions and touched by your kindness to the disadvantaged. If we differ on a few ideas, we do both believe in justice and generosity.

I certainly remember you with your searching eyes and restless frame and quick brain.[46]

Her experiences at school, and later university, were Germaine's escape from what she felt to be an intolerable, shameful situation at home. It was not only the boredom, the ignorance and the philistinism that permeated every family interaction; there was something else, a dark secret or secrets that hung over the household like a toxic brown cloud.

What could it all mean – the half-obvious lies and deceits, the strange behaviours of her mother, her father's silent withholding of affection? She knew she was clever, so why could she not find out what his secrets were? She tried to interrogate him. Who were his parents? Why were there no relations, no cousins from his side of the family whom she could meet and get to know? And what of her mother's indiscretions? Germaine said nothing to Peggy about what might have happened when she was given those knockout drops during the American serviceman's visit to their flat during the war. But she knew. Her mother knew that she knew and that she was smart enough to understand what had happened. Her father, too, could see that a clever girl like Germaine might just succeed in exposing his lies. So he pushed her away. 'I completely mistook the way to his heart. I only threatened him by being so clever. I should have tried to be lovable.'[47]

Reg probably suspected his wife's infidelity, but he kept his suspicions to himself. Peggy must have had doubts about her husband's past too, for there was no one to substantiate his stories about his birth, childhood and youth. His known life seemed to have begun in Adelaide at some time in the 1920s, where friends and colleagues remembered him as a seller of advertising space in the *Adelaide Advertiser*. By the time he met young Peggy Lafrank in Collins Street in 1935, he had moved to Melbourne and become a bon viveur. Full of jokes and clever repartee, he was truly one of the boys, a man about town who liked to watch the pretty girls of Collins Street walk by.

The man Germaine discovered when she began to write *Daddy, We Hardly Knew You* appeared to have been well liked, but when she spoke to his secretary, Joyce, she found out more than she really wanted to know. There was one man, said Joyce, who had no time for Reg Greer. This man's name was 'Mr Bednall'. Joyce had been to his house for dinner and met his family, who, she said, were 'distinguished', 'decent' people. Mr Bednall could see behind Reg's public mask and so, for good reasons, could Joyce. 'Your father was a sensual man,' she said.

Joyce told Germaine about episodes of what would now be seen for what it was – sexual harassment. Her sixteen-year-old bosom was often a source of crude jokes in the office. 'I just laughed it off,' she told Germaine, 'but your father was always brushing past me.' When she came upon him and the other reps 'talking dirty', she would quietly leave. At least they didn't do that in front of her, she said, and she was wise enough to refuse Reg's repeated offers to drive her home, so no serious harm was done. Later, when she had moved upstairs to another office in Newspaper House, Reg told her that his new secretary was much more 'cooperative'. 'I've made the office much more comfortable,' he said. 'I've brought in a blanket. We have wonderful lunchtime sessions.'[48]

The sensitive Joyce had intuited that her boss was not what he seemed.

> He gave the impression of being a well-educated man. But now I come to think of it, he really was mysterious. I've worked in all kinds of jobs all over the world, and I've never worked for someone I knew so little about. Something murky about it.[49]

Germaine could see that there was everything murky about it, and she felt an unaccustomed sympathy for her mother. 'He was a lounge lizard, a line shooter, a larrikin, a jerk.' The evidence, she thought, did not suggest that her father could have been considered officer material in the armed services.[50]

Germaine delved deep into Reg Greer's military record, recalling that he always avoided talking about his wartime experiences. She thought that this may have been because he was ashamed of the anxiety neurosis that caused him to be invalided home after less than two years away. Unwillingly, for she did love her father, she also forced herself to consider the possibility that he had falsely exaggerated his symptoms to procure his discharge from the army. ('I am troubled by a nagging suspicion that the anxiety neurosis was a calculated performance. Reg Greer was not just a salesman, but a crack salesman.'[51]) As an Intelligence Officer attached to a Special Liaison Unit (SLU) he was never involved in armed combat, but the months he spent working long hours underground in the damp, ill-ventilated tunnels under the Lascaris Bastion during the siege of Malta must have been incredibly stressful.

His job was to listen intently for hours on end to a cacophony of radio signals and transcribe information using a 'Type X' machine, an adaptation of the German Enigma machine, the code of which had been finally broken by the British in 1940. Reg's work was an integral, though undervalued, component of the famed British intelligence operation 'Ultra'.

The unglamorous, underappreciated nature of cipher work would not have pleased Reg, but one aspect of it suited him perfectly: the secrecy. Germaine wondered if the army had tried to turn him into a 'deception person', or if they realised 'he was a deception person already'.

> Every member of the Secret Service catches the disease. They all live as if the right hand was not to be trusted to know what the left hand is doing. Once the initial breach has been made in the self, once a man has learned to live a double life, it is a simple matter to live a treble or quadruple life. Did the boffins in Cairo discover that Daddy was a liar, a phony, fitted by temperament and experience to be a member of an SLU pretending to be something else?[52]

Germaine had always known about her mother's wartime adultery – she had absorbed it with those knockout drops – but her father would be dead before she found out the full truth about him. In the meantime, mouths stayed shut as the Greer household soldiered on.

'Do you know where you spent the night before you went to meet your father?' Germaine's aunt once asked her.

'No,' Germaine replied, puzzled by the question.

'With me,' replied her aunt, and waited for it to sink in.

'All night?'

'Your mother picked you up in the morning.'

'I see.'[53]

'I used to think,' wrote Germaine Greer in 1989, 'that truth was single and error legion, but I know now that none of us grasps more than a little splinter of the truth.'[54] When she sought to expose the reality of what happened to her during her childhood and growing-up she knew that, despite her formidable intellect and academic training, she could tell only fragments of what actually happened. Her early life was about much more than the troubled relationship of her parents, her father's apparent rejection of her and her mother's guilt and frustrations. It was also about catching the bus to school, spending long sunny days on the beach, buying ice cream at the corner shop. Her sister's truth about their home life was different from hers, as was her brother's, but on looking back from the person she became to the young person she used to be, she chose her most vivid recollections to shape her narrative. To some, her frank disclosures about her parents are distasteful – 'How could she write all those terrible things about her mother and father?' – but Germaine Greer has always insisted on trying to uncover those 'splinters of the truth' that lurk behind the illusions, comforts and mendacities of ordinary life, and to tell everyone about them. From challenging Sister Cyril to upending conventional views on just about everything, this is what she does. The only complication is that she, like her father, is also a creative performer – she wants to tell and present good stories – and we all know how truth can get in the way of those.

2

A difficult girl

She had the same lone thoughts and wanderings,
The quest of hidden knowledge, and a mind
To comprehend the universe

Lord Byron, *Manfred*

'That was when the trouble started.'

Peggy Greer was referring to the year 1956, when Germaine commenced her studies at the University of Melbourne. A year earlier, Reg had negotiated a war-service loan to finance a pretty Cape Cod–style house in the bayside suburb of Mentone. As Peg saw it, the family had all it needed to fulfil the Australian Dream of the 1950s: parents still married to each other, a father who went off to a regular job in a city office every day, a mother who did not need to go out to work, one academically bright daughter who had won a university scholarship, and two younger siblings doing well at good schools. They would all bring friends home for coffee and have swimming parties at the beach.[1]

But seventeen-year-old Germaine, the source of the 'trouble', was determined to ruin her mother's party. Peggy recalled many anxious nights of lying awake, waiting for her older daughter to come home:

Reg would be full of beer, snoring upstairs. I was worrying about accidents. We were fighting. Reg'd wake up at night. She'd have come home with a boy and he'd discover her in a clinch . . .[2]

As the family sat at the breakfast table, Germaine's father would challenge her about her behaviour of the night before.

'He'd bring it up at breakfast time. She'd come out with f . . . and c . . . and shit at the table. In front of the other children . . .[3]

On the surface, at least, the Greer household at Mentone in 1956 was not untypical of middle- and lower-middle-class Australian suburbia. Many families had their secret sorrows and most dealt with life as Peggy and Reg were attempting to do, by making life physically comfortable and establishing routines. Meanwhile, at university, Germaine was becoming part of a vibrant, exciting world that made her even more aware of the banality at home. She turned angrily on her parents, blaming them for their inadequacy, attacking them as only she knew how, through her shocking behaviour and use of violent language. They were no match for her. They became afraid of her.

On the basis of her matriculation results, which were among the highest in the state of Victoria, Germaine had won a second-ary teaching studentship to study for a four-year Arts Honours degree at the University of Melbourne.[4] This meant that she immediately became a 'permanent' employee of the Victorian Education Department on a salary (allowance) of £8 a week. Her 'classification' was SIT (student in training), the first step on a potentially lifelong career ladder. Her record number, which, she was told, would be hers for life, was 50783.

The secondary studentships were generous to a degree unthinkable in the twenty-first century, but they came with strings attached. The department attempted to treat the SITs as true employees by requiring them to be 'on duty' at the university, even during part of vacation time, and imposing various petty bureaucratic demands like filling out forms for being late or absent from 'duty'. These requirements were all but impossible to enforce in a university environment, and most SITs tried to disregard them, as Germaine certainly did. Only one string could not be ignored. This was the bond, which required students, at the completion of their studies, to teach for three years in an Education Department school, which was often a hard-to-staff country school. The bond called for a guarantor, who was generally, as in Germaine's case, the student's father. If a student 'broke' the bond by failing to meet the teaching requirement, the guarantor would have to repay all costs of the student's salary and training – a significant amount. Most SITs baulked at the thought of placing this burden on their parents, but not Germaine.

One of the most significant effects of the studentships was to allow a very large number of bright young people from working- and lower-middle-class families to attend the university, which, apart from an influx of postwar ex-servicemen on rehabilitation programs, was traditionally the domain of privileged students from Melbourne's more exclusive private schools. Most of the SITs were the first in their families to go to university. Their parents were proud of them, but many were puzzled and concerned by their children's expanding horizons and, to them, alien attitudes: 'I want him to have a good education,' said one mother anxiously, 'but he keeps coming home with all these ideas!'[5]

Some of the SITs' parents took comfort in the knowledge that their children were protégés of the familiar Education Department, which had long been the employer of choice for clever working-class children who became primary school teachers after attending state owned and controlled teachers' colleges.[6] To such people, the department was a venerable authority that respected family values and was immune to all the incomprehensible nonsense being spouted at the university.

That is probably why Peggy Greer appealed to the Education Department for help when Germaine became 'ungovernable' at home.

I said: 'I've got this ungovernable uni student.' I told them she wasn't studying, got all this money and wasn't dependent on me, and didn't take any notice of what we said. I was ushered into a room and I said to the man: 'You give her this money and it's turning her into a tramp!'[7]

The department was not about to act, however, and there was no point in asking people at the university, because they were part of the problem. So seventeen-year-old Germaine's obscenity-filled rebellion continued apace.

Some studentship holders were disconcerted by their first contact with privileged young people from families that were much wealthier and better educated than their own, but Germaine hardly noticed the petty snobberies and subtle class distinctions. She had been a scholarship girl at school and was proud of the fact. At Melbourne University, while she was happy to accept the money from the Education Department each fortnight, she gradually moved away from the future-teacher crowd. Her old school friends, many of whom were also on studentships, recall that she soon became to them a distant, revered figure.

In her earliest days at the university, Germaine was diffident, still seeing herself as a 'freak', embarrassed by her height, but this did not prevent her from making the most of her thespian talents. In May 1956 she starred as Aunt Sylvia, a depressed invalid turned Christian Scientist, in the Secondary Teachers' College production of Noël Coward's *This Happy Breed*. 'A natural comedy flair allied to a distinctive appearance, mark her as ideal for revue,' noted the reviewer of university productions in *Farrago*, the student publication of the University of Melbourne. In June, her performance as 'one of the ladies' who performed in the SRC (Student Representative Council) Revue *Up an Atom* was rated as 'promising'. The reviewers of this production criticised the behaviour of the actors, some of whom were drunk on the last night, created a disturbance in the foyer and had to be sobered up before they could go on stage.[8] Germaine relished it all: she loved a good party, and socialising with the gifted and popular theatre crowd helped her to make friends among people in the trendiest cliques at the university.

Hoping to discover some intellectual underpinning for her lingering fondness for Catholicism, she attended some meetings of the university's Newman Society, but she was never one of those dedicated Catholic students who met daily at 1.15 pm to recite the rosary.[9] The Irish Catholicism of Melbourne circa 1956 could not hope to contain her: as she gravitated to the more radical fringes of student life, she found herself drawn to socially prominent groups of Jewish students, with whom she felt such affinity that she started to identify as Jewish herself.

As the winter of her first year at university closed in, however, she began to suffer depression. Life in the Greer household was as miserable as ever and she grew to detest her daily train journey – sixteen stations from Mentone to the city. Suburban trains were unheated in those days; in peak hour, they were hideously over-crowded and the first- and second-class 'smoking' carriages were thick with cigarette smoke. Germaine developed a cough that turned into chronic, debilitating bronchitis. Her misery inten-sified when somebody stole her one overcoat while she was table-hopping in the Caf and she had to make do with an old Harris Tweed coat of her father's.[10]

As her first-year examinations approached, she was barely managing to stay in control of her life. One blustery day, in despair over a failing relationship with an actor she had fallen in love with, the seventeen-year-old almost fell to her death from the cliffs overlooking the sea near her home. Wearing her father's old coat, she had been following the cliff path, feeling deeply unhappy, when, on an impulse, ignoring all warning signs, she clambered under the restraining fences to position herself at the fragile cliff edge. Wildly, she stared out across the water. 'If you care for me, God, if you think my life is worth saving, you will not let me die!' she cried into the gale.

God's response was to cause the red sandstone beneath her feet to collapse, so that she started to fall rapidly down the cliff face towards the rocks and sea below. It was her father's coat that saved her, as it had caught on a protruding branch. For a few seconds she hung there, halfway down the cliff, until the branch too gave way and she continued to fall, but more slowly, to land on the shingle below. She sat for a moment until a stone that had been dislodged by her fall came down and hit her on the back of her head. So much for God, and her foolishness!

Not long after that incident, she had a breakdown. 'In the last weeks of my first year at university,' she recalled later, 'it looked as if I might follow many a teenager into the twilight of tranquillisers and psychiatric wards,' but the danger passed and she recovered sufficiently to throw away the pills she had been prescribed and pass her first-year exams.

During the long summer vacation, the situation at home became so intolerable that Germaine packed her bags and made her first attempt to leave. She took the train and tram to Carlton, where she was welcomed into the student digs of three male friends. Although she had rung her father to reassure him that she was safe, she found out that he and Peggy had reported her as a 'missing person'. So she went home. 'Who let all the flies in?' said her mother, as her prodigal daughter came through the door.[11]

In spite of showing an unashamed interest in sex, 'going out' with any number of young men, and becoming notorious for the suggestive obscenity of her language, Germaine Greer remained an unlikely virgin for quite some time after she started university: it was not until she discovered that the male students were calling her a cockteaser that she decided her virginity would have to go. The only question was who? There was no shortage of eager males who were prepared to do the necessary, but *her* deflowerer would have to be special.

After careful consideration, her favour fell on a young Jewish man – the impossibly clever and handsome Leon Fink, a law student and head of the Jewish students' society at the university, who had been expressing interest in her defloration for some time. One starry night in April 1957, he and Germaine drove off in his Studebaker to Studley Park, Kew, where the task was accomplished on some blankets that had been carefully laid upon the grass for the purpose.[12]

In her second year at the university, in addition to an increasingly frenetic social life, frequent appearances in theatrical performances and managing to keep up academically, Germaine developed an interest in student politics. By this time, she was becoming an icon as well as a star. She took to dressing as a beatnik, wearing mainly black clothes, painting her eyelids black and putting henna through her hair. Contemporaries recall her dominating presence at lectures and tutorials, her tall figure dwarfing others around the campus, and her loud, exclamatory laughter as she moved around the Caf, obviously aware of the admiring glances that followed her as she paused at various tables to joke and chat with friends.

When she stood, unsuccessfully, for the position of Women's General Representative in the 1957 SRC elections, her platform was equivocal: 'I do not believe in the equality of the sexes,' she proclaimed, 'but the superiority of women in those fields where their talents are of most value.'[13] After her defeat, she continued to agitate for a hairdresser in the Student Union building, but her political activities were now less important to her than her growing involvement with members of the bohemian subculture loosely known as 'The Drift'.

The Drift's origins can be traced back to around 1930, when the economic historian Brian Fitzpatrick would go roistering in dirty pubs with a loud and convivial group of his friends, whom the writer Don Watson described thus:

[They were] the city's unemployed and semi-employed writers and artists . . . there was no unanimity of political opinion but members of the group were uniformly left-wing with varying degrees of radicalism and romanticism.[14]

By 1957, the Swanston Family Hotel in central Melbourne had become the main gathering place for members of the Drift. These were the days when pubs stopped serving alcohol at six o'clock. At around 5.45 pm, the men (women were not allowed in public bars) would stagger to the counters to buy as many glasses of beer as they could carry before the taps were turned off. The tiled, easy-to-hose-down walls that can still be seen outside many of these old pubs are the only remaining evidence of the vomiting and urinating that happened when the drunken men were ejected, sometimes forcibly, after the six o'clock swill.

Because the men of the Drift liked to be with women, because the women of the Drift liked to drink, and because everyone was into defying convention, Drift gatherings were of mixed gender, but they necessarily took place in a room apart from the men-only public bar. (Not that the males-only rule bothered Germaine, who was known to flout it in pubs all over Carlton. 'Don't be ridiculous, child,' she was heard to tell one young student, an aspiring actress of small stature, as she pushed her into the bar of Naughton's Hotel.)

Barry Humphries, who frequented the Swanston Family Hotel in the same period as Germaine, has described this hostelry as a 'picturesque public house . . . which reeked of cigarette smoke, yeast, urine and some unidentifiable disinfectant'. As a rising star of the Drift, Germaine must have felt that she had found her spiritual home. This was certainly Humphries' experience.

> The noise was deafening, and as I stood in that packed throng of artists' models, academics, alkies, radio actors, poofs and ratbags, drinking large quantities of agonisingly cold beer, I felt as though my True Personality was coming into focus.[15]

They were called the Drift because after the beer was turned off everyone would fall into cars and 'drift' on to a restaurant or a party. 'There was no need to issue invitations,' Greer recalled many years later. 'If you gave a party on Friday night, you expected The Drift.'

At home in Mentone, her family problems grew steadily worse. The contrasts between the laissez faire Drift lifestyle and Peggy's fruitless efforts to maintain her version of a 'normal' home could not have been greater. Germaine blamed her mother.

> People think I talk about my mother with contempt. I don't feel contempt for her; I feel a sort of wonder at my mother's personality structure and a great fear, because I suffered intensely because of my mother's personality when I was a child, and I'm supposed to be grown up and have forgotten about it but it's very difficult to forget being terrorised when you were only two feet high.[16]

Loyally, Peggy turned up to Germaine's early theatre performances, but she was an embarrassment: her appearance – dyed blonde hair, heavy make-up and high heels – contrasted strongly with her daughter's fashionable scruffiness. Germaine learned to be selective when choosing which boys to bring home, because her mother was quite likely to open the front door wearing underpants on her head (to protect her hairstyle) and little else, 'except the suntan for which so much was sacrificed'.[17]

In her second year at university, aged eighteen, Germaine left home for good ('the happiest day of my life'). She found work as a waitress in a popular cafe and fell deeply in love with a drummer from the cafe's resident band.

> I had managed to break through the whole Tall/Freak/ Old Maid syndrome I had been born used to . . . The jazz

drummer was five feet two. It was beautiful. All my insecurities crumbled. I was his woman and that gave me special status.[18]

Using her wages and tips from the waitressing job to supplement her fortnightly cheques from the Education Department, she found various types of accommodation, sometimes working as a housekeeper in exchange for lodging, often just sleeping on friends' couches. More than once, she told her *Guardian* readers thirty years later, she returned to one of her temporary homes to find her meagre belongings dumped outside the door and the locks changed.

The rift with her family became permanent: she stayed away and her parents made no attempt to contact her, even though, as she told television presenter Anthony Clare in 1989, it would have been easy enough for them to find out where she was living. One Christmas, feeling lonely, she took the train out to Mentone hoping to spend Christmas Day at 'home'. When she arrived, her mother began to scream hysterically and hid in a cupboard, claiming to be afraid of her daughter. 'I'm sorry, I can't ask you for Christmas dinner,' said her father. 'If I'm good will you come home?' cried her little brother. Germaine assured him that if he was the only person at home she would stay for the next fifty years. Then she walked off to the station to catch a Christmas Day train back to the city.[19]

In those days, mothers of Catholic girls dreamed that their daughters would marry 'suitable' ex-Xavier young men at snowy white weddings in the Xavier College Memorial Chapel. Germaine was not destined to marry an ex-Xavier boy, but she alleged that she had been raped by one. According to the accounts she has given of her ordeal, it happened at a party she attended with the three boys she was sharing a 'swanky flat' with at the time. As the party progressed, the alcohol flowed and the groping intensified. One young man, 'a strapping great rugby player bred up by the Jesuits to Catholicism and banking . . . just the kind of boy my mother would have wanted me to marry', kept pestering her to go outside with him. Despite her protestations that since everyone else was kissing inside the house in full view of each other, he and she should do the same, he persisted; so she accompanied him into the street and into his car, where he bashed and raped her.

Back at the house, all the boys were sitting around the keg drinking beer. She claimed that they were too drunk to realise what had happened to her.

> I'd fucked a few guys by that time. Sometimes it was a mistake and sometimes it wasn't. But when it was a mistake it wasn't forced on me. I really felt as if someone had made me eat shit. I was certain that anyone who looked at me could tell what had happened to me. They could certainly tell that I was beaten up.[20]

No one at the party would take her home, so she flagged down a passing car and explained that she had been raped. Four days later, she was ironing towels at the flat when the rapist appeared at the door. 'Is this him?' her male friends asked, before taking him into the front room and conducting a sort of trial. Convicted as charged, he was banned from attending any more parties at the luxury seaside and ski resorts they all frequented. Never again would he hold up his head in Portsea or Mount Buffalo! Or so they said. Or, so Germaine says they said.

Deflowered by a Jewish student politician, allegedly raped by an ex-Xavier boy, Germaine continued her iconoclastic trajectory through her university years. Prominent feminist Beatrice Faust, who knew Germaine well, had some concerns about her sexual behaviour.

> She had the full convent syndrome: fucking like crazy, swearing, without being fully formed . . . The way she talked about sex was morbid. She could swear about it, but not talk about it.[21]

Remarking on Faust's observations, Christine Wallace pointed to certain 'dichotomies' in Greer's personality – the Catholic girl who identified as Jewish, the bully who could be extraordinarily kind. Then came her tough bravado and vulnerable fragility, both of which could be apparent in her tone of voice and manner. 'Her voice betrayed the vulnerability,' said Faust, 'she had an over-loud, theatrical voice . . . she specialised in swearing in public, audibly across restaurants. When you got her normal voice on occasion it was like a little-girl voice sometimes saying vulnerable things.'[22]

In 2016, Greer appeared as a panellist on the Australian Broadcasting Corporation current affairs program *Q&A*. She chose to play the role of urbane elder statesperson, defending her questionable views on transgender issues so adroitly that none of the other panellists were brave enough to attack her. Only once, in a moment of wry self-deprecation, did she reveal anything substantial of herself: 'I'm not good at falling in love, let me tell you,' she said, contradicting a comment from a young co-panellist who suggested she was 'the voice of experience' on the subject. But then, at the very end of the program, when host Tony Jones asked her, with a respect that bordered on grovelling, if she would return later in the year and spend a full episode talking about Shakespeare, she lost her place in the venerable-guru script and was suddenly transformed, before the eyes of the watching multitudes, into a little girl. She did not say 'Oh yes! Goody! Goody!', but she might just as well have, as she grinned inanely at the camera, clapping her hands like a child for a couple of revealing seconds. The audience applauded indulgently and Jones wrapped up the program. 'I think we've got her! I think we've got her!' he proclaimed.[23]

But back to 1958. Another dichotomy was between Greer's extravagantly bohemian lifestyle and her developing brilliance as a serious scholar, especially in English literature. She was later to say that the teaching she experienced at Melbourne was the best of her life, better than Sydney or even Cambridge. The Professor of English Literature was Ian Maxwell, a gentle, erudite man of Scottish heritage who held generations of students spellbound with his famous recitals of the Scottish border ballads. One of his close friends in the department, Associate Professor of English Keith Macartney, cut an elegant figure around the university in his immaculately tailored clothes and highly polished shoes, a silk handkerchief protruding discreetly from a shirt-cuff.

Macartney, founder of the university graduates' Tin Alley Players, was a driving force in drama at the university for more than two decades. In 1959, he directed Germaine in her performance as Mrs Antrobus in the Melbourne University Dramatic Society production of Thornton Wilder's *The Skin of Our Teeth*. He came to know Germaine quite well, but her extreme behaviour was a bit much, even for him. Of her lifestyle he once remarked, in his exaggerated Oxford English accent, 'It is most ir-reg-ular, isn't it?'[24]

Frank Knopfelmacher, the notoriously right-wing psychology lecturer and political commentator, expressed an opposite viewpoint when he remarked wearily, 'Ah, Miss Greer, you are so unconventional in such a conventional way.'[25]

Of Germaine's two main areas of study, French and English, the first was a disappointment, but she thrived in the English department, where the teaching was generally first class. Maxwell was a pluralist who encouraged variety both in the curriculum, which ranged from Chaucer and Spenser to Eliot, Joyce, Ezra Pound and Auden, and among the views and attitudes of those he chose to teach it. Despite some growing differences and occasional eruptions, the interactions among staff of the English department were disciplined and courteous.

In this atmosphere of academic excellence and liberality, two men of widely differing backgrounds and beliefs flourished. They were the poet Vincent Buckley and the contrarian Sam Goldberg.

Buckley, whose ancestors were among the many Irish who sought their fortunes in Australia in the nineteenth century, had lived in England and worked at the University of Cambridge on the moral criticism of Matthew Arnold, F.R. Leavis and T.S. Eliot, but his heroes were the Irish poets and scholars, and in his own poetry he continually evoked his heritage.

At Melbourne, Buckley argued successfully, against some powerful opposition, for the work of Australian poets like A.D. Hope, Kenneth Slessor and Judith Wright to be included in the English literature curriculum. In 1958 he became the first Lockie Fellow in Creative Writing and Australian Literature. From 1967 he held a personal Chair in poetry.

As a leading figure in the Melbourne University branch of the Newman Society in these years, Buckley clashed with B.A. Santamaria, a fierce warrior against communism, who, with the Catholic Archbishop of Melbourne Daniel Mannix, provided an intellectual rationale for the anti-communist Democratic

Labor Party. A committed Catholic, Buckley loathed Stalinism, but he had no stomach for the repressive anti-communist hysteria preached from the pulpits of Catholic churches – and in Catholic schools like Star of the Sea.

Perhaps it was because Germaine's family, though Catholic, were not of Irish heritage (the Lafranks were of French and Italian descent), or perhaps it was because Sister Cyril's tirades against the Communist Menace so obviously defied rational belief, that she was not drawn to sit at Buckley's feet as so many of her similarly educated fellow students were. The greatest, perhaps the only, pity of this was that her personal canon of literary scholars and writers was English, not Australian: the subjects of her MA and PhD theses were, respectively, Byron and Shakespeare rather than Henry Lawson or Patrick White.

In keeping with her passion for the greats of English literature, Germaine chose the young and brilliant lecturer Sam Goldberg as her chief intellectual guide and mentor at Melbourne University. The charismatic Goldberg, who was known to have a difficult, confrontational and uncompromising personality, did not suffer fools, but that suited Germaine: despite her wariness of orthodoxies, she gravitated to the doctrine preached with furious enthusiasm by him and his disputatious followers. This doctrine was 'Leavisism', a highly disciplined form of literary criticism developed by the Cambridge scholar F.R. Leavis. Leavisism was elitist in that it permitted only the very 'best' of English literature into its canon: Shakespeare, Jane Austen, George Eliot, Joseph Conrad and T.S. Eliot were admitted after careful scrutiny, but even Dickens had question marks over him for a time. This elitism was founded on demanding and disciplined processes of critical inquiry and debate; it was also moralist, in that Leavis and his wife, Queenie, abhorred the 'crass' values of modern industrialist society and culture, and believed in the unique power of superior English literature to oppose and subvert those values.

Novelist Howard Jacobson, who once, at the gates of Downing College, Cambridge, famously and fruitlessly attempted to engage a college porter called Tony in a deep literary conversation in the mistaken belief that he was speaking to the great F.R. Leavis himself, has explained the huge appeal of Leavis for his and Germaine Greer's generation of scholars.

> [I]t was his life's work to re-explore and redetermine that field – an effort, in his own words, 'that was formative and creative' – not merely to compile a list of great or necessary books (about that notion he was scathing) but as a living, changing continuum that made sense of the very concept of tradition, and more importantly still, of Englishness, not as a patriotic notion but as an achievement of the intelligence, of sensibility, and of language. The poems and novels were there before Leavis, but it took him to show us how they spoke to one another.[26]

Poet, and old friend of Germaine, Chris Wallace-Crabbe has described the enduring influence of Leavis on Greer's work. 'Melbourne turned her into a moralist critic,' he said, 'into an anarchist with moral drive.' Christine Wallace concurred: 'The example of Leavis and the Leavisites' mode of analysis and operation formed the rock-solid foundation of Greer's lifelong ability to assert her positions as absolutely, incontestably correct,' she commented.[27]

●

By her final honours year, Germaine had established her own home in an old hayloft at the back of a Victorian terrace house on the corner of Barry and Grattan streets, directly opposite the university's main gates, for which she paid 15 shillings a week in rent. It had no real door: the only access was up a ladder to a trapdoor, and the only ventilation was from a sort of half-door that opened on to a tree. With the help of friends, she managed to haul an old iron stove up through the trapdoor. Apart from heating, the stove was used for two purposes. The first was to cook a large pot of stew which remained on its surface more or less permanently, feeding dozens of people as well as herself. No one caught anything nasty from its likely contamination – probably, she thought, because of the protective effects of the massive quantities of red wine that were generally consumed with it. She also used the stove to warm her feet, which she placed in the oven while contentedly sitting in her old chair and reading her books. Fuel was free, for she used the wooden blocks that were then being removed from the streets of Melbourne as they became macadamised. The blocks had become impregnated with tar, so they burned beautifully.[28]

Invitations to Germaine Greer's loft were highly prized, for by now she was a celebrated figure at the university, as famous for her academic and thespian brilliance, reckless sexuality and capacity for drinking alcohol as for her fruity language.[29]

Each Thursday morning Germaine attended an honours poetry seminar, where discussions among staff and students, heavily influenced by Sam Goldberg and his followers, would rage, often going beyond the set time. On Thursday evenings she would preside over an 'anti-seminar' in her loft, where the seminar students, but not staff, would gather to debate and construct arguments to challenge the positions taken by their teachers. Chris Wallace-Crabbe, who was a fellow student, has described these evenings as:

> A social gathering over flagons of wine, cheese, bread and kabana, in which the members of the Honours class re-discussed the morning's topic without the presence of the staff. This was an occasion of both release and intellectual development which generated great camaraderie.[30]

Towards the end of her final year, however, Germaine began to realise that she was outgrowing both Melbourne University and the Drift. One evening, some new faces appeared at the Swanston Family Hotel. Among them was that of Kathy McMillan, a slim young woman from Sydney with hanging, dark brown hair. Like Germaine, she was dressed in black.

Germaine later described herself as feeling 'wretched and beleaguered without really knowing it' at this time. Kathy was scathing of the Melbourne scene. 'You're a Sydney person,' she told Germaine. 'You're simply in the wrong place. Come to Sydney.'

In 1972 Greer told historian Ian Turner that she 'ran away' to Sydney in 1959 because she felt a lack of 'reasonable criticism' among Melbourne's bohemians. 'I was very much a rational-ist and very much atheistic and not given to romanticism.' She was also becoming critical of a certain kind of elitism among some members of the Drift. 'I don't ever recall anybody arguing that censorship was wrong in any form, that the less elegantly expressed art form of the working class or the illiterate or the poor should have equal representation to the art forms of the Eltham inhabitants.'[31]

The people she met on her first visit to Sydney in 1959 con-vinced her that this was indeed the city where she belonged, but she did not make her final decision to live there until the end of the year, when she finished her degree. Her results – second class honours – were not bad, considering the many distractions she had enjoyed over the four years, but she was mortified, for this was the first and only time in her life she had failed to achieve top academic excellence. By that time she had several reasons for moving away from Melbourne. First, the obligations of her studentship loomed. She was still bonded to the Victorian Education Department, but she had no intention of burying herself in an isolated country school. As soon as she had finished her final exams she simply walked away with characteristic insouciance. 'Poor Reg,' said a family friend, 'she just took off without a care in the world and left him to pay back her bond.'[32] Carefree as she may have been at the time, Germaine did pay her father back some ten years later when she was in a financial position to do so.

The second factor was that her hopes of an academic career had collapsed after her failure to gain a first at Melbourne. The final and most compelling reason was that she had fallen in love – partly with the seductive charm of Sydney's bohemia, but also with Roelof Smilde, a leader of the Sydney Push and its core group of libertarians and anarchists.

The Push was similar to Melbourne's Drift, but there were some important differences. As in the Drift, Push members congregated in the back rooms and ladies' lounges of grubby, beer-soaked pubs. They lived in rented rooms and flats, they dressed with extravagant carelessness, they disputed loudly and passionately, they flung four-letter words around in joyous defiance of the boring conventions of the boring decade in which they found themselves living. They also revelled in the sexual freedom they had managed to argue themselves into embracing.

Frank Moorhouse pithily dismissed the activities of the Push as 'talking, drinking and fornicating'. Barry Humphries saw it as 'a fraternity of middle-class desperates, journalists, drop-out academics, gamblers and poets manqués, and their doxies'.[33]

Clive James was 'enchanted' when he discovered the Push gatherings at the Royal George hotel.

> If you stuck your head through the door of the back room you came face to face with the Push. The noise, the smoke, and the heterogeneity of physiognomy were too much to take in. It looked like a cartoon on which Hogarth, Daumier and George Grosz had all worked together simultaneously, fighting for supremacy.[34]

On the sexual side of things, James was wryly cynical:

> Endorsing Pareto's analysis of sexual guilt as a repressive social mechanism, the Libertarians freely helped themselves to each other's girlfriends.[35]

In James's view, the 'girlfriends' existed outside the male circle of libertarians as a kind of separate commodity, like fruit waiting to be picked. The females of the Push saw it differently: having unrestricted sex with multiple sexual partners made them feel daringly independent, even powerful. However, the truth may have been closer to James's conception, for the women of the Push hardly seemed to notice that, as in the world outside their circle, it was the males who set the agendas, made the decisions, gave the papers and wrote the broadsheets. Male hobbies and interests dominated: going to the races, studying form guides, playing snooker and card games, gambling of all sorts. Push women listened, typed the men's papers and prepared the tea, as well as making themselves sexually available. This was Australia circa 1950s, and Push culture reflected that context more than any of its rebellious members realised.

The women apparently found it unremarkable that their professional appointments with Push doctor Rocky Meyers were much more frequent than those of the men. Similarly, they took in their stride their visits to the abortionist, Dr Crowe, in Elizabeth Street. Push men did not like to use condoms and, in those pre-pill days, abortion was the main method of contraception. When a woman became pregnant, the hat was passed around in the pub to collect the money required – about £60 – for the operation, which was casually known as a 'scrape'. Sometimes a percentage of bets from a card game would be directed towards financing a woman's abortion. (Push men were serious gamblers, and some card games would continue over several days.)

It was with careless humour that Germaine's old friend Margaret Fink, nearly forty years after her adventures in the Push, told writer Anne Coombs about how she and three other female Push members, all teachers at Strathfield Girls High School, were 'up the duff' at the same time and how, at lunchtime, they had all rushed down the street to a public telephone to call Dr Crowe. 'He was hard to get on to. You always seemed to have to ring about eight times.'[36]

The Push women of the 1950s and early 1960s – even Germaine, who was probably the first female to challenge the men on their own terms – were no feminists. How could they be, when the second wave of feminism was yet to begin and the first wave seemed far in the past? The women got along well enough with each other and even formed lasting friendships, but competition for the best men was strong and the notion of sisterhood practically unheard of.

By 1975, Germaine Greer had become well aware of what she may have only dimly realised in 1959:

> While the Libertarians denied the right of anyone else to control the sexuality of anyone but himself [sic] thus challenging the basic unit of the family as described by Engels, they should not on that account be considered pro-feminist. Push men, even as they aged, continued to exploit their prestige, in selecting pretty young women for their preferred mates. They spoke of women in terms that would not seem out of place in a strip-tease club.[37]

Her lover, Roelof Smilde, came to a similar realisation, but for him the process was longer and more painful. 'I think I've been kidding myself for years and years,' he said in an ABC Radio interview, 'that I've been treating women – in an intellectual and social sense – equally, but I don't think I did, and I think a lot of men in the Push [only] came to realise this through the impact of feminism. Bloody hard to do.'[38]

On the whole, the Sydney libertarians were not politically active. Many years later, Germaine Greer reflected that they did not engage with any of the major issues of the time. Like most Australians of that period, they were also blind to the plight of the Aboriginal population.

> I don't understand how we were so insensitive to the aborigine [sic] situation because we saw enough of them around the pub. There was a pub down the road from the Royal George where black prostitutes were regularly to be seen in

various states of batteredness, various bandages and plaster casts around their person. Oh dear![39]

Push members' well-argued denial of the existence of fixed morality, was, however, the crucible for later action, mainly because it rendered all fields of personal conduct and social organisation wide open to question, thereby challenging the old 'certainties' of God, Queen and Country that were already starting to crumble.

ASIO certainly took the Push leaders seriously:

At first meeting with these people one is inclined to regard them as an offshoot of the 'beatniks', but after knowing them a short while it becomes obvious that they are well above the average 'beatnik' intellectually. Their knowledge of Marxism is surprising and their ability to discuss this subject on levels not encountered in the CPA [Communist Party of Australia] is both stimulating and educational.[40]

On joining the Push, Germaine was immediately drawn to the 'scrupulosity' of its arguments.

When I first encountered the dingy back room of the Royal George, I was a clever, undisciplined, pedantic show-off . . . In the flabby intellectual atmosphere of the Melbourne Drift, I had been encouraged to refrain from ungainly insistence upon logic and the connection of ideas, to be instead witty, joking . . . In Sydney, I found myself driven back, again and again to basic premises, demonstrable facts. The scrupulosity that I had missed in my irreligious life was now a part of my everyday behaviour . . . If ever, of anyone, I desire a good report, I desire it of them, my guides, philosophers and friends, the Sydney Libertarians.[41]

It was the intellectual rigour of the libertarians' philosophy that most strongly appealed to Germaine Greer. The ideas of Marx, Wilhelm Reich and Freud were strong influences on her new friends' thinking, but their more immediate inspiration came from the academic John Anderson at Sydney University, where many of them had studied and some had chosen to drop out. Anderson, Challis Professor of Philosophy at Sydney from 1927 to 1958, was an oppositional realist who, over a lifetime of rigorous philosophical scholarship, argued powerfully against idealist-based notions of an absolute morality. This would probably have meant less to people who had never been schooled in such a morality than to those who, like Germaine, had been force-fed it throughout their childhood and adolescence. Utterly unacceptable to the moralists, but irresistible to the libertarians and anarchists, was the argument that universal moral 'truths' are no more than projections of the interests of particular groups, which are translated into 'thou shalts' and 'thou shalt nots'. Any authority, or so the argument goes, can justify its actions by an appeal to God, but, given multiple understandings of 'God', that in itself is proof that no God is there.

The spirit of the 1960s was stirring in the breasts of some Push members before that tumultuous decade had even begun, and already there were some exceptions to their rule of avoiding political activism. One example concerns two prisoners, Kevin John Simmonds and Leslie Alan Newcombe, who, in 1959, escaped from Emu Plains prison farm and killed a prison warder. Newcombe was soon recaptured, but Simmonds remained at large. Push members rather admired Simmonds for his clever way of operating (he was a car thief who used his car radio to monitor pursuing police, then, when they got too close, simply abandoned that car and stole another one).

After several weeks at large, Simmonds was tracked to a swamp near Newcastle. Volunteers were called for, and hundreds of civilians turned out to hunt him down. This manhunt offended the sensibilities of the Push libertarians. Outraged at the thought of one frightened man being pursued by a posse of redneck vigilantes, they produced a poster, which read in part:

WANTED
By . . . 500 fearless coppers
300 righteous treasure-hunting civilians
armed with submachine-guns, pistols and teargas-guns
Using fleets of cars with two-way radios
A helicopter
The State Treasury
And four bloodhounds . . . .
ONE MAN

For defiance, courage, impertinence, enterprise
Theft, audacity, endurance
Alive or preferably
DEAD

Late one night the group went around the streets of Sydney and through some railway tunnels, putting up the posters under the cover of darkness.

According to Anne Coombs, who recounted this incident in *Sex and Anarchy*, her history of the Push, Germaine Greer was said to be the driver of the getaway car. Appealing though this vision is, however, I realised that it could not be true, for Germaine did not get her drivers' licence until several years later, in England. And sure enough, when I discovered, in Greer's archive, her own annotated copy of *Sex and Anarchy*, I saw that she had written beside the relevant paragraph: 'She had never been behind the wheel of a car in her life.'

More satisfyingly, though, the annotation continued: 'Who does AC suppose WROTE the bloody thing?'[42]

Those libertarians who congregated in the back room of the Royal George hotel in the 1950s formed a talented core who would be remembered into the next century, if only because, as Australian philosopher James Franklin has pointed out, some of them can lay claim to a role in bringing about the massive social changes of the 1960s, including and especially the sexual revolution.[43] These changes were a worldwide phenomenon but Push members, including Germaine Greer, Clive James, Robert Hughes and Richard Neville, later travelled to cities like London and New York, and they took their ideas with them. 'Oh pooh!' declared one prominent former Push member in 2017. 'We were doing all those things long before they started in London. We invented them. We wondered what all the fuss was about. They learnt from us!' The same woman, when asked about contraception in those days, replied carelessly, 'Oh, easy! We just had abortions. I've had five.'[44]

But what of Roelof Smilde, he who was such a major reason for Germaine's move to Sydney in 1959? The son of Dutch immigrants, he has often been described as one of the four Princes of the Push, the others being Darcy Waters, Jim Baker and George Molnar. All were former students of John Anderson.

Smilde and Waters were well-built and blond in a Germanic way that some would have described as 'Aryan'. As the two best-looking men they, together with Molnar and Baker, who were less beautiful but more intellectual, were at the apex of the hierarchy and therefore had the best choice of sexual partners. Women who were favoured with more or less regular sexual congress with these heroes enjoyed the highest status of the female Push members. This mirrored the situation in society at large, where good-looking and successful men were often partnered with attractive and gifted women. Even in the Push, thinking had not yet reached a point where it was conceivable that a woman might rise to high rank entirely on her own merits. On her arrival in Sydney, Germaine almost instantly became the top female in the group, partly because of her own brilliance, physical presence and flamboyant personality, but mainly because she was the favoured partner of Roelof Smilde, whom she loved for quite a long time.

Germaine and Roelof met when she was holidaying in Sydney late in 1959, shortly before she finished her degree at Melbourne. After an intense conversation at a Greek cafe after pub closing time, Germaine asked Smilde if he would agree to her coming to live in Sydney. 'I was a little bit startled. It was an unusual request. I don't remember having said anything, but she must've had the impression I was attracted to her. I said yeah, it would be all right'.[45]

In *Sex and Anarchy*, Anne Coombs stated that Roelof was already in a relationship with Push member Roseanne Bonney when he first met Germaine, that Germaine 'supplanted Roseanne in Roelof's affections' and that the sexual jealousy between the two women continued into the 1980s.[46] Greer scornfully disputed this claim. She had never considered Roseanne Bonney as serious competition, she remarked after reading Coombs's book, especially in relation to Roelof. 'I never took Roelof off Roseanne Bonney,' she declared hotly.[47]

At that time Roelof was working as a wharf lumper on Sydney's waterfront. He was also making a living from gambling at the racetrack, driving taxis and playing bridge, at which he excelled. One day early in 1960 he came home to the small terrace house in North Sydney that he shared with friends, to find Germaine on his doorstep. This was the period in which she had taken to emulating Chaucer's lusty Wyf of Bath by encasing her remarkably long and shapely legs in stockings 'of fyn scarlet reed'. He was impressed.

Roelof and Germaine immediately became a relatively monogamous couple. They moved to a house in Glebe and settled into a kind of domesticity, but mainly they were the stars of the Push, carousing at the Royal George, arguing loudly and furiously, challenging convention, dancing, singing, having lots of fun and sex. For a while they were happy. So deeply did she love Roelof that, with typical thoroughness and determination, Germaine even attempted to share his devotion to the horses.

> Sydney has three race-tracks and I served a very hard apprenticeship on all three. For one whole year I had to come to every metropolitan race meeting; I had to bet on one horse and one horse only. I had to lay a uniform stake of five shillings, which went up to ten shillings after a while. The idea was that I was being taught to make a living by gambling . . . I remember it was so boring that I could not bring myself to study the form.[48]

On Friday nights she would fall asleep over the form guide.

Her use of the phrase 'had to' in the above passage is interesting: is it a mark of Germaine's submissiveness in the relationship? Surely not! But try as she might to please her lover, things were not working out. Was this because she and Roelof were over-intellectualising the relationship, as she later claimed? 'I have learned to regret the way I curbed the violence of my obsessive love for a particular Libertarian, so that it became manageable and reasonable and died altogether.' Or was it simply that, like so many women over the millennia, she loved a man who was not ready to make a commitment?

She found a lonely sort of comfort in Sydney's unique beauty:

> When I sometimes got miserable with the people I lived with or with the Royal George, I used to run away to where the footpath was torn up on the [Harbour] bridge and climb down into the rigging underneath it and sit waving my legs above the sea where the wind called the southerly buster blew away all the crossness and all the arguments.[49]

Germaine may well have wanted to have a child by Roelof, but she knew that children were not welcome in Push circles. She also felt that she was not yet ready for motherhood. That feeling may be viewed as commonplace today, but this was the 1950s, when it was usual for women to marry and have children in their early twenties. Push women were hell-bent on escaping such stereotypes, as they asserted their right and even felt obligated to copulate freely, but they were still women of their time, victims of a kind of innocence. Their freedom came at a price, for there were no models of truly liberated women for them to emulate. They were ignorant of female biology, and they seem to have been unaware that their fertility would be compromised as their reproductive years drained away and their bodies suffered the effects of multiple abortions, sexually transmitted diseases and primitive forms of contraception.

The men did not have these problems: many of them later had children with younger women. Roelof, with a new partner, had two daughters in the 1970s. Marion Hallwood, a girlfriend of Roelof's before Germaine, had three abortions while she was with him. 'He said he never wanted children,' she told Anne Coombs. 'I never minded the abortions at the time, but years later, when he had those two children, I was so angry.' Marion never had children.[50]

For all Roelof Smilde's attractiveness and influence over Germaine, he was not the decision-maker in the relationship. In 1959 it was she who made the decision to live with him. Eighteen months later she decided to leave him.

Germaine Greer made many friends in Sydney. Among them was the anarchist poet and Push luminary Harry Hooton, who died in 1961, aged 51. Hooton, who much admired Germaine in her red stockings, had a lasting influence on her development.

> When I last saw him he was dying, just a whisper of himself, but still enormous, the power of his soul filled the little room he lay in. And he called me to tell me he had great faith in me, that he thought I was the woman of the twenty-first century. I didn't know what he meant then, but I think a lot of the things I've done since I've done out of a desire to please Harry Hooton. Too late . . .[51]

At 44, Harry had fallen in love with flamboyant 19-year-old fellow Push member Margaret Elliott. They lived in a flat in Potts Point for several years until his death. She never forgot her first meeting with Germaine Greer. 'She just knocked on our door. I opened the door and here was this phenomenal creature! I'm five feet four and she's six foot. I couldn't believe my eyes! She filled the door frame. Fabulous hair! Just a splendid creature!'[52]

Elliott's love for Hooton did not preclude her from having various tempestuous affairs, including one with Barry Humphries, which continued into the years when Humphries was struggling with the early signs of his alcoholism, and creating his most famous character, Edna Everage. Elliott had more lovers after Harry's death, but eventually married and divorced Leon Fink, the very same clever, handsome Leon Fink who had deflowered Germaine on the grass at Studley Park, Kew, in 1957 and who later became a wealthy property developer.

Margaret Fink was and is Germaine Greer's closest lifelong friend. As young, middle-aged and old women the two have continued to share, across continents, a zest for outrageous behaviour, a zany sense of humour and a raucous enjoyment of *la dolce vita*. Germaine was godmother to Margaret's children, and developed a particularly close relationship with her daughter, Hannah. On her regular visits to London, where the Finks stayed either at Claridge's or at Germaine's house, Margaret – Germaine's 'nice little Australian friend' – was welcomed into Greer's circle of literary and theatrical identities.

In Sydney, Margaret Fink was renowned for the fabulous parties she hosted in her luxurious harbour-side home, where many of the most brilliant and creative people of her generation gathered to enjoy fine food, champagne, butler service and, above all, each other's company. Some of them would stay on for days or weeks. 'Once, between houses, I lived with her,' recalled Max Lambert, Australian composer and musical director. 'For several mornings in a row I sleepily came downstairs and there was Barry Humphries, the next day Clive James, the third day Germaine Greer. I felt like I hadn't woken up, and was still dreaming . . .'[53]

'Margaret had a dinner party one Friday night,' recalls publisher and editor Richard Walsh. 'I was working in Melbourne, aiming to catch a 7 pm flight to Sydney. By the time I arrived it was one of the most chaotic dinner parties imaginable. All kinds of shenanigans. Germaine was there with [her current Australian boyfriend]. They would come and go for a root. Like everyone. Everyone there was paired off. Everyone was pissed or stoned or off rooting. I just walked into it. It was emblematic of the era.'[54]

In 1980, journalist and author Jilly Cooper wrote in the *Sunday Times* about going to a party at Margaret Fink's 'vast Charles Addams pile festooned with creeper'. At first, she said, she thought she was at the wrong house, because of the loud music and roars of laughter that echoed all the way down the street. Inside, she found Margaret presiding over a large table, around which sat '[a]mazingly beautiful people, mostly media luminaries of a slightly indeterminate sexuality'. They were celebrating the birthday of Margaret's boyfriend's ex-boyfriend. (She was still married to Leon at this time, but they had an 'open' marriage.) Margaret was trying to persuade an actor named John to marry his current girlfriend, the actress Kate Fitzpatrick. 'I will organise the wedding,' she cried, 'I will even be a bridesmaid.'

'At my wedding,' said John, looking at his girlfriend, 'you can both be bridesmaids.'

Cooper goes on to record that when Margaret once returned from a visit to Europe she was met by the distraught nanny, who confessed she had been to bed with Leon. 'Is that all,' said a relieved Margaret. 'For a dreadful moment I thought you were going to give your notice.'[55]

Fink, like many former Push members who later went on to distinguished careers, became famous in her own right. A celebrated film producer, her productions include *The Removalists* (1975),

My Brilliant Career (1979), *For Love Alone* (1986), *Edens Lost* (1988, for TV), and *Candy* (2006).

After she left Roelof, Germaine decided that there was a life for her beyond the beer-soaked delights of the Royal George. Because she was ambitious, because she loved to study, and because she had always felt at home in a university environment, she decided to enrol in a Master of Arts degree at Sydney University. This time she had no scholarship. And no money. Had she succeeded in her apprenticeship under Roelof as a professional gambler, she might have earned a living at the racetrack, but as it was she decided to finance her studies through the more conventional means of teaching at various Sydney high schools. By all accounts, including her own, she was a popular, conscientious school teacher in the two years it took to finish her thesis. But she did manage to get herself sacked from one school – a 'middle class ladies' school' – for distributing literature that gave two sides of the Hungarian uprising of 1956 and asking her students to examine both, compare them and check for bias. The school principal, whose ideas were closer to those of Sister Cyril at Star of the Sea than contemporary pedagogical thought and practice, accused her of disseminating propaganda. In vain Germaine protested that she was teaching the girls *about* propaganda.

'Miss Greer, are you a Communist?'

'No.' Useless to argue that a libertarian and anarchist could not be a communist, but she had to go. The parents had objected. It was a fee-paying school.[56]

At university, she was soon back in her element, starring regularly in student theatre and film productions, falling in and out of love, her six-foot figure once again iconic around the campus. But she was not about to risk another embarrassing second-class degree that would destroy forever her hopes of an academic career. She applied herself.

She chose Byron as the subject of her thesis. And why would she not? Forget Roelof Smilde and Leon Fink: George Gordon Byron, sixth Baron Byron, was the archetype of his own creation, the Byronic hero that Germaine had worshipped since her discovery of Steerforth when she first read *David Copperfield* at the age of eleven. Brooding, impossibly handsome, aloof, angry, intelligent, sensual, scorning convention in his determination to pursue his own versions of truth and justice, the Byronic hero is irresistible to women. Often, like Emily Bronte's Heathcliff, or F. Scott Fitzgerald's Gatsby, he has been abused or deprived in childhood: he needs to be mothered and consoled in his rare moments of weakness. And persevered with, as he sorts out his tortured personality. 'Mad, bad and dangerous to know', the Byronic hero takes his pleasure with women as he finds it: he loves and leaves them on his terms.

The most attractive men of the Push were Byronic heroes of a sort, but it was Germaine herself who came closest to the ideal. She and Byron had much in common. Byron's appearances in London society – the handsome seducer stalking majestically through the glittering drawing rooms of Regency London, as described by his biographer Phyllis Grosskurth – are reminiscent of fellow students' descriptions of Germaine striding around the Melbourne University campus in her flowing cloak. Germaine was seducer as well as seduced; her ready wit, awareness of irony and, above all, her towering intellect, all matched Byron's. Like him, she was a star of her generation, like him she was her own theatrical production.

Had Germaine Greer been Byron's contemporary, it could have been of her he was thinking when he wrote:

She was like me in lineaments — her eyes
Her hair, her features, all, to the very tone
Even of her voice, they said were like to mine;
But soften'd all, and temper'd into beauty;
She had the same lone thoughts and wanderings,
The quest of hidden knowledge, and a mind
To comprehend the universe[57]

A mind to comprehend the universe! Little wonder that Germaine was in love with Byron, and that her emotions enhanced her critical judgement of his worth as a poet. But while she quoted him devotedly, and even carried a notebook called 'Byrony' close to her heart, she was shrewdly aware that, in order to achieve the first class honours on which her future career depended, she would have to produce a work of solid critical scholarship that would meet the stringent criteria of some very tough examiners. Schooled as she was in the rigorous Leavisite tradition of her apprenticeship at Melbourne University, she worked solidly, researching meticulously, finding and documenting a multitude of sources, writing with discipline, flair and wit to produce her thesis, 'The Development of Byron's Satiric Mode'.

The only problem for anyone considering this thesis as part of her later body of work – and it was obviously not a problem for her or her teachers and examiners – was that very little in the way of feminist consciousness was to be found in her thesis. Greer's focus, in line with the title of her dissertation, was on the irony and satire in Byron's depictions of his heroes' treatment of women, not on their often contemptuous attitudes towards them. Details of his own life, like his brutal treatment of his wife and mistresses, likely incestuous relationship with his sister and habit of sending his *gondolieri* to buy women and bargain with parents of young girls for their daughters' sexual services, went unremarked.

Most committed feminists would have deplored lines like:

She, in sooth,
Possess'd an air and grace by no means common:
Her stature tall – I hate a dumpy woman.[58]

Germaine would have laughed.

She received first class honours for her MA thesis. When Sam Goldberg arrived at Sydney in 1963 to take up the Challis Chair of English Literature, she accepted his offer of a senior tutorship. Her academic career was at last on track.

Professor Stephen Knight, now of the University of Melbourne, has good memories of the 25-year-old Miss Greer as a colleague and fellow tutor in 1964. Not long arrived in Sydney from England, and still not sure that he would ever adapt to the casual Australian university culture, Knight was grateful for Germaine's friendship. In 2016, he recalled that in her room, which was next to his in the Carslaw Building, she had a fish tank that was occupied by two goldfish. He would hear her clear voice through the thin walls as she conducted her tutorials.

'What are the names of the fish?'

Puzzled silence.

'Correct answer: Form and Content. You can't tell the difference, can you?'

Thus, unforgettably, said Knight, Greer explained a feature of Leavisite criticism to her students, using the well-tried teaching method of illustrating important points with imaginative resources. The young Englishman was impressed. He would later say: 'She was undoubtedly an excellent teacher. And one of the best lecturers – one of the few who could command the Wallace lecture theatre, with its six hundred students. She had a kind of histrionic quality which was quite remarkable, added to her real scholarship.'

Knight remembers her as a popular and interesting member of the English staff. 'She was very tall. You certainly knew when she entered the tea room. She seemed to command the room at once. Everyone would cheer up when Germaine came in.'

Knight particularly recalled Germaine's kindness and willingness to help others. 'There was one young chap from Oxford looking for accommodation in Sydney – Michael Wilding – Germaine was very patient with him, took him around all over the place looking for somewhere to live.'

One conversation, overheard in the tea room, has remained in his mind for the last fifty years.

'Where are you off to this afternoon, Germaine?' inquired a senior staff member.

'I'm going to the races. Can you lend me twenty quid?'[59]

This was the period when Professor Sam Goldberg was furiously recruiting Leavisites, some from Melbourne, to advance his mission to revolutionise the study of English literature at Sydney. Having inspired Germaine, he would have been glad to have her continued support, but he could see that her brilliance would take her far beyond Sydney and that it would be wrong of him to hold her back. So, instead of persuading her to stay, he generously encouraged her to accept the Commonwealth Scholarship she had won to study at the University of Cambridge.

3

Changing skies

Caelum non animum mutant qui trans mare currunt.
They change their sky but not their soul, who rush
across the sea.

Horace, 65 BC–8 BC

Before World War II, opportunities for overseas travel were generally limited to the wealthier classes of Australian society. For most white Australians, setting off on one of the great 'mail-boats' that were almost their only physical connection with their cultural heritage was a dream not often realised. The rest of the world – the real world of their language and culture – was a long, long way away.

Yet many people still thought of the countries of their recent ancestors, especially England, as 'home'. Australian girls like Germaine Greer were brought up on a literary fare of English storybooks and poetry replete with village squires, jolly boarding schools, meadows and stiles. At school, they were taught British and European history; they drew maps of the British Isles in their copybooks, and they absorbed the values of the Empire, values that were only starting to become reconceptualised as those of 'The British Commonwealth of Nations'.

What does it mean to grow up in a land of droughts and flooding rains and endless suburbs while your head is filled with visions of the Tower of London and leafy reaches of the Thames? In 1989, Germaine Greer, in her column for *The Independent* magazine, reflected on that experience.

> Thirty-five years ago, in Australia, I learnt by heart Browning's poem 'Home thoughts from abroad'. I had no idea where abroad was. I was in it. I did not think of England as home, rather as the centre. I lived somewhere on an outer edge of a geographical suburbia called The Commonwealth. My head was stuffed with Englishness. I knew more about hedgehogs and squirrels than I did about echidnas and possums.[1]

Having her head 'stuffed with Englishness' also caused the young Germaine Greer to develop an enduring love of English and European literature, and an uncomfortable feeling that her own country could never fully nourish and sustain her. She had a point: culturally, the Australia she left in 1964 was changing but it was still, as Ian Britain described it in 1997, 'too circumscribed a stage to contain such a high-octane performer as herself'.[2]

She was not alone; other young Australians felt the same, and the times were right for them. In the 1960s, as fares to England became cheaper, jobs abounded and wages improved, the ships that carried thousands of immigrants to a new life in a new land did not return empty but instead were filled with the youth of Australia, in search of adventure. To London they went, and if it was not quite the London of their storybooks, and if the Londoners treated them with a kind of amused contempt, they cared little. They lived in Earls Court bedsitters, got drunk at the Down Under club and worked as secretaries, nurses, teachers, labourers, whatever they could find, until the summer, when they set off in their campervans to discover Europe. They were seeking home, but most of them would have to go back to Australia to find it.

By the time she arrived in England, Germaine had already eclipsed the great majority of these young Australian expats. Her first experiences in England were not of Earls Court but of Cambridge. As the winner of a Commonwealth Scholarship, she had achieved not only academic success, but instant access to a world of privilege.

Having chosen Cambridge over Oxford, largely because her beloved Lord Byron had studied there, Germaine moved in to rooms on the first floor of a comfortable Newnham College hostel, with a diamond-leadlight casement window through which Clive James would eventually effect entry. As an 'affiliated student' she was expected to study for the Tripos, a bachelor's degree that normally took three years but which scholarship holders like herself were permitted to complete in two. The underlying assumption of this requirement was that Australian degrees were inferior versions of the Oxbridge models they tried to copy. At first Germaine agreed with this judgement, but as soon as she hit her straps she changed her mind. 'I thought [the degree] I had probably wasn't good enough,' she later recalled.

I was completely wrong. Cambridge offered an inferior version of the same thing. After the first term, I realised they were not going to teach me anything so I transferred to the PhD programme.[3]

Clive James, who also won a scholarship to Cambridge, later declared that it was 'by force of argument' that Germaine had got herself registered as a PhD student. Maybe there was a trace of envy on his part, for after only a few months in England

she had streaked ahead not only of most of her young compa-
triots who were enjoying themselves in London, but of other
Commonwealth Scholarship holders as well, including himself.
Academically, she was a compulsive high-achiever: he was not.
The university library, he said, 'swallowed her up . . . like a
tomb'. Fiercely resenting any interruptions to her work, she filled
her rooms with books and settled down to unremitting study. She
managed to make time for some other pursuits, like acting, but if
James is to be believed, study came first. Or perhaps she was just
making excuses for not wanting to go to bed with him.

'I didn't ever sleep with Clive James,' she told an interviewer
in 2000:

> That was the whole point, I never fancied him. I said about
> him a long time ago that Clive was a very witty man, but
> not sexy. I said it to his face. I was doing this talk show and
> I said, 'The thing about you, Clive, is that you're very witty
> and very interesting, but you're just not sexy.' And he said
> 'I know.'[4]

Academically, and socially, university life for female students
was improving by the time Germaine arrived at Cambridge in
1964, but there were still traces of the discrimination women
had suffered for most of the first half of the twentieth century.
They were not formally permitted to graduate until 1948, social
interaction between students in the segregated male and female
colleges was discouraged, and some lectures were closed to
women. 'Women were lacking from our lives,' Nigel Nicolson
wrote of Oxford in the 1930s. 'We knew that they existed
somewhere in the outer suburbs linked somewhere to our great
monastery, but we never met them.'[5]

By the mid-1960s, however, women were starting to become more visible around the university and some of them were occupying positions of influence. The two Cambridge dons who guided Greer's study at this time were Professor Muriel Bradbrook and Dr Anne Righter. As powerful, successful women who had defied every limitation imposed on them, they also by example strongly influenced her later feminist thinking. Bradbrook, 55 years old when Germaine arrived at Cambridge, had studied for her first degree at Cambridge in 1930 but, being a woman, was not permitted to graduate: she received her certificate, onto which the word 'titular' had been inserted by hand, in the mail. She sat through the daytime lectures of Sir Arthur Quiller-Couch, who addressed his audience as 'Gentlemen', but was not permitted to attend his evening lectures on Aristotle's *Poetics*, because they were closed to women. Later she studied under F.R. Leavis, wrote several influential books, travelled widely and established herself as an eminent Shakespearean scholar. Awarded a Chair at Cambridge in 1965, she was the first female Professor of English in the university's long history. Bradbrook led the Renaissance seminars that had a profound effect on Germaine's thinking, and it was she who persuaded Germaine to choose Shakespeare as the subject of her thesis.

Anne Righter was an American scholar, six years older than Germaine, who later became a professor under the name of her second husband, the theatre director John Barton (co-founder, with Sir Peter Hall, of the Royal Shakespeare Company). After graduating summa cum laude from Bryn Mawr College in the United States, Righter was awarded her doctorate at Cambridge in 1960. Published as *Shakespeare and the Idea of the Play* in 1962, her thesis was supervised by Muriel Bradbrook. In 1974, Righter (then Barton) became the first female fellow of New College, Oxford. She and Germaine formed a lasting friendship.

While Germaine Greer's affection and admiration for both Muriel Bradbrook and Anne Righter are beyond question, she was dismissive of that breed of older (but still called 'New') academic women, belonging to the earlier wave of feminism, to which both of her mentors were connected. The stereotypical old New Women, she wrote in an unpublished draft of the 'Summary' to *The Female Eunuch*, had rejected their femininity; they dressed like men and 'eschewed' the company of women.

> The heavy-footed tweed-clad New Women who presided over my college were too inefficient, too crabby, too joyless, to serve as ushers into a new wave of life. They were so consciously elitist that most 'silly' girls felt they were better off left outside their charmed circle. Most 'normal' girls hastily denied any interest in liberty which in those days was called 'emancipation'.[6]

When dining in college, Germaine was struck by the contrasts between the 'sour faces and shapeless bodies' of the female dons who sat with the principal at the high table, and the pretty young women who sat with her at the students' tables – the 'Jennys and Valeries and Lindas and Sues – very dull girls indeed', whose conversation was 'as vapid and girlish as you might expect at lunchtime in Selfridges Canteen'.[7]

What did those girls have to look forward to if they wanted to escape the world of the desiccated old New Women? To become a faculty wife, perhaps? But even this door seemed closed to them: at faculty parties Germaine noted that most of the male dons seemed to have married 'decorative and tranquil women who could scarcely speak English'. And Cambridge men continued to choose debutantes from London as their trophy partners for the May Balls.[8]

It would be only a few years before Germaine Greer and other feminists of the second wave would offer new models and alternatives for the Jennys and Valeries and Lindas and Sues, but in the meantime Professor Bradbrook and her colleagues had to be tough as they continued to battle against discrimination in academic life.

Nor was it easy for male and female students to break free of the gender-based restrictions imposed by hundreds of years of custom and tradition. Things had improved since 1938 but, like Nigel Nicolson and others before him, Clive James bemoaned the paucity of female company in clubs and societies around the university. He feared that the university library may have absorbed most of the women as it had 'swallowed up' Germaine, since there seemed to be so few of them about. 'The relative absence of a civilising female influence made it all the easier,' he said, 'to get disgustingly drunk.'[9]

James, who had known Germaine at the University of Sydney and in the Push, was delighted to rediscover her at the Cambridge University Footlights Dramatic Club. They met at an audition for the first of two 'smoking concerts', known as 'smokers', that were given by the club each term. The results of these auditions were the basis upon which candidates were selected for Footlights membership, but no female had ever been admitted to the club in its long history. Even Germaine, on this occasion, was doubtful that she would succeed.

The venue for the audition was the club room above the MacFisheries fish shop in Falcon Yard. As James tells the story, he was wearing a rented dinner suit and Germaine a satin dress she had modified herself to contain her generous bosom. (James noted that 'she was always a dab hand at the household tasks against which she later rebelled on behalf of all women-kind'.)

The smell of halibut wafted through the floorboards as the two performed a sketch in which James, as Noël Coward with a Chips Rafferty accent, played opposite Germaine's Gertrude Lawrence. 'I was awful, she was great,' said James, 'so we both got in.'[10]

Eric Idle, the club president, was delighted that his long-cherished plan to admit women to the club had been realised, but others were not happy.

> Up until then, women could appear in Footlights revues only as guests, and most of the dons who congregated around the club's small but thriving bar made it piercingly clear that they had preferred the era of good, straightforward transvestism, with properly shaved legs and no nonsense about it.[11]

Germaine was as unimpressed by those dons as they were by her. 'This place is jumping with freckle-punchers,' she told James in broad Australian. 'You can have it on your own.' Nevertheless, the two went on to perform in many a Footlights revue. Particularly popular was Germaine's nun-striptease routine in which, dressed as a Carmelite nun in a costume she had run up herself, she stripped to a brief bikini.

The 1960s marked a stellar period in the Footlights club's history. Its membership included John Cleese, Peter Cook, Eric Idle and David Frost. Julian Fellowes, Charles Mountbatten-Windsor, Kevin McCloud and Stephen Fry came later. Women were noticeably absent from the membership lists in the first half of the century, but this changed after Germaine was admitted. The name of Miriam Margolyes, who is two years younger than Greer, appeared on the lists shortly after Greer's. Other female names followed. Most of the better-known members up to the present time have gone on to careers in film, comedy, drama and broadcasting, but there are also journalists, politicians, diplomats and Peers of the Realm.

Clive from Kogarah and Germaine from Mentone were in fine company, but there were big differences in their attitudes to study. In the present vernacular you might say she was 'focused' while he was not. This was brought home to him when he moved into a room in the ancient, half-timbered Friar House in Bene't Street and discovered that he would have to suffer not only the smell of curry from the Pakistani restaurant on the ground floor, but also the Neighbour from Hell, his old friend from the Antipodes, in the room next door.

Germaine had also chosen to move to Friar House because of its quaint atmosphere and cheap rent.

> In something less than a week, [Germaine], who in another time and place might have run the sort of salon that Goethe and the boys would have swarmed around like blowflies, had already transformed her room into a dream from the Arabian nights. Drawing on her incongruous but irrepressible skills as a housewife, she had tatted lengths of batik, draped bolts of brocade, swathed silk, swagged satin . . . Aristotle Onassis had married Jackie Kennedy in vain hopes of getting his yacht to look like that.[12]

But Germaine had created her bower for a more serious purpose.

> She had a typewriter the size of a printing press. Instantly she was at it, ten hours a day. Through the lath-and-plaster wall I could hear her attacking the typewriter as if she had a contract, with penalty clauses, for testing it to destruction.[13]

She loved to study and she loved to excel, she was determined to forge a career in academic life, but her relentless determination to do well at Cambridge had an additional motive: she did not want to go home to Australia. All Commonwealth Scholarship holders knew that at the end of their studies they would be expected to return to their native countries to become flag-bearers of British learning, values and culture; for the generosity of their Commonwealth benefactors was grounded in the fading but stubbornly enduring ideals of Empire-building. The students also knew, however, that the best of them would be allowed to stay and make their careers in England with its great universities, libraries, museums, galleries and easy access to Europe. Their passports still declared them to be British subjects, and they saw no disloyalty in remaining at the 'centre' of the Commonwealth rather than at its culturally impoverished periphery. Germaine knew she was among the best of the scholarship holders, and it was almost a corollary to being the best that she should be permitted to remain where she was.

The title of her PhD thesis was 'The Ethic of Love and Marriage in Shakespeare's Early Comedies'. Her stated intention was to 'explore the relationships of lovers in a way that cannot be explained by reference to established convention'. This was breaking new ground, especially important in the field of Shakespearean studies, where so much had already been written that scholars found it difficult to discover new areas to explore.

In a response to a query from the University of Melbourne Archives in 2015, Greer said that the seven research notebooks she had written in 1965, and which are now housed in the Germaine Greer Archive at the university, were 'possibly more interesting' than the thesis typescript itself. Unlike most scholars, who did not have the language skills to read the European plays of this tradition in their original French, German, Italian, Latin or Spanish, she considered herself sufficiently fluent in those languages to argue that Shakespeare was not imitating a continental tradition. This, she said in 2015, was the main point of her research. Each notebook has a name that corresponds to the places she worked in, e.g. the Bodleian at Oxford, the British Museum, the Marciana in Venice. Notes are written mostly in English, but also in French, Latin and Italian.

The Shakespeare sections of Greer's research notes do not make easy reading, as University of Melbourne archivist Rachel Buchanan found when curating the Greer collection in 2016. After prising out dozens of rusting staples from ripped, fragile papers, staining her fingers in the process as the staples fell apart in her hands, Buchanan initially found the material daunting and not of great interest to a modern scholar like herself.

> [H]ere I was wading through dozens of folders of notes about 16th and 17th-century men who wrote plays, poems, sermons and pamphlets: Shakespeare; Lyly; Browne; Sidney; Spenser; Nashe; Jonson; Webster; Dryden; Donne; Sir John Davies; Samuel Daniel; Butler.
>
> Once I had got through the individual blokes, there were many more folders about Renaissance literature, Jacobean drama and, of course, William Shakespeare's early comedies . . .[14]

She was moved by the evidence of Greer's scholarship, but wondered:

> aside from a future biographer, what sort of researcher would ever want to look at these bits of old paper? . . . The

records appeared absolutely academic, in the most disparaging popular definition of that much abused word. Where was the Greer liberation, feminism, fire?[15]

Buchanan found an answer to this question when she asked herself another one: 'What happens if you read *The Female Eunuch* not for evidence of feminism but for evidence of Shakespeare?' Taking up her 2006 Harper Perennial Modern Classics paperback edition of Greer's book, she discovered that many of the names she had been cataloguing from Greer's PhD research notebooks also appeared in the text and footnotes of *The Female Eunuch*.

Half of the references in the Sex sub-section are Renaissance-era writers. Ditto for The Stereotype. Most of the sources cited in The Ideal are at least 400 years old: Shakespeare, Spenser, Sidney, Daniel, Wyatt, Nashe, anonymous Elizabethan ballads, they are all named in a couple of dense pages in the sub-section The Middle-Class Myth of Love and Marriage.[16]

Nineteen years earlier, Christine Wallace, who did not have the advantage of access to the Greer archive, had noticed that parts of the 'Middle-Class Myth of Love and Marriage' chapter of *The Female Eunuch* looked 'suspiciously like off-cuts from her doctoral thesis'. There was far more of Shakespeare and the Renaissance in the chapter, she said, than of modern matrimony and Mills & Boon.[17]

And there, perhaps, is the secret, or one of them, of *The Female Eunuch*'s success. Feminist writers until that time had sourced most of their material from contemporary or comparatively recent accounts of women's struggle for independence. Greer approached the subject from another angle, that of her work as a humanist scholar. An essential requirement of her study for the PhD was to learn about the rich, centuries-old literature about humankind's experiences of love and marriage – the stories, the plays, the folklore, the characters – that would inform not only her thesis, but also her later writing. This was the labour for which she was 'swallowed up' in libraries in England and Europe, and which fed the clattering typewriter that drove Clive James to distraction.

All of this is to say that, as Buchanan correctly stated and Wallace suspected, Greer's PhD studies substantially influenced her later writing as a feminist. But what happens if we turn the question around to inquire what evidence of feminist thinking is to be found in her thesis? The plays she chose to write about were *The Two Gentlemen of Verona*, *The Comedy of Errors*, *The Taming of the Shrew* and *Love's Labour Lost*. Of most interest with regard to feminism is her treatment of *The Taming of the Shrew*.

Shakespeare adapted the central ideas of this play from various folktales dealing with the notion of the shrewish woman, the 'scold', often punished by the cruel scold's bridle, who talks too much and too loudly, is a scourge to her menfolk and must be tortured until she either submits or is burned as a witch. The play's characters are Katharine (Kate), the elder daughter of Baptista, a wealthy merchant of Padua, and Petruchio, who is prepared to marry Kate, sight unseen, because of her father's wealth. This is a commercial transaction. Kate, the shrew, is embarrassing her family by her rebellious spirit and ungovern-able tongue. Her younger sister, the sweet and generous Bianca, has fallen in love with Lucentio, a student who is of good family, but custom decrees that she cannot be courted by him until her difficult older sister has found a husband. So everyone but Kate is relieved and delighted when the dashing Petruchio persuades Baptista to agree to the marriage, which is to take place almost immediately.

Petruchio arrives late to the wedding. He is wearing a strange assortment of old clothes and is mounted on a broken-down horse – all calculated to insult Kate. Already he is turning out to be something of a Byronic hero who puzzles and intrigues her as he rides roughshod over her protestations. Refusing to attend the marriage feast, or to allow his new wife to attend, he carries her off through the mud to his country house, having told everyone that she is now his property and he can do what he likes with her.

> She is my goods, my chattels; she is my house,
> My household stuff, my field, my barn,
> My horse, my ox, my ass, my anything . . .[18]

In their new home at Verona, Petruchio teases Kate unmercifully, denying her food and clothing, declaring mockingly that nothing is good enough for her – the meat is not cooked properly, a stylish new hat is not fashionable, beautiful clothes do not fit properly. He disagrees with everything she says and forces her to agree with whatever he says, no matter how absurd. Gradually, cold, tired and hungry, Kate gives in.

In the meantime, Bianca has married Lucentio, and Hortensio, friend of Petruchio, has married a rich widow. At a banquet to celebrate Hortensio's marriage, the three new husbands stage a contest to see which of their wives will come to them first when summoned. Everyone expects the sweet Bianca to be the first to obey, but to general astonishment, it is the tamed Katharine who, to demonstrate her submission to her husband, declares herself willing to place her hand beneath his foot, declaring:

Thy husband is thy lord, thy life, thy keeper,
Thy head, thy sovereign; one that cares for thee,
And for thy maintenance commits his body
To painful labour both by sea and land
To watch the night in storms, the day in cold,
Whilst thou liest warm at home, secure and safe . . .[19]

And so on, in the same vein, announcing that she is ashamed for her sex of women who disobey their husbands They 'are bound to serve, love and obey,' she simpers.

Petruchio, having won the bet, is delighted: 'Why, there's a wench! Come on, and kiss me Kate!' he exclaims joyfully. And off they go to bed.

In the years between 1594 (the approximate date of the play's first appearance) and 1967, when Germaine completed her thesis, many critics struggled with *The Taming of the Shrew*'s apparent misogyny. One reading has it that the play is sincere – Petruchio rightly and successfully tamed Katharine; another sees it as a farce, and yet another suggests that he has simply fallen in love with her and she with him in a meeting of minds and bodies. A popular twentieth-century interpretation was that Katharine's submission was faked. In a 1929 film version, the actress Mary Pickford as Kate winks at Bianca as a sign she does not mean a word of what she is saying. Elizabeth Taylor, playing opposite Richard Burton (now *there's* a Byronic hero!) in Zeffirelli's 1967 film, delivers the final speech then sweeps out, leaving Petruchio looking foolish in front of the wedding guests.

On 8 June 1888, Bernard Shaw wrote what may have been the first strong feminist criticism of the play in a letter to the *Pall Mall Gazette*, where he declared the play to be 'one vile insult to womanhood and manhood from the first word to the last'.[20] Later scholars have created more nuanced interpretations, taking into account the context of the social changes of the Renaissance period. Emily Detmer, a feminist Renaissance scholar, locates the play within a contemporary public discourse about using new methods to control women that were starting to replace crude wife-beating, especially in more cultivated society. 'Gentlemen' like Petruchio thought it beneath them to physically abuse women. Detmer suggests that:

Shakespeare's *The Taming of the Shrew* acts as a comedic roadmap for reconfiguring these emergent modes of 'skilful' and civilised dominance for *gentle*men, that is, for subordinating a wife without resorting to the 'common' man's brute strength.[21]

Detmer goes on to describe Kate's surrender to Petruchio as 'something other than consensual, as, in fact, a typical response to abuse'. Substituting psychological torture for physical mistreatment, she argues, does not alter the central fact that a woman is being abused: it is no more than an insidious change of method, which may even 'work better' in achieving the old, despicable aim of female subjugation to the male.[22]

In recognising Germaine Greer as probably the best-known feminist of the twentieth century, and a Shakespearean–Renaissance specialist scholar to boot, one might have expected that her discussion of *The Taming of the Shrew* would address the types of concerns raised by Detmer and others, but no. Not a bit of it! Petruchio's claim that he is 'born to tame her', Greer writes in her thesis:

> rings like the greatest compliment he could pay her, and shows her a way to end her fruitless revolt; Petruchio vaunts like some hero who must ride a horse never before mastered, or draw an enchanted sword out of a rock.[23]

Christine Wallace struggled to reconcile the central arguments of *The Female Eunuch* – 'the feminist bible of the 1970s' – with the views Greer expressed in her PhD thesis, especially the chapter on *The Taming of the Shrew*. 'The feminist reader,' she concluded, 'encounters the uncomfortable possibility that Greer thought shrew-taming in the style of Petruchio and Kate could lead to happiness for women.' Like Detmer, she argues that when Petruchio uses methods other than violence in his campaign to subjugate his new wife, he is simply replacing physical cruelty with psychological abuse.[24]

Yet in *The Female Eunuch*, first published in 1970, two years after Germaine Greer received her doctorate, the view she expresses of Kate's 'taming' is essentially the same as in her thesis.

> Kate . . . has the uncommon good fortune to find Petruchio, who is man enough to know what he wants and how to get it. He wants her spirit and energy because he wants a wife worth keeping. He tames her like he might a hawk or a high-mettled horse, and she rewards him with strong sexual love and high loyalty . . . The submission of a woman like Kate is genuine and exciting because she has something to lay down, her virgin pride and individuality . . . Kate's speech at the close of the play is the greatest defence of Christian

monogamy ever written. It rests upon the role of a husband as a protector and friend, and it is valid because Kate has a man who is capable of being both, for Petruchio is both gentle and strong (it is a vile distortion of the play to have him strike her ever).[25]

'How could it be,' asks a puzzled Wallace, that Greer – 'highly intelligent, worldly, striking, striving – why would she of all people condone without a disclaimer women's longing for men who are capable of exercising dominion over them?'[26]

Why, indeed!

•

Always a driven, efficient worker, Greer finished her PhD thesis well within the time allowed by her Commonwealth Scholarship. In her introduction to her essay collection *The Madwoman's Underclothes*, she described how and where she completed the final draft. No more libraries, no more confinement to her room in Friar House; she had decamped, alone, with her books and a red typewriter, to a remote village in Calabria. Here she lived for three months in two rooms on the top floor of 'an isolated clump of stone buildings in sight of the sea'. The floors were terracotta, the walls 'of velvety whitewash'. Outside were brilliant cornfields, a grapevine and an *uliveto* – an olive grove – planted with 'the oldest olive trees I have ever seen, each with a girth of eight or nine feet'.

Her routine was to get up before dawn, wash at the well (there was no running water in the village) while she watched the sun emerge from the grey sea, and sluice her floor with well-water so that the evaporation would keep the rooms fresh.

Then she would drink thick black coffee and apply herself to the red typewriter.

She also developed close friendships with the local people, discovering in the process that her 'certainty' of the superiority of her urban education and culture was probably unwarranted. 'Three months of living with some of the poorest peasants in Europe,' she wrote, 'has turned that certainty upside down, and it has never righted itself.'

'Where is your husband?' asked Maruzzo, the eight-year-old peasant boy who liked to keep her company. 'Why did your mother send you away?'[27]

Germaine Greer formally received her PhD at a ceremony in the ancient Cambridge Senate House in May 1968. She had been happy during her three years of study, but from the first day, when other new students were showing their parents around their rooms, the lecture theatres and the magnificent surrounds of the university, she felt alone and different – cut off from those ordinary family connections that were part of the lives of others. On graduation day, as she observed the mostly upper-middle-class parents rushing about to photograph their successful offspring against famous landmarks like King's College and Erasmus's Bridge, she was keenly aware that she was an outsider, although she found some excuse in being Australian. In one way she was actually more relieved than sorry that Peg and Reg were not there, for she knew how utterly out of place they would have been in those hallowed spaces.

Nobody photographed me . . . not when I knelt resplendent in medieval red and black with my hands drawn in prayer within those of the Vice Chancellor. Germaine Greer, Philosophiae Doctoris Cantabrigiensis. I collected my degree by myself. There was no victory supper, no champagne. I had worked all my life for love, done my best to please everybody, kept going till I reached the top, looked about and found I was all alone. My parents were too ignorant even to appreciate what I had achieved.[28]

As one of the most brilliant graduates ever of a Cambridge PhD program, Germaine Greer achieved her aim of remaining in England. In 1967 she was appointed to Warwick University as an assistant lecturer. Already she was developing three distinct and wildly contrasting personae: the first was that of Dr Greer, scholar, university lecturer in English literature, an academic at a time when academics were fewer and much more revered than they are now. Her second persona was that of an actress. On the basis of her appearances in the Footlights productions she had made many friends in the theatre world and established a reputation as a talented performer. It was these contacts and this reputation that secured her a role on the Granada Television program *Nice Time*, filmed live each week in Manchester, where she appeared as herself, a co-presenter with Kenny Everett and interviewer in popular comedy sketches. Watching these sketches today on YouTube, the viewer is struck by her beauty, her figure-revealing costumes, the professionally constructed hairdos and her accent, in which only a faint trace of Australian is discernible.

Her third identity was that of a leading light in London's counterculture of the 1960s, a role in which, mainly at weekends, she relaxed into hippiedom, her hair styled in an electric Afro, her clothing the colourful 'ethnic gear' and jangling, extravagant jewellery of the period. Joyfully and recklessly, she allowed herself to become drunk on alcohol and stoned on drugs with her many friends in the worlds of the underground and rock music. She took her sexual pleasure as she found it.

By the time she went to Cambridge to take out her degree, Germaine was well established at Warwick University, but once again she felt herself to be an oddity, for she was almost alone in being female among the carefully selected number of talented individuals the new university had recruited to build its academic credentials. Many of the men had female partners to whom Germaine was unable to relate. As a single, beautiful, sexually liberated and talented woman, she got along well with her male colleagues: she flirted, engaged with them intellectually, and even had sex with those she found attractive, but she did not fit in to their cosy, couple-orientated world of academic dinner parties and entertainments. Inevitably she fell foul of some of the wives and girlfriends who, as she discovered, resented her and gossiped about her behind her back. Much of their nastiness went over her head, for she herself was too big a personality to indulge in cheap forms of invective, but in time she came to despise those women for their pettiness and dependency. 'I had made it in a man's world,' she wrote in the draft Dedication to *The Female Eunuch*. 'And I reaped the fruits of the rarity of this phenomenon. I enjoyed other people's husbands without risk to my freedom, and I was repaid by their infatuation . . . I mocked the women who had sacrificed liberty for security.'[29]

Yet she would write her book for them.

Living in a rented bedsitter at Leamington Spa, near the university, Germaine was often lonely, but there were compensations. Shortly after her arrival at Warwick, she was in the office collecting her first pay cheque (which she thought depressingly lean) when she fell into conversation with the only other female don in her faculty, the sparkling Gay Clifford, who would become her lifelong friend.

Four years younger than Germaine, Gay was probably her intellectual equal, although a series of unfortunate events in her life would prevent her from realising her full potential. She had enjoyed a privileged upbringing in a well-to-do, supportive family who lived in London. At Oxford, she had achieved a double-first in English literature. She was fiercely ambitious and competitive, physically beautiful and possessed of the same wicked sense of fun and humour as Germaine. At staff meetings, where they were outnumbered by colleagues who were not only of a different gender, but who had very different philosophies and world views, they were bound, as Germaine said many years later, by a kind of 'tacit solidarity', since they were also the hardest-worked members of the faculty.[30]

Like Germaine, Gay was not popular with the faculty wives, so the two misfits did most of their socialising with the students, who loved and admired them as much for their colourful avant-garde dress and behaviour as for their fine teaching. 'Miss Clifford was a bit of a thrill. She wore crimson suits in a sea of professional grey . . . she plied you with advice on haircuts while combing through your essay on Piers Plowman with a red pen . . .' commented one of her students.[31]

The 1960s were the heady days of student demonstrations, and Dr Greer and Miss Clifford were on the students' side. In February 1968, when protesting students occupied the Warwick University registry, the two young staff renegades cheered them on. These were also the years of anti–Vietnam War 'demos', in which Germaine, as an Australian, felt obliged to be involved. She was convinced that there were political dossiers on herself and on Gay, who was a socialist, in the Vice-Chancellor's files.[32]

Nevertheless, she worked hard to build her professional credentials and she generally managed to maintain a modicum of decorum so as not to offend the local academic community. Her escape valves were London's counterculture and the Granada studios in Manchester, where she went for the filming of *Nice Time*. Ever since her Melbourne University student days, she had scorned what she believed to be the academy's tendency to take itself too seriously. She found that, as a bohemian, hippie and actress, she could lighten up and release the tensions brought on by intense work and study: like her father before her, she was good at performing, and it was through performances of various kinds that she found her escape from the confronting solemnity of the academic grind.

The University of Melbourne Archives recently released a rare video of Germaine Greer appearing on *Nice Time*, apparently nude, in a bathtub full of milk. Obviously enjoying herself, she sponges her long arms and legs seductively, at one point revealing a glimpse of her naked breasts. Deeply shocking in those innocent times![33]

British journalist Linda Grant, writing in *The Guardian* in 2013, recalled watching *Nice Time* as a child. In retrospect, she saw the program as:

> the high water mark of the sexual revolution's innocence, co-presented by Kenny Everett, Jonathon Routh and Germaine Greer. Greer had already been arguing against the constriction of bras and I recollect her dancing around on my parents' TV, exposing her breasts. Apart from the male excitement of undoing them, bras were a symbol of restraint.[34]

Tellingly, Grant goes on to make the point that Greer and the emerging band of her second-wave feminist sisters had yet to come to terms with: brassieres may well have been 'a symbol of restraint', but their removal was seen by some males as a sexual invitation, signalling to them that 'the braless dollybird was instantly accessible'. Women were still innocent – or ignorant – of the fact that some men (Grant cites notable examples from the 1970s like television personalities Jimmy Savile and Stuart Hall) would seize on the concept of women as 'liberated chicks' as a convenient rationalisation for their sleaze.

> These men . . . were taking advantage of the sexual revolution, regarding all younger women as easy meat for exploitation . . . Male predators could embarrass and bully you into believing that fending off unwanted advances was something your grandma had to do to protect a modesty and virginity now out of date.[35]

In London, Germaine had many friends. Some, like Richard Neville and Barry Humphries, were from Australia; some were rock stars; nearly all were part of the capital's hippie culture. Before she acquired a pad of her own, friends invited her to sleep on their couches or, as in the case of disc jockey and broadcaster John Peel, in a spare room.

It was while she was staying in Peel's house that she first met his friend, the equally famous rock star Mick Farren. In his memoir *Give the Anarchist a Cigarette*, Farren recalled that meeting and the events that followed. Peel, he wrote, had invited him to travel up to the Mothers Rock Club in Birmingham to see The Who in concert. When he arrived to pick up Peel at his house, he discovered that there was to be another passenger, 'an angular Australian in a Thea Porter A Class Groupie costume'[36]. 'Hey hey,' he thought. 'Who the hell is this?'

On the ride to Birmingham, Farren went from 'interested' and 'fascinated' by Germaine to 'captivated'. She seemed to be interested in him too. 'The woman was so damned bright, and the more attention I paid her, the more I sensed a reciprocal stream of pheromones.' After the concert, which was memorable, Peel announced his intention to drop Germaine off at her flat in Leamington, as she had to teach at the university the next morning. Farren was dismayed. 'That's a pity,' he said. 'I had hoped we could go on talking.' Germaine's solution was simple. He should come and stay at her place.

What followed was a night of 'boudoir sex, conversation and red wine', and then an intense affair that lasted for some months before she decided she had had enough of him. Farren had fallen in love and could not stop thinking about her, but from the start he had reservations. She was so incredibly clever. 'To say she was uncomplicated is like describing quantum physics as a brain teaser,' but there was also a kind of strangeness about her that made him wary.

> In her brilliance, I feared an oddness festered. She was sensual, but cerebral in that sensuality . . . I think she enjoyed her liaisons with low-lifes on an earthy level of lust.[37]

Before the end of her affair with Farren, Germaine moved out of John Peel's spare room, having decided to accept an invitation to take a studio at The Pheasantry, 152 Kings Road, Chelsea.

Nobody lived at The Pheasantry except by invitation: the necessary credentials were creativity, bohemianism, iconoclasm and recognised talent in the arts. The building itself, built in the mid-nineteenth century, was originally used to raise pheasants for the royal court. By the 1960s and 1970s it had become a rather shambolic collection of studios, with a members-only club in the basement. Eric Clapton, who lived at The Pheasantry, tells in his autobiography of how he and George Harrison used to take acid and write songs at the club. Filmmaker Philippe Mora recalls:

> Our Pheasantry scene was a kind of cultural catalyst and melting pot. R.D. Laing would drop by and say we were normal and everyone else was crazy . . . Bob Whitaker [a] talented photographer, lived around the corner . . . Germaine Greer lived downstairs, working on a book . . . George Harrison would drop by . . .[38]

Germaine did not have to wait until the underground scene became fashionable before she joined it in London – she had been a hippie back in the days of the Royal George, before the word was invented – but she took a little longer to embrace rock. Her Australian milieu was the pubs, where there was no music, and the jazz cafes like the one in Melbourne where she had fallen in love with the Greek drummer. In England, her music preferences only changed when she discovered the psychedelic delights of the Rolling Stones, and decided to become a groupie.

Among her many close friendships in London, none was more significant than her association with 'the boys from Oz', including journalists Richard Neville and artist Martin Sharp, the creators of *Oz* magazine. (Her studio at The Pheasantry was just below Martin Sharp's.)

> What luck they met, bouncing out of their campus newspapers, the start-up lads of their generation. What a good mix: Sharp, surely the most talented pop artist Australia has produced; Neville, mischievous, convincing, the money-

raiser who was able to find enough pretty girls to sell OZ on street corners . . .[39]

The Australian *Oz* was launched in Sydney in 1963, two years before Prime Minister Menzies sent troops to Vietnam. Its targets, attacked mainly through satire, were prejudice against coloured people and homosexuals, censorship, values that sent young men off to war in defence of the indefensible and everything that got in the way of them having sex as often as they felt like it.

After only three months of publication, and having gained a readership of eight thousand, the editors of the Australian *Oz* magazine were charged with obscenity, fined and acquitted. Later they were charged again, found guilty and sentenced to jail terms. The case included some memorable moments, but with the aid of brilliant lawyers – including John Kerr, who would later become the Australian Governor-General who famously sacked the Prime Minister Gough Whitlam, and Neville Wran, future Premier of New South Wales – the convictions were again overturned.

Richard Neville moved to London, epicentre of the counterculture, in 1966, and immediately set about establishing the London *Oz* magazine. He was staying at his sister Jill's flat in Clarendon Road with his Australian girlfriend, Louise Ferrier, when his old friend Germaine Greer turned up one afternoon for tea. Richard thought that Germaine seemed unhappy. Decorously dressed in a cashmere twin-set, pearls and tartan skirt, and wearing a beehive hairdo, she paced restlessly across Jill's carpet, complaining that the only English men she knew were 'either queer or kinky'. Richard, who was working hard on setting up his London *Oz* magazine, suggested that she might like to write an article on the subject of English males for the first issue. 'I'd love to,' she responded. 'I've already got a title: "In Bed with the English".'

Louise could hardly contain herself after Germaine left the flat. 'Incredible! Incredible!' she kept exclaiming. Germaine was still the amazing creature Louise had met at Repin's cafe in Sydney, the first woman she had known to say 'fuck' in public.[40]

In England, as in Australia, and the United States at that time, opposition to the war in Vietnam was growing exponentially. Thousands of people, especially the young, were marching and demonstrating in the belief that if enough people showed their anger, politicians would listen and the war would be brought to an end. Many Australians objected to their government's scare-mongering rationale for conscripting young men to 'serve' in the war. There was no evidence, they insisted, that Australia was under threat of communist invasion from Vietnam, China or anywhere else.

In his memoir *Hippie Hippie Shake*, published in 1995, Neville records how, on May Day 1969, a group of Australian expatriates that included himself, Louise Ferrier and Germaine Greer assembled in the Strand to join an anti-war protest. Chanting 'Ho Ho Ho Chi Minh' and holding the Australian flag high, they marched towards Australia House, where they halted. Someone produced a box of matches and started a fire. Everyone was screaming, tussling with the flag as, 'larger than life, Germaine thrust herself to the fore and hurled the flag into the flames, shouting, "We are all Viet Cong, we are all Viet Cong."' Neville was shocked, in spite of himself. 'However much I shared and identified with her rage, an ingrained respect for my dinkum Aussie Dad and his beliefs prevented me from endorsing what she did to the Southern Cross.'[41]

Some months later, when the 'dinkum Aussie Dad' was visiting his son in London, Richard and Louise took him, 'The Colonel', out to see the sights, including 10 Downing Street and the Arts

Lab in Soho. And who should they run into but Germaine Greer! Her hair was in an Afro, she was wearing heavily embroidered garments from Rajasthan and her long arms and fingers were festooned with Indian bracelets and rings.

Immediately, she launched into a dissertation on marijuana. 'Have you ever been stoned, Mr Neville?' she asked the Colonel politely.

'I gave up smoking, my dear, after I got pneumonia.'

'The first rule of pot is don't get caught.'

The Colonel eyed her speculatively. 'You'd be a good catch, my dear.'

They discussed being body-searched for drugs. 'Let them try and body-search me,' said Germaine provocatively.

The Colonel considered the possibility. He asked Germaine if she lived nearby. Yes (she had just moved into her studio at The Pheasantry).

She took the Colonel by the arm 'How long are you in town, Mr Neville?' she purred.

'Not long!' cried his alarmed son, and hailed a cab. 'Write us a piece about pot,' he called to her as they made their farewells. Germaine goosed the delighted Colonel. 'God, Germaine!' muttered Richard to himself as he pushed his father into the taxi.[42]

By this time Germaine's article 'In Bed with the English' had appeared in the first edition of Neville's London *Oz* in 1967. In it she claimed never to have had sex with an Englishman. Rather, she had been reduced to the role of sisterly adviser on sexual matters like contraception ('there had been improvements on *coitus inter-ruptus*') and venereal disease ('Sweetie, those are lice. You are not so much diseased as dirty.'). In an attempt to 'sample' the country gentry, she wrote, she had attended a party where, all night, she had put up with the 'braying' of the assembled aristocrats.

At party's end the host, who had hopefully removed his shoes and socks in preparation for a bout, chased her out into the garden. Taking advantage of his bare feet, she attempted to escape across the cricket ground that separated his property from the house where she was staying. He followed her in hot but crippled pursuit, eventually catching up with her on the pitch, where they rolled about for a bit. She berated him for his lack of loyalty to the cricket club and lost a fifteen-guinea earring. Then she was up and off again. 'The last I saw of him,' she said, 'he was remorsefully smoothing and patting the ravaged wicket.'[43]

Englishmen were politely outraged by the article. In Soho, Peter Cook, actor and satirist, publicly set fire to a copy. Another Englishman, Rod Lake, offered to take her to bed and change her mind. Ever the entrepreneur, Richard Neville set up a meeting between Greer and Lake in a pub. He wrote about it in the fourth edition of *Oz* but, as he was forced to admit, Germaine jumped into a taxi and escaped.

The *Oz* piece for which Germaine Greer is probably best remembered is 'The Universal Tonguebath: A groupie's vision'. According to Neville, this article was conceived early one morning when he and Germaine met accidentally in the dining carriage of a northbound train. He was on his way to Reading. She was going to Manchester to shoot some scenes for *Nice Time*. As they waited for the tea they had ordered separately, she told him about her recently developed passion for rock music and musicians. 'Oh?' he said, surprised. 'I thought you were strictly Bach and Verdi . . . I thought you spent all your spare time in libraries.'

'No, no,' she assured him, 'I've been rushing off to rock concerts . . .'

Her epiphany, she declared, had occurred at the Granada studios. 'The place was full of smoothies and groovers being cool, and this sweaty rocker with his underpants showing just blasted off . . . You know, I even find Engelbert Humperdinck horny-making. Those high-fronted shiny mohair trousers . . . ohhh . . . with a length of rubber hose. Evil. No wonder those lonely housewives cream their jeans . . .'

The waiter served Germaine with her pot of tea but ignored the thirsty Neville – probably, they both thought, because of his long hair. Not right, opined Germaine, sipping her own tea contentedly as she went on to describe how a group of musicians had 'eyeballed' her naked breasts as she was dressing for a show, and how she had once listened to some rock stars enjoying a group fuck in a hotel room adjacent to hers with the door ajar.

As the train reached the outskirts of Reading and Neville remained tea-less, Germaine 'shuddered with pleasure' as she uttered the words that would define the yet-to-be-written 'Universal Tonguebath'. 'You see, Richard . . . the group fuck is the highest ritual expression of our faith – but it must happen as a sort of special grace.'[44]

'The Universal Tonguebath' appeared in issue 19 of *Oz*, early in 1969. On the magazine's cover is a magnificently psychedelic picture, created by Martin Sharp, of Germaine and Vivian Stanshall of the Bonzo Dog Doo-Dah band. The bespectacled Stanshall gazes ahead pensively as Germaine, hippie-ness personified, with wild hair, flares, and multiple bracelets and rings, peers out from behind his shoulder, coyly extracting his clearly visible penis from the fly of his black-and-white striped trousers. 'OZ talks to DR G – the only groupie with a Ph.D in captivity', proclaims the blurb on the cover. Inside, the article appears with the caption 'Staff writer Germaine talks to Dr G, a celebrated (and over educated) international groupie.'

What follows is Germaine Greer interviewing herself.

In the days before Beatlemania, she wrote, there were two kinds of musicians' birds – the musos' old ladies, and the scrubbers. The rock'n'rollers treated the scrubbers badly, taking out all their aggression on them, picking them up and throwing them away as the mood took them. The jazz scene was different.

But then jazz met rock, and the girls who had been sitting helplessly around club walls 'arose with their listening eyes and danced alone, opened out their beauty in the various light and sex flowed back into the scene and lapped all around them'.

Dr G had been slow to embrace rock music, wrote her 'interviewer', but when she met Simon Dupree and the Big Sound in a television studio she began to understand. The first pop star she 'actually pulled' was the lead singer in a 'nowhere' group that was performing at a ball in the country, and whom she actually did not 'dig'. Many others followed. Her own distinguishing characteristic, the one that set her aside from other groupies, was that she was a 'starfucker'.

> You know [starfucker's] a name I dig, because all the men who get inside me are stars. Even if they're plumbers, they're star plumbers.

The article continued with a brief reference to drugs: 'I don't know. I mean everyone uses the sacrament Acid . . .' She had had a 'magical' multiple orgasm experience with a pop star on heroin, whom she still felt involved with although she had heard that he had recently fallen off a bandstand and that he got sick a lot. 'I guess it's unemancipated or something but I won't call him . . . I love him you know, him and a thousand others as they say.'[45]

Was she, as the hippies would have said, 'for real' when she wrote this article? Initially she denied it ('My life is private') (!), but three years later, in an article for *POL* magazine, she explained that 'Dr G was also me', and that she had discussed, in the *Oz* piece, 'the rock musicians I have known and loved . . . and the life led by people who are caught up in the rock culture'.[46]

In the summer of 1971, the editors of *Oz* were once again charged with obscenity. During the famous London *Oz* trials that followed, people rioted outside the court and the crowd burned an effigy of the judge. Colourful barrister, and author of the Rumpole stories, John Mortimer, with the assistance of a young Geoffrey Robertson, appeared for the defence. The trial had many bizarre and hilarious moments that delighted the press and public. In one session Mortimer found himself in the embarrassing position of having to explain the meaning of 'cunnilingus' to the judge. The *Oz* editors were eventually convicted and sent on remand to the psychiatric unit of Wandsworth prison, where their long hair was chopped off. Richard Neville appeared on the steps of the prison, defying the governor's orders not to speak to the press. 'Fuck the governor!' he declared. Eventually their convictions were overturned on appeal.

Germaine was unable to support her friends by giving evidence at their trial. By that time *The Female Eunuch* had become a worldwide bestseller, she had become rich and her life was being transformed. When the editors of *Oz* were standing in the dock at the Old Bailey, she was in Italy, in search of a tax haven.

•

In her leisure time, Germaine loved to walk about the London streets, her imposing figure hardly less noticeable in the world metropolis than it had been in the surrounds of Melbourne and Sydney universities. Usually she would meet up with friends for a meal or a drink at a pub. One Saturday morning, late in the winter of 1968, she was walking through Portobello Market when she spotted fellow Australian Derek Brook drinking outside Finch's pub with a tall building-worker whose jeans were spattered with concrete over his working boots. The attraction between Germaine and this fine example of rough trade, whose name turned out to be Paul du Feu, was instant and mutual. Only later did she find out that he had a very good degree in English literature.

In his memoir, *Let's Hear It for the Long-Legged Women*, du Feu recorded how, after joining him and Brook at the pub, Germaine had sipped Guinness from his glass and then asked for a half-pint of the same for herself, stroking his face, confiding to him her need to get 'well fucked', and telling him he had an 'odd sort of beauty'. Later, after she had taken a break to keep an appointment for afternoon tea with a member of the British aristocracy at his townhouse in Blenheim Crescent, she again met up with du Feu. They went back to Brook's flat and from there to a Notting Hill pub, where they drank whisky with Guinness chasers till closing time. Germaine remarked that du Feu should get new false teeth, since the ones he was wearing didn't seem to fit, but then, undeterred by the teeth, she accompanied him back to his flat for the night.

In his account of the relationship, du Feu remarked that, on that first morning in his flat, after a long night of sex, Greer asked him to make her a cup of tea. When he twice 'got sidetracked', she raised herself up on one elbow, saying, 'Listen sport, I've asked twice for a cup of tea and all that happened was I got fucked. D'you reckon if I asked for a fuck I'd get a cup of tea?'[47]

Matters progressed swiftly from there. An entry in Germaine's diary for Thursday 30 May 1968 records that at 9.30 am she invigilated in the Old Library at Warwick. The entry continues,

'Catch the 1.35 to London, Euston. 3.45 Harrow Road Registry Office to get married.'

Her diary entry for 31 May shows that she was back again at Warwick, invigilating at 2 pm. For the following day, Saturday 1 June, there is just one diary entry – a single, capitalised word – 'DISASTER'.

Further diary entries show that on Monday 3 June, she took the train to Manchester to film *Nice Time*. On Thursday 13 June, du Feu arrived '6-ish' to stay with her at Leamington Spa. He left on Saturday at 2.14 pm. On Monday 17 June, she had to finish an article on humour that was due that day. On Tuesday she got her hair done. On Friday, after attending an examiners' meeting, she went down to London. On Saturday 22 June, she 'left Paul'.[48]

So the marriage lasted just three-and-a-half weeks. Du Feu claimed that the trouble started barely two hours after the wedding ceremony. They had gone for a drink at the Dennis Club in Paddington, and Germaine provoked him to fury when she danced with one of the club's regular lesbian customers. Du Feu attacked her, and she attacked him back, accusing him of possessiveness, and they both got very drunk, mainly on whisky. She told him she would like to have two or three children by different fathers, but none by him.

When he went to Leamington Spa the following weekend, Germaine, according to du Feu, spent most of the time marking students' exam papers and getting drunk, like him. Back in London, he rented another, better flat in Shepherd's Bush from a friend. Germaine had told him she liked cooking, so he decided to use his building skills to make a home that would include a pleasant kitchen for her. He bought flowers and vases and new cooking utensils, and even ordered a stereo for her to listen to choral music, but it was all to no avail. When she next came to London and they met at Euston station she immediately launched into a long account of an argument at the examiners' meeting she had just attended at her university, which was of no interest to him. Her monologue continued in the taxi and she was infuriated when he tried to change the subject. They drank and fought for the whole weekend. She refused to use her new kitchen, accusing him of trying to turn her into a domestic slave. Early on the Monday morning, having chosen to sleep in an armchair, already fortified by half a bottle of whisky, she packed her Gladstone bag and left him for good.[49]

That was his story and Germaine later claimed that there was no truth in it. Yet, factually, her own accounts were not so very different from his. For many years she was reluctant to speak about her marriage, but in 2004, in one of her regular pieces for *The Telegraph*, she responded to a recent *Daily Mail* story written by journalist Helen Weathers, under the headline 'I was Mr Germaine Greer'. Greer remarked that Weathers could have saved herself the trouble of contacting du Feu in America, where he was then growing tomatoes, by simply recycling bits from his book, which he had sold to the publishers for US$60,000 in 1972 (more money, she said, than she had received in her advance for *The Female Eunuch*). What Weathers did not know, and Paul had not told her, she continued, was that when he met her he had only recently been discharged from a hospital where he had been treated for alcoholic poisoning. In the early stages of their acquaintance he had 'soft-pedalled on the booze'. When they decided to marry she 'made certain conditions that he appeared to accept', but by the time she found herself on the train headed for the registry office, she knew she was 'in deep trouble'.

> When the waiter on the train asked me why I looked so sad,
> I said: 'I'm going to marry a drunk,' and burst into tears,
> so he gave me a free bottle of Liebfraumilch to cheer me up.
> I was so miserable that I drank it.

Germaine's version of dancing with the lesbian at her bridal celebration is slightly different from du Feu's.

> The grim ceremony over, the bridal party went to a Bayswater
> club to celebrate. A sweet-faced old lady in men's clothing
> asked if she might dance with the bride, I stepped into her
> arms for a turn around the room and my drunken husband
> offered to fight her.

On her wedding night, she claimed, a drunk du Feu forced her to sleep in an armchair. She remembered 'every insult, every jeer, every threat, every humiliation'.

Her version of the ending of the relationship is also different from his. It wasn't because of the rows, she said:

> I don't do rows. We were at a Sunday afternoon drinks party
> in a studio off Ladbroke Grove. He turned to me and sneered
> (drunk as usual): 'I could have any woman in this room.'
> 'Except me,' I said, and walked away for ever.[50]

A previously unseen account of the marriage, written by Greer herself in 1969, appeared in 2013 when the first draft of *The Female Eunuch* became available in the Greer archive. Prepared to suit the purpose of the book, this account has a strong feminist orientation. She had decided to marry, she wrote, 'in a moment of inattention to what I knew was the intrinsic character of the institution'. As soon as she had been asked to sign the register, she realised that 'something awful had happened'. No longer 'free, busy and rich', she had become enslaved.

> Sure I had security and legal protection, so has any inmate of Her Majesty's prisons. What I had before offered my husband in joy was now his to demand. I would be allowed to earn my own living, although I would be taxed as an appendage of his, and even to sleep with other people if he chose. [Greer's emphasis]

She had 'been prepared to learn the role of a wife as well as I could', she claimed improbably, given 'time and adaptability', but all too soon she discovered that neither was to be accorded to her, and she was told that she did not understand what being a wife was.

And so another version of the end of the marriage was put forward. This time it was du Feu who was portrayed as having taken the initiative.

> The threat held over was that of abandonment, a singularly meaningless one in this case, and eventually, after being told to go, like a Muslim wife, three times, I went on the fourth, with a great sense of liberation.[51]

The Greer archive has also made public a sad little letter to Germaine from a friend of du Feu's first wife, who was concerned about the effects of the negative publicity on his first family – du Feu had two sons who were then aged fourteen and sixteen. Germaine replied that Paul du Feu's activities had been 'an embarrassment' to her, as they surely must have been to his wife and children. However, he was not commonly known as his first wife's husband, she wrote, but as 'Mr Greer'. She felt concern for the wife and even more for the two boys, but she could do nothing to mitigate the embarrassment she shared with them.[52]

•

The relaxed Dutch pornography laws made Amsterdam a mecca for the counterculture in Europe in the late 1960s and early 1970s. Germaine and her friends soon gravitated to that scene. Some of the main players were herself, Richard Neville, Jay Landesman, Michael Zwerin, Jim Haynes and Heathcote Williams, plus Bill Levy and his partner Susan Janssen (known as Purple Susan).

In the summer of 1969, Bill Levy, his fellow expatriate American Jim Haynes, Heathcote Williams, a London-based magazine editor, Williams's girlfriend, the model Jean Shrimpton, and Germaine Greer met to form the first editorial group of the Amsterdam-based pornographic magazine *Suck*. Haynes would later say that *Suck*'s first mistake was made at that initial meeting when the five participants failed to realise they should have stopped talking and made love together. Instead, Williams and Shrimpton went off briefly to have sex in another room.[53]

Copies of *Suck* magazine, which are probably quite valuable because of their rarity, are now accessible in the Germaine Greer Archive at the University of Melbourne. They do not make pleasant reading. Some articles are harmless enough – best described as adolescent sexual smut – but others that include graphic descriptions of bestiality, incest and abuse of children are nauseating, even to a twenty-first century audience. Almost nothing appears to be off limits.

In addition to her editorial duties, Germaine wrote a satirical gossip column for *Suck* under the by-line 'Earth Rose', in which she mercilessly exposed some very private and intimate details of her friends' lives. Her targets also included a (named) male who, according to Earth Rose, had recently recovered from a case of the clap. In view of the state of his foreskin and disinclination to wash, she declared, readers should not attempt closer contact with this person. And Martin Amis did not like giving head. 'You have been warned,' she advised.[54]

Greer understood and exploited the pulling power of Earth Rose's tittle-tattle, but she continued to believe that *Suck* should be a serious, non-exploitative vehicle for a 'clean', liberated brand of pornography. In keeping with this philosophy, some of her contributions to *Suck* were serious, clinical and proselytising to the point of being boring. Her advice for women on how to care for their vulva without using chemical products, in order to avoid pruritus and leucorrhoea, for example, is medically sound and has a fine moral ring to it, but it is not very entertaining. When she invited women to taste their vaginal secretions – if possible by sucking or, if they were not supple enough to reach, by inserting a finger – she was being absolutely serious.

Germaine was convinced that, by openly and freely discussing and exposing all facets of human sexual activity, *Suck* magazine was performing a valuable service to society. She particularly wanted to change the traditional pornographic emphasis on women as passive objects of male fantasy to one of active female involvement and enjoyment. The problem was that the other editors were not quite on her wavelength. They agreed with her to an extent but their baser instincts apparently got the better of them – old habits died hard, and they eventually decided to go with titillation over education.

Later, Germaine would claim that she had agreed to join the editorial board of *Suck* because she saw the magazine's potential as an 'antidote' to 'exploitative' pornographic papers like *Screw* and *Hustler*. She had tried, but failed, she said, to ensure that male bodies featured in the magazine, and that the art was erotic – 'away from the tits 'n ass and the peep-show syndrome'. 'My co-editors were quite happy to let me expound my utopian sexual theories,' she wrote in 1985, 'and utterly indifferent to them.'[55]

In September 1969, shortly after the first edition of *Suck* had been published, author Tom Wolfe had dinner with Germaine Greer, Jim Haynes and other *Suck* people at Alexander's, a restaurant on the Kings Road. Wolfe did not take to Germaine; 'She was a thin, hard-looking woman with a tremendous curly electric hairdo and the most outrageous Naugahyde mouth I had ever heard on a woman,' he wrote in an article for *New York* magazine.

Wolfe went on to describe how, upon becoming bored, Greer had set fire to her hair with a match, and how the waiters had to put it out with napkins, making a noise like 'pigeons taking off in the park'. Also bored, Wolfe was as unimpressed with *Suck* as he was with its editors.

> *Suck* was full of pictures of gaping thighs, moist lips, stiffened giblets, glistening nodules, dirty stories, dirty poems, essays on sexual freedom, and a gossip column detailing the sexual habits of people whose names I assumed were fictitious. Then I came to an item that said, 'Anyone who wants group sex in New York and likes fat girls, contact L—— R——,' except that it gave her full name. She was a friend of mine.[56]

Nor was Wolfe impressed by Haynes's attempt to convince him that *Suck*'s founders and contributors were committed sexual libertarians rather than smutty attention-seekers. As Germaine's hair blazed away, Wolfe studied Haynes's face for signs that he was joking, but the American was alarmingly in earnest. With growing horror, Wolfe realised that sex for these people had become a kind of religion, existing on a plane far beyond mortal venality – 'Beyond Irony. Whatever it had been for [Haynes] once, sex had now become a religion, and he had developed a theology in which the orgasm had become a form of spiritual ecstasy.'[57]

As well as being responsible for producing regular editions of their magazine, the *Suck* editors were the organisers of two very popular 'Wet Dream' Film Festivals, held in Amsterdam in 1970 and 1971. Germaine was a member of the 1970 judging panel (later described by Richard Neville, who was also a judge, as 'eight libertarian loudmouths') that awarded first prize to Bodil Joensen for *A Summer Day*, which featured the beautiful female protagonist having sex (lovingly) with her animals. The Walt Disney Memorial Award went to Christie Erikson's film *Snow White*, in which the little men perform some interesting sex acts on the young heroine. Germaine's votes went to Jean Genet's 1954 classic *Un Chant d'Amour*.[58]

Most of the events at the festival were films or film-related, but there were some live acts. The sexual libertarians relished the pornography just as much as they worked hard to provide intellectual justification for it, but, as Wendy Bacon, Richard Neville and others have related, even they displayed unfortunate remnants of 'bourgeois mentality' when they interrupted a performance by Austrian artist and actor Otto Muehl at the Kosmos meditation centre. His act, at which Germaine, wearing high-heeled boots and a fur coat she had bought with some of the early profits from *The Female Eunuch*, was present, started with two assistants coming on stage shouting 'Throw off your repressions'. Then the two young women entertained the audience with some lesbian fun. All quite kosher, until Muehl arrived with a goose. His plan was to cut off its head, place a condom on the neck and fuck one of the girls with it. He had done it before, but on this occasion he had overestimated the tolerance of his audience. On seeing Muehl's glinting knife, many of the sexually liberated 'freaked out'. 'If you kill that goose, we'll fucking kill you!' screamed one. Then, suddenly, Heathcote Williams leaped onto the stage and tried to pin Muehl down. Muehl fell off the stage as Williams grabbed the wildly flapping goose and passed it to Anthony Haden-Guest, a British journalist, who ran off with it. Fighting broke out in the audience as Muehl clambered back on the stage, confusedly declaring his right to employ the goose's head as he chose. As Richard Neville tells the story, a white-faced Heathcote Williams remained on the stage, weeping. Then: 'Germaine sweeps to his side, her face radiating gratitude, compassion, even love.'

'Only Heathcote had the courage to stop the violence,' she shouted. 'Muehl's antics are sadistic and stupid . . . Six million Jews went to the gas chambers because of pigs like Otto . . . I will not sit through violence in the name of art.'[59]

When the uproar died down, Muehl simply walked contemptuously to the centre of the stage and shat on it. Maybe, as libertarian journalist Wendy Bacon suggested, people were just thinking of the goose's welfare – why else would they have been outraged? But she felt this explanation was 'rather spurious' as they knew animals were killed every day. Perhaps this was just their way of rationalising their continuing inhibitions.[60]

Muehl went on to pursue a more sedate, though often controversial, career as an artist until his death in 2013. The goose was taken to an Amsterdam canal barge, where it lived happily ever after.

4

The Female Eunuch

> I wish to persuade women to endeavour to acquire
> strength, both of mind and body . . .
>
> Mary Wollstonecraft, *A Vindication of the*
> *Rights of Woman*

It is the morning of 21 April 1969. In Leamington Spa, England,
Germaine Greer is setting down her first thoughts about the
book for which she does not yet have a name, but which will
make her enduringly rich and famous. Today, she writes, is 'the
day on which my book begins itself, and Janis Joplin sings at
Albert Hall. Yesterday the title was "Strumpet Voluntary", what
shall it be today?'[1]

In Leamington Spa – as in London, Toronto, Sydney,
Auckland, Washington DC – women brought up in the Western
tradition are still contented (or miserable) to live the lives of busy
domesticity for which society has conditioned them. They have
no idea of the extent to which their lives are about to change.
Consider, for example, Cheryl Davis, who lives in East Doncaster,
Melbourne, Australia.

In Australia it is already evening. As Germaine takes up her
pen on the other side of the world, Cheryl is reflecting on the
day just past. She has completed all the tasks she set herself.

After she drove her children to school, she had gone to Box Hill to choose the material for her new curtains. Then there was the food shopping, cooking, cleaning and getting the house tidy for Jim when he came home.

Cheryl is thirty years old. Born in 1939, she is the same age as Germaine Greer. At fifteen she left school, where she had taken the 'commercial girls' course, to become a typist and filing clerk in the mailroom of the head office of a large bank in the city. She found the work boring, but enjoyed the company of the other girls and the boys who brought up the heavy bags of mail and prepared the correspondence for the girls to sort. The boys earned more than the girls and nearly all of them suffered from acne. They laughed and joked a lot, but they knew they would be bank managers one day if they could earn the approval of the men who supervised their work. Cheryl, over the filing, thought only of Jim, who would become her fiancé, and how she would spend her next pay on items for her glory box.

Cheryl is very pretty – dark haired, green eyed. She is intelligent, too, but she does not yet know it. Germaine's book will change that. Jim, whom Cheryl married when she was 20 and he 23, is tall and handsome. At 33 he is on his way up, proud of his wife and children, neglecting no opportunity to show them off to the senior management of his firm.

Each morning Jim leaves for work in his company car, a large, late-model Peugeot (his company is French-owned). For Cheryl he has bought an old, second- or third-hand Renault 750. It is not very reliable or even safe, but the children are still small and can all fit quite comfortably in the back.

Cheryl Davis does not know that Germaine Greer is about to write a book about her. Nor does she know that, in 1963, an

American woman, herself a wife and mother of three children, had already written a book about her.

> As she made the beds, shopped for groceries, matched slipcover material, ate peanut butter sandwiches with her children, chauffeured Cub Scouts and Brownies, lay beside her husband at night – she was afraid to ask even of herself the silent question – 'Is this all?'[2]

Betty Friedan's *The Feminine Mystique*, which sold three million copies in its first three years of publication, described the situation of millions of middle-class women like Cheryl. Representing their situation as a problem, 'the problem that has no name', Friedan painted a depressing picture of stunted creatures whose sole identity was that of unpaid servant to their families. The problem's archetype was the American housewife who had dropped out of college to take on the 'stifling' role of full-time wife, mother and homemaker. Symptoms of her dilemma included inexplicable fatigue, chronic depression and blisters that broke out over her arms and bled.

Women everywhere wrote to Friedan expressing their gratitude that, at last, someone was aware of their plight. Her book has been credited with sparking off the second wave of feminism.

•

On 1 December 1955, after a tiring day at work, a black woman, Rosa Parks, was riding on a racially segregated bus in Montgomery, Alabama, when the driver asked her to give up her seat in the coloured section to make room for a white passenger. She refused and was arrested. Her action ignited a long civil rights protest in Montgomery and she was hailed as the mother of the civil rights movement.

In September 1957, nine black students tried to enrol in the all-white high school in Little Rock, Arkansas. They were beaten, abused and spat upon until federal troops were called in to protect them. In 1958, black 'sit-ins' happened across the country, as blacks demanded an end to segregated seating in cafes and drugstores.

Then came the Freedom Rides, when activists, black and white, rode on buses through the Deep South to integrate seating on buses and the use of facilities at bus stations. This was a dangerous mission; buses were firebombed and activists were attacked and beaten by angry mobs of white men. In Birmingham, Alabama, an FBI informant reported that the police commissioner Bull Connor gave the Ku Klux Klan fifteen minutes to beat up the freedom riders before moving in to 'protect' them. One rider was so badly beaten that he needed fifty stitches to his head.

Yet, despite the civil unrest in their country, throughout the 1950s and into the 1960s millions of white families in America continued to relax after their days' labours to consume doses of popular culture on television. The stories reassured them that the world was not changing as fast as it might seem. In situation comedies like *Leave It to Beaver*, white families lived in comfortable houses behind white picket fences, pretty mothers worried over nothing more serious than their children's squabbles and handsome fathers returned home from the office each evening to sort everything out. This was the dream Peggy Greer was pursuing when she persuaded Reg to buy the Cape Cod–style house on Melbourne's bayside – the dream Germaine so aggressively rejected.

Peggy's precocious older daughter was not alone in realising that the old certainties were crumbling. June and Ward Cleaver's measured efforts to teach their son, 'the Beaver', the values of truth, justice and the American way did not at all gel with the events viewers had just witnessed on the nightly news. How could America be a fair, prosperous society, a model to the world, when so many of its citizens were being beaten and vilified, thrown into jail without just cause?

Then came Vietnam, and the illusions died forever when, for the first time in history, the horrors of war came into families' living rooms. Even at the beginning, when the media made great efforts to support US involvement, it was impossible to ignore the pictures of villages being destroyed and children being burned to death. Horrified citizens in all Western countries became aware of the massive injustices that were being committed in their name. Outraged that their country was the chief perpetrator of an unjust war abroad and massive racial persecution at home, the youth of America, both black and white, gravitated to the great protest movements that were shaking the world.

None of this was lost on Germaine Greer: increasingly, she was swept up in the excitement and rebelliousness of the times. Like many other activists, she soon became aware of the similarities between discrimination based on colour and on gender. Clearly it was a short step from understanding that if black people were being discriminated against because they were black, women were similarly oppressed because they were women.

Rosa Parks's famous refusal to give up her seat on the bus reminds us that, from the very beginning, women played a pivotal role in the civil rights movements of the 1950s, 60s and 70s. They led and joined the sit-ins, rode on the Freedom Rides and suffered beatings and jail terms. They turned up in their thousands at the Lincoln Memorial to hear Martin Luther King Jr speak in 1963. Lessons had been learned: the turbulent times provided a ripe context for protest; men in power showed that they would listen and act – however reluctantly, and however contested the field – in response to organised voices of dissent; men and women, black and white, could work together for change.

But despite the heroism of Rosa Parks and others like her, many male protestors assumed that women would play only a supporting role in the movements – typing meeting minutes, washing dishes, making the men feel good. Several people spoke along with Martin Luther King outside the Lincoln Memorial at the March on Washington, but not one was female, and that fact was hardly remarked upon. When future Mississippi governor Ross Barnett spoke the infamous words, 'The Negro is different because God made him different to punish him,' in 1959, surely some people must have considered the implication for women. Did being different from men mean that women deserved to be punished?[3]

In Washington DC on 28 June 1966, at a conference on the status of women, twenty-eight women gathered in Betty Friedan's hotel room to found the National Organization for Women. On a table napkin, Friedan wrote the acronym NOW. She and black activist Pauli Murray then proceeded to draft (also on a table napkin) a statement of purpose that declared:

> the time has come to confront, with concrete action, the con-
> ditions that now prevent women from enjoying the equality
> of opportunity and freedom of choice which is their right, as
> individual Americans, and as human beings.[4]

By the end of the decade a substantial feminist literature was emerging. In the United States, Kate Millett, already battling crippling mental illness, was writing her groundbreaking *Sexual*

Politics, and Gloria Steinem gained national and international fame following the publication of her article 'After Black Power, Women's Liberation'. The media's appetite was whetted. Women's liberation was about to become big business.

•

Germaine made her first visit to New York at Christmas in 1968, while she was on vacation from her job at Warwick University. The visit is significant because of the connections she made with prominent men and women of the counterculture, whose life-styles and attitudes were a powerful influence on the book she would start to write a few months later.

She had decided to stay with Lillian Roxon, whom she first met in Melbourne back in her student days. They had met up again in Sydney, where both were members of the Push, but did not become close friends as Lillian left Sydney in 1959, the year Germaine arrived.

By the time Germaine appeared in New York, Lillian, the New York correspondent for the *Sydney Morning Herald*, had become a popular personality in the rock and underground scene, the centre of which was the famous Max's Kansas City restaurant, hangout of rock royalty and artists like Andy Warhol, Leonard Cohen, Janis Joplin, Jane Fonda and their friends, who congregated in the back room. Germaine realised that Roxon was well placed to introduce her to these people, the cream of New York 'hip' society. Because it was customary for Push members to seek each other out on their travels, she had decided, without asking, to stay in Lillian's flat.

The journalist Robert Milliken would later note that the two women were a study in contrasts: Lillian was 36, attractive, short and tubby, with shoulder-length fair hair. Germaine, 29, was very tall and dark. On her first visit to Max's she created an instant impression, strikingly attired in an 'embroidered satin antique jacket from the Chelsea Antique Market, her Bessarabian Princess's Defloration robe, a black net and silver belly dancer's vest and see-through chiffon velvet elephant pants'.[5]

When she turned up at Lillian's small apartment on East 21st Street expecting to stay there, Germaine discovered that she was not welcome. Lillian, who was already suffering from the asthma that would eventually kill her at only 41, and anxious about her recent weight gain, was struggling to meet her publisher's deadline for her *Rock Encyclopedia*, which was destined to become an icon of its genre.[6] Her flat was overflowing with books and papers and she told Germaine she did not have room for guests. Instead of offering her couch, she had booked Germaine into the Broadway Central, a cheap hotel which she thought was all her friend could afford.

Thirty years later, Germaine told Robert Milliken about the episode. She had been prepared to doss on Lillian's floor, she said, because that was the way of the Push. Enough people had dossed on her floor. But Lillian had refused to have her. 'She just did not want me there.'

So she found herself a lone nonentity in New York, relegated to a hotel which, as she was later to find out, had been the scene of a number of homicides. When she arrived to check in she was informed that her room would not be ready before midnight. 'As I stood there,' she told Milliken, 'all kinds of human flotsam and jetsam were creeping up to the desk, junkies and madmen . . . It was like dropping someone into a snake pit.'

That evening she went to a gathering of some academic friends at an apartment on Riverside Drive, near Columbia University, where she met up with the English novelist and historian Andrew Sinclair. Appalled to hear where she was staying, he insisted on returning to the hotel with her. They couldn't use the lift because someone resembling a corpse was being brought down in a wheelchair, with a cigarette in its mouth to make it look alive. Taking the stairs, they were confronted by a drag queen screaming that the police were after him because he had not paid his taxi fare. 'How much is your cab fare?' asked Germaine. 'Ninety-five dollars,' he replied. 'Where the fuck did you come from, Mexico City?' she cried as she continued up the stairs to spend her first and last night in her room.[7]

Sinclair, in his account of the episode, confirmed that the body in the wheelchair was 'a stiff'. 'How do you know he is a stiff?' Germaine asked him. 'Because they can't light the cigarette in his mouth,' he replied. His recollection was that the drag queen had asked him for twenty dollars and he had given him two.

'We did not even kiss good-night,' Sinclair reminisced, 'but we have continued to respect each other mightily – she's a fine woman.'[8]

Next day Germaine moved to another friend's apartment on 110th Street, on the edge of Harlem, a long way from Lillian on 21st Street.

In May 1971, Lillian Roxon told her side of the story of Germaine's visit to New York.

I had just developed asthma . . . My home was covered in newspapers and pages of my manuscript. New York was in the throes of a cockroach plague, I was exhausted and bad-tempered and definitely NOT in the mood to entertain anyone, let alone a lady larger than life . . .[9]

When she told her friend that she needed to be left alone, she continued, Germaine showed no sympathy. 'She said, without a trace of compassion, that it was all in my mind, and the love of a good man would solve everything, her usual solution . . .'

Despite the inauspicious start to her holiday, Lillian was Germaine's golden ticket into the elite of New York's rock-art culture. Roxon's New York friends remember her introducing Germaine to the Warhol society at Max's. 'There is no way you could have paid anyone to do the PR that Lillian did out of her heart and out of her belief in her friend,' declared Danny Goldberg, close friend of Lillian, rock fan, author and 'fixture' at Max's.[10]

> [S]he brought Germaine Greer to Max's for the first time. She said, 'This is my friend Germaine and she's going to write this book, she is really important, she's really famous in Australia,' and she introduced her to everybody and it ended up with Germaine being on the cover of *Life* Magazine. That was all Lillian.[11]

But the relationship between the two women was fraught. On one occasion, Germaine arrived at Max's and attempted to join Lillian's party. For no reason (this is Germaine's version), Lillian 'just ripped into me. She abused me up hill and down dale – everything about me. My face, my hands, my feet, my voice, my mind . . .' Germaine swore that she did not retaliate. 'I just sort of sat there with tears running down my face'. Then, she said, she left quietly.[12]

By this time, in 1968, Betty Friedan's NOW was well established. The wider female liberation movement was flourishing, but on this, her first visit to New York, Germaine's heroes and heroines were not the demanding political figures of renascent feminism but rather the artists, musicians and rock stars who lived their freedom and expressed it in song, dance and disgraceful behaviour. On holiday in one of the greatest cities of the Western world, she found women who had broken free of the stereotypes. It would be for these women, and for women everywhere who would heed their message, she declared, that she would write a book.

> It was the women I have met in London and New York, bloody but unbowed, riding the waves of achievement and failure with a valiant attempt at equanimity, still warm, still tough, still sensuous and lovely, sometimes marvellously neurotic. These are my sisters and through them I have learnt to recognise the female principle. The woman who decides to trust to herself, her uncertain beauty and half-disciplined mind and make her own rules for existence in this white man's world, walk into the wilderness like the Duchess of Malfi, and dares the unknown.[13]

She would eventually dedicate *The Female Eunuch* to five of these women (though in an original draft there were eight). The first woman named is easily identifiable as Lillian Roxon.

> This book is dedicated to LILLIAN, who lives with nobody but a colony of New York roaches, whose energy has never failed despite her anxieties and her asthma and her overweight, who is always interested in everybody, often angry, sometimes bitchy, but always involved. Lillian the abundant, the golden, the eloquent, the well and badly loved; Lillian

the beautiful who thinks she is ugly, Lillian the indefatigable
who thinks she is always tired.[14]

Lillian was appalled when she first heard about this classic
example of Germaine's infamous venom from her friend Tony
Delano, an Australian journalist who was working for the
Sunday Mirror in London. 'He thought it was lovely. I thought it
was simply horrible,' she told Robert Milliken.[15]

There it stands to this day – the first paragraph on the first
page of every edition of the book that has been read by millions
over nearly fifty years. Would it have been different if Lillian had
let Germaine sleep on her couch?

•

Little has been known about how Germaine Greer came to write
The Female Eunuch until recently, when her archive became
available to researchers.

Her Warwick University diary for 1969, now housed in the
University of Melbourne's Germaine Greer Archive, shows that
on 17 March she met her friend Sonny Mehta, the commissioning
editor for the publishing house MacGibbon & Kee, an imprint
of Granada, at a cafe in Golden Square in Soho, London. She
told him that her agent, Diana Crawfurd, had suggested that she
should write a book about female suffrage. Germaine was not
interested but Mehta, astutely aware of the commercial potential of books in the rapidly growing field of feminist literature,
managed to persuade her to think about writing a book about
women that was not limited to the question of suffrage.

Still predominantly an academic, a part-time actress and a
weekend hippie, the Germaine Greer of this time was not formally

involved in any of the organised feminist movements. She was dismissive of the by-now old, tweedy 'New Women' of first wave feminism, and she was bored by most of their modern counterparts. Yet Mehta's proposal appealed to her. As a libertarian, she had long despaired of the condition of women, whose lives she saw as blighted by the constraints of marriage, the nuclear family and the institutions of religion and the state. She was also well aware of the media's interest in the new feminism. Included in her preliminary notes for *The Female Eunuch* are some handwritten pages with the heading 'TFE' ('Women's Liberation is dead trendy these days' crossed out) in which she notes that:

the 1969 'second wave' of women's liberation manifestations were very much a ['media mani' crossed out] phenomenon of the sinister forces in our society which we call the media. From pulling in millions of pounds, lire, dollars, and what have you ['from' crossed out] on brainwashing women into demanding emulsified fats, perfumed douches, liver-corroding analgesics and other consumer 'products' which are as necessary to keep our economy on keel as the threat of war or anarchist insurrection the newspapers ['sold their advertising brochures' crossed out] kept up their circulation and thus their advertising by inventing a new sensation. Women's Liberation.[16]

After her meeting with Sonny, she returned to her bedsitter in Leamington Spa to prepare a proposal for him. At first, she thought her book would be a series of essays about a 'problem'.

My book on women, for which I have not yet devised a title will be a collection essays of what it is like to be a woman in 1969. The aim is not to present a plan, or even a series of certainties or correct observations, but a correct statement of a problem. The problem is not one of personal happiness (although doubtless women will decide that there is no problem except a personal one for individuals like me) but the problem of female identity.[17]

The development of the pill, she continued, was having a stronger influence on women's emancipation than getting the vote, accessing education or equal pay. It was now time to 'clear the decks for whatever progress will take place, by discerning what is old, retrogressive, spurious in the culture offered to women in what is still a male society'. Already she had conceived the notion of 'female castration', and she was convinced that the most important factor in overcoming it was the development of women's understanding of themselves as fully sexual beings.

I believe that the most important factor in overcoming female castration is the beginning of awareness, otherwise I should not bother with a book at all.[18]

'Saw Sonny. Gave him synopsis. Talked till 5 am', reads her Warwick diary entry for 29 March 1969. Of course, they talked about the book. Because they were both aware of its commercial potential, they agreed that Germaine should not write an 'academic' book that would attract only a limited readership. It would have to be a blockbuster. On fire with enthusiasm and excitement, she wanted to create something sensational, 'outrageous', that would shock the world into making 'revolution for the hell of it'.

Opposing the predicament of women would come as naturally to Germaine as fighting the oppression of black Americans had come to leaders of the civil rights movement across the Atlantic. To many the similarities appeared to be self-evident. Greer's heroes were her friends Abbie Hoffman, who wrote the book she quoted in her synopsis, *Revolution for the Hell of It*, and other male radical American writers like Eldridge Cleaver, a black activist and an early leader of the Black Panther Party, whose memoir *Soul on Ice* is a classic statement of black alienation and oppression in the United States.

> I shall describe some ways of being <u>outrageous</u> which I privately think also mirror some of our deepest desires, so that women can make revolution for the hell of it (my book is aware of ['Jerry Rubin' crossed out and replaced by 'Abby [sic] Hoffman'] too) which is the only kind at all likely to succeed.[19]

A collection of typed and handwritten notes, preliminary drafts and reflections preserves Germaine's first, surprisingly well-formed, ideas about her book. She goes straight to the heart of the problem, even showing a prescient awareness of the having-it-all-syndrome that would plague women in the decades ahead. Already she recognised, as established feminists like Friedan apparently did not, that creating the political and economic conditions for females to join the male hierarchies, even on equal terms, though necessary, would not be enough. Women would need to look deep into their own bodies and souls to find solutions to the dilemma of their oppression. ('What oppression?' cried the Cheryl Davises of the world, thereby proving Germaine's point.)

She reflected on her attitudes towards her own sex, and on her own situation as a woman who had been successful in a male world. She was certainly not about to write out of love for women.

> I have suffered a great deal at the hands of women, nuns, nurses, sexual rivals, and I had as a result, no interest in their problems at all. I would no more have written a book for my people than the first black senator would be likely to join the Black Panthers. I had made it in a man's world and I reaped the fruits of the rarity of the phenomenon. I enjoyed other people's husbands without risk to my freedom, and was repaid by their infatuation.[20]

In her musings about what she would write in her book, and why, Greer looked back on her own life, painting a picture of herself as a young girl, probably but unknowingly a prodigy, who discovered herself to be out of step with most of her contemporaries. At school, she was mostly clever enough to disguise or adapt to that fact, but at home, every day, she observed with frustration her mother's pathetic attempts to please her husband and family, to look attractive, to conform to the stereotypes, and she knew that she herself could never be like that. Even as a child she believed that the God who had made her too tall had decreed that she was to be an oddity, a misfit. She would have to learn to develop 'tactics' to deal with that misfortune, so devastating for a little girl who only wanted, like all children, to belong.

Those tactics eventually brought her freedom, but it came at a price.

I can have no credit for inventing the tactics: they were forced on me as a freak – too tall, too clever, too noisy – at a very early age.[21]

Her reflections continued. As a university student, after a shaky start, she had begun not only to understand her situation, but to see it as superior to that of the common run of women. She met congenial people, male and female, and followed her convictions with growing confidence, eventually coming to realise that the freak was now being perceived as an icon. She must be doing something right. At first, she said, the 'tactics' of her unusual lifestyle 'merely functioned', but later she was able to develop a rationale for them. Now, at Warwick, on the cusp of writing her book, she rejoiced that she had 'made it in a man's world' and 'reaped the fruits of the phenomenon'.[22]

She had promised Sonny Mehta that she would write a book about women, but she knew, and he perceived, with the excitement of a publisher who stood to make a lot of money from a book, that her preoccupations were not simply with the male/female divide or even the many ways in which women, like blacks, were oppressed. Her issue was with the dilemma of womanhood itself. What was it about women that had placed them in their present state?

As she prepared to write *The Female Eunuch*, Greer was grappling, in a very personal way, with the notion that lumbering men with the blame for women's troubles was attacking the wrong problem. Women would need to look within their own beings to discover, at the most profound levels, what it meant to be female, and, more specifically, what aspects of their 'femininity' were contributing to their oppression.

Importantly, her experiences of living within the counter-cultures of the United Kingdom and the United States had taught her that there were ways of being female that did not bend to the stereotype. The women to whom she would dedicate her book had shown her that it was possible to subvert 'the docile womanhood of the world'. She would begin by questioning 'the commonest presumptions about women, first her body, then her soul'.[23]

The Female Eunuch was first published by MacGibbon & Kee in London, in October 1970, just eighteen months after Germaine's discussions with Sonny Mehta in the Soho cafe. The publishers, unprepared for the book's explosive success, could not print extra copies fast enough to meet demand. The cover alone would become iconic. Designed by artist John Holmes, it shows the naked torso of a white woman separated from the rest of the body. Suspended helplessly from a pole, the torso has a handle protruding from each hip and the genitalia are missing, as in most dolls. 'She has tits because the iconography of commercial sex allows them,' Greer explained to her friend Gershon Legman in 1972. 'No energy, she just hangs there, like the hunchback girl in the dirty joke. She is also equipped with handles on her hips, troops for the use of.'[24]

As a graphic representation of the book's title, the figure sears into readers' minds an unforgettable image of what the book is about. In 1971 Greer told an interviewer from the *New York Times* that she saw the title and cover of her book as 'an indication of the problem'.

Women have somehow been separated from their libido, from their faculty of desire, from their sexuality. They've become suspicious about it.

Like beasts, for example, who are castrated in farming in order to serve their master's ulterior motives – to be fattened or made docile – women have been cut off from their capacity for action. It's a process that sacrifices vigour for delicacy and succulence, and one that's got to be changed.[25]

In her summary to *The Female Eunuch*, which is published in the opening pages of many editions of the book, she noted that, by the mid-twentieth century, the militant ladies of first-wave feminism had grown old, the main force of their energy had drained away, and their 'evangelism' had withered into 'eccentricity'. Yet, two generations earlier, these women had opened the cage door for women. Why was it that 'the canary had refused to fly out?'[26]

The problem would not be solved, she believed, until essential questions about the kind of liberty that would set the canary free were understood and resolved. Political activity would be essential, but women could not afford to wait until the old paternalistic structures decided to give way. They would have to learn to understand themselves before they could arrive at a definition of their present condition.

> . . . it is absolutely essential that women arrive at a correct
> description of their present plight in order not to incorporate
> its present aspects in a new order; so I have come to write
> a book.[27]

Thus, 'Body', the first chapter of the book, begins with an assessment of the female body, which Greer describes in meticulous detail in the sections 'Gender', 'Bones', 'Curves', 'Hair', 'Sex' and 'The Wicked Womb'. In this first group of topics, she explains her theory – the central argument of the book – that the bodies of women have been effectively castrated for the convenience of men. The vagina has become unmentionable to the point of obliteration, its natural odours disguised by all manner of expensive unguents; women's bones are wasted by dieting and poor nutrition; body hair is shaved or waxed away; curves are exaggerated or disguised; sexuality has become passivity. The wicked womb is commonly seen as the source of all female problems – hysteria, menstrual depression, the multitude of imagined weaknesses for which women are judged to be unfit for active participation in those activities men have claimed for themselves.

Greer wants women to develop a clear perception of these perversions and to seek to recognise the true nature of their bodies, by physically examining and probing their most intimate nooks and crannies without feelings of guilt. Provokingly, with her usual eye to the impact of shock tactics and the market value of sensationalism, she even suggests that they taste their own menstrual blood – 'if it makes you sick, you've a long way to go, baby'.[28]

Introducing the second chapter, 'Soul', Greer paints an exotic yet tragic picture of the feminine stereotype.

> She is the crown of creation, the masterpiece. The depths of the sea are ransacked for pearl and coral to deck her; the bowels of the earth are laid open that she might wear gold, sapphires, diamonds and rubies.[29]

Once upon a time, she continues, it was only the wives of aristocrats who could 'lay claim to the crown of creation'. Only their feet were small enough, their hands white enough, their waists narrow enough, their hair sufficiently golden to display the wealth and status of their owner-husbands. Then the burghers' wives caught up with the aristocratic ladies and now, in our own time, most women can pamper and adorn themselves as proof of their husbands' success in the world. But what of their souls?

The stereotype is a soulless doll. Her value is determined only by the extent of her attractiveness to men, and no hint of independent thought or action must be permitted to impede her allure. She may stand by a motorbike in an advertisement, for she is a great seller of the world's goods, but she must not ride it. Her expressions may provide tantalising glimpses of smouldering lust, but she may know lust only as irrational submission. She must betray no suggestion of humour, curiosity or intelligence, but she needs to project happiness, for an unhappy woman becomes a man's problem wife. She must be young and hairless, her body buoyant; most importantly of all, 'she must not have a sexual organ'.[30]

In 'Love', the third chapter of *The Female Eunuch*, Greer suggests that 'an attainable ideal of love' might resemble the kind of relationship suggested by Maslow, in which two 'self-regulating' personalities come together under 'an autonomous moral code', free from imposed restrictions. 'The essential factor in self-realization is independence, resistance to enculturation.' There are strong hints of the conflicts Germaine herself has experienced in attempting to give and receive such love.

A woman who decided to become a lover without conditions might discover that her relationships broke up relatively easily because of her degree of resistance to efforts to 'tame' her, and the opinion of her friends will usually be on the side of the man who was prepared to do the decent thing, who was in love with her, etcetera . . . Her love may often be devalued by the people for whom she feels the most tenderness, and her self-esteem might have much direct attack . . . Even if a woman does not inhibit her behaviour she will find herself reacting in some other way, being outrageous when she only meant to be spontaneous, and so forth. She may limit herself to writing defences of promiscuity, or even books about women. (Hm.)[31]

She goes on to describe the common 'perversions' of love in the twentieth century, notably those portrayed in romantic literature. In this most entertaining chapter she paints a perfect picture of her Byronic hero – 'He has more than a hint of danger in his past conquests, or a secret suffering or a disdain for women. The banked fires of passion burn just below the surface . . .' The first of these heroes, she points out, were Rochester, Heathcliff, Darcy and Lord Byron himself. Later novelists, like Georgette Heyer and Barbara Cartland, had attempted to create their counterparts. There is Heyer's hero Lord Worth, the Regency Buck with world-weary eyelids, who rescues his helpless young heroine from the evil intentions of the Prince of Wales, and Cartland's Lord Ravenscar, who covets lovely Amanda's tiny body. Particularly titillating is Cartland's description of poor, ineffectual little Amanda, arms and legs flailing in fruitless resistance, becoming exquisitely aware of Lord R's 'rising passion' as he carries her masterfully to the sofa.[32]

Amanda has no power in this terrifyingly delightful situation. 'How could such a delicate little thing kick a peer of the realm in his rising passion?' queries Greer; but, wryly, she acknowledges that she herself cannot claim to be fully emancipated from the dream. 'For three weeks I was married to him.'[33]

What Heyer, Cartland and their ilk strategically refused to recognise, Greer argues, is that female objects of male fantasy are not Lord Worth's young lover or Ravenscar's Amanda but 'the opulent tigresses of thriller literature', The Poison Maiden and The Great Bitch. The latter category, 'those extraordinary springing women . . . wheeling suddenly upon the hero, talons unsheathed for the kill', are a familiar sight in men's and boys' comics. They also appear in the fantasy creations of writers like Ian Fleming, in which the aggressively male hero carries a phallic armoury of weapons to attack the female. In this part of her book, Greer also quotes the notoriously misogynistic Norman Mailer, whom she was soon to meet and debate in New York (and to whom she would inevitably find herself attracted), as another famous exponent of the genre: 'She was a handsome woman, Deborah, she was big. With high heels she stood at least an inch over me. . . .' he wrote – prophetically, as it turned out.[34]

With such perceptions of the impossible polarities between male and female, Greer's critique of 'The Middle-Class Myth of Love and Marriage' towards the end of the Love chapter comes as no surprise. The key word here is 'myth'. Wives like to deceive themselves into believing their husbands to be strong, rich, handsome, et cetera, when they know at a deeper level that they are actually 'paunchy, short, un-athletic, and snore or smell or leave their clothes lying around . . . It never occurs to them to seek the cause of their unhappiness in the myth itself.'[35]

Readers who have got this far into *The Female Eunuch* may be excused for thinking that, as Winston Churchill once famously said of democracy, the institutions of marriage and family are the worst forms of social organisation, especially for women, but they are better than all the others. What practical alternatives can there be?

Greer's only suggestion is a utopian fantasy whose chief value is that it allows us to see how she, at the age of thirty, perceives her own life and future. She has already made one disastrous attempt to marry and is unlikely to do it again. She is highly intelligent, highly educated, highly successful. She believes that she has seen through the myth of love and marriage and has escaped becoming its victim. Sex is freely available to her, she does not need a man's money to support her. There is just one problem. Her body craves a baby. And how can she care for that baby in the absence of its father? Where can she find the time, to say nothing of the inclination, to care for 'his' needs? What sort of life would it be for her child, cooped up in a city flat all day while she is off at the university?

She is aware that she is not alone. Other brilliant women like her are also deciding not to reproduce, and for similar reasons. After much deliberation, she conceives a plan, inspired by the months she spent in the village in Calabria, that she and a group of like-minded women who wanted to breed could purchase a farmhouse in Italy. Immediately after giving birth they could take their children to live on this property and leave them there. They, the mothers, and even the fathers and some friends, if they so wished, could visit the children for longer and shorter periods, to rest, enjoy themselves, even work a bit. Her child would not even need to know that she was 'his' mother:

> If necessary the child need not even know that I was his womb-mother and I could have relationships with the other children as well.[36]

And the problem of who will look after the children's daily needs? Well may the reader wonder who will change the nappies of these children. Who will feed them, bathe them, toilet train them, suffer their crying in the sleepless nights? And who will clean the house? Look after the garden?

No problem at all: a local family will take care of all the tasks the birth mothers are much too busy and important to attend to. Somehow, the woman or women of this simple family will not need to be counted as women who might also want to become emancipated!

And so the book proceeds towards its blockbuster conclusion. 'Women have very little idea of how much men hate them' is a horrific wake-up call. Surely, one thinks, it cannot be true, but she marshals the evidence: the habitual put-downs, the casual abuse, the snide references to sexual conquests, the nasty names for women and their sexual parts. With her usual academic thoroughness she lists what must be nearly every male-invented term for women: cow, bitch, douche-bag, pig, pig-meat, dog, drab, slut – and more. Then for their vaginas: meat, snatch, pussy, slit, crack and tail. Then she retells the story of the gang rape of the prostitute Tralala from Hubert Selby Jr's *Last Exit to Brooklyn*, who suffers violation after violation in a car, only to be abandoned, presumably left to die, by the fifty or so crowing men who argued among themselves and drank beer as they waited their turn. Tralala's nipples were destroyed by the cigarettes the men stubbed out on them, her lips were split, her teeth broken, her body soaked in urine, and a broomstick was shoved 'up her snatch'.[37]

'Punished, punished, punished for being the object of hatred and fear and disgust, through her magic orifices, her cunt and her mouth, poor Tralala,' wails Greer. The Cheryl Davises of the Western world cried out in anguish: Can it be true? Do men really hate women that much? What secrets are hidden in our husbands' dark hearts? Do they all harbour private fantasies like the rape of Tralala? Is this why they won't let us into their pubs? Is that what they talk about there? But *why*? When we women try so hard to please them!

More dispassionately, Greer noted that as long as men continued to act out their accustomed roles, feminists would see them as The Enemy. But when both sexes were brought face to face with the myths of the all-powerful male – the Omnipotent Administrator – and his opposite, the Ultra-feminine, women might see that men were only the enemy in the same way as 'some crazed boy in uniform' is the enemy of another like himself. 'One possible tactic is to try to get the uniforms off.'[38]

The forms of 'Revolution' Greer outlines in her final chapter differ from other feminist prescriptions for change in that they demand little or nothing of men. It is up to women to change the world by their own new insights and actions. First they must learn to understand that they are collaborators in their own oppression. They are the ones who flee to marriage for security, thereby pledging their lives away for ever; they are the greatest consumers of goods, both household and personal; they are the providers of the cheapest form of labour, slaves of the nuclear household, which is the chief unit of consumption. Once they realise their true situation, the answers become clear. They must not marry. If they are already married they should run away, leave their children if necessary. They should live with their sisters in various forms of social organisation which they will be free to sort out for themselves. Men will be around, but women will not belong to them or provide cheap services for them. Even paternity is to be denied, as the idea of family shifts from nuclear to collective.

Thus will the present state wither away, all by itself, and the suffering proletariat will be spared the conflict of a masculine, Marxist reversal of their condition. But she fears that not even the Marxists will be behind her. 'They might even identify the authoress [sic] as an anarchist and first for the firing squads . . .'[39]

In the popular mind, *The Female Eunuch* has come to be thought of as a seminal text of second-wave feminism, but from the time of its original publication the book's connection to the women's movement has been tenuous, and Greer's relationship with her feminist sisters in the United Kingdom and the United States has been problematic. In February 1984, eight of the most prominent feminists in England – Sheila Rowbotham, Angela Phillips, Reva Klein, Liz Heron, Judith Hunt, Hilary Wainwright, Kate Falcon and Gail Lewis – wrote, in a letter to the *Sunday Times*:

> Just to avoid misunderstanding, can we make it clear that Germaine Greer never involved herself in the women's movement in this country. Judging by the romantic nonsense she spouts about her Italian lovers she has had little contact with the Italian movement either. Her thoughts are her own and they are based not on history, not even on the present, but on a sentimental misalignment of information plucked from a dozen sources, countries, cultures and centuries.[40]

By January 1971, *The Female Eunuch* was already a sensation, though it had been in the English bookshops for less than three months. Thousands of copies had been sold in England, America and Europe, and it had been translated into eight languages. From all over the world, Germaine received letters from excited women who told her that this book had changed their lives. Of these many, many letters, one stands out as being representative and especially perceptive. It came from a young Australian high school teacher who was soon to start exerting her own lifelong influence on millions of women and men. Her name? Helen Garner.

Reading what you write, I find my mind working fully and joyfully for the first time since – I was going to say since I had my daughter nearly 2 years ago but it has just struck me that it could well be since I was a child and read night and day in that drunken total way which I feared I would never do again.

She explained that she was a teacher at Fitzroy High School in Melbourne, that many of the young women at the school were reading the book and that she and other female teachers were chafing against the ignorance and condescension of many of their male colleagues.

A lot of the young women at the school are reading your book and I know that it is encouraging us to feel that we are <u>right</u> when we know the men are talking shit and that it is time for us to say so and to start changing the school the way we know in our bones it <u>must</u> be changed . . .

Whenever I am listening to one of the men talking shit to me about the value of corporal punishment or some such monstrosity and whenever I feel that awful feminine defer-ence eroding my urge to fight back I call to mind your picture on the back of The Female Eunuch and I think 'Fuck, <u>she</u> wouldn't stand here silent, and neither will I.'[41]

Another letter, headed 'UNSOLICITED TESTIMONIAL', written before *The Female Eunuch* was published, was as enthu-siastic, but even more prescient than Garner's. Germaine had sent the proofs of her book to Clive James, whose admiration of her work, to that point, had been touched with the wry cynicism of an old friend who knew her every mood. All of that changed when he read the proofs. 'It is without question the most important single thing yet to emerge from our generation of Australian exiles,' he wrote, 'polemically energetic in the most Shavian way, epigrammatic in a fashion that I knew you capable of in speech but not in prose, and above all assembled beyond anything I expected.'

When he had first heard about her project, he continued, he had predicted it would turn out a joke. How wrong, he now admitted, he had been.

> Well, it has turned out a triumph and the measure of that is how it made me examine the assumptions by which I had decided it would be a joke. The book is aimed at me . . . it wasn't going to kick the romanticism out of me but it'll kick some daylight in.
>
> Allora. Fame is yours.[42]

An article first published in *Rolling Stone* magazine on 7 January 1971 provides a fascinating insight into the person Germaine Greer was in the short interval between *The Female Eunuch*'s initial success and her subsequent fame. The writer of the article was Robert Greenfield, journalist and music critic, who was then on the staff of *Rolling Stone*.

The setting of Greenfield's report is a London film studio, on the set of a picture starring George Lazenby, the erstwhile James Bond, who was playing a gun runner who gave it all up for flower power. It is Sunday afternoon and the room is hazy and crowded; members of the cast lounge around in studied poses, smoking and drinking. Everyone is stoned and/or drunk. Germaine Greer, silver-knit flapper's hat pulled over her ears, holds court in a corner of the room near Chrissie Shrimpton, who is 'drifting through a doorway like some Victorian butterfly'. Lazenby is around somewhere. In the film, Germaine is playing the sister of the female protagonist. The plot seems simple enough. 'George wants to fuck [the female lead],' Germaine explains sweetly. 'She says no. Peace, flowers, love. He asks her for some head. She says no. Well, the whole thing is unreal. She should plate him in the middle of the scene.'

Greenfield is intrigued by the duality of Germaine's lifestyle. 'Although she tends to defy definitions and skirt boundaries,' he writes, 'Germaine exists primarily in two worlds – the "I say old chap" very British artsy-literary-academic sphere and the oop-shoop-shangalalang-a-jingabop of the music business.' She tells him about her trip to New York as a groupie, waking up in the hotel with the bodies of young rock stars all over the floor, everyone about to start the day with a joint. But she draws the line at heroin, which those same boys had asked her for the last time they were in England.

The day's interview closes with Germaine telling Greenfield that she has already been paid a great deal of money for her book and is about to make much more. She will need to go to America to avoid tax.

Two weeks later she and Greenfield meet again at the Charles Clore Pavilion in Regent's Park Zoo. Germaine, fresh from lunch with writers Ken Tynan and Mary McCarthy, is an hour late, smelling of gin. She talks again about her coming trip to the United States. She will not bond with the political feminists over there, she declares; she prefers ('digs') the Redstockings, a libertarian radical group whose views were closer to her own. Those women who were learning karate to fight men, she opined, would be better off making love to them.

That seemed to be Germaine's solution to everything, thought Greenfield. 'If your landlady is hassling you, ball her. Want better care from your doctor? Make it with him.'

Five o'clock comes and the attendant wants to close the Mammal House, but Germaine hasn't seen the wombat.

> 'It's closing time,' a zoo attendant shouts.
> 'Where's the wombat?' Greer asks blithely, pushing past.
> 'It's closed, lady,' the attendant explodes, red in the face. 'It's closed. Get out!'
> 'I bet he hasn't gotten his rocks off in months.' Germaine says, turning to go back. 'What if I went down on him?'
> Someone takes her arm and leads her gently away.[43]

For a short time after the publication and dramatic success of *The Female Eunuch*, Greer's relationship with her fellow editors and supporters of *Suck* remained, for the most part, cordial and occasionally intimate. Eventually, however, cracks developed in the *Suck* partnership that no amount of intimacy could paper over. Differences of belief and perception were always part of the enterprise, but significant shifts in Germaine's relationship with the other editors only started to occur after she became a celebrity. Jim Haynes and Bill Levy, her male co-editors, were proud of their colleague's phenomenal success, but they had difficulty coming to terms with it. Talented and ambitious as they and most of her friends of this time were, none was a match for her, and it was with mixed feelings that they began to realise she was moving up and away from them.

Matters came to a head in 1972, when Germaine agreed to send some photographs of her naked self to Jim Haynes on the understanding that one would appear alongside pictures of all the editors of *Suck*, including Jean Shrimpton, that would be published in a book about the Wet Dream Film Festival. From Amsterdam, Purple Susan wrote that 'everyone' was waiting eagerly for the photographs to arrive, but she did not tell Germaine what Haynes and/or Bill Levy were planning to do with them.

Among the photos was one of a naked Germaine in a yoga pose that showed her lying down with her splayed legs thrown back over her shoulders, her buttocks and genitalia presented to the camera and her raised-up face grinning mischievously through her legs. The photograph is clearly pornographic, but unlike most porn of the era, the woman, Germaine, is seen to be actively and happily in control, confronting the world through her legs, as opposed to appearing as a passive object.

She had thought that picture and others, including one of her naked, sucking her toenail, rather good, so she decided to let the *Suck* people keep them, but she was devastated when Jim Haynes or Bill Levy – or someone; it never quite became clear who was responsible – chose to publish her yoga-pose picture in the next edition (issue number 7) of *Suck*. Dismayed, she felt that this was not only a betrayal of her trust, but almost certainly a commercial decision, for by this time Germaine Greer, Celebrity, was ripe for exploitation. When Haynes chose to hawk that issue with its scandalous photograph of her around the Frankfurt Book Fair, she was distraught.

> Knowing my feelings about it and the fact that I was appalled at such a crass exploitation of the situation, you then took the SUCK in question and peddled it around the Frankfurt Book Fair. Now you may consider that I am very strong and can take whatever you dish out; that's pretty much like telling somebody they have a face that's made for kicking . . .

'I am not ashamed of my collaboration with *Suck* in the past,' she concluded, 'but I think I'd have to be a raving maniac to associate with *Suck* in the future.'[44]

Haynes, for his part, steadfastly maintained that it was not his but Bill Levy's decision to publish the photos, and that he had advised Bill to consult with her before printing.

'I HAD NOTHING TO DO WITH SUCK PUBLISHING YOUR PHOTOGRAPH,' he wrote to her in March 1973.[45] And one year later:

> Our one-sided altercation has left me a bit shell-shocked. I say one-sided because I never felt any antagonism towards you, only frustration. I wanted to hug you tenderly and warmly and say 'Hey Germaine, it's me, Jim. I have done you no harm, why are you angry with me?'[46]

Germaine was convinced that Haynes and Levy had used and exploited her. Haynes saw it differently. Their relationship, he believed, covered two distinct periods – pre– and post–*The Female Eunuch*. In the first, carefree, period, they shared a kindred view. 'You were stimulating and exciting to work with and more and more I felt our friendship grow closer.' In the second, post-*Eunuch* period, he was proud of her, but he saw 'a steady and slow transformation . . . and during this period, which has not ended, you became more and more of a media personality and with this came pressures from all sides . . .'[47]

Haynes continued to try to mend the relationship into the early 1990s ('Some people never learn, I know, but nevertheless I send you best wishes for the 90s.'[48]) but Germaine would have no part of him. When Sarah Harris from the publishers Faber & Faber approached her for a contribution to an autobiography he was writing, she replied acidly that she was unsympathetic to him and to his 'friendship industry', which struck her as 'facile and basically exploitative, as does American friendship in general, I regret to say'.[49]

Jim Haynes was right. The post–*Female Eunuch* Germaine Greer was a very different person from her pre-*Eunuch* days – more aware of her commercial value, and warier of being exploited for it. As an international celebrity, she found herself living in a world where her every utterance might be reported or distorted in the media, and where spicy morsels of news about her private life were worth money and influence to informers. From carelessly blithe hippie she metamorphosed into a media-savvy professional. She remained loyal to some of her old friends in the counterculture, but her new fame and wealth set her apart from most of them, and many were envious of her success.

After the *Suck* debacle, Germaine felt that being with some old friends had become an 'embarrassment and humiliation' so intense that she would have to abandon them.

> Stuff it [Levy] might want to be a friend, but he behaves like an enemy and this is true of many other people who have been close to me and have done cute things like ring PRIVATE EYE with details of conversations that I have had with them . . . All of which is called exploitation . . . or parasitism . . . I am afraid I have given up a great many of my friends . . . Madness is catching and I feel sick and crazy . . .[50]

In an effort to maintain her academic career in the wake of the success of *The Female Eunuch*, she had initially chosen to take leave rather than resign from her job at the University of Warwick, but as she continued to struggle with the demands and pressures of promoting her book and her ideas, especially the necessary travel, she decided to seek new avenues for her talents. In 1972, she resigned from the university. Always inclined to be a loner, she now became alone in a more poignant sense – the private person behind the public celebrity.

An old Australian friend has described the Germaine Greer of the early 1970s as 'hungry and lustful – like most lapsed Catholic girls', but this underestimates her capacity for falling in love. She herself has said that she was never very good at love, and her life is testimony that her romantic relationships do not last. In several cases the imbalance between her brilliance, riches and phenomenal success, and the comparatively ordinary lives of her lovers, was part of the problem. This was almost certainly the case with Tony Gourvish, the man she was involved with when she was writing *The Female Eunuch*.

At the beginning of that relationship, Gourvish was doing well in his own right as a manager of the rock band Family. In 1970–71, this band was very successful: it had appeared on the same concert bill as the Rolling Stones and scored fifth in a *Melody Maker* popularity poll behind Led Zeppelin, the Beatles, The Who and Pink Floyd.[51]

Gourvish certainly seems to have been on Germaine's mind as she wrote some of her rough preliminary notes for *The Female Eunuch*: 'I LOVE YOU TONY XXXX', she scrawled at the bottom of one page of text, references for the 'Soul' section.[52]

While on a major tour of the United States in 1971, Gourvish wrote to 'dearest Germaine' from Buffalo, New York, telling her that he found her letters 'an incredible turn-on'. He was disappointed that she would be unable to meet him at the airport, he said, but perhaps that would be better as 'I fear my emotions would run to tears of joy and love. Still you must ring me on the Wednesday night so that I can feel that much closer to you.' Upon his return he would share with her – 'my love' – every detail about the tour, he would kiss her all over, and they would stay in bed 'all day and all night Friday, Saturday, Sunday, never let you up. No work for either of us!' For the whole of that tour, he wrote, he had felt close to her 'in mind and body'.[53]

This was the language of a committed relationship; they were living together and she had even taken to referring to him as her 'Old Man'. ('Old Lady' was also a term of choice for 'wives' of the counterculture.) She wrote to Lillian Roxon, asking her to spread the word about Gourvish and Family among her influential friends in New York and at Max's Kansas City. Gourvish, for his part, was trying to come to terms with Germaine's imminent success and fame: 'The cover of your book looks very together, and I [sic] really very happy for you, and for anything you do. NO BULLSHIT.'[54]

But by 1973 their love had cooled to a conflicted friendship as her wealth and fame increased and his diminished as Family, which had seemed so promising, failed to reach the heights of other groups like the Stones. She began to suspect that he was taking advantage of her generosity when he made free use of her car, a Mini Cooper, in London during her absences abroad. He had also taken to wearing her favourite wolf-fur coat, and seemed to believe it was his. From Italy she wrote to her secretary, Franki Roberts, asking her to repossess the car and to call the police if necessary. Tony was more astonished than appalled, but Germaine was feeling used, betrayed and suspicious. 'Cut the crap and tell me WHAT THE FUCK ARE YOU UP TO instead of writing letters about how badly I'm treating you,' she wrote.[55]

Gourvish had believed Germaine was happy to share her possessions – that was the way of the counterculture, after all.

And she had led him to believe that the coat was a present. 'Surely there must be some other reason for this attack,' he wrote. 'Am I to be held to blame because I cannot afford to buy the car? I would if I could . . . Please don't do this to me without understanding my complete lack of understanding as to what I have done.' But Germaine was obdurate. 'If you behave like a half-bred cretin you must expect people to be annoyed. Franki was going on her information, which was probably largely based on an impression she got of you as yet another one of my shitty friends (she's seen a few in action).'[56]

The friendship managed to limp along for a few more years. In 1976, she allowed him to live for a while in the basement flat at her house, but by the time he left she had had enough of what she believed to be ongoing exploitation of her good intentions towards him. She reminded him that he had failed to pay rent and bills. He argued that the few possessions he was leaving behind would square his debts.

Germaine gave up on him. 'You have used and abused this house for less than £20 a week,' she wrote scathingly. 'My attempts at explaining what I wanted were met with hysteria . . . In other words you dealt with me dishonestly and you are still doing so. In the past, I wrote off the wolf coat and the Mini. What I have done before I could have done again, except that this time I am writing you off because it wasn't even fun.'[57]

The American author Marilyn French said of Germaine Greer that she had a big soul. French could have added that Germaine was also generous and egalitarian by nature, not the type of person who would discard old friends on the climb to fame and fortune, neither of which she had deliberately set out to achieve. As time went on, however, and more of her friends behaved badly, she was increasingly suspicious of their motives. In some instances, her own motives were also questionable. Handing out largesse to less fortunate friends put her in a position of power. She expected gratitude, if not obeisance, but this was not always clear to those whom she had helped. Because she had encouraged them to see her as their equal, with no strings attached to her generosity, they were baffled when their Lady Bountiful turned on them and accused them of leeching off her.

Thus Jim Haynes's judgement appears to be vindicated: the success of Germaine Greer's first book brought about seismic changes, not only in her life circumstances but also in her psyche and the ways in which she related to her friends. In time, she managed to adjust to her new status, but much of her correspondence shows that she remained suspicious and conflicted – as attracted by promises of intimacy as she was wary of them. For the rest of her life she would make sure to keep frantically busy, warding off personal doubts and fears with productive activity. She would also get angry, often, for anger is an excellent defence mechanism.

5

The commercialisation
of Germaine Greer

'Tis the white stag, Fame, we're a-hunting,
Bid the world's hounds come to horn!

Ezra Pound, 'The White Stag'

On 7 September 1968, four hundred feminists gathered on the Atlantic City Boardwalk outside the Miss America Pageant to protest what they called 'the degrading, mindless boob-girlie system'. The women marched and shouted slogans; they carried placards, gave out pamphlets and even crowned a hapless live sheep to illustrate the similarities between pageants and livestock competitions at county fairs. The marchers also threw a number of female-targeted products into a 'Freedom Trash Can'. These objects included false eyelashes, high-heeled shoes, pots and pans, make-up, girdles, corsets and bras. Nothing was burned on this occasion because the protesters couldn't get a permit – the Atlantic City Boardwalk was made of wood – but this did not prevent the media from inventing stories of how the women had burned numerous items of underwear, most notably their brassieres.

This was the era when anti-Vietnam protesters were burning all sorts of things – their draft cards, the American flag, whatever else came to hand – and the bra-burning story provided a brilliant counterpoint to those activities, never mind that it wasn't true. The press response to the Atlantic City protests was predictable – crazy women, 'dykes', 'commies', 'uglies' doing crazy things, attacking the foundations of American society, an insult to decent women, where would it all end, and so on. At least some of the newspaper reports were funny. Pulitzer Prize winner Art Buchwald, writing in the *New York Post*, suggested a few things no one else had thought of. American women, he said, beautiful though they undoubtedly were, needed all the help they could get to stay attractive to men. And thanks to the boundless efforts of science and the beauty industries they were getting it: 'it is now impossible for anyone to know where God leaves off and Maidenform takes over'. The protesting women might believe that by getting rid of the beauty 'hardware' they would gain sexual independence, but they were mistaken, he opined. Even with all the aids presently at her disposal, a woman was hard-pressed to distract a male from his manly pursuit of making money long enough for him to look at her. Without those aids she would be finished; the clock would be turned back to those cave-dwelling days when men liked to batter women about the head without even glancing at them.

> It was only, after the women started rubbing petals on themselves, and putting dust on their cheeks and red clay in their hair, that the men stopped batting them around.
>
> As we saw in Chicago, there are still many men who would like to club women over the head, if they're given the slightest excuse, and there's no better excuse for hitting a woman than the fact that she looks just like a man.[1]

Buchwald, of course, was joking, but some media commentators expressed similar sentiments without a hint of irony.

The antics of the media-created 'uglies', 'dogs' and 'commies' remained newsworthy into the 1970s, but the savvier commentators recognised that the commercial value of unattractive women is limited even when they are being pilloried; ultimately, they become a bore. It is the glamour factor that sells magazines and television programs. Beautiful faces, long legs, glamorous poses, shimmering dresses, airbrushed everything. Outrageous unfeminine behaviour had sparked media interest in the new movement, but how long would it last? How long would women's lib survive if it remained the preserve of Ugly Bettys?

This absence of the glamour factor in women's liberation was a relatively minor issue for the media, but it was a much greater problem for the feminists. No individual provides a better example of this than Kate Millett, a committee member of Betty Friedan's NOW, whose groundbreaking book *Sexual Politics* was published in the United States only a few months before *The Female Eunuch*. Originating from her PhD dissertation, the book vigorously attacked romantic love ('a means of emotional manipulation which the male is free to exploit'), monogamous marriage and the nuclear family ('patriarchy's chief institution'). Memorably, Millett pounced on the sexism in books by the male novelists D.H. Lawrence, Henry Miller and Norman Mailer. In its first year of publication *Sexual Politics* sold eighty thousand copies and was reprinted six times. In August 1970, Millett was featured in a *Time* cover story, 'The Politics of Sex', which called her book 'remarkable' and congratulated her on having provided a coherent theory about the feminist movement.

But writer and supreme male chauvinist Norman Mailer was lying in wait for her. In his essay for *Harper's Magazine*, 'The

Prisoner of Sex', he called her 'a pug-nosed wit' and a 'Battling Annie'. She had no proper literary sense, he asserted; how dare she question the genius of writers like Lawrence and Miller (and, by implication, himself)?[2]

The turning point for Millett came when she was speaking about sexual liberation at Columbia University in November 1970. A woman in the audience asked her to declare herself a lesbian. Kate hesitated, then responded quietly: 'Yes, I am a lesbian.' Only a couple of weeks later, on 8 December 1970, in an article titled 'Women's lib: A second look', *Time* commented that Millett's 'admission' would cause people to turn away from feminism in the belief that all feminists were lesbians. That did happen, and members of the movement, including Betty Friedan, did not thank her for it. Nor did gay activists, who censured her for not coming out sooner.

Millett later argued that it was at this time, with the publication of *Time*'s second piece, that the figure of the feminist as lesbian first became fully manifest in the press and popular culture. She may have overestimated her influence, however. The stereotype is hundreds, if not thousands, of years old, apparent in stories of the burning of witches and many other forms of abuse. In the early twentieth century the media had seized on it to discredit the feminists of the first wave, and some journalists were now sharpening their knives to do it again for the second.

Millett continued her work into the twenty-first century, but she was a tortured soul, plagued by personal trauma, bouts of serious mental illness, hospital admissions and treatment with electro-shock therapy. For a few months after the publication of *Sexual Politics* the media had tried to turn her into a celebrity, but lust for fame and wealth was not in her. 'Microphones shoved into my mouth . . . "What is the future of the

women's movement?" How the hell do I know – I don't run
it . . . The whole thing is sordid, embarrassing, a fraud . . . I'm
vomiting with terror . . . why have you made me a curiosity?'
she wrote.[3]

The demons that caused the sensitive Millett to flee publicity were foreign to Germaine Greer. She was excited by the
power of the media to generate change (as well as fortunes
and power for performers like herself). She relished the irony
that those very media outlets might use their influence to shame
gullible females into awareness of the humiliating circumstances
of their lives.

> Most of her life [the average housewife] has served fashion
> without demur, and now the media have created the fashion of
> female liberation. At last the fucking media look like they are
> hoist with their own petard.[4]

Greer and her publicists also realised that while portraying
feminists as freaky lesbians had solid news value, the ethics of this
approach were questionable and its appeal was likely to sour. As
an attention-getter, women's liberation had started a new trend,
but the trend was based on the 'tiny' reality of elites like NOW,
the Redstockings, the New York Radical Women movement
(organisers of the Atlantic City Miss America protest) and the
rapidly proliferating groups of local consciousness-raisers. These
women were exceptional but not mainstream.

> Of course, most women are not radical leftists, or unmar-
> ried university students, and the luxury of such theorising
> is not accessible to them in any way at all. Mrs. Smith who
> tends a bottling machine by day and husband and kids

morning and night has no use for a reading list however exhaustive.[5]

Until and unless a new angle could be found, the second-wave feminist movement would be in danger of becoming a modern, but no more attractive or useful, version of the first wave. The images of ill-fitting suits, shapeless felt hats and threatening umbrellas would be replaced by sagging breasts, hairy legs and smelly underarms. In popular culture, the women of the new feminism might well go the dowdy way of the old.

Germaine Greer arrived in New York early in 1971 to commence her promotional tour for *The Female Eunuch*. No longer the relatively unknown person who Lillian Roxon had sent off to the sleazy Broadway Central Hotel a couple of years earlier, she was now a celebrity, accompanied everywhere by her own British television crew.

The tour began with a disagreement between Greer and McGraw-Hill, her American publishers, about where she would stay in New York. They had booked her into the famous Algonquin Hotel, a sophisticated retreat for the classier members of the international literati. But Germaine did not yet consider herself to be classy. She was still a groupie and she wanted her friends from the rock and underground scenes to be able to visit her and enjoy having sex with her as she and they pleased. So she demanded that her booking be changed to the Chelsea Hotel, famous refuge of writers, musicians and artists, where she knew she would be in congenial company.

Bob Dylan had lived at the Chelsea Hotel; Nancy Spungen would be found stabbed to death there, allegedly by her boyfriend, the Sex Pistols' Sid Vicious; Dylan Thomas was taken from his room in the hotel to the hospital where he died; Leonard

Cohen's song 'Chelsea Hotel No. 2' is about a sexual encounter he once had at the Chelsea with Janis Joplin.

Germaine's publicists did not quite get it, but, mindful of her market value, they tried. They even sent a basket of fruit up to her room as a welcoming gesture. 'I guess they consider it inappropriate to send flowers to a female revolutionary,' Germaine later commented.[6]

Perhaps it was because she was the daughter of an advertising man that Germaine realised the value of the glamour factor in journalism. As her comments about Mrs Smith at her bottling machine show, she was keenly aware that most women did not want to read some frustrated academic's complicated theories about female oppression; nor did they want to spend their lives tut-tutting over untidy-looking women who wore no make-up and refused to shave their legs or use deodorant. Mrs Smith and her sisters craved excitement, and Germaine Greer was happy to give it to them.

In the May 1971 edition of the high fashion magazine *Vogue*, Germaine appeared as the glamorous face of feminism alongside all the other long-legged, airbrushed models. The main black-and-white picture, which now hangs in London's National Portrait Gallery, depicts her sitting on a beanbag, long legs askew, wearing low-heeled knee-high boots, a skirt and scarf, and a paisley-patterned coat that she made herself (and which is now displayed in the National Museum of Australia). Her natural eyebrows have been plucked to extinction and replaced by carefully pencilled arches, reminiscent of Greta Garbo. Her hair is luxuriant and make-up highlights her eyes. Around her, the walls are covered in necklaces, bags, bracelets and scarves. In this picture she is enigmatically straight-faced, even deadpan, but in other photos of the series she is laughing, her head thrown back.

These fabulous, now-famous *Vogue* photographs were taken by society photographer, and husband of Princess Margaret, Lord Snowdon.

Vogue had also invited Kate Millett to be interviewed but, according to Kathleen Tynan, the author of the article that accompanied the pictures, she declined because such magazines perpetuated a negative image of women as objects of ornament rather than as persons. A small photo of Millett appears alongside Snowdon's photographs of Greer. She is smiling in a friendly way.

Tynan's article opens with a flattering description of Greer's appearance: '. . . just under 6 feet tall, boldly dressed and bra-less with a long pre-Raphaelite face and a voice that can be coaxingly soft or stridently vulgar . . .' Millett, whom Tynan had met previously at a launch party for *Sexual Politics*, is described as 'short, rather plump, with long brown hair, a particularly soft voice and an open smile'. Millett's book is erudite, says Tynan, and she is a hardliner, but it is Greer who makes us laugh.

And so, Germaine Greer, tall, glamorous, beautiful, funny, is positioned as the insouciant face of the new feminism against poor short and dumpy Kate, who takes herself too seriously. Tynan does not neglect to mention Millet's sexual orientation, contrasting it with Greer's cheerful heterosexuality: 'Germaine can't understand why you should mind if you make it with her man.'[7]

The hype continued. 'Saucy Feminist That Even Men Like', announced the famous headline on the cover of *Life* magazine on 7 May 1971. In the cover photograph Germaine Greer is sitting with her feet up on a park bench. She is utterly carefree, laughing, pointing at something behind the camera, multiple rings on her fingers and silver bangles on her wrists. She is wearing a dress of a dark material, flat-heeled shoes and her paisley patterned coat. Her hair looks wild and free, but was probably expensively arranged to look that way; she is professionally made-up. Inside, five more photos show her in a variety of roles – the academic leading a seminar at Warwick University, the suede-skirted free spirit collecting firewood in the English countryside, the activist marching in an anti-Vietnam war protest and, perhaps most tellingly, the laughing hippie, cuddling up to filmmaker Dick Fontaine on a bed in the Chelsea Hotel. 'The feminist who is against sexism but not sex' is the caption to a photo of a pensive Germaine sitting on a paisley couch.

Thus the image was built. Greer's views on unrestricted heterosexual sexuality complemented the glamour factor as she challenged women to replace submissiveness with 'cuntpower'. The American media would feast on this beautiful woman who was telling everybody to go out and enjoy good, feisty sex. 'Why does Hamlet let Ophelia die?' asks a student at the Warwick seminar described in the *Life* article. 'Because she's such a bore! That's why he lets her die,' Greer replies. 'Because she's such an insipid and disloyal little bitch.'

> Miss Greer was everything those messy American feminists were not: pretty, predictable, aggressively heterosexual, media-wise, clever, foreign, and exotic . . . Her philosophy, as outlined in *The Female Eunuch*, could be expected to appeal to men: women's liberation means that women will be sexually liberated; feminism equals free love. Here was a libbie a man could like.[8]

The message was clear. Away with all the Ophelias who were boring their husbands shitless, and in with Petruchio's Kate, who would give them a run for their money! What was not to like about that?

The Greer publicity machine was running hot. On 18 May, soon after the publication of the *Life* cover story, Germaine became the first woman ever to address the National Press Club in Washington. This was a momentous occasion for the Press Club, which had only recently opened its doors to women. The president of the club introduced her as 'an attractive, intelligent, sexually liberated woman' and a lecturer at 'Wor-wick University'. She spoke about the appalling ways newspapers treated women – their trivialisation of issues like childcare, breast cancer and contraception. Remarking on the fact that women were generally represented not as real women but as fantasy creatures who appeared only as adjuncts to the men, she reminded the press of their professional obligation to speak for the whole population, rather than just the male half of it.

At the conclusion of her speech the president presented her with a National Press Club tie. She said it would be useful to keep her hair out of her eyes when she marched in demonstrations. To a question from the floor: 'If there were only three people left on earth, yourself, Teddy Kennedy and Norman Mailer, who would you choose?' she replied that if she had to breed with either it would be better if the earth came to an end immediately. The audience loved her. At the conclusion of the performance – for a performance it was – she stayed on for several hours drinking in the bar with the mostly male journalists.[9]

The address at the National Press Club followed one that became the most talked-about and powerful performance of her American tour. This was her starring role in a 'dialogue' on women's liberation between herself, three other feminists and the archenemy of the women's libbers, Norman Mailer.

Mailer, born into a Jewish family in 1923, was famous as a journalist, novelist, filmmaker and political activist. His novels are intensely physical; his (always male) heroes seek love that is inevitably orgasmic, body-oriented, power-hungry and usually violent. His books are filled with graphic, vicious depictions of sex.

Married six times, Mailer had nine children. In 1960, at a party, he stabbed his second wife, Adele, with a penknife, puncturing her pericardium and nearly killing her. She refused to press charges but he was convicted of assault and given a suspended sentence. Feminists often pointed to this incident as an example of the sexual violence that, they believed, lay at the heart of his work.

Dark, brooding, Byronic – few women could resist him. Germaine, always susceptible to the type, confessed that she 'wanted to fuck' him long before she met him in New York. He was interested in her, too, and the commercial potential of bringing these two powerfully attracted adversaries together was clear to many, including the two protagonists. The event would be:

> a nuptial ceremony celebrating the amorous public encoun-
> ter of the chief representatives of the warring factions: the
> educated goddess from abroad and the general of books and
> machismo at home. The warring parties found each other
> attractive.[10]

It was arranged that the debate would take place in New York University's Town Hall on 30 April 1971, under the banner of the Theatre of Ideas, an organisation that had produced similar evenings of intellectual performance. 'It became a standing joke,' wrote Germaine later, 'that I would seduce Norman Mailer and prove to the breathlessly waiting world that he was . . . the world's worst. In an article for *Listener*, I wrote that I half expected him to blow his head off in "one last killer come" like Ernest Hemingway.'[11]

Kate Millett had refused an invitation to participate in the debate, as had prominent feminists Gloria Steinem, Ti-Grace Atkinson and Robin Morgan. Those who had accepted, along-side Germaine, were Jill Johnston and Diana Trilling, both literary feminists, and Jacqui Ceballos, head of the New York chapter of NOW. The plan was that these would be the women who would bring Mailer's sexual fantasies to life in front of a national audience of notables, who had paid the then large sum of US$25 for the privilege. Like the hero of *The Prisoner of Sex*, he would have:

> that particular part of his ghost phallus which remained in New York – his very reputation in residence – not only . . . ambushed, but . . . chewed half to death by a squadron of enraged Amazons, an honor guard of revolu-tionary (if only we could see them) vaginas.[12]

It emerged later that, in the lead-up to the debate, Mailer was privately organising publication rights for a book with the New American Library, instead of McGraw-Hill, the usual publisher for materials arising from the Theatre of Ideas. He had also supplied D.A. Pennebaker with funding to film the debate. (The full documentary movie that arose from this footage, *Town Bloody Hall*, which was released in 1979, survives to this day as a powerful record of the night's events.)[13]

At the time, the female participants in the debate, including Germaine, knew nothing of Mailer's entrepreneurial activities.

'The Mailer–Women's Liberation title fight,' Germaine later wrote, 'was being set up for maximum exploitation, yet none of the women knew anything about it.'[14]

Greer met Mailer before the debate in a 'snot-green' dressing room at the Town Hall where, she said, he was being photographed like a matinee idol.

'You're better looking than I thought,' he greeted her.

'I know,' she replied coolly.[15]

In her account of this meeting Greer does not mention that her own photographers and publicists were there alongside Mailer's. Nor does she mention that Mailer was holding up for the photographers not his own book *Prisoner of Sex*, but *The Female Eunuch*.

She had been doing her homework on his latest book and, in her notes for the debate, she had written on a card his own remarks about D.H. Lawrence:

. . . yet [he] was locked into the body of a middling male physique, not physically strong, of reasonable good looks, a pleasant to somewhat seedy-looking man, no stud.[16]

Her intention was to use them to attack Mailer at an opportune moment in the debate.

Germaine's attire for the evening was variously reported as 'elegance, furs and jewellery', but the reality was that her choice of a strappy, ten-shilling black dress ('slinky') and cheap fox fur (one pound at a market) was designed to mock the Hollywood fantasies of middle-class American women. The local press did not catch the joke, but as Pennebaker's film shows, Germaine did look elegant in spite of herself, and the sexual tension between her naked-shouldered self and Mailer was palpable.

The audience was as celebrated as the debaters. Betty Friedan was there with an entourage, as were people like Susan Sontag, Stephen Spender and Sargent Shriver. 'Obviously,' said Jill Johnston, 'somebody had spread the word that you didn't count if you didn't make it to this one.'[17]

Johnston herself was planning to misbehave. Widely known as a crazy lesbian feminist with extreme views, she had started the evening drinking with friends and co-conspirators at the Algonquin Hotel. Lurking in the Town Hall lobby before the 'Command Performance', coffee-to-go in one hand, baby bottle of martini in the other, she intended to leap across the orchestra pit 'Fairbanks style', storm the stage and open the proceedings by kissing Germaine. But Shirley Broughton, the organiser of the evening, managed to outwit her, and she found herself embracing Germaine behind the closed curtain.

Johnston was an outsider in women's liberation circles. A year before the debate, Betty Friedan had denounced her lesbianism, declaring her to be 'the biggest enemy of the movement'. Now she was mischievously delighted to defy Friedan and the rest at this gold-plated event.

> So here was a sick, dirty, dangerous lesbian appearing on sacred puritan anglo-Jewish territory and by their own invitation.[18]

Like everyone else, Johnston knew in advance that it was Germaine Greer, that unlikely 'provincial from Australia', who was the drawcard.

> [I]t was the preference of the moderator for a glamorous impudent foreigner from Australia which made this event

very much what it was supposed to be. The prospect herself satisfied everybody's expectations by her advance interest in the moderator. Germaine's obsession with Norman seemed to me in fact foreign and embarrassing. She had already told me she wouldn't mind fucking him.[19]

The women gave their speeches in alphabetical order, with Jacqui Ceballos going first. Germaine, seated at Mailer's right, was second; she was introduced by Mailer as 'that distinguished, young and formidable lady writer, Miss Germaine Greer, from England'.

In a well-modulated Australian/British/American accent, Greer spoke about the aggressive dominance of the masculine artist in Western culture. Her speech was thoroughly researched, well prepared and erudite. Norman Mailer accused her of 'diaper Marxism' but otherwise held his pose of gallant adjudicator. He and Germaine appeared to be exchanging private jokes.

The real fun started when Jill, the third speaker, got up to speak. She was wearing patched jeans and a jacket with a Union Jack patch sewn to the sleeve, the purpose of which seemed to be to show that she was the true Brit, not Germaine, as Mailer had declared. She started with an attack on Greer's provincialism.

'Were you born in Australia?'

Germaine (graciously): 'Yes, I was.'

Jill (aggressively): 'I was born in England. I can't help it. That was just the first thing I thought of.'

She continued with her speech: 'All women are lesbians except those who don't know it yet . . .' The audience listened politely.

She made a couple of jokes. Mailer was not amused. He said her time was up. 'You've written your letter, now mail it, Jill!'

Then, suddenly, two women, dressed like Jill in torn jeans and jackets, crashed onto the stage and started to kiss and fondle each other. Laughing, Jill joined them on the floor and they all writhed about for a bit. The audience roared.

Mailer forgot to behave like an old-world gentleman. 'It's great that you pay $25 to see three dirty overalls on the floor when you can see lots of cock and cunt for $4 just down the street,' he shouted.

The party was getting dirty. 'C'mon, Jill, be a lady,' he begged, but she was determined to continue with her speech. He decided to call a popular vote as to whether she should be allowed to continue. 'If you don't think I've got enough fairness to do the count properly you can come and get this mic away from me,' he shouted at the audience.

A vote was taken and the 'No's won – or so he decided – and Jill left the stage with her giggling companions.

After this, Diana Trilling's speech, delivered in an up-market, supercilious drawl, was anticlimactic. Obviously bored, Germaine tried to upstage her by passing little notes to Mailer. Trilling showed that she did not think much of her as she needled her into a verbal stoush, which a disdainful Germaine clearly won, remarking wearily that it was characteristic of 'oppressed people' that they fought among themselves. She was right. The debate was starting to look like a bitch-fight between the warring feminists on one side and Germaine and Norman on the other. She never got to use her D.H. Lawrence quote on him.

By question time the audience was well warmed up. Mailer tried manfully to assert control but he was outclassed. 'Be accurate, Betty,' he admonished Betty Friedan, who asked the first question. 'Norman, I will define accuracy for myself,' she replied acerbically. Then Susan Sontag quietly took him up on his use of the word 'lady'. He vowed never to say it in public again, then proceeded to do so at least three more times in the next five minutes.

When asked what colour ink he dipped his balls in to write, Mailer delighted the audience when he replied 'yellow', but he reverted to low-class nastiness when he called one female member of the audience 'Cunty', and screamed 'Fuck you!' at another. At times, he appeared to lose his cool completely. 'I'm not going to sit here and let you harridans harangue me.'

Pennebaker's cameras rolled.

Germaine was enjoying herself, throwing back her mane of hair as she laughed and continued to exchange private jokes with Mailer. Apart from one moment of exasperation, when she coined the peculiarly Australian phrase 'Town Bloody Hall', she had, to use Mailer's language, behaved like a 'lady'. (Afterwards she credited her convent education for keeping her to the rules of the debate.) It was not until the final question that she unleashed her talons upon a hapless member of the audience, the writer Anatole Broyard.

'I would like to ask Germaine Greer, as having a peculiar aptitude for this question, to describe, perhaps in the form of a one-act play, what it would be like to be a woman and to have the initiation and consummation of a sexual contact. . . .' he announced sententiously.

It was at that moment, Germaine said later, that she felt Mailer's hackles rise with hers. Simultaneously they sensed the weakness in this foolish creature and smelled his blood. 'Attagirl! Sick him,' Mailer hissed as Greer closed in on her prey.

'Why do you ask that question?' she demanded icily.

The atmosphere in the hall became electric as her capacity to inflict pain was laid bare.

'I tried to make my question un-polemical,' he protested.

'Balls you did!'

The young man floundered. 'I don't know what women are asking for. Now suppose I wanted to give it to them . . .'

Germaine went in for the kill.

'You might as well relax, honey, because whatever they're asking for, it's not for you.'[20]

And so, to the delighted applause of the audience, the debate ended. Mailer invited Germaine for a drink after the program, but she declined. She also declined to have sex with him. *Suck* magazine was prepared to pay her for an account of a bedroom scene, she said, but it never happened. 'I liked Mailer, but not enough. I disliked him too, and that's not enough either.'[21] Part of her was becoming sickened by the media's (and Mailer's) rapacious attempts to exploit her as Norman's love object. It is also possible that she was finally getting over her obsession with men of his type. She had loved several in Melbourne and had suffered at least one breakdown for her pains; she had lived with one for a year or so in Sydney and had married another for three weeks in London. It was time to move on.

Taking a yellow cab back to the Chelsea after the debate, she was attracted by the cab driver, David, a much younger and more malleable type than Mailer. She would form a relationship with him.

My cab was being driven by a corrupt child of my own generation [Mailer was sixteen years her senior] with a white angelic face (marked a little from experiences on the streets and in reform school) who was to become famous on the West Coast as my 'bodyguard'.[22]

In 1979, the famous Anglo-American journalist Christopher Hitchens went to see *Town Bloody Hall* with his friend John Marquand. Writing to Germaine afterwards, he told her he had thought she looked 'exceptionally beautiful'. 'Miss Trilling is a pretentious bore,' he declared, and as for Jill Johnston, 'that daft tart . . . she is revealed as a crypto-bully girl'. But it was Germaine's put-down of Broyard, the 'smug, ignorant twerp of an art dealer', that delighted him most. 'Marquand, who knows him slightly, clapped until his palms were sore. Likewise the rest of us.'[23]

The Mailer debate proved good for business. As the *Female Eunuch* promotional tour continued across America the hype intensified, sales of the book went up and up and the media (and the author) reaped immense profits. Most reviews were lightweight, for the press was more interested in her appearance, sexuality and personal charisma than serious feminist arguments, but it was largely because of the publicity that Greer's more complex ideas started to reach their intended audience – the women of America. She became their first convincing feminist role model. When they sat down to watch television at the end of their days of cooking, cleaning and driving their children to school, they could view this charismatic woman trading jokes and verbal blows with top male talk-show performers like Johnny Carson, David Frost, David Susskind and Dick Cavett. Hers was the new face of feminism – not a drab, angry old man-hater with whom they could never identify, but a young, educated, beautiful woman who was on their side, who gave voice to their deepest misgivings about their lives, and who was pointing the way to what they might become. Wives who watched the shows with their husbands had a whole new armoury with which to argue for their freedom, and the husbands were thrown off guard by this woman's personal attractiveness.

Germaine knew exactly what was going on.

The only reason . . . I ever submit to the commercialization of Germaine Greer is to help women in the home, to raise the self-image of women, to spread the movement on the widest possible base. My aim is to demonstrate that everything could be otherwise, and joyously otherwise.[24]

Among Germaine Greer's many television successes on the US tour was her appearance on the high rating late-night talk program *The Dick Cavett Show* for a 90-minute discussion among panellists who represented different ideological positions about feminist issues. On 14 and 15 June, after one successful performance as a guest, Germaine hosted the show. She chose not to play the role of independent adjudicator of the various opinions, but rather to use the program as a platform for her own ideas. On her first night the topic was birth control and abortion, on the second it was rape.

The availability of the Germaine Greer Archive has opened up dramatic new possibilities for researchers to assess the impact of her television appearances on the lives of ordinary people. The archive includes over four hundred letters written by viewers who watched those two episodes of *The Dick Cavett Show* in June 1971. Of these letters, about 80 per cent are positive.

The minority who criticised her claimed that she had gone beyond her role as moderator to impose her opinions on the panellists. A Mrs Wardell N. Weeden called her 'a pompous ass who has no business sitting in the interviewer's seat'. One woman wished a 'social disease' upon her; others described her as 'disgusting' and 'looking like a worn-out whore'. Most of the negative letters were from women and most criticised her appearance – her 'unkempt' hair, her failure to wear a bra, her 'gaudy' attire.

The majority of viewers who wrote to Greer after watching the show, however, commented on her intelligence, honesty and courage in facing issues that other television performers avoided because they were too controversial or too difficult. One woman, commenting on the abortion discussion, wrote, 'It is a fresh breeze to hear the taboo words of menstruation, ovulation etc. discussed in open conversation. The import to individual women of now being included in polite conversation that goes some-where is immense.'

Rebecca Sheehan, lecturer in US History at the University of Sydney, who researched these letters in depth, recognised that their study opens up new possibilities for understanding how feminist ideas were disseminated, to 'write expanded and more nuanced histories of second-wave feminism and its reception, and to remember that movements do not operate in a vacuum'.

> Through Greer, feminism moved from the theoretical realm to the worlds of everyday people, where it had the potential to make a real difference . . .
>
> In the force of their comments and the very fact that these letters were written . . . these viewers tell us how extra-ordinary it was to see a woman such as Germaine Greer on television in 1971.[25]

Sheehan also remarked on the 'tensions' between Greer and prominent American feminists at this time. Germaine, who since her convent days had refused to conform to any orthodoxy, was never about to become a paid-up member of the sisterhood. Many feminist critics were galled at her book's success. They were enraged when male critics like Christopher Lehmann-Haupt of the *New York Times* compared it favourably with Millett's ('it is everything that Millett's book is not') and furious that, in contrast to Millett's castigation of men for their brutality against women, Greer, as she annoyingly admitted, appeared to like them.

Inevitably, Germaine's media masters often arranged for her to speak on the same platforms as other prominent feminists. Her own accounts of two of these encounters are revealing. In one, which appeared in *The Guardian* on 8 February 2006, after the death of Betty Friedan, she recalled how, in 1972, she, Betty and Helvi Sipilä of the United Nations had been guests of the Women's Organization of Iran.[26]

She began her account by dissociating herself from Friedan's central beliefs about the causes of women's subjugation.

> According to Betty, what happened was that women's sexuality was emphasised at the expense of all their other talents and attributes. What Betty saw as sexuality, I saw as the denial and repression of female sexuality. The Female Eunuch was conceived in reaction to The Feminine Mystique.[27]

Then she went on to tell of how the Shah of Iran, who was still in power at that time, had placed some of his courtiers at the women's disposal. According to her, these men found Betty's imperiousness utterly disconcerting and they struggled to meet her unreasonable demands. It was the same with the elegantly dressed aristocratic ladies with bleached hair who were the feminists' escorts. Again and again, said Greer, these ladies begged her to explain Betty's behaviour. 'Please, Mrs Greer, she behaves so strangely, we think she may be drinking. She shouts at us, and when we try to explain she walks away. Sometimes her speech is strange.'[28]

Germaine was irritated by the way Betty insisted on taking over her, Germaine's, allotted speaking time, and by her complaints about younger feminists (like her) who talked dirty. As they travelled around in an air-conditioned Cadillac, Betty, refusing to speak to the other women, would rest her head against the leather seats and close her eyes. Eventually, tired of her companion's antics and of pretending to admire contrived examples of the Shah's achievements, Germaine organised a side-trip for herself to Shiraz University. The night before the trip, Betty swept into her room, 'fetchingly clad for bed in a cascade of frills and flounces'. 'Whuttzes extra trip they've laid on for tomorrow?' she demanded to know. 'I've told them to cancel it! I've done enough!' By that time Germaine had come to know Betty well enough to refrain from telling her that the trip had not been arranged to include her. Diplomatically, she allowed her to believe the visit had been cancelled and she went alone, as planned.

At the end of the tour, after the farewell party, Friedan was furious when she discovered that the male dignitaries and ministers all had their own cars to take them back to their hotels, while she was expected to share a Cadillac with Germaine and Helvi. Already seated in the car, the two women looked on while Betty, refusing to get in, stood in front of the Cadillac in her spangled crepe de Chine, yelling, 'I will nutt be quiet and geddina car. Absolutely nutt!' Eventually, another car was sent for her.

In her closing remarks, perhaps realising that her comments were in the nature of an obituary, Greer made a belated attempt to set the record straight.

Betty was disconcerted by lesbianism, leery of abortion and ultimately concerned for the men whose ancient privileges she feared were being eroded. Betty was actually very feminine, very keen on pretty clothes and very responsive to male attention, of which she got rather more than you might think. The world will be a tamer place without her.[29]

Jill Johnston wrote another account of Germaine Greer's touring experiences with an American feminist – in this case herself. This article appeared in the *Village Voice* on 22 April 1971, just eight days before the Town Hall debate. Johnston had been scheduled to appear with Greer in a 'TV thing' called *The Arnold Zenker Show* in Baltimore. She described how she met Germaine at the station and they took a taxi to the Sheraton hotel, where Jill asked Germaine if she wanted to share a nightcap. Initially, Germaine refused, but then she changed her mind and the two women settled in at the bar for a discussion about their sex lives. Germaine ordered a large beer. She confided to Jill that she always wore skirts to cover her 'big ass' (interesting in view of her comments, made half a century later, about Australian Prime Minister Julia Gillard: 'You've got a big arse, Julia, just get on with it!')

Jill asked her how long it had been since she had been in love.

'Not for ten or fifteen years,' she replied. (Roelof?) But she was in love with Jamaica.

Then, according to Jill, 'she tells me how a black lesbian she knows sometimes gets it off on her'. Germaine followed this up with an account of how she once 'fixed up' a young couple who were unable to please each other sexually. The female 'fell for' Germaine, who was able to teach her what she needed to know to satisfy her boyfriend. Germaine then did the same for the bloke. He too fell in love with her, but eventually they got it all sorted out and the two young lovers lived happily ever after.[30]

Jill claimed that, later in the night, on her way to bed, Germaine rapped on her door twice. Jill decided not to accept the implied invitation.

The next morning, 7.30, at breakfast, Jill found herself admiring Germaine's breasts in her knit wool top. She wondered why she plucked her eyebrows.[31]

Germaine's friendship with Lillian Roxon endured during her promotional tour of the United States – but only just, as the tensions in the relationship grew. Lillian was still living in the flat which Germaine had declared to be full of cockroaches. Her book, *Lillian Roxon's Rock Encyclopedia*, published late in 1969, was widely acclaimed as an authority on popular music culture. She continued to be a valued friend of many of the cream of rock culture in New York and a regular at Max's Kansas City, but her health was deteriorating badly. Working full-time as a journalist as well as writing and promoting her *Encyclopedia* had taken a huge toll, and her asthma was becoming life-threatening.

Germaine made the most of her limited time in New York during the tour in 1971 and on subsequent visits, choosing to stay at the Chelsea, live as rambunctiously as the publicity machine and tight schedules would allow, and immerse herself in the culture at Max's. Lillian was still smarting from Germaine's remarks about her in the Earth Rose column of *Suck* magazine, where her supposed friend had identified her by name and suggested that anyone who wanted group sex in New York and who liked 'fat girls' should contact her. Nor could she ever forgive Germaine for her remarks in the dedication to *The Female Eunuch*.

'Germaine Greer and her double-edged dedication changed my life and is she ever proud of herself!' she wrote to the editor of the Australian publication *Nation* on 15 May 1971. And to Germaine: '. . . it was both flattering and devastating to be in the dedication. I realised how devastating when someone said to me: "That chick must sure hate you." I'll have to learn to live with it.'[32]

But Lillian had no doubts as to the quality of *The Female Eunuch*. She was 'knocked out by it'.

> I think it is an extremely important book though I'm willing to bet that you, characteristically, don't know what the important parts are. It's such a virtuoso performance that one is dazzled by that and it takes a while to pick up on what the book is really saying . . . Better than Millet's book, it affected me more than *The Second Sex* [by Simone de Beauvoir] . . . I spent all weekend feeling shaken and overwhelmed.[33]

Germaine tried to brush off the hurt she had caused her friend. When she wrote to Lillian from London to ask her for the favour of mentioning Tony Gourvish and Family to her friends in New York, she offered an apology of sorts: 'Sorry about Earth Rose's indiscretion – I really didn't expect that we'd get any significant distribution in NY . . .' She even suggested that, should Lillian get any calls in response to the *Suck* piece, she should record the dialogue and send it to *Suck* for publication. 'People are very weird,' she wrote.[34]

Lillian's response was generous: 'I finally saw the *Suck* column. Very <u>mean</u>, but funny of course. I came off pretty lightly considering who had the crabs, whippings, etc.'[35]

Yet the bickering continued. Furious when she heard that her friend had been talking and writing about her relationship with Gourvish 'in the bitchiest way', Greer complained to

Louise Ferrier: 'If she's still around you might tell her that I nearly caught a plane to NYC just to punch her in the teeth. I just wish she'd ignore me. PR from Lillian equals poison relations.'[36]

Louise tried to remain neutral. 'She bitches as much about you as you do about her,' she told Germaine. 'Anyway, as I may have said to you before, I think your whole thing with her is quite ridiculous and unproductive. However, I do think Lillian had every right to be genuinely hurt by your column in *Suck* and I think that is underneath it all the bit that did it.'[37]

In the same letter, Ferrier also warned Germaine that there was an 'element in the London Underground that really hates success'. Some people, she said, would dislike Germaine for that reason alone.

Lillian Roxon made her last appearance at Max's early in August 1973, wearing one of her glitziest gowns and a feather stole. She was clearly very ill, overweight and bloated from the drugs she had been prescribed for her asthma. On 10 August, alone in her flat on a suffocatingly hot New York night, she suffered a fatal asthma attack and was found dead there a couple of days later. She was 41.

In a letter to her friend Nika Hazelton, written shortly after Lillian's death, Germaine confided that she felt 'as if a great nail had been driven through [her] sternum'. She could hope only that she would 'get used to it, like I did to all the other nails'. She was full of regret that she and Lillian had never managed to resolve their differences, but, strangely, she was still painting herself as Lillian's victim. 'I hope it means that in future, instead of creeping off to lick my wounds, I follow through my grievances while there is still time.'[38]

Another letter addressed to 'Dearest Lonni' on 30 September (no year) stated:

I did not hate her, although I am utterly convinced she hated me and did me all the harm that lay in her power. The press-cuttings that ill-wishers always used to send hit me in the face like spittle, and I'd fret my gizzards to rags trying to work out whether she was telling the truth or not. She was obviously proud of the dedication to *The Female Eunuch* because she made damn sure that everybody knew about it and even based her whole lying story of being an intimate of mine (which she never was) upon that evidence, but all she ever said to me about it was that I had forced her to have the flat fumigated, as if John D. Rockefeller himself hasn't got cockroaches. I think I always imagined that one day it would come right, especially if I became un-famous again and Lillian could matronise me more successfully. She could not have hurt me as much as she did if I hadn't loved her.[39]

Derryn Hinch, the Fairfax media group's New York manager in the early 1970s, was Lillian's 28-year-old Australian friend and boss at the time of her death. He was one of the last people to see her alive, when he called at her apartment on the night before she died to pick up tickets for a Helen Reddy concert. The heat that night was unbearable but she did not let him in because, she said, her flat was too stuffy and messy. She had no air conditioning. They stood at the door, talking, for fifteen minutes. It was he who later identified her body in the Manhattan morgue.

At the Melbourne International Film Festival in 2010, at a question-and-answer session after the premiere of the documentary *Mother of Rock: The life and times of Lillian Roxon*, based on the book of the same name by Robert Milliken, Germaine Greer clashed furiously with Hinch. Of all the 'fuckwits' in

Fairfax's New York bureau in the early 1970s, she railed, Hinch was the 'biggest fuckwit of them all'. He was responsible for the punishing deadlines that had tormented Lillian, and he had paid her so poorly that she was forced to eat the 'crap' that added to her weight problem.

It had not taken her forty years to reach this conclusion. At the time, she deeply regretted that she could not be present at Lillian's funeral, and, even more, she hated to think that Hinch and his Fairfax colleagues had made all the big decisions about the disposal of Lillian's body and her effects. She was glad to hear that Lillian's good friends Danny Fields and Bob Hughes had been there at the funeral, she told Nika Hazelton, for she hated to think 'of the whole jamboree concocted of the greasy, crumpled sneaking spies that she used to smuggle into my room at the Chelsea'. The letter continued:

> Reading between the lines of Derryn Hinch's account, I have that horrid, usual feeling that in death, Lillian fell into the wrong hands. The idea of three hundred journalists meeting among flowers to pay tribute is to me at least quite horrifying. The SMH worked her quite literally to death never letting her do any serious reporting, never offering her any promotion. Admittedly she was a hack, a gutter gossiper without any respect for facts, but that is what the Australian Press made . . . For Hinch to be smug and appreciative of her over her poor dead bloated body really churns my entrails.[40]

But Hinch had some facts on his side. On the night he called at Lillian's apartment to pick up the Reddy tickets, he had been appalled at the conditions she was living in. 'She looked hot and flushed because it was a mid-summer night. I said "Lillian, you've got to get yourself bloody air conditioning or get yourself a better apartment" and she was like "You don't pay me enough."' But when he was helping to sort out her effects after her death, he discovered that she had more than US$60,000 in her bank accounts – more than enough to afford a better apartment, air conditioning and decent food. Also, Hinch was not acting alone in managing Lillian's final affairs. Most of this task fell to her family, including her brother Jack, who flew to New York from Melbourne as soon as her death was discovered. It was mainly Jack who decided to use Lillian's estate to set up a memorial trust in her name, to help Australian asthma researchers study overseas.

Derryn Hinch was not the only villain in Germaine Greer's perceptions of the events surrounding Lillian Roxon's death. She also lashed out at the US medical establishment for failing to provide effective treatment. Not untypically, these attacks appear to have been driven as much by her personal spleen, unresolved issues in her relationship with her friend and the need to apportion blame as they were by feelings of loss and loyalty. Hinch certainly thought so: 'she's such a bitter old person,' he said in 2010. 'In her dotage, Greer has become the female Malcolm Muggeridge.'[41]

Before her death, Lillian provided a much more generous assessment of Germaine than Hinch's. To David Harcourt, on 14 May 1972, she wrote, 'She is by the way . . . not a "rival" since no one can hold a candle to her particular brand of pizzazz but she is someone I have quarrelled with often enough to truly love. She's braver, crueller and bawdier than I'll ever be, also more generous and patient.'[42]

●

By the time Germaine Greer left the United States at the end of her tour, *The Female Eunuch* had reached the top of the American bestseller lists. Sales were booming in Australia, too, but her countrymen and women did not quite know what to make of her. To many, she was one of the harbingers of an exciting, uncertain future at a crucial period when, as political journalist Graham Freudenberg noted, the country was experiencing 'a brilliant balance between hope for better things and satisfaction with the present; between expectation and experience; between a desire for change and enjoyment of the present'.[43]

Like their American counterparts, the Australian media had begun to exploit 'women's lib' in newspaper articles and on television and radio talk shows. Australian women marched, held meetings, attended conferences and published their ideas. Housewives became involved in local consciousness-raising groups, and many were thinking about going back to school or university and moving into paid jobs. In traditional female occupations like teaching and nursing, groups of women got together to assert their rights. Noticing, finally, that men were being promoted faster and dumping the women with all the mundane jobs, they took action. The subtle innuendos and insults that in today's terms would be called sexual harassment in the workplace would continue for many years yet, but in the meantime, exploits like charging into the men's washroom to remove pin-ups of naked women were not only fun, they were symbolic of major cultural change.

When she returned to Australia in December 1971 to promote the paperback edition of *The Female Eunuch*, Germaine Greer had become a colourful celebrity who was of huge interest to the international media. After having virtually divorced herself from her parents, she was now a very different person from the rebellious teenager who had escaped from her mother's house in Mentone all those years ago. Coming back to Melbourne – Melbourne the provincial, Melbourne the supremely suburban, Melbourne the unavoidably dull – must have been difficult for her: she was still deeply conflicted and not yet ready to confront the demons of memory that seemed to wait for her around every corner of her home city.

She was awkwardly and briefly reunited with some members of her family, including her sister Jane and brother Barry, but she did not get to see her mother because Peggy had fled overseas, ostensibly to avoid all the media hype but mainly to avoid the daughter of whom she claimed to be afraid, as her daughter claimed to be afraid of her. Nor did she see her father.

There were compensations: at her friend Winsome McCaughey's house, in the inner-city suburb of Parkville, Germaine and her old friend Ann Polis met up with a group of like-minded female friends. She was comfortable with them, but there were others who had discovered her celebrity status and sought to capitalise on it. She had to fend off not only a curious media but invitations from socially ambitious hostesses who would once have scorned her but were now threatening to lionise her.

On 12 January 1972 she was photographed at Melbourne airport on her way to board a plane to Sydney, where the promotional hype was about to start. Fashionably but casually dressed in a light midi-skirt and candy-striped top, handbag slung across one shoulder, the soon-to-turn-33 celebrity feminist and author refused to talk to the hungry press. 'I am still on holidays. I have nothing to say until I am working,' she announced regally.[44]

As in America, Australian journalists and their readers were more interested in Germaine Greer's personality and private life than they were in her ideas and opinions. 'She's brilliant, she's witty, she's outrageous. She talks like a cross between an English don and a sailor,' reported an *Australian Women's Weekly* journalist who interviewed Germaine in her luxury hotel room overlooking a sparkling Sydney Harbour in February 1972.

The 'green-eyed, chestnut-haired' Greer seems to have treated the *Weekly*'s female reporter to a classic performance, as she gave a highly personal account of her unhappy relationship with her mother, her parents' unfortunate marriage, her first kiss from the rough labourer who squeezed her 'poor little budding breast', her embarrassment at being tall, and so on. Only when she was asked about her marriage did she threaten to 'clam up'. '[A]nything I say about my husband sounds libellous.'

The article was light on factual detail, but it did describe how Greer had recently won the hearts of male journalists at a 'packed' press conference in Sydney when she had told them, with a grin, that women's lib could be very sexy.[45]

In March 1972, no longer feeling quite so up close and personal, Germaine Greer complained on television that the Australian media were treating her like a superstar. 'They're much more interested in, you know, my going to bed with someone or my having VD or my getting a divorce than they are in the actual issues which I've come here to promote,' she protested.

This was all too true, but hardly surprising in a land that was still half asleep in the sunshine. In the same television program, a reporter asked some randomly selected women in the street about their views of women's liberation.

Reporter: Do you think you need liberating?
Woman 1 (vaguely): Oh, from certain things. Not like they're preaching though.

Reporter: What sort of things?

Woman 1 (chuckles, looks away): I don't know what to say. I don't know much about this.

Woman 2: No, I don't either.

Woman 3: I don't – I think women should be feminine.

Woman 4 (agreeing and nodding her head): No.

Woman 5: What's it about?

Woman 6: No.

Woman 7 (laughing): I'd rather be under the thumb.

Woman 8: No, I'm perfectly satisfied as we are.

Woman 9: No, I think it's a man's place to be head and that's all there is about it.

Woman 10: I think it's a lot of nonsense really.

Woman 11: I'm old-fashioned and he's old-fashioned but we just believe in the same things, like I believe a woman's place is in the home.[46]

Later, the program showed a group of senior girls from Sydney Church of England Girls Grammar School (SCEGGS), who expressed more informed opinions than the women on the street. They had all studied *The Female Eunuch*, a copy of which was in the school library. To the reporter's question, 'Does Germaine Greer's book *The Female Eunuch* offer *you* a way of life that would appeal to *you*?' they replied in the affirmative, although comments like the following suggested a growing divide based on gender and generation.

My father has voiced many opinions that he didn't think it was a good thing and that it made many women dissatisfied with the life they had without, sort of . . . and when they couldn't really improve it or that they themselves would be frustrated in their efforts. And so they were just going to be making them unhappy, a lot of women who were previously happy.[47]

The Australian reviews of *The Female Eunuch* were more sensationalist than serious. Thelma Forshaw's review in Melbourne's *The Age* was not only trivial but offensive. A freelance reviewer, who was a generation older than Greer, Forshaw called her piece 'Feminist yen for a grizzle and a bit of rough'. 'King Kong is back,' she began, before going on to argue that Greer was attempting to return women to their primitive state of caveman days, when they needed to be 'restrained' by superior males. The castration Greer had drawn everyone's attention to, she claimed, amounted to no more than this ancient civilising influence of male over female.[48]

Five days after the publication of Forshaw's article, *The Age* devoted its entire Correspondence section to readers' responses. Most were critical of Forshaw's views and annoyed that a quality newspaper like *The Age* would publish such a 'scurrilous personal attack'.

But Elsie Fry of Macleod agreed with Forshaw.

After reading the review I am convinced that the book is the product of a perverted mind and I feel it is such a pity for *The Age* to lower its high standards by publishing such unhealthy ideas.[49]

Sydney continued to be the hub of Germaine Greer's publicity whirlwind of television appearances, press conferences and countless interviews. When she gave a lecture to a packed audience at her old stamping ground, the Wallace Theatre at the University of Sydney, her performance was more polished but no less riveting than that of the young Miss Greer, promising academic, who, not so very long ago, had lectured regularly in that renowned space.

The harbour city was also the scene of Germaine's political activities in Australia. Sensing her country's changing mood, as the Labor Party marshalled its resources to bring twenty-three years of conservative government to an end, she volunteered her support, marched in anti-war and women's liberation demonstrations, and gave evidence at the obscenity trials of two journalist mates, Wendy Bacon and John Cox. Yet, perhaps unfairly, her old friend Beatrice Faust described the Greer of this time as a 'political bonehead'. 'I should not have thought,' she wrote in *Australian Humanist* in March 1972, 'that she had a political bone in her body. I suspect that she may have, and that this is between her ears.'[50]

As if all this was not enough, her social life was frenetic. She was living in the then-raffish neighbourhood of Paddington with Phillip Frazer, the young founder and editor of Australia's first rock music paper and several counterculture magazines. They shared the house out of mutual convenience rather than mutual attraction, for she was involved in a wild affair with Mike Willesee, a charismatic Australian journalist and television personality whose high-profile marriage to a former Miss Australia was in the process of breaking up, and Phillip had multiple entanglements of his own to juggle. He recalls that time with great fondness.

> We would talk a lot. She was reflective, intelligent, well-read, and original: she always thought outside the box. She also made no apologies for being her. And even though she was of that generation born just before 1946, who came of age

before the 1960s' twin technological life-changers – the Pill and electronic music – she celebrated them for their transformative power. Still, I occasionally sensed her 1950s convent-girl self at work, affecting what made her twitch and holding on to a fundamental belief in the definability of right and wrong.[51]

At every opportunity, Germaine partied strenuously with loyal old Push friends like Margaret Fink, and newer acquaintances like Frazer, who were at the apex of the Sydney Left and rock-music scenes. ('Raced off Robert Plant the other night,' she confided casually in a letter to a friend in London.[52])

Her love for Willesee, however, was serious, reciprocated, and complicated in part by his wife's undisguised fury and determination to confront her. She realised that the affair would have to end but she thought she was probably in too deep for that to happen – yet.

I think I'm travelling around the bend, having fallen in love with a marvellous madman who has Australia conned into thinking that he's a solid current affairs commentator, of which more when I see you. All I shall say at this stage is that I'm fighting it. Not sure that I'm winning though.[53]

This affair continued for some years as Germaine's visits to Australia became more frequent. She was even named as the co-respondent in Willesee's divorce case, but over time the relationship cooled as the busy demands of their work and travel kept them apart, and they both enjoyed multiple sex partners. As with many of Germaine's former lovers, Mike Willesee remained a good friend long after they had both moved on to new challenges and new lovers.

Germaine had been commissioned to write a column for *The Australian* newspaper while she was in Australia, but for various reasons she was sacked after she had written only one piece. Her old friend Richard Walsh, from the Push and Australian *Oz* days, who had become the founding editor of *Nation Review*, was delighted when she agreed to write a weekly column for his paper instead.

> She would arrive at around 5.30, bash away at the typewriter and be finished by 7. She was very fluent. She wouldn't stay around afterwards and have a drink with the boys. Everyone else was kind of nervous. She would treat the junior staff in a fairly imperious way. By that time, she was a celebrity and she acted like one.[54]

Early in March 1972, Germaine Greer left Australia briefly to stir up a storm in the gentle country of New Zealand. Her publicity team had arranged an exacting schedule that included a television photo shoot on the beach at Islington Bay with prominent New Zealand feminist activist Sue Kedgley.[55] According to a report in the *Canberra Times*, Germaine was dressed for the stunt in knickers she claimed to have bought at Coles in Sydney for 30 cents, and a similarly cheap boys' singlet. No bra, of course. Sue was wearing pink knickers, in which the elastic appeared to have failed, and a black nylon see-through bra.

This episode was only the start of the excitement. Everywhere Germaine went, the citizens of this peaceful land, where not a lot was going on, flocked to hear her speak. 'For the first time in New Zealand,' said one commentator, 'a radical women's liberationist was given the sort of media coverage normally accorded to royalty. Suddenly the dangerously subversive ideas of Women's

Liberation were being discussed on prime-time television and on the front pages of daily newspapers.'[56]

The incident that led to the greatest publicity coup of all happened at a packed meeting at the Auckland Town Hall. It was a twist of fate that Germaine dressed for the occasion in her *Oz* obscenity trial T-shirt and (as usual) no bra. Contrived though the episode may have been, however, even she probably did not realise that she was about to face her very own obscenity trial.

The background to the incident was that left-wing politician Mr Tim Shadbolt, who would later become the Mayor of Invercargill, had recently been arrested for saying 'bullshit' over a loudspeaker. It was reported that, as she was speaking at the meeting, someone passed Greer a note informing her that Shadbolt was in jail. Delighted at this opportunity to use one of her favourite attention-getting tactics, she inserted a couple of 'bullshits' of her own into her speech and added some 'fucks' for good measure. 'Now they'll have to arrest me too,' she said happily. Which they did.

The Auckland Magistrate's Court was so crowded for Germaine Greer's 'trial' that Sue Kedgley had to climb through a fire escape at the back of the building to get into it. Outside the court, six hundred people chanted, swore, and threw rotten eggs and jelly beans at police. Twenty-nine people were arrested. Auckland had never seen anything like it!

Inside the courthouse, Greer sacked her lawyer and conducted her own defence in front of Mr D.G. Sinclair, Stipendiary Magistrate. The proceedings soon became Gilbertian as the first witness, a married woman with grown-up children, rose to give her evidence. She had heard Greer use the word 'bullshit', she said, and had complained to the police.

Woman: She used it at least three times. I don't know what it means for sure.

Greer: Are you saying that you don't know what the two separate words mean – bull and shit?

Woman: No.

Greer: Didn't you know it was excrement?

Woman: I didn't know if it was excrement or semen.

Greer: Do you think 'rubbish' is an adequate word to use instead?

Woman: No – not so emphatic.[57]

Greer was acquitted on 'bullshit' but convicted for 'fuck'. The magistrate imposed a jail sentence, but since she did not have time to go to jail in New Zealand, she offered to pay the NZ$40 fine instead. (Which, incidentally, she did not do, even when plaintive demands followed her back to the United Kingdom.)

She left Sydney on 22 March 1972 to fly back to England via India and Bangladesh, where, she told reporters, she intended to investigate the rape of Bengali women during the war with Pakistan. She joked that she was leaving Australia for her health: 'One more day of Australian newspapers and I'll have a plastic bag instead of a colon.' Shamelessly, considering how she had used the press to generate publicity, she criticised the media for 'interposing' themselves between herself and the public.[58]

On a personal level, Germaine's return to Australia after such a long absence was difficult. She was not yet ready to confront the demons of her youth and childhood. That would come later. For now, she would seek peace and acceptance in other lands.

I think I've outlived my usefulness here anyway . . . So I'll go back to England where they accept me as just another person . . . I'll go back there for a while and see how the indigenous movement here develops, see if Australians begin to listen to their own women as a result of my having been here. If they don't lend ear to what's being said, then [her voice becoming anguished], Australia, goddamn![59]

6

Wind of Tizoula

O Wind of Tizoula! O wind of Amsoud!
Blow over the plains and over the sea,
Carry, oh, carry my thoughts
To him who is so far, so far,
And who has left me without a little child.
O wind! Remind him I have no child.

Anonymous[1]

Germaine Greer's transition to international celebrity was not achieved without pain. She lost some old friends along the way, but made new ones among some of the richest and most powerful people in the world. In her archive are to be found many gold-lettered invitations to star-studded events, dinners and parties, from members of the British aristocracy, famous writers, actors, artists and musicians, diplomats, prominent politicians and captains of industry. In the United States, as a long-time civil rights activist and supporter of the Left, she gravitated towards the Democratic side of politics, which, at that time, meant the Kennedys. Her publicists, anxious to maximise the connection, organised for her to meet Kennedy family members, including Sargent Shriver, husband of Eunice Kennedy. She and Shriver became good friends; he entertained her at expensive New York society restaurants and on at least one occasion was her 'date' at Max's Kansas City. When *Harper's Magazine* commissioned her to cover the Democratic National Convention that gave George McGovern the presidential nomination in 1972, Germaine publicly and privately supported the Kennedys, helping Shriver to gain the vice-presidential nomination.

Like many Australians, Germaine Greer was no monarchist. In 1954, she and her sister Jane had been taken to see the young Queen Elizabeth and her handsome husband Phillip on their first official visit to Australia. The two girls were lifted onto a trestle in the midst of a flag-waving crowd. Germaine had her little flag too, but as the Daimler drove past their spot, something about the way the gracious Queen was smiling and waving – maybe it was the monarchical condescension – got under her skin: she became an instant republican, a position she has held ever since. As soon as she got home she tore up her collection of Royal pictures. 'That was the end of my love affair with Lilibet,' she was later to write.[2]

Nearly twenty years later, in England, she made the acquaintance of Lord Snowdon, husband of Princess Margaret, when he photographed her for *Vogue* magazine. That was her first but by no means her last encounter with British royalty. In an article published in *The Telegraph* in 2002, she recalled a meeting with Princess Margaret at Porto Cervo in Sardinia, more than thirty years earlier.

Porto Cervo, on the stunningly beautiful Costa Smeralda, is a luxury resort made famous by the Aga Khan IV in the 1960s as a village retreat for the cream of international society and a berthing place for their super-luxury yachts. In the summer of 1971, Germaine travelled there on her green moped and by ferry in response to a telegraphed invitation from theatre critic and close friend Kenneth Tynan. In her saddlebag she was carrying a draft of an adaptation of Aristophanes' *Lysistrata* that she had prepared at his request. Tynan, who was hoping to produce the show in London starring Laurence Olivier the following January, was impatient to see her and her script, and she herself was hot with excitement about the venture.

In the end, the project came to nothing; that version of *Lysistrata* was never performed and Germaine's visit to Porto Cervo ended, literally, in tears, after she fought with Tynan and took off precipitately early one morning on her moped, without farewells. The only thing that made the visit memorable, apart from her bizarre mode of transport, was her dinner with royalty.

Greer and Tynan were the guests of Michael White, British theatre impresario and film producer, whose credits included *Monty Python and the Holy Grail* and *The Rocky Horror Picture Show*. White's connections were impressive and no one was surprised when an invitation arrived from Princess Margaret and her husband for White and his house party to join them for drinks at their holiday flat nearby. Stuffed in her saddlebag, apart from the *Lysistrata* script, Germaine had carried only a toothbrush, a red bikini, and a cotton jersey dress which, she thought, though crushed, showed off her brown bosom and shoulders rather well. Clad in this dress and otherwise unadorned, hair awry, she prepared to make the acquaintance of HRH. She knew she should curtsey, so she practised before she left, but when they arrived at the flat, which she thought modest ('neither a chandelier nor a footman in sight'), Margaret saw her first and startled her by barking 'Good evening,' so she did not have time to twist her knees into the required position. She knew that one should not sit while a member of the royal family is standing, and had read in some women's magazine that the princess was a stickler for protocol, so she was careful to remain standing in her presence. This created another problem. She was so tall. The princess was so tiny. She felt herself to be looming. 'For God's sake sit down,' commanded Margaret. Drinks were served.

Then Margaret announced that they were all invited to 'K's' for dinner. K was Karim Aga Khan, descendant of the prophet Mohammed and one of the ten richest royals in the world. Born in 1936, the same year as Ken Tynan and three years before Germaine, he was then 35 years old.

To reach the Snowdons' holiday flat the party had travelled by motorboat. By the time they arrived at their destination, Germaine's hair, unruly enough to begin with, had been whipped totally out of control by the wind. She carried no handbag, brush or comb. 'Go into my room,' said Margaret. 'You'll find every-thing you need on the dressing-table.' And sure enough, on the glass-topped table she discovered exotic perfumes of every kind, powder boxes and silver-backed ivory brushes and combs. Over-whelmed, she sat staring, frozen, in front of the mirror. Then Princess Margaret came up behind her, took the largest brush, and started to brush her guest's lustrous hair in long strokes.

> She worked unhurriedly, as a little girl might brush her mother's hair, attentively, silently, careful not to tug at the tangles or catch my ears with bristles, keeping the static controlled with her free hand, oblivious that I was watching her in the mirror. After a good five minutes, she laid down the brush, said, 'You'll do,' and went out to join the others.[3]

Over dinner at the Aga Khan's house, Germaine sat next to Tony, Lord Snowdon, who entertained her with unkind comments about the royal family. When the pudding arrived, a confection of white spun sugar, she joked that it looked like one of the Queen Mother's hats. Tony laughed so uproariously that Margaret, seated at the other table, asked what the joke was. Germaine felt sorry for the princess, noticing how Snowdon would evade her touch and avoid her glances.

In the years that followed, Germaine had many opportunities to exchange pleasantries with Princess Margaret (and manage to curtsey). 'Each time,' she commented, 'I was left with a vivid impression of a real person condemned to live her life as a pantomime.'[4]

Germaine had travelled to Porto Cervo from Tuscany, where she was renting 'Il Palazzone', a woodcutter's cottage near the town of Cortona. She had chosen Tuscany as a refuge, first from the glare of publicity that now, after her book's success and her triumphant American tour, pursued her everywhere, and second from the British taxation system, which threatened to come down hard on her newly acquired wealth from the success of *The Female Eunuch*. In the summer of 1971, writing from Il Palazzone, she told lawyers for her old friend Richard Neville that she could not return to England to give evidence in his support at the *Oz* obscenity trials because of the taxation laws that were forcing her to spend significant periods of time out of the country.

From Il Palazzone she corresponded with David Greville, Lord Brooke, soon to become the eighth Earl of Warwick, who was also a friend of the Snowdons. While lecturing at the University of Warwick, she had become a regular visitor to his home, Warwick Castle. There she had formed a lasting friendship with this urbane peer whose father, the seventh earl, was one of the richest men in England. (It was Brooke with whom she had arranged to take tea at his London house in elegant Blenheim Crescent on the afternoon of her first meeting with Paul du Feu.

Du Feu was impressed when she told him she would need to keep that appointment before rejoining him later back at the pub on the Portobello Road.)

In one letter from Il Palazzone, she told Brooke that she was feeling 'paralyzed by homesickness' for England. The *Oz* trials were going badly for her friends back in London, and they were facing jail terms. 'The *Oz* scandal has upset me,' she wrote, 'so that I cannot imagine what I am doing in impotent isolation in a country where the newspapers clatter egregiously about people going to hospital for overdoses of marijuana.' She was surrounded, she continued, by a host of minor Italian nobility, 'every vulgar little speculator selling off his patrimony before [new laws on land ownership] are passed'. Unlike David, who had a strong sense of service to his country, she wrote, these '*nobilacci*' were selfish, greedy parasites.

Brooke, tongue firmly in cheek, replied, 'Naturally, I support the Italian nobility.'

On 29 August 1971, she wrote to tell David Brooke about her visit to Porto Cervo and her dinner with royalty at the Aga Khan's house. She had thought that Snowdon was 'pretty much at the end of his tether . . . he behaved distinctly worse than I did, although I wasn't trying, and I think he was'. It seemed to her that Snowdon was deliberately provoking 'HRH' so that she would send him off for good, but 'the Princess seems just as resolute that this shall not happen'.[5]

The Germaine Greer of 1971 was, as her friend Richard Walsh would later describe her, a 'lusty' woman who never went too long without a man in her bed. Il Palazzone was the scene of several love affairs, including one with a New York taxidriver called David (presumably the same David who had been called her 'bodyguard' in America). She confided to her friend, the academic and poet Clive Bush, that she had been 'enduring' an off-and-on relationship with this young man. He was physically beautiful but otherwise 'thoroughly unpleasant'.[6]

Il Palazzone was also the venue for what was possibly her most famous interview for a publication – Hugh Hefner's *Playboy*, the magazine that aimed to turn soft porn into an art form. Inside *Playboy*'s glossy covers were pages and pages of extraordinarily lovely women displaying their naked breasts and buttocks in strategically lit poses. This was hardly the stuff of feminism, but *Playboy* also provided serious intellectual content, mainly in the form of interviews with writers, poets, politicians, engineers, academics and economists. Its editors believed that an article on Germaine Greer would show the magazine at its best, by paying attention to the important intellectual issue of women's liberation while engaging with its current embodiment who, fortuitously, happened to be a very sexy and beautiful woman.

On 8 July 1971, *Playboy* editor Nat Lehrman contacted Greer's agent, Diana Crawfurd, in London, about the possibility of him doing an article on her. 'I'd like to state our motivation as clearly as I can,' he wrote, 'we think Dr Greer is a brilliantly articulate spokeswoman for an important point of view, as well as a delightfully witty and intelligent person in all regards. The fact that she is consummately sexy as well has not influenced our desire for the interview – I think . . .'

He understood, he continued, that Greer was living in a small town near Florence and would probably stay there till October. He would be prepared to travel there and to stay for at least a week, so that he could do the interview 'in small doses, over a week or two'.[7]

With Germaine's agreement, Lehrman flew from the United States to Rome, then drove 140 miles to the hills above Cortona to discover her in her cottage. He had expected her to commend him for his effort, but she was unimpressed. 'I'd planned to sneak out tonight to see a play in Montepulciano,' she greeted him, 'but you *would* show up on time. Just like a *bloody* American.'

Nor did she hold back in her comments about his magazine.

> It's not just the centrefold I disapprove of, it's all the other images of women in *Playboy* . . . all those bleary faces and those haggard men and those pumped-up women in their see-through dresses, with everybody's nipples poking out and those fixed, glittering, maniacal smiles on the girls' faces . . . Or the jokes . . . not to mention the cartoon. They all give the illusion that fifty-year-old men are entitled to fuck fifteen-year-old girls – especially if they are given diamond bracelets – while fifty-year-old women are too repulsive to be seen with – you display your girls as if they were a commodity. Sex ought not to be that.[8]

Australian writer and journalist Keith Dunstan, who remarked that the Germaine Greer of this time was the best-known Australian in the world – comparable only with Dame Nellie Melba – described this *Playboy* interview as 'the ultimate accolade'.[9]

•

Some months after her interview with Lehrman, Germaine, still in love with Tuscany, bought a pretty cottage, 'Pianelli', in the Montanare di Cortona. It was here that she found her greatest peace and happiness. 'I loved that house so much,' she said years later, 'that I have been able to survive the loss of it only by sternly forbidding myself to think about it, let alone write about it.'[10]

It was through her old friend from Warwick, Gay Clifford, that she discovered Pianelli. The two young women had remained firm friends and enjoyed many riotous times together in England and Italy, but their friendship was complicated by a mutually ungovernable urge to compete against each other for personal and professional success, and for men.

Germaine was living at Il Palazzone when she first visited Pianelli as a guest of Gay, who was spending the summer of 1971 there with her lover, Michael. 'She pays through the nose for an exquisite hideaway at a wild desolate and utterly lovely place known as "Pianelli",' Germaine wrote to Clive Bush, 'where she whiles away the days with a student lover . . . bathing naked in the sun.'[11]

At Gay's invitation, Germaine laboured up the hill on her moped to that 'exquisite' little house and immediately fell in love with it. She had to have it!

Gay would have loved to buy Pianelli for herself, but it was Germaine, now flush with money and success, who was able to raise the money without blinking. Gay was vexed when she realised that the friend with whom she had been happy to share her beloved Pianelli had become its owner – the piper who stood ready to call all of the tunes in *her* house.

With Germaine, it is sometimes difficult to tell when her natural generosity of spirit is overtaken by a compulsion to control the lives of others in her orbit. She has shared all of her homes with other people, never expecting payment, and she has been especially kind to people in need. There is evidence in her own correspondence and in newspaper articles written by and about her that suggests her relationships often soured and mis-understandings multiplied when she tried to make decisions about her protégés' needs and wants, showing a careless disregard of their own desires and feelings. As a supremely capable and intelligent person herself, she simply could not understand how some of them could be (in her view) so stupid.

Stupidity was never an issue in Germaine's relationship with Gay Clifford, for both women recognised each other's brilliance, but Germaine's purchase of Pianelli is one example of her failure to be aware of the effect her actions might have on others. This marked the beginning of a long period in which arguments over money – Germaine wanting to help her friend and Gay resenting her for it – could not be resolved. Generously, Germaine had assumed that Gay and Michael would continue to stay at Pianelli as often as they wanted, without paying rent, but she failed to consider that Gay, who had lived in and loved the house before her, might not wish Germaine to become her benefactor.

Germaine had looked forward to spending her first night as owner of Pianelli with Gay and Michael but, in the event, they chose to move out and sleep elsewhere. Deeply hurt, surprised and disappointed at being left by herself in her new house, she later suspected that they had taken this action as some kind of (undeserved) revenge or punishment 'so that I could gloat over my new acquisition alone'. Agonising over the reasons for Gay's behaviour, she lamented the subsequent rift in the friendship, which went on for several months. Why could her friend not simply accept her generosity? What difference did it make that she, rather than some absentee landlord, was now the owner of Pianelli? Had Gay, unwarrantedly, believed herself to be the 'true' owner because she had lived there first?

'Gay clearly felt that the little house was no longer her territory and used it much less than I would have wanted,' Germaine wrote wistfully after her friend's death. But she also confessed that she herself had run the house as an 'autocracy'.[12]

Her rift with Gay Clifford was not the only problem that unsettled Germaine in those early days at Pianelli. She had commissioned several labourers to carry out substantial building works, and between their demands and meeting the needs of guests with whom she wanted to share her good fortune, her nerves were strung almost to breaking point. So much so that, as she wrote to her friend and secretary, Franki Roberts, who was looking after her affairs in London:

> I seduced the bull-dozer driver, actually it was done with so much dispatch that he may have thought he raped me, my metabolism being strung to such a pitch that kept me half-swooning with accumulated (and utterly impersonal) desire. Oops. He has eyes as yellow as French headlights and the original up-curving cock that you find on the satyrs in Catherine the Great's boudoir. He is actually an ignorant ego-maniac but I have always found silk purses much more interesting than sow's ears.[13]

Pianelli stood at the end of a very long road that wound uphill through a picturesque valley. It was small, simple and well-proportioned, on eight acres of land with views stretching across the mist to the Apennine Mountains. There were few modern comforts to start with – not even electricity – but Germaine made the house into a home for herself and for the many visitors she liked to entertain there. Some friends came with their families, and shades of her fantasy of shared parenthood in a remote village surfaced as she helped to care for and entertain the children.

Her homemaking skills often surprised visitors. Her house, like her wardrobe, reflected her distinctive sense of style, colour and fabric as well as her proficiency with her needle and sewing machine. She had carefully selected her furniture for quality and charm, and had even arranged for some pieces to be made by local craftsmen from regional materials. She was also a first-class cook who liked to use herbs and other fresh produce from her garden in her recipes.

This classic, white-themed Italian garden of roses, lavender, fruit trees and a large range of temperate plants and shrubs was her great joy. One of her visitors, the Australian artist Jeffrey Smart, described 'a most splendid and scholarly rose garden, as well as a kitchen garden'. His use of the word 'scholarly' was well chosen, as Germaine's knowledge of plants and flowers was encyclopaedic, and she tended her garden with academic thoroughness as well as botanical flair.[14]

To complement her herb garden, she had a small laboratory where she made herbal tinctures and medicines, thus harking back to medieval times when 'wise' women were the chief practitioners of the healing arts, and every convent had its garden of therapeutic plants and herbs tended by nuns. At one stage she even produced medicinal plants on a commercial basis, supplying iris, lavender, camomile, mistletoe and rue for homeopathic industries.[15]

She was dividing her time between London and Pianelli when she first met legendary film director Federico Fellini in August 1975. He was about to start work on *Casanova*, for which he would later win an Academy Award, at the Cinecittà studios in Rome, where all his films were made. One of the casting directors suggested that Germaine should be given an audition for the role of the giantess. On a very hot day, the hottest of the year, according to the account she wrote for *The Guardian* in 2010, she set off along the Autostrada del Sole to have lunch with Fellini and the film crew. By the time she arrived she was looking very sexy

1954 class photo, Star of the Sea. Germaine is sixth from the right in the back row. *Germaine Greer Collection – University of Melbourne Archives*

Germaine speaking to fellow protestors at the first ever women's liberation march in London, in March 1971. More than four thousand women took part in the demonstration. *Shepard Sherbell/Corbis via Getty Images*

Photo of Germaine Greer and Vivian Stanshall of the Bonzo Dog Doo Dah Band, from the same photoshoot as the controversial cover of *Oz* issue 19. *Estate of Keith Morris/Redferns/Getty Images*

Germaine outside the entrance of the Chelsea Hotel in New York City.
Bettmann/Getty Images

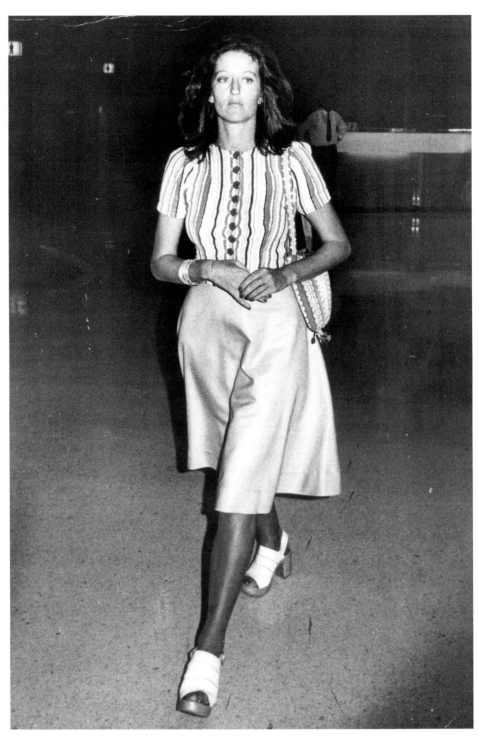

Germaine at Melbourne Airport in January 1972, about to board a flight to Sydney to begin promotion for *The Female Eunuch* in Australia. *The Age/Fairfax Syndication*

Germaine Greer with Christopher the cat at home in London, 1980s.
Homer Sykes/Alamy Stock Photo

Photo of Pianelli. *Germaine Greer Collection – University of Melbourne Archives*

The garden at The Mills, with cat Shanghai Jim walking along the path. *Germaine Greer Collection – University of Melbourne Archives*

Germaine in her garden at The Mills, May 1994. *Mike Forster/Daily Mail/ Shutterstock*

Germaine at an event for the publication of *The Boy* at a bookshop in Piccadilly, London, 2003. *Rune Hellestad/Corbis via Getty Images*

Germaine in the Baillieu Library at Melbourne University, where she began her academic career, after selling her archives to the university in 2013. *Angela Wylie/Fairfax Syndication*

(at least, that is what she implied in her article). She had been sweating so much that her hair was flattened against her head and her flimsy dress clung to her otherwise naked 36-year-old body. Ignoring the fact that she must have been uncomfortable and, probably, smelling, Fellini could not take his eyes off her. 'Fellini kept watching me as I chatted with the crew, moving his head slightly as if he was studying the planes of my face, narrowing his eyes.' No one mentioned the part of the giantess during lunch and she decided she did not want it anyway.

Fellini, then 55, was a notorious philanderer who, according to one biographer, liked to talk about 'the insatiable dragon' he kept in his pants. He gave Germaine a copy of the *Casanova* film script, 'then very much a work in progress', asked her for her opinion and suggested that she might consider taking the part of Madame Châtelet in a scene where Casanova meets Rousseau. After the lunch she took the script home, studied it closely, and then wrote to Fellini suggesting that Madame Châtelet should not be reduced to a huge-breasted nurse for the senile Rousseau. Fellini, obviously drawn as much by his memories of her sweaty body as her helpful comments, decided to visit her.

In her *Guardian* article, she told of how Fellini arrived at Pianelli one day in a large blue Mercedes and, with obvious intent, sent the driver away till the following morning. They talked at length about the film, but Germaine wondered if he was really listening to her as his eyes raked her body and he whistled between his teeth from time to time. Suppertime came and she wanted to cook for him, but, valetudinarian that he was, he insisted on making his own plain risotto with just one leaf of basil. He drank no wine.

There was never any question, said Germaine, of their not sleeping together in her bed. He changed carefully into the brown silk pyjamas with cream piping he had brought in a small overnight bag, and carefully hung up his clothes for the morrow. Not wanting to let truth get in the way of the story, she claimed that he then made a quick call to his wife, actress Giulietta Masina, at home in their apartment in the Via Margutta, and followed it up with more calls to Giulietta every couple of hours. This is a nice touch, but it could not have been true, as there was no telephone, or even electricity, connected at Pianelli at this time.

Germaine chose not to provide details of her first sexual encounter with Fellini. But she gave her *Guardian* readers a fair idea of what went on in the big bed. He was horrified that she slept with all her windows open. When the oil lamps were extinguished, a small bat came in through the open window and circled the room. Fellini, according to Germaine, was terrified. A bat had flown into his hair when he was a child. Did she not know that? She replied that any bat would have a better idea of where his hair was than he did. He began to pant, and she kept two fingers on his pulse, which was beating around 'like a frog in a bucket'. When he apologised for frightening her she assured him she had not been frightened, but was simply wondering what she would tell the press if he 'carked it' in her bed.

As he had planned, Fellini left next day, promising to buy her a generator so that she would no longer have to depend on the bat-attracting oil lamps. He fulfilled his promise and sent his own electricians to install the equipment. 'Now, every time you turn the lights on, you'll think of me,' he said.

From then on, says Greer, the relationship 'was self-limiting, because I wasn't always available'. She continued to spend time with him on the sets of his films at Cinecittà. She teased him about the way he directed the storm scene in *La città delle donne*, 'flying back and forth on a huge dolly, calling for "Thunder! Lightning! Rain! More lightning!" like God Himself'. The two exchanged letters for almost twenty years before Fellini died on 31 October 1993, one day after his fiftieth wedding anniversary.[16]

•

Pianelli was not the only house Germaine bought after the financial success of *The Female Eunuch*. In 1973 she decided to buy a house in London's gentrifying Notting Hill area. The one she chose was at 54 Cambridge Gardens, a relatively quiet street off Ladbroke Grove. It had five storeys, including the basement, and a porch with pillars and six doorbells. Once the grand home of nineteenth-century gentlefolk, it had decayed into a kind of rooming house – a warren of kitchenettes, bathrooms and bedsitters with shilling-in-the-meter heating – just the kind of cheap accommodation expatriate Australians used to seek out in the 1960s. Germaine was now not only the owner of this conglomeration, but a person with the means, taste and connections to turn it into a grand home for herself.

Her first challenge was the squatters and graffitists who had taken over the house. In the British legal system, squatters can only be dealt with through civil procedures, and in the counterculture circles that Germaine still favoured there was considerable empathy with their plight. Most liberal-minded people saw no good reason to disapprove of the homeless who chose to occupy houses left vacant by wealthy people who could afford to own more than one property. Germaine was not surprised that squatters were living in her house when she bought it, but any moral dilemma she may have felt about putting an end to their occupancy did not prevent her from having them evicted. On Tuesday 3 September 1973, Franki Roberts wrote to her employer, who was strategically away from London at Pianelli.

The squatters were evicted from the house at 6 am this morning . . . there were only 3 squatters in residence and they surprised them, as the squatters were prepared for a fight – i.e. pots of paint etc., slogans strung outside the house and such, but from what I gathered from them there was no trouble. Mind you they had 50 police there. There was also an eviction at 48 Cambridge Gardens, a West Indian family squatting there in Notting Hill Housing Trust property and Mr Stocks said he advised the Sheriff to evict them at the same time to distract from activity at your house . . . I was bothered at [Greer's] flat from 10 on by the BBC, radio and press people asking about the squat and at 1 pm this afternoon about a dozen squatters and friends held a demonstration outside the flat in Gloucester Walk, with slogans etc.[17]

Germaine was later to claim that one of her reasons for choosing the house was its 'magnificent' graffiti, one of which, said to have been written by the poet Christopher Logue, spelled out, in foot-high block capitals, 'Boredom is counter-revolutionary'. The truth was hardly less romantic: authorship of the piece was later attributed to a band of anarchists and revolutionaries called 'King Mob'. This group, whose fundamental ideas and principles must have been close to Germaine's, was known for its incendiary graffiti across London, the most celebrated instance being a slogan painted along a half-mile section of the London Tube between Ladbroke Grove and Westbourne Park stations, which read:

Same thing day after day – tube – work – dinner – work – tube – armchair – TV – sleep – tube – work – how much more can you take? – one in ten go mad, one in five cracks up.

In 2007, in an article published on the revolutionary website Revolt Against Plenty, a former member of King Mob recalled that Germaine's house, being in a dimly lit side street off the regular police beat, was easy to spray-paint. For the record, he said, they had also sprayed 'This too will burn'. When they discovered that it was Germaine Greer who had bought the house and evicted the squatters living there, they returned to do 'a bit of further spray-painting after the midnight hour'. People around Notting Hill (by whom he could have meant his fellow squatters and revolutionaries and/or the new left-leaning gentry who were moving in to the area) were feeling indignant about her actions. Before their onslaught on Germaine's house, the group had set fire to Paul McCartney's Mercedes, and the writer of the article (recalling in 2007 his youthful strength and how good it had felt to pick up a huge potted plant and slam it through the car's bonnet) regretted that the police, whom Greer had called to spoil their adventure, had succeeded, largely because he and his friends were 'out of our brains on grass and Portuguese bagacao'. But they did manage to set fire to one of Germaine's skips.[18]

From the moment she first saw 54 Cambridge Gardens, Germaine thought she had realised her dream: high ceilings, shutters, cornices, a house of noble proportions and gentle warmth. The architectural firm she chose to help her with plans for the conversion was renowned for its modernist buildings and sensitive social housing projects: there was some tension between her vision and theirs, but eventually they managed to create a house of style and grace. At considerable expense, they made three gardens – back, front and roof – and transformed the attics into a double-height, open plan workroom-cum-library. The many small bedrooms were reduced to three, there was a conservatory on the first-floor landing, and the pitch-pine kitchen and reception area on the ground floor became the main living room in which Germaine, as the self-described 'hostess', could entertain friends while she cooked.

It was a big house for one woman and she was determined to share it, but the sharing was not without its difficulties. As ever, Germaine was torn between living up to her desired self-image as generous friend and patron, and putting up with the foibles of those she chose to shelter.

The result was a beautiful, calm and spacious house that I always shared with friends, from whom I never demanded any rent. Only the tenant of the basement flat was expected to pay rent, which didn't prevent people living as my guests in the main house from describing me as their landlady.[19]

Among her guests was the then-fledgling star Pamela Stephenson, who practised singing every morning. Loudly.

In a very short time, however, noisy singers, unappreciative guests and the plight (or nuisance) of the squatters came to bother Germaine less than the steady drain of money from her bank account occasioned by her grand house. All too soon, a combination of unwise investments, the economic slump of the 1970s and harassment by the Department of Inland Revenue forced her to sell her home at a substantial loss, to an accountant who made a good profit when he in turn sold it to a film producer a couple of years later.

•

1975 was an unforgettable year in Australian politics – the year of the Dismissal, when the governor-general chose to sack an elected prime minister. Most Australians, even many of those who had opposed the Labor Party and its policies, were gobsmacked. Before the December election that closely followed the sacking on 11 November, many people who had never taken an active interest in politics turned up at local Labor Party branch meetings to support Gough Whitlam. Members of the Women's Electoral Lobby went into overdrive.[20]

Like many of her countrymen and women, Germaine Greer was outraged at what she believed to be a basely motivated abuse of Australia's constitutional system of government. It was unthinkable, she told a *Sunday Times* reporter, that the Australian people should choose to replace the socialist Whitlam with the patrician Malcolm Fraser, who would destroy all of the Labor government's achievements of the past three years. Why would they want a man like Fraser for their prime minister anyway?, she demanded to know. His eyes were much too close together.[21]

Having lost no time in returning home to offer her support to the Labor Party, she chose to stay in Canberra at the home of her friend, Labor minister Susan Ryan, telling her that she expected to be a useful ally of the Left in the hard-fought electoral campaign to come. She had many friends at the highest levels of the Labor Party, including the former prime minister and his wife, but her country was still not ready for her, and the Australian press continued to deride and shame her. Shell-shocked, the Labor Party mandarins feared that she would be a liability rather than an asset to their cause, and her offers of assistance were politely refused.

The mid-1970s were not happy years for Germaine. To ease the financial pressures that were becoming a major worry, she was spending about three weeks every few months in the United States, lecturing on feminist issues. Lucrative as this was, it was also disruptive and exhausting. She longed for change, but she was not sure how to achieve it.

Changing men was one way, and, as she told Sydney journalist Hilary Roots in an interview for the *Australian Women's Weekly* in January 1976, her custom was to combine this with cutting her hair. She complained about people's nosy interest in her appearance but then went on to provide more details about it. She used to pluck her eyebrows because she didn't like them, she said. She had tried bleaching them and combing them and plucking them into all sorts of shapes, but now she just cut them with scissors. And lest people be wondering about her hands, 'I put formaldehyde on my nails,' she said, 'to help them grow.'[22]

She had come to Australia to help out with the election, she explained, but there was another reason. She wanted to visit the gynaecologist who had looked after her in her Sydney Push days. 'Of course I wanted to see Labor win,' she said, 'but I also came back to see my old doctor.

'I want to have a baby. He operated on me and diagnosed me correctly . . . before, so I thought I'd give him another go.'[23]

This 'old doctor' may have been the one Germaine later talked about with her friend Liz Fell, who was also a left-wing journalist. Known to some women in Push circles, this man specialised in treating various gynaecological disorders by removing an ovary and one fallopian tube. Germaine and Liz both had abdominal scars from being operated on by him. Neither woman ever went on to have a successful pregnancy.[24]

If she had a baby, Germaine told Hilary Roots, she would give up the US lecture circuit. 'I'd have to cool it a lot, even for my pregnancy, because no doctor would ever agree to my doing all that flying. If I ever get pregnant, it's going to be a bumpy ride for everybody, baby included.' She was 'coy' about whom she might choose as the father, but believed there was no shortage of suitable candidates (and three in Australia alone). As resolutely opposed to the idea of the nuclear family as ever, she believed that the people who shared her house in London would welcome a child. They were all getting a bit bored and jaded, she said, and it struck her that children were just what they needed to brighten them up. Or, she might establish a household somewhere else. She had not abandoned her earlier idyll of a cooperative parenting arrangement in a simple, probably Mediterranean, environment, with a peasant couple doing all the domestic work. And she definitely intended to breastfeed.[25]

Over the years, Germaine Greer has publicly shared much of her personal gynaecological history in print and interviews. In May 2000, she wrote an article for the first issue of *Aura* magazine in which she described her longing for a baby in the 1970s. In this article, under the heading 'The truth is, says Germaine Greer, I was desperate for a baby and I have the medical bills to prove it', she traced the reasons for her inability to bear a child. As a student, she explained, she had had a contraceptive device called a Gräfenberg ring inserted into her uterus.[26] The device had been accidentally expelled, painfully cutting into her cervix in the process and causing infection. Her fallopian tubes were severely damaged and she underwent complicated surgery. The gynaecologist who performed the operation told her afterwards that she would never conceive a child.

This doctor was wrong, she said, and she did become pregnant, but the pregnancy went badly. Fearing that she would become 'the impoverished single mother of a handicapped child', she arranged to have an abortion which, in the event, coincided with a natural miscarriage and a violent haemorrhage that exploded all over the abortionist's Savile Row suit. Again, she was told that another pregnancy was virtually impossible; again, the medical advice was wrong.

The article continued: a couple of years later, she heard that one of her students at Warwick was pregnant and unable to pay her rent. Germaine invited her to come and live with her at her flat in Leamington Spa. She herself was only spending two or three nights a week there at that time, so she generously agreed to give the young mother her bed while she herself slept on the couch in the living room.

Baby Ruby screamed every night from eight o'clock till midnight for the first three months, but Germaine did not mind at all. She nursed her and walked her and soothed her until she fell asleep. She was smitten. 'I found her scrumptious, delicious, ineffable, adorable . . . Ruby lit up my life in a way that nobody, certainly no lover has ever done.' Germaine became Ruby's godmother and surrogate mother, continuing to share her homes in Italy and London with the child's natural mother, Renee, whom she supported for some years.

Ruby was thirty years old when Germaine wrote her article for *Aura*, and by that time there were many other godchildren. 'Ruby probably has no idea how much I loved her or what a difference she made to my life,' she mused. But it was all a long time ago. Now, in 2000, her life was 'full of baby surrogates, animals and birds that need nursing, that run to meet me when I open the door, as Ruby used to, all those years ago'.[27]

Germaine knew that her reproductive system was severely compromised. When the old and trusted gynaecologist in Sydney failed to restore her fertility, she told the *Aura* journalist, she commissioned a Harley Street gynaecologist to perform a long, expensive and complicated operation that left her with one healthy fallopian tube and a uterus free of fibroids.[28]

In 1977, she met a young man who, she decided, would make an excellent father for her baby. He was James Hughes-Onslow, old Etonian, six years her junior and a freelance writer. As he told the story more than twenty years later, they first met when he was covering the story of that year's Notting Hill Carnival for *The Spectator*. It was a sultry Saturday evening, racial trouble was brewing, and Germaine was sitting on the balcony of her house at 54 Cambridge Gardens reading a new book on Byron that she had been commissioned to review. He looked up, they fell into conversation and she invited him to join her on the balcony, where she gave him a lecture on the causes of racial tension in Britain generally and Notting Hill in particular. Then he returned to the street, where he was attacked by group of drug-affected black youths, who left him in the gutter.

When he came to his senses, he decided to return to Germaine's house. She comforted him, gave him food and drinks and offered him a bed, though not with her. Soon, other victims of the riots, black and white, followed. She looked after them all as the troubles continued over the weekend. 'Germaine had a powerful, caring side to her nature,' commented Hughes-Onslow. 'I noticed a strong maternal tendency which was sadly underused.'[29]

Two days later, they chanced to meet at the Bloomsbury offices of *The Spectator*, where he was delivering his article on the riots and she her review of the Byron book. Germaine invited him to go with her to a party being held by socialite Olga Deterding in her Green Park penthouse. Perceiving them as a couple, some guests at the party tried to ingratiate themselves with him in the hope that he would bring her to dinner at their houses. He declined because, he said, he disliked dinner parties where he didn't know anyone.

Soon Germaine invited him to Pianelli, where they embarked on a love affair, with the intent of conceiving a child. He admired her domestic arrangements and noted how she 'communed' with her cats and with Lisa, her housekeeper, who, although she addressed her as 'La Dottoressa', clearly respected her as a fellow survivor in the tough Tuscan hills.

One evening they visited a vineyard owned by the Lamborghini family. Germaine enthused over the venture as an example of how the wealthy were supporting the local community. Hughes-Onslow disagreed, arguing that the family were using the vineyard as a test site for their latest capitalist enterprises. She called him a cynic, but, later, at dinner with the Lamborghinis and speaking in Italian, she used his arguments 'with devastating effect, and far more lucidly'. 'How clever it is to be able to change your mind so quickly and so completely, but ultimately, how confusing for her,' he thought.[30]

The gossip columnists soon picked up on the news that Germaine had chosen James Hughes-Onslow to become the father of her hoped-for child. He was not averse to the idea. 'I had noticed Germaine's caring instincts and thought she would make a wonderful mother. I was flattered to have been chosen as the father of the child and looked forward to having a useful role in the child's life as well as hers.'

He sought clarification of the situation. Was the baby to be recognised as his or not? Germaine assured him that he was indeed the man she had chosen to be the father of her child, and even consented to discuss the possibility of marriage, but in spite of her regular visits to the London clinic and several more romantic trips to Tuscany, no baby eventuated. She thought it might be his fault and even sent him off to be medically tested, but eventually she gave up on him and started an affair with another handsome old Etonian, the writer William Shawcross, who, being already the father of a three-year-old son, was not required to give further proof of his virility.[31]

•

Germaine's lecture tours of the United States continued through the 1970s, barely keeping her financially afloat and often leaving her miserable and exhausted. Each tour was physically gruelling in that she was required to fly across the country (and she disliked flying), enduring brief hotel stays in city after city within very short time frames. At each venue, she had to perform before audiences who had paid a high entrance fee to listen to her views on sex, birth control, abortion and women's rights. Ever the consummate performer, she rose magnificently to every occasion and the newspaper reviews recorded strong attendances and enthusiastic responses everywhere she went. The lectures became an important aspect of her influence and success in transforming the lives of an entire generation. In 2018, many of the ideas and propositions she expounded in those American lectures have become orthodox – even humdrum. In the mid-1970s, they were revolutionary.

Since the release of relevant documents in Greer's archive, researchers have gained powerful new insights into this period of her life. Of these documents, none is more significant than her 'Long letter to a short love, or . . .', written to journalist and writer Martin Amis in 1976 (she never completed the title).

At more than thirty thousand words, this letter was indeed long, and the man to whom she wrote it was short – only five feet four inches tall and embarrassed about his height. They had had a brief affair but he was in a committed relationship with fashion journalist Julie Kavanagh. Germaine had multiple lovers in England and the United States. On the face of it, Amis was not her usual type, but academic and journalist Margaret Simons, who discovered the letter in Greer's archive in 2014, put her finger on the probable nature of his attraction for Germaine when she noted Kavanagh's comment that Amis's former misgivings about his physical unattractiveness 'had given way to Byronic magnetism', so that 'everyone was after him . . . from Germaine Greer to [magazine editor] Mark Boxer'.[32]

Before she left for Heathrow, en route to one American tour, Greer spoke with Amis on the telephone and he suggested that she write to him while she was away. So she bought a hardback A5 notebook (now housed in the archive). While waiting for her delayed flight in the British Airways lounge, 'for all the world as if I was rich and famous', she started to write.

Amis became her imaginary companion for the duration of her trip, much like those pretend friends with whom some lonely young children have endless conversations, or that mysterious personal God and all the saints and angels Catholics are taught to confide in.

For every city, she had a story for her lover. In Las Vegas – a place she detested – she told him how she drove, hooting and waving encouragingly, through streets lined by striking hospitality workers. She wondered how the celebrities – Sammy Davis Jr, Ann-Margret et al. – were managing to find something to eat. Warming up TV dinners perhaps. In British Columbia, where she was finally able to obtain a decent cup of tea, 'a young swollen pallid person' fainted at her lecture when she was talking about the horrors of IUDs. In Chicago, her luggage, containing Amis's novel *Dead Babies*, was left behind and she panicked. 'God how glad I am you're here . . .' she wrote pathetically. In Montana she had a restorative sauna. 'My breasts seem to have climbed back to their usual position and the furrows in my face have shrunk away . . .' Then on she went to Phoenix, Seattle, Vancouver, Calgary and Jerome, Arizona, where she discovered the county's female sheriff 'complete with hand tooled belt, silver and turquoise buckle, tear gas canister, revolver and handcuffs'. On a two-day break from the circuit she hired a Gran Torino sports car and drove 820 miles around Arizona, 'tearing around the backblocks at high speed', and spending a night in a fake log cabin with a view of the Grand Canyon.

She mostly travelled alone, but she had an American sexual partner, based in Detroit. He satisfied her physically, but his 'undemanding mind' irritated her and made her restive. Her advice to him, to 'try fucking first and talking later', seems to have worked, for she reported to Amis that once a certain 'crustiness' was overcome, their sexual encounters became smooth, 'like crème brulee'.

The worst thing she got from this lover was pubic lice, also known as crabs. She told Amis how she discovered the little creatures. (In 1993 she provided more detail in an article for *The Guardian*.) At the time, she was staying at the superluxurious Beverly Wilshire hotel in Los Angeles, where she met 'dear Woody Allen' on the steps. She may also have run into Elizabeth Taylor, who was staying there as well. Having identified the crabs, with the help of a large magnifying mirror, in her eyebrows and 'goodness knew where else', she spent the rest of the evening in her sumptuous bathroom, hunting for more until she had discovered 'two adults, a teenager and assorted eggs', which she methodically placed in an ashtray. She assumed that she had contracted them from her Detroit lover, but it was possible that she may have had them longer, and may even have passed some on to Amis. 'The unspeakable question is could I, by any concatenation of adverse influences have given them to you?' She rang her boyfriend in Detroit, who 'pretended' to be furious with her when, in her opinion, it was her turn to be furious with him.

The next morning, Sunday, she went downstairs to Hernando's Hideaway, the hotel restaurant, where she found the famous pop star Frank Zappa and his wife Gail quietly enjoying coffee over the morning newspapers. They invited her to join them and, having done so, she launched into the sad tale of her crabs. Far from being shocked or surprised at her frankness, Zappa, proclaiming himself to be an authority on crabs, declared that he would take care of it. He called for his car, a black Rolls-Royce with smoked glass windows, and in it they set off for Schwab's drugstore. 'Blue lotion!' demanded Zappa loudly, to the amazement of the young 'would be Lana Turners' who were draping themselves across the stools by the counter in this, the most famous drugstore in the world. 'Blue lotion please, for the crabs!'[33]

One annoying consequence of the crabs was that she felt she could not carry out her plan of contacting her occasional lover Warren Beatty. She feared that he might not appreciate her, in her infested state.

Upon arrival back home in London, Germaine wrote the final entries in her notebook. Exhausted and miserable, she despaired when she found that her entire earnings from that lecture tour would be consumed by bills that had arrived while she was away. She decided that the letter would never be sent. At some level, she recognised the image of Martin Amis she had created for the chimera it was.

> This despairing cry to someone who hardly exists will never be heard . . . It is better for him and for me that this book remains closed. I do not care as much as I wish I did, and

> he is not what I wish I cared for . . . For a month and from
> 6,000 miles away, I loved him well.

And, at an even deeper level, she had come to understand that her image of Amis was a self-image, an imposition of her alter ego upon the idea of him, created to assuage her own feelings of loneliness and abandonment.

> How can I dismiss you, my own darling? I have no choice.
> In the month that has passed since you telephoned and bade
> me begin my letter, I have come to rely on you absolutely, but
> I have also made you in my own image, simply imposed my
> alter-ego upon you, and with it all my passion, and alas all
> my loneliness. I dare not allow irrelevant reality to intrude
> upon this self-indulgence.[34]

•

Before the second wave of feminism, few people had bothered to consider the question of why the visual arts, over the centuries, had been so persistently the preserve of men, and no one had written about the absurdity of this situation. It is a mark of the success of the women's movement that at least six books on the subject had appeared by the end of the 1970s, but if this was a bandwagon, Germaine cannot be accused of jumping aboard when she wrote her second book, *The Obstacle Race*; first, because her contribution to the sexual revolution had been so influential in creating the interest, and second, because, as she had remarked as early as at the Town Hall debate in 1971, the question of why female artists did not achieve like men had been on her mind since she was a precocious little girl. The idea of writing a book about it had been growing in her mind for a very long time.

Germaine is a natural scholar who rarely feels more in control of her life than when she is sitting in libraries fossicking through books and papers and other evidence of human endeavour. She also loves art and never tires of exploring galleries and museums. This is the side of her character that is the most straightforward, and it has not changed from the days when Clive James tried in vain to extract her from the library at Cambridge. In the later 1970s, the work of researching and writing *The Obstacle Race* provided a merciful escape and distraction from the horrors of dealing with banks and accountants, facing up to the likelihood that she would be permanently infertile, and trying to get along with people who annoyed her. It also meant that she would earn some money to replenish her alarmingly depleted finances.

In seeking answers to her question of why no woman has achieved the stature of artists like Leonardo da Vinci and Michelangelo, Germaine's research led her to the work of virtually unknown female painters like Natalia Goncharova and Berthe Morisot, and to those whose contributions were impaired by their subservience to men they loved, such as the German modernist Paula Modersohn-Becker. The nineteen chapters of the book are divided into two sections: 'The Obstacles' and 'How They Ran'. In the first section, which is a feminist analysis, the obstacles are identified as 'Family', 'Love', 'The Illusion of Success', 'Humiliation', 'Dimension', 'Primitivism' and 'The Disappearing Oeuvre'. The second part of the book deals with the actual achievements of female artists. Organised chronologically, it focuses on the genres in which women excelled: flower painting, still life and portraiture.

The book was published in 1979 and reviews, as she had feared, were mixed. Critics acknowledged that she provided valuable insights into the difficulties faced by women artists in a field that had long been dominated by men, but they were quick to point out that her professional areas of scholarship were literature and feminism before art. Art historians remarked that she was more at home writing the first section of her book than the second. Some also criticised her tedious habit of laboriously detailing lists and examples, and her failure to engage more fully with complex theoretical issues.

> Although the author has obviously done an enormous amount of research on her subject, her discussion here is weakened by a conflict between the attempt to deal incisively with the various complex theoretical issues involved in women's creative achievement and an effort to attain scholarly and historical completeness.
>
> . . . in these historical chapters one tends to bog down in lists, ponderous as the 'begats' in the Bible, of the once- or near-famous and their relatives and supporters.[35]

The *London Review of Books'* review of *The Obstacle Race* was scathing, and strangely misogynistic, almost as if its writer, the feminist Brigid Brophy, wanted to conduct a personal vendetta against Greer. She could find nothing to praise in the book, accusing Greer of having a 'one-eyed' view of history and of providing only limited explanation as to 'why women artists have, on the whole, painted so abysmally'. Like other critics, Brophy picked up Germaine's annoying penchant for making long lists of examples.

> Ms Greer has searched written records and the reserve collections of galleries for every mention and trace of a woman painter. Her findings are numerous but seldom lively and she

has relentlessly put them all in. Her text is weighted down, sometimes twice to a page, with mere lists, which, since there *are* notes at the back, could with more kindness to the reader have gone there.[36]

The 1970s had brought Germaine Greer international fame; they had seen her become rich; they had allowed her to make friends among some of the most exciting people of her generation. Yet, by decade's end, she was unhappy. 'Oh I'm neurotic. Is there any doubt about that?' she told Liz Fell in 1979.

> I don't have any enduring relationships of any sort except with animals and plants. Human beings come and go . . . Oh shit, why would I be happy? What reason would I have to be happy? I mean, I'm happy enough, I've got me garden, got me cats.[37]

In the European autumn of 1979, she left England for America to take up a post as visiting Professor at the University of Tulsa in Oklahoma and, subsequently, founding director of the university's Center for the Study of Women's Literature. Tulsa was geographically and intellectually a long way from the Europe of Greer's cultural roots; it lacked the sophistication of New York or Washington and did not even have the charm of southern towns like Charleston or New Orleans. So why would she go there?

Her first reason was the dire state of her finances. Records in the Greer archive show that on 13 November 1978 she received a writ notifying her of the case 'The Commissioner of Inland Revenue v. Dr Germaine Greer of 54 Cambridge Gardens London W 10, Defendant', to be heard in the High Court of

Justice, Queen's Bench Division, regarding her failure to meet her taxation commitments. Eight months later, the debt still unpaid, she was informed that the Solicitor of Inland Revenue had been instructed to commence bankruptcy proceedings against her for the non-payment of £37,095.70 in tax, plus interest.

On 19 June 1979 her accountant argued, unsuccessfully, on her behalf.

Our client had extraordinary success with her first book, some ten years ago. She made very proper and adequate reserves for her taxation liabilities. That reserve was invested in what we believe was a most reputable and secure finance house, Vavasseur Limited. In the slump of 74/75 and the virtual liquidation of Vavasseur, that reserve was wiped out. What remaining funds Dr Greer had were invested in a property which, equally disastrously, slumped . . . She wasn't fraudulent or negligent . . . Since that time her income has not been sufficiently substantial to meet these old tax liabilities, although she has made valiant efforts and has in fact paid substantial sums to you.[38]

Disaster was averted, eventually, after the accountant pointed out that bankruptcy proceedings would not produce any further payment and could indeed jeopardise her further income and payments. He was supported by Germaine's friend and agent Peter Grose, who feared that if she were not treated with sympathy, she would be unable to work. 'Authors are not machines and cannot be made to produce on demand,' he wrote. 'For the better part of a year now, I have seen concern over her financial situation begin to dominate her thinking, and this tax question is her most pressing worry.'[39]

The University of Tulsa was not offering a huge salary, but the appointment would take her out of the country and leave her advisers to manage the negotiations with the Department of Inland Revenue in her absence. She could rent out the flat she had bought in London after selling her house, while living rent-free at Pianelli and the university.

She also went to Tulsa because she was invited to undertake work that interested her and that she felt to be important. She wanted to resume the academic career she had left when she resigned from Warwick University in 1972, and she wanted to keep investigating and promoting the work of female writers. She worried that art historian reviewers of *The Obstacle Race* would accuse her of 'not [knowing] me arse from me elbow' (which they did), but in discovering and chronicling the lives and work of women in her own professional field of literature, as the Tulsa appointment would empower her to do, she would be on safer ground. The provincial university might have been relatively small and unknown outside the United States, but it was far-sighted enough to offer support for her ground-breaking work. No comparable invitation from Oxford or Cambridge or any other more prestigious institution had come her way.

Obviously, too, she wanted a break – not just a holiday but a break from London, the epicentre of all the economic, social and emotional complications of her life. She knew she was at a turning point. Forty years old, her groupie days long behind her, the excitement of the first flush of celebrity a bittersweet memory, her hopes of becoming a mother in tatters, she took comfort, as always, in the constancy of her work.

She was still nervous about how *The Obstacle Race* would be received by readers. 'I have a feeling of vertigo about this

book . . . I wish I'd done it better. I wish I were doing it over,'
she confided to *People* magazine journalist Andrea Chambers in
1979. 'I don't know what I feel . . . if I feel jealous or like I'm
going to be left, I'll tear my throat out before I let it show. I hate
it whenever I feel my control is slipping. When I do, I just get in
the car and drive. I spend all my time leaving people.'

Her plan was to spend half the year in Tulsa and the other
half at Pianelli, where she hoped to retire. 'I'm happiest farming
my land with my bottom in the air and my hands in the mud,'
she told Chambers. 'I'll be stark naked and brown as a nut. At
the end of the day, I'll come home and take the cat out of the best
chair and I'll read and write fiction . . . I hope, of course, that the
men will come and go.'[40]

She later told journalist Richard Boeth that she had chosen
Tulsa 'because it was a rich university that didn't know quite
what to do with its money'. As it turned out, however, she had
to fight many a battle with the university's administration to get
the funds she needed to realise her dream of setting up a first-rate
scholarly institution dedicated to women's writing and staffed by
women. 'It *was* rich,' she told Boeth, 'and it *doesn't* quite know
what to do with its money because it hates to spend it.'[41]

Shari Benstock, who took over the directorship of the Tulsa
Center for the Study of Women's Literature after Greer left in
1983, has described her as an inspiration to the Center's small
academic staff and graduate students, but Germaine struggled
to maintain her patience with some of them. The seven students
who were helping her to prepare an early manuscript for
hand-printing, she told Richard Boeth, were 'in scholarly terms
simply illiterate . . . Not one could name an English poet of the
eighteenth century. One thought maybe Kipling . . .'[42] Tulsa was
proving hard work.

Her base at the university was 'the Red House', a small cottage on campus that was surrounded by parking lots and dead trees. It was here, in 1980, that Greer established the journal *Tulsa Studies in Women's Literature*, which was the first, and for a time the only, one in the world that was dedicated to the study of women's literary history.

Benstock wrote about Greer's work in Tulsa with a reverence that bordered on adulation, but as in her pre-*Eunuch* days at Warwick, when she was a serious academic on weekdays and a groupie and contributor to underground magazines at weekends, the Tulsa Germaine Greer, if Andrea Chambers' *People* article is to be believed, had another life. This Germaine, wrote Chambers, liked to hoon around the county in a rented Mustang with a bottle of Jack Daniels under the seat. At night, she would sit in the smoky corners of what, in Tulsa, passed for bohemian bars, drinking copious quantities of bourbon and encouraging the local performers in the vernacular. 'Gawwwd damnnnn!' she would cry out, and 'Yip!', her dark hair thrown back, her long legs splayed. 'I think I am a potential alcoholic,' she confided to Chambers, 'and I can't afford the only drug I like, which is coke.'[43]

It was now two years since she had undergone the complex operation that, she continued to hope, might restore her fertility. She had been forced to acknowledge the effects of her lifestyle on her body, but she still liked men and she still believed in liberated sex. The raunchy males of Oklahoma were much to her taste. 'Let me advise any unhappy career girl in New York to hightail it down here,' she said. 'It's like Rome. Men follow you in the supermarkets.' Nevertheless, as she went on to explain to a fascinated Chambers, she was now practising periods of sexual abstinence, and she was less enthusiastic about sex than of yore. '[I]t takes a fair amount of persuasion to get me back on men.' She was no lesbian, she declared, but she looked to women before men for emotional comfort. 'For support, it's women. I sleep with men. I don't expect anything else from them.'[44]

In April 1980, she received a letter from a young French girl who was about to move out of home to live independently with a girlfriend. The letter was typical of many she received, in which the writers confided the most intimate details of their lives and asked her for advice. Depending on her inclination and workload at the time, she would reply to some of these letters with a brief comment or apology for not having time to write more, and to others sagely and at length. Her reply to the French girl's letter is an example of the latter.

In this sweetly naive letter the young girl confided the secrets of her relationship with her boyfriend and her uncertainty about how to respond to his sexual advances, explaining that, unlike Germaine Greer (parts of some of whose books she said she had read), her parents were very conservative. She begged the older woman for advice as to what she should do about her boyfriend and how she should live her life.

In her reply, Germaine opened her heart to this young stranger.

> Love is difficult; friendship is even more so. You ask me if I have children. The answer is No. If I have friends, permanent friends – the answer is that I don't know. It has been a bad year for friendships for me. There have been all kinds of misunderstandings and estrangements but I still believe as long as my friends are alive even if they are estranged from me there is hope that they will come to trust me again. Most of my friends are married and it is my experience that

in times of conflict the couple asserts itself at the expense of the outsider. The family has a kind of dreadful durability which undermines and outlasts everything else, by force of exploiting and consuming it.

You do not tell me what you do; in the last analysis, it is our work that keeps us sane and makes a rudder for all those ups and downs.[45]

About one month after her reply to the French girl, Germaine wrote to her friend and agent at that time, Gillon Aitken, telling him that she had found a new 'swain' in Tuscany. His name was John; he was a 'transplanted Englishman' who liked to walk across the hills between their houses, bringing her orchids he had picked along the way. He was 'strong and practical', and her maid and the *contadini* (farmers) respected him because he was a hard worker. A photograph now in the Greer archive shows a relaxed, bearded, handsome man of around forty years old – strong and practical, just as Germaine described him. He is driving a tractor. Germaine is seated behind him, smiling.[46]

She also told Richard Boeth about John. 'He's completely non-verbal . . . he dreams in shape and line . . . None of my boyfriends is ever an intellectual or an academic. I think it's restful to look for people who are restful to be with, to rescue you from the treadmill . . . Clever women should marry truck drivers.'[47]

Germaine's letters to John tell of her many frustrations with the university administration at Tulsa and the effort she was putting into establishing her Center. They are loving, gentle letters. She writes of how much she longs to be with him and how much she misses 'his eyes upon [her] and his sandpaper hands'.[48]

In Germaine's absence, John employed his skills generously at Pianelli, rewiring the bathroom, fixing the plumbing, installing furniture, and doing heavy work in the garden with tractor and plough. He was sleeping in her bed (with the two cats) three nights a week, attending to all the practical tasks like getting the telephone connected and new cupboards delivered. Lisa, the maid, came up every day to work in the house and garden and feed the cats.

In one letter, John told Germaine about some interesting local gossip. The word in the village was that he and Germaine were planning to marry at Christmas. He had not been able to discover the source but he suspected that Lisa had been 'doing a few sums'.[49]

Were they indeed planning to marry? It would seem so. On 3 April 1981, her accountant Alan Patten wrote to her from London: 'You raise the possibility of marrying a UK citizen who is resident in Italy.'[50]

And on 25 September 1981, her solicitor wrote:

Dear Germaine,

Alan Patten tells me that you have confirmed your probable marriage plans to him and wish to know how they might affect your position in the UK . . . I understand that your intended husband, although a UK citizen, is not resident in the UK . . .

PS I hope you will ensure that we know about your wedding arrangements. I do not wish to read about them for the first time on the front page of The Sun.[51]

Was it because Germaine was in love with John in the autumn of 1980 that the man to whom she was closest in Tulsa at this time was the writer David Plante, who was gay? She had known him in London and in Italy, where he had a stone cottage in the same district as Pianelli. Now, in September, they met again in the unlikely setting of the University of Tulsa, where Plante had been appointed writer-in-residence for the autumn term.

Plante arrived in Tulsa a couple of days before Germaine returned there from Italy, also for the autumn term. On her arrival, it was arranged that the Dean would take both of them to dinner at a Chinese restaurant with his wife and children. When he and Plante drove up to the glitzy hotel where she was staying, she was waiting for them in the shade of the portico, carrying her shoes in her hand. Plante was surprised when he saw that her feet were broad and stubby. He had always thought of her as a kind of flawless goddess.

> I had, before, thought of her as beautiful beyond any fault. I had thought of her, large, standing high above me and looking down upon me, a very beautiful, public woman. Her feet made her, in one small part, a private woman.[52]

In the car, Germaine complained loudly to the Dean about the quality of the champagne in her hotel. No French to be had, only Californian, what a fucking provincial place she had come to! But Californian champagnes could be quite good, protested the Dean. Not good enough, she replied rudely. At dinner, she held the floor, lecturing her companions on the subjects of abortion and contraception. The situation was desperate all over the world, she told them. Infanticide was practised in certain cultures by smothering the baby or by placing a stick across its throat and standing on both ends. Plante could see that she had lost all awareness of her audience. He realised, with a kind of awe, that she was obsessed by the problems of the world. 'What's to be done?' she kept asking. 'About unwanted children, what's to be done?'

Plante was given an office in Germaine's Center, on the opposite side of the kitchen from hers. On a white-hot day, Plante, Germaine and a male friend of hers, a native of Tulsa, worked happily together in the air-conditioned building, drinking champagne and eating chicken as they painted the interior walls of the cottage 'Liberty' red, Germaine's choice of colour for two rooms which she called the 'ventricles' of the heart of the Center. Plante stripped to his underpants. Germaine complimented him on his buttocks and caressed them. ('I like a nice ass.') She, as usual, wore no underclothes and he was aware of the power of her body under her thin dress. He paused often to kiss and embrace her, paint brush in the air. Whenever the other man turned around she poked her tongue out at him. Plante did not know or care if they were lovers.

Afterwards, when the friend had left them, Germaine told Plante that this man had been with her at Pianelli, but that he had disappointed her by being 'unaware' of the beauty around him. He was so insensitive, she told Plante, that he was incapable, even, of being aware of the vastness and glory of his own Tulsan sky.

Not so Germaine: 'She was always aware,' said Plante.

At 'home', in Tuscany, John, her new love, was also aware as he awaited her return. He was worried that she was overstraining herself and he was happy with her news that she and David had taken a short holiday together over the Thanksgiving period. His letters to Germaine are those of a domesticated househusband to an absent wife. He is no scholar – the letters contain many misspellings – but his handwriting is firm and he is articulate, even lyrical at times, as he describes the beauty of the countryside and the views across to the mountains. He could never live in any other place, he wrote.[53]

Germaine's letters to John tell of the long hours she is working to make her Center a success. As Plante remarked, this was the one area of her life over which she had total control.

[S]he arrived early in the morning and left late at night, and while she was there telephones rang all the time, typewriters clacked, papers appeared to fly about, and she, exuding the scent of patchouli, kept it all going . . . when she was away there was an air of quiet withdrawal among the students.[54]

As David Plante's friendship with Germaine deepened during the time they spent together at Tulsa, he observed her curious habit of revealing to groups of virtual strangers details of her life that most people would only share with a close friend. She rarely discussed personal matters with him, but once, at a party, he found her telling a full room of people about her family. Surprised, but wanting to know more about her, he found a chair, sat down and listened with everyone else. Similarly, he learned about her problems with showing affection when he was part of a larger audience to whom she disclosed that when greeting an ardent lover at an airport she would 'grow rigid' and ask him if he had had the plumber in or the car repaired. And how she did not like to share a bed with a man she had just made love with, but preferred to sleep on the floor beside the bed.[55]

Eventually, Plante concluded that Germaine Greer was interested only in public issues, not personal ones. 'You can't presume to be intimate with her. Even in private, she's public,' he confided to a friend.

I don't think Germaine really has friends, close friends, and I think she doesn't because she's not interested in her relationships, she's not interested in herself. She's only interested in other people, and that, somehow, depersonalizes her interest.[56]

But still he thought he loved her.

Meanwhile, in Tuscany, John was still dreaming of Germaine, longing for her return to Pianelli. Germaine kept his letters and copies of her letters to him. They are now contained in a special envelope in the 'General correspondence' section of her archive. Most are undated; they carry headings like 'Friday' or 'Thursday the somethingth'. However, the final letter from John is dated – '16.11.81'. He writes with enthusiasm about her 'grand idea' that they should spend Christmas in New York. 'How much I love the Autumn here,' he says, 'and how much I love you.'[57]

The marriage did not eventuate. John and Germaine remained friends.

Later, after she returned to live in England, Germaine was so incensed when she discovered that David Plante had written about their time together in Tulsa in his book *Difficult Women* that she vowed never to speak to him again. It mattered nothing that he had offered to show her what he had written and invited her to amend it if she wanted to.

I despised him for being so ready to change his work, and also because – though he made a great parade of sensitivity – he had no idea how deeply I would resent being made to utter namby-pamby Plante-speak like a dummy on his knee.[58]

7

Recalibration

Shout for joy, O barren one, you who have borne
no child . . . For the sons of the desolate one will be
more numerous than the sons of the married woman.

Isaiah 54:1

In her third major book, *Sex and Destiny*, which was first
published in 1984, shortly after she returned from Tulsa to
resume her life in England, Germaine Greer faced up to the challenges that confront women as they approach middle age. Now
in her fifth decade, she wanted not only to express her views
on women as they reached that stage of life, but also to apply
her blowtorch to larger questions about human fertility, sterility,
abortion, birth control and, for her, the very personal dilemma
of 'barrenness'.

Her repeated use of this word, 'barrenness', together with
much of the content and mood of *Sex and Destiny*, is reflective of
her religious upbringing. As always, she detested orthodoxies and
was appalled at the thought of women's lives being controlled by
the men of the Catholic Church. She was never about to return
to her roots and speak up in support of the Pope, but by the time
she sat down to write *Sex and Destiny*, in the early 1980s, she
had come to the other side of a personal rebellion and wanted to

share the lessons she had learned. In her youth she had joyfully defied the repressive beliefs of her religion and culture, but now, as she faced the physical and emotional consequences of her adventures, she needed to explore what it had all meant. Was unrestrained sexual freedom really in the best interests of women? Was loss of fecundity – barrenness – the price to be paid for denying the natural connection between sexual congress and new life? How could she explain to herself and her sisters not only her own personal disappointment and despair at the loss of her fertility, but the dangers confronting unwitting young women who were setting off on the path she had so recently travelled?[1]

With apparent but by no means exclusive reference to her own experience, she describes in *Sex and Destiny* many of the physical problems that can make a woman infertile: fallopian tube obstruction, pelvic inflammatory disease as a result of infection, abdominal surgery, abortions, curettes, and insertion, expulsion or removal of an IUD. She covers the lifestyle factors of smoking, alcohol abuse, medications, stress and the postponement of pregnancy until later in a woman's reproductive life, and does not forget to mention the expensive medical interventions that exist to counteract the loss of fertility, with their false hopes and promises.

Like a caring mother or older sister, she sets out to inform young women about the possible negative consequences of recreational sex. She found examples galore and lists them all. One is infection by the gonorrhoea bacillus, which, she explains, is a malign organism that is 'uncommonly well adapted for dwelling in humans' and may be asymptomatic. Other organisms with similar effects include the Chlamydiae species of bacteria and common fungal infections like *Candida albicans*. With her usual attention to detail, she explores every clinical component of the many ills that sexually transmitted diseases can inflict on the female human body.[2]

Only belatedly, it seems, had she come to realise that male bodies not only have less to lose from casual sex than women's, but that men are better protected by the patriarchy. She notes that while the bodies of travelling rock stars are looked after by the commercial entities for which they generate profit, the bodies of the women who service them are not. On every tour, she explains, the young men are given supplies of broad-spectrum antibiotics to treat any unwanted side effects of their sexual activities before they move on to their next gig. It is unthinkable, she comments, that a multimillion-dollar performance might be ruined because the lead singer has a 'prurient greenish-yellow discharge leaking through his tight white satin trousers'. No one would think of the women the young musicians might have infected, apart from the inconvenience of leaving them as a possible source of infection for the next group of men they pleasured. 'Many a young woman,' Greer comments, 'returns from her adventure sterile, and when, years later, she sits tense and miserable with the doctor who is doing her infertility workup, she can no longer remember that dreadful stomach ache and fever that she treated with erythromycin . . . somewhere between Agra and Benares.'[3]

For intellectual and spiritual inspiration, she returns, as always, to literature: Shakespeare, Yeats, Lawrence, Joyce, Robert Graves, Joseph Conrad and the rest – those writers for whom fecundity, she believed, was always 'the underlying principle of a moral system in which productivity and creativity were the metaphors'. Even the hard-headed Clive James, she noted, had recognised 'the fructive energy' in Jane Austen. ('She chose Art [over sex] and put all her fructive energy into it. The force she shapes to her symmetrical designs is the force that shapes the world.'[4])

T.S. Eliot, she reports, had recognised fecundity's 'barren' opposite:

> Industrialist society was to be seen as a barren landscape inhabited by Hollow Men, important debased creatures performing meaningless tasks in rented accommodation, with only the barest recollection of a virile time when they fought at the hot gates.[5]

Readers of *Sex and Destiny* who expected a succinct, well-argued exposition of Greer's latest ideas on the condition and circumstances of women's lives fifteen years after *The Female Eunuch* were disappointed. With its 500-plus pages of dense writing and often unnecessary detail, the book is not an easy read, and is less coherent and less powerful than her first book.

Respected critic Michael Mason, in the *London Review of Books*, pointed out that *Sex and Destiny*'s three central arguments – first, that genital, recreational sex is overvalued in our culture; second, that birth control programs in the third world are unnecessary, ineffectual and cruel; and third, that families that stress the procreative relationship are preferable to those which stress the conjugal relationship – are not well connected. Each of these arguments, he says, deserves consideration, but her treatment of them both individually and as a cluster of ideas is 'poor' and 'even unprincipled'. Specifically, he points to her 'obsessive' bias against the West in favour of the developing world. While noting some merit in her contention that the West does not have the right to impose its ideas about birth control on other societies, he points out that this does not justify Greer's position that all non-Western procreative practices and customs should be inviolate. This applies in particular to her apparent endorsement of practices such as infanticide and clitoridectomy. It also applies, he argues, to her apparent sanctioning of the practice, still used in some societies, of 'culling' disabled babies at birth. (Some tribal mothers, Greer noted approvingly, 'bashed their new-borns' brains out with a rock' when social and other circumstances warranted).[6]

Following the publication of *Sex and Destiny* in 1984, newspaper editors were inundated with letters from people who accused Greer of turning her back on the feminist credo through which she had made her mark with *The Female Eunuch*. She herself had anticipated this kind of criticism.

> Such an attack upon the ideology of sexual freedom, usually, and quite correctly, called permissiveness, must seem shocking coming from a sexual radical, as the present writer professes to be. It is galling to find oneself lined up with bigots and body haters, as it were circumstantially, when the point of opposition to contemporary sex religion is that it is based in a dreary, circumscribed and thoroughly predictable version of human libido.[7]

Galling though she may have found her supposed place among the bigots and body-haters, there could be no resiling from her new position (remarkably similar to that of the Catholic Church) that the concept of untrammelled recreational sex divorced from notions of child-bearing and rearing was selfishly narcissistic, ultimately boring, dangerous for women and destructive of the best conceptions of family life. From these considerations, it followed, for her, that the West's attempts to impose its sexual values and practices, especially its newer methods of artificial birth control and sterilisation, on developing societies were ethically unacceptable.

Some of Greer's readers who had paid a heavy price for their sexual freedom could see what she was driving at. 'M/s Germaine Greer may be responsible for more women being sterile due to blocked tubes than any other female guru in recent history,' wrote one of her correspondents. 'We girls believed [Greer's earlier claims that problems of VD and unwanted pregnancy were easily solved], but many of us realized years ago that now, as always in shifting relationships, it is the woman who pays the price. I am glad that M/s Greer has come to the same conclusion and I admire her for having the courage to say so.' This woman, who called herself 'a victim of the former state of affairs', signed her letter only as 'W.H.'[8]

W.H. understood Greer's arguments better than critics like moral philosopher Peter Singer, who claimed that *Sex and Destiny* made it hard to see her as a feminist at all.[9] W.H. could see that, belatedly, and probably on the basis of her own experience, Greer had come to realise what her more cautious sisters back in the Push days could have told her then: men can and do manipulate the notion of sexual freedom to suit themselves, and the consequences for women can be dire. *Sex and Destiny*, like *The Female Eunuch*, was concerned with the power imbalance between men and women. Greer's book was not anti-feminist; she had simply reached another stage in her life and, as always, she wanted to explore and share her new insights.

After her return to England from Tulsa in 1983, Germaine continued to travel widely for pleasure and work. She never tired of visiting the theatres and galleries of continental Europe;

she liked America and had many friends there. As a working journalist and humanitarian, she was also advancing and disseminating her knowledge of the people and cultures of developing countries – India, Ethiopia, Pakistan and others – becoming ever more convinced that Western influences were depriving them of much that was of value. Her visits to Australia were also becoming more frequent.

In the late 1970s, after she sold 54 Cambridge Gardens, she bought an apartment in West London at 20 Westbourne Terrace, where she lived for several years when she was not at Pianelli or travelling. From this, her London base, she could readily access everything she needed and valued for her work and cultural life. She was also able to enjoy a satisfying social life with friends who, as well as old mates like Richard Neville and Martin Sharp, included some of the most significant literary and artistic figures of the day. Her archive provides accounts of amusing dinners and lunches with congenial company at hotels, restaurants and private homes. She took every opportunity to spend time with Australian visitors, including Margaret Fink and her family, who generally stayed with her or at Claridge's.

Before the rift caused by his 'sin' of writing about her in his book *Difficult Women*, the writer David Plante and his partner, the well-known art publisher Nikos Stangos, were regular members of her social circle. In his memoir, *Becoming a Londoner: A diary*, Plante provides some fascinating insights into Germaine's social world at this time in her life. One of his descriptions is of a dinner party he attended at her apartment in Westbourne Terrace, where she served individual soufflés, boiled mutton with a caper sauce, and rhubarb sponge, everything prepared on a huge cooker in her kitchen with its many ovens and hobs. The wines, he noted, were exceptionally good.

Germaine had organised this dinner in honour of the Australian writer David Malouf. Among the guests were poet Stephen Spender and his wife Natasha, a concert pianist. The telephone rang constantly during the meal and other people, including broadcaster, journalist and politician Melvyn Bragg, kept arriving. Germaine, who was doing everything herself, seemed frazzled. 'I had the vivid sense of a woman entertaining completely on her own who was frantic that she wasn't up to the entertainment.' She did not sit down and relax with her guests but, 'like an Italian peasant woman', prepared the courses and served them while her guests were eating. Everyone commented on the excellence of her food, but she kept apologising, saying it wasn't good enough.[10]

Plante, whose intense interest in human behaviour often led him to delve into the personal lives and characters of the people he would later write about, looked to items in Germaine's home that might provide insight into the kind of person she was. For a start there was the huge cooker, testament to her love of preparing good food. There was also a large chest of drawers lined with mother-of-pearl. When Plante admired it, she offered it to him, saying she didn't like it. 'So I saw in her an attraction to the extravagant and, at the same time, indifference to that extravagance . . .'[11]

This apparent oscillation between passionate engagement and sudden indifference, Plante believed, extended to her personal relationships.

> She can be so intimate, taking one's chin into her hand and staring into one's eyes as if one were the only person in the world, and then she turns away and she sees something altogether unrelated to one that leaves one totally apart, leaving one to wonder what that intimacy was all about.[12]

Germaine also socialised with Plante and Stangos at their flat. On one occasion the historian Steven Runciman was among the guests. After meeting Germaine, he was inspired to compose a limerick, which he subsequently sent to Plante:

They told me to stay clear
Of the formidable doctor Greer
But, in spite of her learning
For all my discerning
I find her rather a dear.[13]

At one stage, Germaine acquired the flat that adjoined hers and made plans to combine the two units into one large residence, but by 1984 she was growing tired of the London literary scene and the stressful congestion of city traffic and life. The time she had spent in developing countries, especially famine-struck Ethiopia, had convinced her that Western urban society had lost touch with the most basic and essential human values as practised in other cultures. She was happiest in Tuscany, but felt cut off there from the world of books and culture that was so necessary to her. The planned displacement of the Reading Room of the British Museum where she, like so many other famous writers, loved to work, was the last straw.[14]

On 9 January 1985, she wrote to her old friend and mentor, Professor Anne Barton (previously Righter):

I've been going through a minor brain-storm recently and have decided to return to Cambridge for good, if I can find the right house not too far from the university library as the car flies. Since I got back from Ethiopia I find I'm tired of London and the looming dismantlement of the British Museum Reading Room is severing the only bond.

I am not, however, tired of life. Dr Johnson being wrong about that as he was about everything else.[15]

Later in 1985, she found an enduring solution to her dilemmas in a property, The Mills (then known as Mill Farm), at Stump Cross, near the town of Saffron Walden in Essex. On first sight it did not seem to be what she was looking for. The building had originally been a terrace of cheerless one-up one-down houses for farm labourers and their families. New owners had renovated it to make it one house, but it was very close to a road that led to a busy roundabout only two hundred yards away. This road and roundabout were at the end of an access road for the M11 motorway. Visitors might notice the noise, she said, but she would grow accustomed to it. After deciding to buy the property and renovating it extensively, she lived there most of each year into the second decade of the twenty-first century.

After moving to The Mills, she was made an honorary fellow of her old college, Newnham, and given unrestricted access to the Cambridge university libraries. She also set up on her property a small but successful publishing house, Stump Cross Books, which continues to make available works by female writers. In a separate building from the main house, above a large garage, she set up her 'workshop' for writing and research. This pleasant and generous room was where she, her administrative assistants, and various helpers, students and scholars could apply themselves to her many projects. This space was also used to store her growing archive, before it found its final home at the University of Melbourne in 2013.

Why did she choose this initially unpromising house at such a noisy location? The answer is at least twofold. First, the property was less than half an hour's drive to Cambridge and its libraries. Second, it was the country – 3.6 acres surrounded by rolling Essex fields – and she looked forward to transforming the house and garden into the kind of domestic paradise she had achieved at Pianelli. Eventually, one acre of the property became a garden to complement the house, with roses, honeysuckle, lavender and as many exotic plants as she could encourage to survive in the English climate. In the second acre she planted a wood, where she had a bed in the form of a platform raised about four feet from the ground with a foam mattress for sleeping on on summer nights. (Occasionally she would take a bottle of gin with her.) Sometimes it would rain on her, and this she quite liked, choosing to move only when her bedclothes became saturated. An orchard and vegetable and herb gardens in the third acre supplied fresh produce for her table; eggs were collected each morning from the geese and hens, each of which had a name. Then came the domestic animals, Livingstone the parrot, Mollie and Margot the standard poodles, and her beloved cats, Christopher, a red-and-white Persian, and Shanghai Jim, a silver shorthair. Jim liked to sleep outside when it was not too cold, but Christopher, who competed with Livingstone to sit on Germaine's shoulder, preferred to sleep with her in her bed.

Inside the house, the generously proportioned drawing and dining rooms were furnished on quite a grand scale, with luxurious couches, carefully selected antiques and pictures, rich drapes, and interesting rugs on the parquet and stone-flagged floor. Upstairs were three bedrooms, including her own with ensuite dressing room, and a cosy, well-stocked library with comfortable seating and a television set. Guests could stay in the house or in one of several outbuildings that included a small, self-contained cottage. Most rooms had distant views across the Essex countryside; the rear windows of the main house overlooked a walled garden with colourful herbaceous borders and a small stream that flowed to a waterfall and then down to a sunken pool beyond.

In the regular columns she wrote for several newspapers over nearly three decades, Germaine referred to 'everyone' who lived with her at The Mills. But who was 'everyone'? In 1999, James Hughes-Onslow, he who, long ago, had failed to fulfil Germaine's dream of making him the father of her hoped-for child, visited her at The Mills with his wife and four children. He wrote about her habit of referring to her household as 'We'. Who did she mean by this 'We', he wondered: 'Does she refer to her occasional lodgers, her cats, her poodles or her geese?'

'When I have visited her with my wife and family,' he continued, 'I have felt a sense of sadness touched with envy . . . She is a generous and loving person who does not deserve to be lonely in her old age. I suspect this is why she is always busy.'[16]

Usually, 'everyone' seemed to be the young people, mostly students, whom she described in her columns as 'OPCs' (Other Peoples' Children) or 'NPGs' (Non-Paying Guests). All were expected to work in the house, garden or workshop in appreciation of their board and lessons from Germaine in how to do literary and historical research. On the whole, the arrangement worked well. Never able to suffer fools, she occasionally despaired when one or more of them seemed lazy, stupid or unwilling to perform their assigned tasks, but she became very fond of others, like the 'sparkly girl' who was so eager to work and to learn. She employed a small paid domestic staff: a housekeeper, an assistant to manage her correspondence and appointment diary, and a gardener. All were necessary for the smooth running of the household, especially when she was away, as she often was, at Pianelli, on journalistic assignments, or on lecture circuits and tours to promote her books.

Readers of Germaine Greer's regular columns, especially Country Notebook, which was published weekly in the Saturday edition of the *Daily Telegraph* between 1999 and 2005, became familiar with her daily doings at The Mills. There are some memorable self-portraits of her rising early to cut lavender, picking strawberries and currants, black, red and white, and deciding what to do with the surplus of apricots and other fruit picked in the orchard – only so much could be frozen and turned into jam.

When journalists Polly Toynbee and Jill Tweedie drove down to Essex, one glorious summer's day in May 1988, to visit Germaine for lunch, they found her in her kitchen preparing chapattis. Laid out on the table in the stone-flagged dining room, on a sunflower yellow cloth, were salads of curried potatoes, chickpeas and broad beans, guacamole, and a cold bottle of white wine.[17]

Conversation over lunch was brisk. Without rancour, the three women discussed the changes wrought by second-wave feminism in the twenty years since Germaine had written *The Female Eunuch*. Germaine was not optimistic. Younger women were still mincing around trying to please men, she opined, 'speaking in baby voices, and acting helpless'. They had yet to learn the lesson she had tried to impart: to take control of their own bodies and lives in order to live freely. Moving on to abortion, she spoke up in favour of motherhood. Every woman wants her child, she declared. The problem was that society did not provide the necessary support. She herself, she reminded them, had given practical and emotional aid to several needy unmarried women who wanted to keep their babies. She had many godchildren.

After lunch they moved out into the garden. Christopher was stalking a small animal and Germaine did not restrain him. 'It's a rat,' she declared; but the other two women could see that it was a tiny vole, native to the area. Christopher played with it for a while before it escaped into a bush, while Germaine watched indulgently. Later he caught and ate it all except for the head. Germaine was not dismayed. 'She is besotted by her pets,' commented Toynbee.

Perhaps feeling slightly queasy after this grisly episode, Tweedie wandered off to chat with some of the people, whom Toynbee later described as 'waifs and strays', who were currently living at Germaine's house. She is a 'generous host to various passers-through, she always has a collection of the wounded,' she later commented in her account of the visit. She also reflected on the abuse Germaine Greer had to suffer from so many people whom she did not know, and who did not know her. 'Small minds, small spirits affronted by the sheer size and magnetism of the woman.'[18]

Germaine certainly did not see her household as a lonely refuge for the lame and the halt. In 1994, in conversation with writer Duncan Fallowell, she remarked on the similarities between her vision for The Mills and L'abbaye de Thélème. Her reference was to that part of Rabelais' *Gargantua* that describes the Abbey as a kind of utopia where the giants, male and female – all of noble birth, all well-educated with cultivated tastes – lived together under only one rule: '*Fais ce que voudras.*' (Live freely, do what you want.) The inmates of the Abbey could rise from bed when they felt like it, eat and drink when and what they wanted, enjoy their pleasure as they found it. The vision is libertarian, qualified by elitism.

Les gens libres, bien nés bien instruits, conversant en
compagnie honnête, on par nature un instinct et aiguillon,
qui toujours les pousse á de façon, verteuse et fuir le vice;
ils nommaient cela honneur.

(People who are free, well born, well instructed and conversant with honest company, have by nature an instinct and motivation which always makes them act in a virtuous manner and shun vice. They will call this honour.)

So well-educated were the giants that they could read, write, play harmonious instruments, speak five or six languages and write prose and poetry. The men were skilled in riding and jousting, the women, sweet and agreeable, were adept at needlework and other feminine pursuits.

'I don't have a partner. But I have a household ... at the moment,' Greer told Fallowell.

It really is the Abbaye de Thélèmes. Music, painting, laughter, gardening, extremely sensual, very Mediterranean. There's Rita. James and Tom – they're graduate students at Cambridge. Christopher and Shanghai Jim – they're two cats. Livingstone, the parrot. Cecil, the gardener. Paul, the gardener's boy ... My ambition is to run a secular monastery of refined pleasures. But I am perfectly happy to be by myself. The great luxury is to be utterly alone.[19]

As well as being an accomplished cook and hostess, Germaine Greer was a much sought-after guest: her archive holds a multitude of invitations to private and public gatherings of every kind, most of which she politely refused. Although certainly not a recluse, she tended to avoid larger gatherings or to leave early, especially when she did not know most of the company well. In some of her columns, evidence is to be found of her failure to recognise the effects of her appearance and behaviour on others, and of the misunderstandings that could result: on one occasion, for example, when she turned up to a gathering with 'filthy' nails and leaves in her hair she was surprised and annoyed when she overheard someone saying, 'You'd think she'd make an effort.'

'If only they knew,' she commented enigmatically.[20]

For many celebrities, New Year's Eve is a time to see and be seen, but for Germaine it was usually a time of private contemplation. She received some quite spectacular invitations to celebrate the change of the millennium at various events and venues, but she chose not to accept any of them: her plan was to keep to her usual New Year's Eve practice of sorting and ironing her linen in peaceful solitude.[21]

As it turned out, however, when it came to the point she changed her mind and decided to give a millennial bonfire party, which was a great success. The next day, the first of the new millennium, she was out driving her bobcat to dig a 25-metre (80-foot) land drain from one of the goose ponds, for watering the roots of the apple trees in the orchard.

All of Germaine's households reflected her almost religious belief in cooperative living arrangements where groups of like-minded people would share the goods and labour – a socialist model. She wanted everyone in her house to live comfortably, do their fair share of the work and be kind to each other. But it seems she never came to terms with the fact that, in her houses, the system was more capitalist than socialist. *She* owned the wealth and the means of production, and she was not about to give them away. Whenever she came to suspect that any of her protégés might be leeching off her wealth she would turn on them angrily.

Inevitably, complications and conflicts arose. There are many examples. When one friend, whom she had helped in a time of trouble, departed from the house after running up a large telephone bill, leaving a mess and failing to return the house key, she complained about him to a mutual acquaintance, who told him what Germaine was saying about him behind his back. Immediately, he wrote to his former benefactress, protesting his innocence. She replied savagely, accusing him of being 'mentally ill'. She did not want him to pay the £400 phone bill, she informed him, for this was a small price to pay for being rid of him. 'Use the money to pay for your psychiatrist. He's paid to listen to your raving; we weren't and very boring and self-obsessed it was too.'[22]

This friend, like most who became the targets of her anger, retired to lick his wounds and wait her out until she was ready to resume the relationship. Similarly, young Cambridge don Paul McHugh, another good friend, was deeply hurt when she humiliated him in one of her newspaper columns, but he did not want to sever his bonds with her. The son of a New Zealand judge, he never forgot her kindness to his family when she sent magnificent flowers – orchids, lilies, roses, carnations – when his sister, Pauline, was killed in a car accident; but when Germaine wrote her scathing piece about him in *The Independent* of 23 July 1991, he was not going to let her get away with it. 'Your piece in today's *Independent*,' he wrote to her, 'was cruel, vicious, slanted and unnecessary.'

However inept or foolish I may be, I certainly don't think I deserved such sustained public humiliation. The article makes it perfectly plain to most of my colleagues of whom you are speaking/complaining, and it belittles and degrades me. I just cannot understand how or why you would treat me in that way . . . There was no sting in the tail at the end, no warmth or loving ever surfaced, but a succession of lashing and whipping and scornful abuse. It was wrong, hurtful and harmful. You cannot treat one who is so fond of you in such an ad libitum fashion.[23]

It seems the damage Germaine did to this friendship was eventually repaired. Paul and his partner, Andy Hardwick, invited her to their civil partnership ceremony in 2006. (She was unable to attend because she was in Australia at the time.)

Significantly, most of the people Germaine attacked did not want to lose her friendship. Jim Haynes is an early example; another is Ken Tynan, who refused to allow the quarrel they had at Porto Cervo to fester. The day after their disagreement he wrote to her saying that he had been 'astonished' to hear her roaring away that morning on her moped. When she failed to reply, he wrote again to assure her that he still loved her, 'very much'. She was contrite. 'I wonder sometimes if I'll ever learn. It's like banging my head . . . Sometimes the blinds of ego go up and one can see nothing, especially if one feels embattled from the outset.'[24]

But not all conflicts were resolved. Greer's rift with Australian actress Kate Fitzpatrick, for example, never healed: it ended as it had begun, bizarrely. Seven months pregnant by a French architect from whom she was separated, Fitzpatrick was being sheltered by the Australian ambassador in Rome when Germaine, who was more of an acquaintance than a friend, discovered her plight. The thought of rescuing this temporarily defenceless compatriot was irresistible to her, as was the idea that having a baby, a real live baby whom she might almost claim as her own if it was born on her property, might at last be within her grasp. She telephoned the embassy repeatedly until a desperate Fitzpatrick agreed to come to her. The visit started well, although Kate had her reservations.

On the first night, Germaine cooked a wonderful meal of chicken, vegetables and couscous. It was a very pleasant and welcoming introduction. The only cloud was introduced by her free-range cats, who gave me the mother of all asthma attacks. At one moment she kissed one very near its bum and I remember thinking no woman who kisses a cat on the arse is going to kiss my baby.[25]

After that, nothing worked out. It was winter and the heating in the house seemed to be regulated to save on the bills. Like other guests who were sharing the household at the time, Kate was expected to work to earn her keep. Her hostess and protector decreed gardening in the frozen cabbage patch, very difficult for anyone, but torture for a woman who was seven months pregnant. Most bizarrely of all, Germaine was insisting that the baby be born in her own bedroom at The Mills, rather than in a hospital or its mother's room. Without a car, Kate was trapped, and Greer refused to let her go. It was only with the aid of sympathetic friends that the frantic actress eventually managed to smuggle herself out.[26]

Some of Germaine's friendships have lasted a lifetime, but most of these are with people she sees only intermittently – Margaret Fink, who lives in Sydney, is one; another is Ann Polis in Melbourne. Even in England, partly because of her peripatetic lifestyle, her relationships, though warm and loving, do not include the intimate, regular contact that most people expect of a close friendship.

For nearly twenty years, up to and including Germaine's purchase of The Mills, she enjoyed a volatile friendship with Gay Clifford, her old colleague from the University of Warwick. The relationship was fun-filled, competitive, high octane, a meeting of minds. They holidayed together, raced across the motorways of Europe in cars of doubtful roadworthiness, flirted with drivers and passengers in passing cars, infuriated the local gendarmerie and carabinieri. On one occasion they sped across a frozen landscape in an unheated old car, wearing thick fur coats and pretending they were in a troika. On another, they were pursued down the Autostrade by a man in a late-model Ferrari. He kept weaving in and out of the traffic, first passing the two women, then slowing down so they would have to pass him. At every roadside cafe he gestured, inviting them to lunch. Germaine was all for accepting, but Gay, the driver, pressed on until she had to pull aside for petrol. Seizing his chance, the Ferrari driver screeched up behind them. They all got out of their cars and looked at each other. He was stunned by the unexpectedly tall stature and beauty of these two Amazonian women. They took one look at him and collapsed into helpless laughter, for he was short and squat, pot-bellied and bald.

One Christmas at Pianelli, Germaine awoke to find that her friend had placed at the foot of her bed a red stocking filled with small presents she had chosen with extraordinary taste and care: six little tortoiseshell buttons, a phial of bergamot oil, a marzipan cat, a necklace of Venetian glass daisies, a nutmeg holder. Germaine wondered then if she understood anyone as well as Gay understood her.

But the friendship was marred by petty conflicts and mis-understandings. The two continued to share good and bad times, but Germaine's life was so crowded that those times were often rushed, and she hardly had time to notice, as her relationships collapsed around her and hoped-for babies never arrived, that Gay was falling into depression, physical illness and alcoholism. According to Germaine, 'she made herself a mad maenad who terrorised hostesses, devastated dinner parties, mumbled or bawded her way through poetry readings, amazed and appalled her students, and had occasionally to be dragged, unconscious, out of the lavatories at University College.'[27]

One evening, about a year before Germaine left London to live in Essex, she invited Gay to a dinner party at her flat at 20 Westbourne Terrace. She was annoyed when Gay failed to appear, putting it down to her growing eccentricity and unreliability. Eventually, the downstairs bell rang, but there was still no sign of Gay. Twenty minutes later, Germaine went down and found her friend wandering around the stairwell, completely disorientated. Later she deeply regretted that she had mistaken the signs of serious illness for drunkenness.

Then, on Christmas Eve 1984, disaster struck when Gay's brain was devastated by a cerebral haemorrhage. Germaine visited her in hospital, lay her head beside her friend's on the pillow and read to her – mostly the poems Gay had written herself. She was not sure if Gay had any brain function at all, for she could only respond with distressed, incoherent sounds.

At the time of Gay's collapse, Germaine was frantically busy with radio, television and speaking engagements, her travels, her writing, negotiating the sale of her London properties, buying The Mills and deciding how she would renovate it. Hoping to find a way of helping Gay's parents, Freddie and Pam, to look after Gay, she hit upon a plan to build a special accommodation unit at The Mills for her, and to become responsible for her care. 'We could make you up a set of study-bedroom and own bathroom,' she wrote to Gay. 'Please understand that I'm not making this offer out of pity because I think Pam and Freddie can't cope . . . I want my big house to be useful and alive.'[28] And in another letter, written on 16 March 1986, 'Please let me look after you in my impersonal way for a space; Freddie and Pam need a rest from you as much as you need a rest from them. And dammit, I need to feel useful from time to time . . . My motives are not that I wish to feel myself a great and grand-hearted prima donna at your expense. I simply want the great relief of having you to talk to . . .'[29]

This letter suggests great generosity but also a lack of empathy on Germaine's part. She had not yet understood that Gay was now a different person, much diminished in her ability, who could not be cajoled, as in the old days, into accepting her largesse. Reality asserted itself, however, when she took Gay to Pianelli for a four-week holiday in July 1986. When they came back to London she had to tell Pam and Freddie that her proposal to provide sheltered accommodation for Gay at The Mills was not going to work, for Gay needed far more help than she would be able to give her. 'After living with Gay for a month,' she wrote, 'during most of which time I was her sole companion and nurse, I have unwillingly come to the conclusion that she is a very sick woman indeed. From some points of view, taking her to Pianelli was simply silly.'[30]

Pam and Freddie Clifford's letters to Germaine at this time are full of love and gratitude. With the wisdom of an older generation, Pam, especially, was able to recognise in Germaine the qualities of steadfastness and loyalty added to intellect and a sense of fun that had charmed so many of her friends and acquaintances, from the nuns at Star of the Sea to Federico Fellini.

In the years that followed, Germaine grew ever closer to Pam and Freddie, who had taken their daughter home to their house in London and, later, acting on Germaine's suggestion, to a house they had bought in Gloucestershire. Over time, with the best treatment and medication, Gay regained the ability to speak, but she had little sense of time and space, very little short-term memory, and was dependent on her loving carers for most of her physical needs.

Before Gay died, Germaine initiated a project that gave her parents great solace. She decided, with their help and involvement, to collect and publish Gay's poems. 'I know this book cannot be sold on the poetry alone,' she told a representative of the publisher, Hamish Hamilton. 'It is important to think of it as a hybrid, the story of a friendship, an account of poetry and fragments of an elegant mind that has been smashed.' The book, titled *Poems by Gay Clifford*, was published in 1990. The long introduction, written by Germaine, gives a love-filled yet honest account of their friendship.[31]

Germaine also gave the address at the thanksgiving service for the life of Gay Clifford, which was held at Holy Trinity Church, Minchinhampton, on 6 August 1998. Speaking without notes, she provided insight not only into the friendship, but also into her own capacity to sustain relationships. 'Gay Clifford was my friend,' she began. 'To be a writer's friend is a difficult thing. As a friend I am disloyal, distracted, forgetful, busy. I regard myself, really, as a rather hopeless sort of friend.'[32]

Some who considered themselves to be Germaine's friends were inclined to agree with her. All too often, partly because of her frenetic way of life and partly for other reasons to do with her conflicted personality, relationships that may have become close, even intimate, did not develop. Her association with one fellow Australian, publisher and founder of Virago Modern Classics Carmen Callil, is a case in point.[33]

Callil (who was made a Dame of the British Empire in 2017) and Germaine Greer had much in common. Carmen was born in Melbourne on what she described as a Black Friday – because it was one of the coldest days on record – in July 1938. Germaine was born in the same city three weeks after *the* famous Black Friday, 13 January 1939, then the hottest day on record. They grew up living a few kilometres apart on Melbourne's bayside, Carmen in the wealthy suburb of Brighton, Germaine in nearby Elwood and Sandringham. Both were educated in Melbourne convents, Germaine at Star of the Sea, Carmen at Loreto Mandeville Hall. Both attended the University of Melbourne in the late 1950s.

Over the years, some reports in the media created a false impression that the two Australians were close friends who had been at school together in Australia. They had known each other at Melbourne University, but their association did not develop until they found themselves mixing in the same literary circles in 1960s London and having to cope with what Carmen later described as the 'occasional tedium of British superciliousness' towards Australians. The two met frequently when Callil was heavily involved in the publicity for the publication of *The Female Eunuch* in Britain. Sonny Mehta was a mutual friend.

Later, Carmen recalled that, despite the similarities in their respective backgrounds, Germaine always seemed quite indifferent to her. 'She was a star and I was not and I always found her entirely uninterested in me,' she recalled in 2017. 'Years and years later, I realised this was not anything in particular but part of her general personality i.e. the price she paid for her genius and fame was – perhaps – lack of great interest in the minutiae of other peoples' lives or the sort of things that make for close friendships. I could be wrong.'[34]

In her write-up of a conversation between herself and Carmen Callil published in *Vogue* magazine, Germaine pointed out the media's mistake in assuming that she and Carmen were close friends. 'We do not know each other very well,' she wrote. 'Both of us are feminist to the marrow, and both of us have a taut and difficult relationship with other feminists who underestimate the struggle we have had and overestimate the degree of acceptance we have had from the male establishment. We have come to expect less loyalty and less consideration from our sisters than from any other quarter.'

The discussion moved on to friendship. In the past, said Carmen, she had made some efforts to become closer to Germaine. One Christmas she had even come to see her, but Germaine had no time to talk to her. Did Germaine have any close friends? Carmen described her relationship with several women whom she spoke to on the telephone at least three times a week and saw most weekends. Germaine had fallen silent, but Carmen persevered. Did Germaine have any friends like that? 'No, I don't,' she responded.

Carmen speculated that this may be because Germaine was travelling all the time – or maybe because she was 'daunting'. Germaine sidestepped the issue, shutting off further discussion of this thorny question. 'She told me she could not put me on her friends' list and phone me three times a week, because I was a genius. I'm no more of a genius than Carmen Callil is a bitch. By such stereotypes are women still pitted against women.'[35]

Germaine Greer may well have struggled with issues involving intimacy and close friendship, but her concern for people in need seemed to increase as the years went on. In 1994, she placed an offer in *The Big Issue* for homeless people to write to her, care of the magazine, and tell her why they might like to live with her. Other newspapers picked up the story and, predictably, her generous but naive request elicited responses from numerous fake homeless people, mainly journalists in search of good copy. She welcomed the first man who arrived on her doorstep with such friendliness and courtesy that he left, ashamed and embarrassed. The second was a curly headed boy on crutches. He carried a bedroll that was strangely clean, and offered to cook and work in the garden. Germaine took his (expensive) jeans to wash while he had a bath, and then she cooked for him. At 11 pm another imposter arrived. His mouth reminded her of a pig's anus, so she got rid of him. The next day, the phone rang constantly with more pleas from the 'homeless'. By now the press were hovering, planes were circling over her house, and photographers managed to capture images of the man with the challenged mouth as he walked away from her door disconsolately. The boy on crutches remained safely inside until Shelley, Germaine's assistant, who agreed with her employer that he was probably brain-damaged, took him to the supermarket to buy some food and underwear. When they returned, Germaine tried to teach him how to bake bread.

That night he left quietly after going through her bathroom cupboard and listing the contents, which he subsequently revealed in the three-page article he wrote for the *Mail on Sunday*. He left £30 and a note of thanks, signed with his true name, Martin Hennessey.

'He was a slug who trailed his slime across my doormat,' wrote Greer in her regular *Guardian* column, declaring her intention to sue Hennessey and the *Daily Mail*. *The Guardian*, however, was having a field day with the story. 'Having got on the wrong side of Germaine Greer in her student days,' wrote Simon Hoggart in that newspaper on 8 February 1994, 'I know she is a persistent and effective hater. Mr Hennessey's next few decades are going to be disagreeable.'[36]

Germaine demanded a retraction and threatened to sue. In the same week, she faxed *Guardian* journalist Joanna Coles, who had called her 'promiscuous', informing her that this statement was actionable.[37]

She may or may not have been a good hater, as Simon Hoggart claimed, but she could certainly be lethal in response to perceived insults. In 2000, the disc jockey John Peel disclosed in a BBC television interview that he had been seduced by Germaine Greer in the 1960s. Sensing a good story, editor of the *Daily Telegraph* Richard Preston asked Germaine to respond. He was not disappointed. She regarded John Peel as a friend, she wrote in her next column, and did not want to 'dish the dirt on him', but since he had not extended the same courtesy to her . . .

So unremarkable was the alleged sexual encounter, she continued, that she had no memory of it. She could remember, however, accompanying him to a concert at the Albert Hall, wearing shoes with four-inch heels and 'swishing' along in gunmetal blue silk trousers. It was a glorious summer day and she was enjoying herself until, out of the blue, Peel informed her that he had gonorrhoea. She suffered through the rest of the concert knowing that she would have to run the gauntlet of the 'Clap Clinic' the next morning and make some embarrassing phone calls to people she had recently had sex with.

If any reader doubted her story, she said in conclusion, she was prepared to offer as evidence her blue card from the clinic with its negative results, and a photograph of herself and Peel sitting on the stage of the Albert Hall on the day of the concert.[38]

She may well have wanted to deal similarly with some of those disturbed people whose letters she kept in a special drawer of a filing cabinet, labelled 'Nutters', but they were too many, and most of them chose to be anonymous. Some of these letters were very nasty indeed. Religious nutters sent her copies of biblical texts, accusing her, often in the most vile terms, of corrupting others by being corrupt herself. One Muslim man wanted to take her as his second wife. They could be married at the Egyptian Embassy in Canberra. 'I will take you by force! I want a son, remember, but a daughter would be nice too. We will have a house by Christmas!'[39]

Some threatening letters were of the chain variety, attempting to pass on the evil. Many were obscene and venomous. 'Shut your mouth fucken bitch or I'll slam you in your fucken mouth and give you equal rites [sic]' being one example among many. Some were self-righteously censorious, but still hurtful: 'This surely is woman's role to make a haven for her family, and in doing so to bring the greatest happiness it is possible to have . . . I am afraid you will never know this.' Some letters were endearingly eccentric. One anonymous man who signed himself 'Old Pink Male Person', for example, told her he sincerely believed she should be elected Pope.[40]

A file in Unit 79 of the General Correspondence section of the Greer archive contains thirteen letters that, in accordance with Germaine's directions to her assistant, have never been opened. These letters, and many others that were opened, were from well-known Australian actor, theatre director and writer Peter O'Shaughnessy, who, for more than thirty years, insisted on bombarding Germaine Greer with unwanted demands for her friendship and recognition of his talents.

O'Shaughnessy, nearly twenty years older than Germaine, had been a leader in the Melbourne Drift; he was a well-known identity at the Swanston Family Hotel in the 1950s and, later, the Royal George in Sydney. A mentor of Barry Humphries and acquaintance of Push stars including Margaret Fink, he had, over the years, followed Germaine Greer's career with an interest that bordered on obsession. His letters to her go back at least as far as 1982. At first, she tried to acknowledge them politely but made it clear she was not interested in resuming a by-now defunct relationship. He persevered. In July 1999, he wrote seeking an invitation for himself and his daughter and grandson to spend a weekend with her at The Mills so that he could share with her his ideas on Shakespeare. Exasperated, Germaine made her position clear. Through her assistant, she replied: 'Professor Greer desires me to inform you she has no desire to entertain you and your family at her house or to discuss Shakespeare with you.'

By 2011, Greer felt herself to be increasingly under siege as the letters kept coming. O'Shaughnessy had even started to pester Margaret Fink, recalling their old association and demanding that she use her influence with Germaine to get her to talk to him. Matters came to a head in 2013, when the now-octogenarian O'Shaughnessy embraced digital technology to denigrate Greer on his website and threaten to publish personal information about her, including her address at The Mills, on Facebook and Twitter. Distressed, Germaine considered legal options, including an injunction, but she knew that any such efforts to silence him would be nerve-racking and expensive. Tension mounted until the issue was resolved by his death, at age 89, in July 2013.[41]

The real worry was that written threats from all sorts of disturbed people would be followed by action. Typical of the generous side of Germaine's nature was that she worried about the welfare of her mentally ill correspondents. When she received a letter from an anonymous young person who threatened to show up in Cambridge during May Week, dressed as Johnny Rotten, and do 'one last pogo' to the strains of 'God Save the Queen' before setting fire to herself and jumping into the River

Cam, she forwarded it to the Cambridge Constabulary. 'You will understand that I could hardly live with myself after getting such a letter if I did open my local newspaper and found that a young person had died in this way, and I had done nothing to prevent it,' she wrote in a covering letter. The police replied that they were liaising with the university authorities; the writer had been identified and 'those responsible for this young lady have been alerted to her problems'.[42]

The outcome of some correspondence with another young girl was much less satisfactory. On 23 April 2000, guests who arrived to take Greer out to dinner discovered that she had been taken virtual hostage in her home by a besotted, apparently deranged nineteen-year-old student from Bath University, who kept calling her 'Mummy' and clinging to her legs. More of the story unfolded during the subsequent court case, in which the girl was acquitted of charges of causing actual bodily harm and imprisonment, but convicted of harassment. This young woman had been exchanging letters with Greer for some time, regarding her as 'a spiritual mother figure'. Realising that the girl's letters were becoming increasingly frequent and disjointed, Germaine asked her to stop writing, but the letters kept coming. On 21 April, the student arrived at The Mills, saying that she was camping out in a nearby field. Germaine took pity on her and allowed her to sleep for one night in a spare room. The next day she drove her to the closest railway station, but at about midnight the young woman was back at the house, frantically ringing the doorbell. Greer called the police and the girl was carried off by two officers, only to return the next day, which was when the assault occurred. The two women struggled violently for two hours; furniture was broken and a telephone was ripped from the wall before Greer's dinner companions arrived and the 'siege' ended.

The following day, a cool Professor Greer held an impromptu press conference outside her home. 'I am not angry,' she told the assembled journalists, 'I am not upset. I am not hurt. I am fine. I haven't lost my sense of humour. I am not the victim here.'

In court, with her parents in the public gallery, the young woman said: 'I knew it was wrong but I did it. I went to hug her and there was a struggle. I was continually confused by her. I never knew whether she wanted to see me or not. I saw her as a motherly kind of figure, but it was not infatuation.'[43]

Six years later, Germaine was enraged when she discovered that an Australian playwright, Joanna Murray-Smith, had written a play that was obviously based on this incident, and that the main protagonist, played by Eileen Atkins, was a caricature of herself. *The Female of the Species*, a satire about second-wave feminism, tells the story of Margot Mason, celebrity feminist and author of bestselling tracts '*The Cerebral Vagina*', '*Madame Ovary*', '*Love and Other Four-Letter Words*' and '*The Complete Insignificance of Male Sexuality*', who lives more or less alone on a rural estate in the English countryside. As the play opens, Margot, who is suffering from writer's block, is ending an abusive telephone conversation with her publisher when the French doors to her study open to admit Molly, a former student of hers, who threatens her with a gun and handcuffs her to her desk. Molly is obsessed by the belief that reading *The Cerebral Vagina* caused her mother to give her away as a baby before she killed herself. Following the feminist credo, she, Molly, had herself sterilised to preserve her creativity, but felt destroyed when her teacher, Margot, told her she had no talent.

The play proceeds to its hilarious conclusion when Margot's daughter, Tess, Tess's caring but dull stockbroker husband, the high-voiced publisher and even a macho taxidriver turn up to join in the argument, all commenting on Margot's lewd books, her inconsistent views and her failings as a mother and a woman. Tess agrees that her mother deserves to be shot.

In July 2008, Murray-Smith was less than convincing when she claimed that Margot Mason was not a character portrait of Greer. ('It would take a braver woman than me to write about Greer directly.') Greer herself was not deceived. 'She holds feminism in contempt,' she told *Telegraph* journalist Laura Clout, calling the play 'threadbare' though she claimed not to have read it. 'What are they doing putting this play on in the West End?' she queried regally before taking aim, with devastating precision, at twin targets Murray-Smith and a country she had reason to dislike: 'Auckland in New Zealand, maybe . . .'[44]

In more serious vein, Greer later drew attention to a problem faced by all celebrities – the conflation of their public image with their personal lives. The invasion of her home by the young student happened only three years after Princess Diana's death had opened the eyes of a shocked public to the damage that could be done to vulnerable people – celebrity status notwithstanding – by the media's greedy attempts to satisfy the prurient appetites of their mass audience. In a piece for the BBC's Radio 4, Greer commented:

> Murray-Smith . . . has not yet realised that [Margot] is a real person who lives in England. [The young girl] was then a 19-year-old student (not one of mine) who was suffering from Obsessive Compulsive Disorder . . . She is still probably under an injunction to keep 15 miles away from me but she inveigled the magistrate into giving her permission to visit the Cambridge University Library where there is so little in the way of surveillance or security that gentlemen

so inclined can bugger each other ad libitum in the privacy of the stacks.

Eileen Atkins will do a very good impersonation of me, and I'll bet no one has warned her that this could place her in immediate physical danger. How the perpetrator will react to an impersonation of herself is incalculable. In the play she has a gun. If she turns up with a gun again, I've had it.[45]

Murray-Smith's attempt to inquire into the private life of the public institution that was Germaine Greer caused her, like David Plante and others who attempted the same feat, to be attacked and vilified by her subject. Of these intrepid people, none is more significant than Christine Wallace, who, in the 1990s, wrote the first (and, to date, only) biography of Germaine Greer, titled *Untamed Shrew*.

Wallace is a respected Australian journalist, writer and academic. At the time of writing *Untamed Shrew* she was a member of the Canberra Press Gallery writing for the *Australian Financial Review*. She had previously written a biography of the then Liberal Party Opposition Leader John Hewson, who lost the so-called 'unlosable' 1993 federal election to Labor's Paul Keating. As well as underlining the extent and roots of Hewson's neoliberal policy agenda, Wallace's biography included previously undisclosed details of his tax minimisation practices, taking some paint off a leader who had been considered 'above' politics. Swimming against the tide of press gallery opinion, she was one of only three journalists to correctly predict a Keating win.

Still in her thirties when she wrote her biography of Greer, Wallace was a strong feminist of the younger generation that profited from the gains of the second wave but was beginning to question some of its assumptions. One aim of the biography was to investigate 'the profound disjuncture' in the way Greer's books were received by the majority of baby boomers versus the committed feminists among them. Wallace noted that more knowledgeable feminists, especially senior figures in the American women's liberation movement, had serious reservations about aspects of Greer's approach. Why were 'Germaine' and '*The Female Eunuch*' still so often, in the 1990s, the first words from the mouths of 'ordinary' women in Australia, Britain and even the United States when one raised feminism, at the same time as her books were virtually invisible on the reading lists of the burgeoning Women's Studies courses at universities? Wallace set out to solve that conundrum and puzzle out how and where Greer fitted into the feminist pantheon.

Wallace could see the value of following an approach that combined biography with critical review, and believed it was important to capture the convictions and achievements of significant second-wave feminists like Greer before they were lost in memory or obscured by later work. 'Rediscovering the value, as well as dismissing the dross in their pioneering contribution is a valuable endeavour for a movement prone to historical amnesia,' she wrote in her foreword to *Untamed Shrew*.

Before she started work on the biography, Wallace wrote to Greer outlining the project and requesting help, beginning with an interview. Greer's response was perfunctory and rude: she accused all biographers of being parasites and demanded Wallace wait till she, Greer, was dead before writing about her. Wallace replied, engaging with the substance of Greer's arguments. Surely it was better, especially in the case of someone who had led as full a life as Germaine, to be able to check and correct stories, eliminating errors and falsehoods, while Greer was alive? Had not Greer herself written extensively about living subjects without compunction, including close family members, so wasn't there a consistency problem inherent in the rebuff?, she continued. Greer wrote back via her agent, telling Wallace to 'publish and be damned'. Little did Wallace know that respected biographer Hazel Rowley had only just prior to this exchange received the same bruising treatment from Greer. So shaken was Rowley she decided to work only on dead subjects in the future, and so big an imprint did the exchange make that it would be mentioned in recollections at Rowley's memorial service.

Undeterred, however, Wallace went ahead. She explained to those she approached that her biography was not authorised but that authorised biographies in any case often lacked credibility, tending to the hagiographical. Her own approach, she said, would be independent, sympathetic and critically engaged. She began in Melbourne, talking first with Greer's mother, well before Greer issued her threat to 'kneecap' Wallace should she do so. Then Wallace sought out friends and teachers of Greer's from Star of the Sea convent school and Melbourne University, then friends in Sydney from Sydney University and the Push. Wallace then went to the United States, where she interviewed titans of second-wave feminism including Kate Millett, Gloria Steinem and Jill Johnston about Greer, before going on to England.

'There was an inverse relationship between proximity to Germaine and a willingness to talk,' Wallace said.

> Everyone in Australia, where people are not easily intimidated, and likewise the US, happily contributed, but in England there was a reluctance which deepened the closer one got to Cambridge near which Greer lived. People seemed genuinely fearful of Greer's rage. As one person who declined an interview said, "We have to live with her."[46]

Wallace did not give up hope that Greer might ultimately be persuaded to understand how well motivated the biography was and, despite the brutal opening rebuffs, asked Greer twice more for interviews: once before leaving the United States to come to England, the other while she was in Cambridge, to no avail.

Greer's column in *The Guardian* on 31 October 1994 was influential in shutting down sources in England against Wallace. Those who wrote about the lives of living people, she opined, were akin to malign, flesh-eating bacteria that fed off living organisms and caused them 'toxic shock, paralysis and death'. Other, probably libellous, epithets for Wallace included 'dung beetle', 'amoeba' and 'brain-dead hack.' She expected that her friends would refuse to speak with Wallace. 'Nobody actually wants to sit down and have an hour's conversation with a tapeworm.' Her friends could make their own decisions, but they would no longer be her friends if they chose poorly. Even more was she appalled that Wallace had had the effrontery to request a meeting with herself, in Cambridge. 'I'd no more want to clap eyes on this individual than I want to study a slide of my intestinal flora.' Then she switched from bullying attack to pathetic victim mode: after she made the mistake of reading former husband Paul du Feu's book about her, she wrote, she was 'so crippled with self-doubt that I could hardly manage the simplest intellectual task. Writing was entirely beyond me.'

Greer also wrote to her solicitor in an (unsuccessful) attempt to have the book blocked or, at least, modified. She enclosed a copy of a letter of protest she had written to the managing editor of Pan Macmillan, Wallace's publisher. Once again, she claimed that the chief cause of her opposition was a desire to protect her family. She was concerned about her mother, 'who is nowadays very disinhibited and can talk with great violence', and her uncle, who was dying of prostate cancer. 'My own privacy is a lost cause,' she said (truthfully, but conveniently overlooking the fact that she herself had been the chief source of information about herself and her mother). 'Is there anything I can do,' she continued, 'to limit the damage to my unfortunate family? Wallace is not the first, and I fear she is far from the last to hit upon the bright idea of ripping me off.'[47]

Members of the Canberra Press Gallery are not known for their timidity or oversensitivity to criticism. Wallace was tough, but she was deeply wounded by this public attack on her professional integrity. Her response to Greer, published in *The Guardian* of Wednesday 2 November 1994, was elegant and to the point. 'Germaine Greer's rich organic metaphors made interesting reading. However, like compost, her analysis contained much heat but no light.'[48]

When she had tried to persuade Greer of the obvious benefit of writing about living people rather than dead ones, Wallace continued, Greer had failed to respond. Nor had she cared to comment on the fact that she herself had written freely, often abusively, about living figures ranging from her own mother to Mother Teresa. 'The contradiction glares,' said Wallace, with obvious justification. When Jill Neville, long-time expatriate Australian writer in London and Richard Neville's sister, went ahead with a planned interview despite Greer's *Guardian* tirade, Wallace was touched that not everybody had run scared. As they sat together in The Three Greyhounds pub in Soho, Neville comforted her that writing books was never easy in the best of circumstances, and that these circumstances were particularly difficult.

Greer never relented. While preparing the book for publication, Wallace wrote another polite letter to her subject requesting permission to reproduce a photo of her by Diane Arbus. Greer simply annotated the letter 'Ignore'.

Most people assumed at the time that Greer's opposition to Wallace's biography was based on privacy concerns, given her subject's flamboyant lifestyle. But, as Wallace pointed out, no one could write anything about Germaine's life that Germaine had not already copiously written about herself. In the end she concluded Greer's wrath was fuelled by intellectual insecurity: that she worried that her oeuvre did not hang together well on close inspection and would not stand up to scrutiny. Wallace did indeed find that body of work contained twists and turns that Greer failed to reconcile as she moved from one theme to another, and sometimes outright contradictions. However, she also concluded that this did not undercut Greer's significance in the second wave as a great international populariser of feminist revolt, especially among 'ordinary' women. Greer was a maverick feminist, she wrote, whose refusal to surrender her sovereignty as a woman inspired others to assert their own.

Nevertheless, Germaine continued to rail against and threaten the reception of a book that intelligently recorded and generously judged her achievements while sympathetically handling her human frailties and flaws. Wallace believes that Germaine's attacks on *Untamed Shrew* led to fewer people reading the book than otherwise would have – as it turned out, a Greer 'own goal'.[49]

•

Germaine Greer was in her mid-forties when *Sex and Destiny* was published in January 1984. Soon to become moderately happy and settled at The Mills, she had friends, admirers, detractors and enemies aplenty, but there were no enduring romantic partners, no children – just herself, with her brilliant, restless mind, her frequent headaches and other health problems, her complex, difficult personality, her garden and her animals. Maybe now was the time to confront the personal demons, rooted in her childhood, that she had hitherto been unable to exorcise.

She had seen relatively little of her family in the years since she left Australia for England in 1964. Her mother was still working on her tan and figure on the beach at Mentone, but, perhaps inspired by Germaine's success, she had also studied to pass her matriculation. Like so many women who had not been able to go to university in their youth, Peggy took advantage of one of the government programs that followed the feminist revolution to study for an Arts degree, majoring in literature and Italian.

In spite of her claim to be an advocate for women's education, Germaine was scathing about her mother's efforts: 'She's now taking some ludicrous academic course,' she told *Sydney Morning Herald* journalist Tina Brown. 'I do disapprove of the taxpayers' money going on educational programs invented to keep old women off the streets.'[50]

When Germaine travelled to Australia in 1971–72 to promote *The Female Eunuch*, Peggy Greer was not at home to greet her daughter, for she had flown off on an extended European trip to escape – so she said – all the commotion of journalists beating at her door. Germaine spent only a few days in Melbourne, ostensibly with 'family', in December, before she flew on to Sydney for the 'business' part of her promotional tour. It seems that she did not see her father at that time either, for she said later that they met again for the first time in 1981, seventeen years after she left Australia for England.

This meeting, which she describes in her most personal book, *Daddy, We Hardly Knew You*, must have been extraordinarily upsetting for both father and daughter. They had lunch in a popular Melbourne restaurant – two good-looking, stylishly dressed people. Reg was his most charming self – 'suave' and 'droll'. Their conversation was light, peppered with wit and ironic humour, for they were both good at that sort of thing; but a mass of unspeakably painful memories and regrets welled up through the banter, threatening to overwhelm them.[51]

A couple of days after the lunch Germaine telephoned her father. Maintaining his facade of jovial man about town, he tried to make a joke of what had happened to him after he left the restaurant. He had been walking across Princes Bridge, he told her, to where he had parked his car, when he had felt violently sick and soiled himself in the pants of his beautiful cream silk suit.

Germaine told her father that she would like to see him again, but Reg politely refused her request. Germaine realised, not for the first time, that beneath all the bonhomie, Reg Greer was a severely damaged man. She was a source of stress to him and he could not again allow her to puncture his fragile defences.

In 1984, Jane Greer, now Jane Burke, telephoned her sister in England to tell her that their father wanted to see her. After hurriedly getting her affairs in order, Germaine set off for Melbourne, where she found her father living in distressing circumstances.

> . . . a hostel, a shabby weatherboard house where derelicts
> of one sort or another could be fed and housed two or three
> to a room in return for their pension cheques, out of which
> the management would take its profit.[52]

When the two sisters arrived at the house, they were met by the proprietor, a grubby individual wearing a singlet and shorts, a cigarette hanging from his mouth. He showed them into a room where an assortment of broken, ill-cared for old men sat in front of a booming television without watching it. 'They were all too busy cackling, raving, mouthing obscenities, scratching themselves or cursing. Over all hung a miasma of frying fat and the scent of tinned baked beans.' In a chair at the back of the room sat Reg Greer.

Jane fled out into the garden, weeping, as Germaine approached her father. Courteous as ever, he rose to greet her and take her arm. They went to his room, which was bare of all possessions. It seemed to Germaine that he had nothing and was nothing.

True to form, she blamed her mother for turning Reg out of his own home and committing him to this awful place, an accusation Peg later denied. Knowing that their father had certain rights and privileges as 'a returned man', Jane and Germaine went straight to the Returned Services League (RSL). Characteristically for them both, they went to the man who was at the top of the organisation, Bruce Ruxton, the controversial, iron-willed president of the Victorian branch. Ruxton was as stubborn and self-opinionated as Germaine. Unlike her, he was an arch-conservative, but he had a sharp sense of humour to which she immediately responded. He was notorious for his loud mouth and his views on every topic, from feminism to imperialism, were at the opposite ends of the spectrum to Germaine's. Yet the two formed an immediate bond which would grow into a lasting, if unlikely, friendship. Their correspondence is now held in the Greer archive: like a proud uncle, Ruxton would regularly cut out articles about Germaine from Australian newspapers, affix them to a sheet of paper, and send them to her.

Reg had never been an active RSL member, although he had worn the badge to prove his wartime credentials. He did not go to reunions or march on Anzac Day, but with Ruxton's powerful support, his military records were soon located and his medical diagnosis, 'Anxiety Neurosis', discovered. 'We've got more old soldiers suffer from anxiety neurosis than heart disease,' said Ruxton. 'There's no need to distress the old man anymore.' A place was found for him at an RSL retirement home and Germaine returned to England. She did not see her father again, for he died in April 1984, about three months after her final visit to him.

Reg's death left Germaine utterly conflicted. Here was the man whom she had tried so hard to please throughout her childhood, but who had constantly pushed her away, physically and emotionally, the non-father who took no interest in her achievements, who was unfailingly polite, often amusing, but never truly present in her life. Even in death he had rejected her. 'The greatest grief of my whole life,' she told writer Duncan Fallowell, as he was interviewing her in 'the velvety luxury of the Montcalm Hotel in London's West End' (she drank champagne throughout), 'was realising it was too late . . .' Unlike her mother, sister and brother, she was not even mentioned in her father's will.[53]

She could see herself in Reg Greer, his long face and limbs, his hands, his ability to charm, his skill as a performer, his nose for an advertising or promotional opportunity. In getting to know him, might she finally come to understand herself?

But how would this be possible after death, when so much about his life remained a mystery? She knew he had been somehow connected with army intelligence and the top-secret Enigma project. She knew that after his service in Malta he had been sent to Deolali in India, where there was a psychiatric institution for war-damaged soldiers. Had her father perhaps been treated there with electroconvulsive therapy to erase all memory of the secrets he must never be permitted to divulge? Had the army turned him into a zombie; a silent, manageable zombie who was not so much unwilling as incapable of embracing his little child when he came back from the war?

Such were Germaine's thoughts when she returned to England after her father's funeral. As usual, she shared them with friends in literary circles, including publishers. They soon realised that there was a story here, and that this story, if told by Germaine herself, would have high commercial potential. She needed no convincing, and after some wheeling and dealing managed by herself and her agent, she agreed to accept the very large sum of £110,000 from the publisher Hamish Hamilton as an advance on a chronicle which would describe her search for her father across four continents.

'Hamish Hamilton have paid me a lot of money to write a book about [Reg],' Germaine told her mother, in answer to Peggy's question as to why she was doing this. She felt she could not begin to explain the rest of the truth about her motives, and she thought her mother would find the money incentive easy to understand. 'Gee, I'm glad I don't have to do that to earn a crust,' replied Peg.[54]

Germaine started to write this, her most personal book, which she called *Daddy, We Hardly Knew You*, at Pianelli in the European winter of 1986, nearly two years after her father's death. In her desk, she found the old notebook in which she had begun to plan *The Female Eunuch*. She opened it and commenced: 'Here we go, Daddy, in at the deep end. . . .' Two days later, she drove away from her cottage, alone, down the hill, to begin her latest journey to the other side of the world. Her little elderly cat followed her out to the gate and watched her leave. She did not know that she would never see him again.

Daddy, We Hardly Knew You tells of Germaine Greer's attempts to discover the truth about her father, but it also reveals how she began to find out the truth about herself. In the third chapter she describes how, on the first leg of her journey of discovery, she was already made to feel alienated from her homeland. On her arrival in Melbourne, not able to understand the Greek Australian accent of the taxidriver who drove her from the airport, she insulted him by trying to communicate with him in Greek. 'Did I think he couldn't understand English or something? Impossible to understand that it was I who couldn't understand Australian.' Then came her experience at a Melbourne racetrack when she attempted to take a bottle of champagne out onto the lawn, only to be told, when she protested that this was acceptable in Europe, to 'go back to where she came from'. She was used to hearing this in Europe, she commented, but it felt strange to be ordered out of her own country. Could it be that she had no country of her own?

The book goes on to tell of the long search for her father that took Germaine from Tasmania, where she believed he had lived as a child, to outback Australia, where he said he had gone jackerooing, to South Africa, where he claimed to have been born, to India and Malta, where he served in the war. She spent hours and hours fighting the petty intransigence of clerks in libraries and public records offices; she sent letters off to a multitude of people whom she thought might know something about an Eric Reginald Greer; she appealed to listeners and viewers on the radio and on TV; she trawled the newspapers of countries from five continents. She found hundreds of Greers and even, in Ireland, a Greerstown. She became a Greer expert. Various Greers wrote to thank her for helping them add information to their family trees, but she found no evidence that her father had ever been a member of any Greer family. He was not a Greer, and therefore, neither was she.

What she finally managed to find out about her father – the truth – was this.

His whole life was built on a series of lies and a spiv-like bravado that came easily to him, especially as a young man. When he attended the military recruitment office in Collins Street in 1941 to volunteer for officer training under the Empire Air Training Scheme he lied in almost every detail of the information he provided. He was not born in South Africa; his parents were not English; the father he described as 'Robert Greer' never existed; he completed no public examinations at the high school he attended for only two months in Launceston; he played little or no organised sport; he was never an officer cadet, never a journalist and, at that time, had never been manager of a newspaper office or department.

Reg Greer probably never knew his legal family name. It was not Greer. It was not even Greeney, the name Germaine eventually discovered on his school register. It was King, and the story of his birth and subsequent adoption is tragic, though not untypical of the period.

His biological mother, Germaine's grandmother, was Rhoda Elizabeth King, the daughter of a poor family of convict stock, who worked on the estate of a prosperous landowner near Deloraine, Tasmania. In her teens, Rhoda went into service in Ulverstone, a small town some one hundred kilometres from the larger city of Launceston. At Christmastime 1903, she became pregnant, left her job, and fled to Launceston. Her child, Germaine's father, was born in a small house in Middle Street, Launceston, on 1 September 1904. Unable to keep her baby, Rhoda gave him into the care of Emma Greeney, a married woman who had recently lost a child of her own. The name entered on the birth certificate was Robert Hamilton King.

He had been given his mother's surname in accordance with the custom of the time for 'illegitimate' children. The space for the father's name was left blank. Germaine suspected that it was probably 'Hamilton', since this name did not appear on any records for the King family.

On 9 November 1904, Emma Greeney took 'her' five-week-old baby to St John's Church in Launceston to be christened Robert Henry Eric Ernest. A father's name which looked something like 'Hambett' was entered on the baptismal certificate, but it was scrawled and hard to decipher. Germaine suspected that the curate who made the entry was protecting someone, for there was a Richard Robert Ernest Hamilton who was living in Ulverstone at that time as one of the town's most upright and respectable citizens. He was born at Colenso, north-west of Ladysmith, near Durban, South Africa, in 1865, and educated in England. In 1895, he was married to a Tasmanian girl by a Reverend Robert Beresford, the same Reverend Beresford who was vicar of St John's Launceston when little Robert Hamilton King was christened there in 1904. Richard Hamilton and his wife had three daughters who were born in 1897, 1902 and 1908 respectively. Germaine had no doubt that this man was her biological grandfather.

Hamilton had prospered as a businessman, commission agent, and representative of the Holyman family's White Star Line of steamers. He was a secretary of the Ulverstone City Council and of the Leven Harbour Trust. There could be no possibility, Germaine commented sardonically, that such a man would seduce a young servant girl and turn her out. 'Respectable men do not seduce the help when their wives are pregnant or busy with young babies.' And a 'bad ignorant girl' like Rhoda King would not compromise Mr Hamilton's reputation by declaring him to be the father of her child. All of what Germaine had discovered about this man was 'irrelevant'.

> It is also irrelevant that he was tall, narrow-chested, had a moustache, a long face, a narrow nose, deep-set eyes, very fair skin and rode a bicycle around Ulverstone.[55]

Rhoda King never saw her firstborn son again. Eventually she married and had ten children. She died in 1968.

As Germaine discovered, Reg Greer had covered his tracks well. It was only because of her professional skills as a researcher and writer, her access to resources, including the media, and the financial support provided by Hamish Hamilton's generous advance that Reg Greer's cover was, eventually, blown. Her father had left just enough truth among his lies to enable her to discover him as Eric Greeney, who was indeed born in 1904, not in Durban, South Africa, as he claimed, but Launceston, Tasmania. It was to this small, undisturbed little town at the end of the world that she returned to assemble the last pieces of the jigsaw.

Perhaps unwittingly, at this final point of discovery in her story, Greer provides her readers with a most revealing picture of herself. Her hosts and fellow guests at the seedy hotel where she spent the night before meeting the Greeney family had probably never seen the likes of her – striking in appearance, obviously wealthy, rumoured to be famous in some mysterious way, she carried with her suggestions of a world that was only vaguely within their ken. Yet she was obviously, like them, an Australian: familiar though foreign. She was quite alone.

In the stifling privacy of her hotel bedroom, the imposing celebrity figure becomes a vulnerable woman, her loneliness all the more apparent because she is unaware of it. She does not spare herself. Had she ever really loved her father? Had she ever really loved anyone? ('Don't *say* that!') Had he rejected her because he was afraid her cleverness would expose his lies? Why did he become a toff? She must have known that he was a fraud, why had she not admitted it to herself? Surely her mother must have known. Why had she not told Germaine? In broad Australian, she berated herself: 'You never gave the poor bugger a second thought. After you left home you never wrote, never called.'

'You sound like my mother,' she cried.

'Who did you think I was?' came the answering voice.[56]

The next morning, she made telephone contact with her father's family. 'Mrs Greeney,' she began. 'This will seem rather an odd request. Are you related to Ernest Henry Greeney?'

'Yes,' replied Mrs Greeney. 'He's my husband's father.' She called Mr Greeney to the phone.

Germaine started again. 'My name is, or rather was . . . Germaine Greer. I'm the daughter of Henry's brother, Eric . . . I'm quite a well-known writer.' She was floundering, suddenly afraid that she was committing that sin – mortal in Australia – of sounding superior.

He helped her. 'Would you like to come and see us?' he asked. 'I'll see what I can find out from the other foster brothers and sisters.'

'I beg your pardon? Did you say *foster*?'

'Oh yes. They were all adopted. Didn't you know?'

At 2.29 that afternoon, Germaine found herself knocking on the door of the Greeneys' modest bungalow in suburban Launceston. Mrs Greeney had baked a fruitcake while Mr Greeney had gathered the family to meet their unlikely cousin. He had also visited his aunt's house to find old photos, among which was one of Emma Greeney, Germaine's adoptive grandmother, wearing a high-necked dress with a cameo brooch at the throat.

She was told that in 1920, when Germaine's father, Eric, turned sixteen, Emma and her husband were fostering eight children, of whom Eric was the much-loved second-eldest. Emma had cared for them well. All of them – Ernest, Eric, Eli, Hazel, Gwendoline, Dulcie, Kathleen and Bessie – eventually 'made something of themselves'. Now, in January 1988, as Australia was preparing to celebrate two hundred years of European settlement, their descendants, including the famous writer, actor and academic Germaine Greer, were gathered to eat fruitcake and drink cups of tea. No one had seen or heard anything of Eric since the day in 1921 when the young man sailed away to the mainland on the SS *Nairana* with a company of actors.

Germaine dedicated her book to her three grandmothers. The first was her mother's mother, Alida Jensen Lafrank, who had loved her and been kind to her in her childhood; the second was Emma Wise Greeney, who had raised young Eric with love; the third was Rhoda Elizabeth King, her father's biological mother, the young servant girl who was deceived by her respectable married employer and forced to give her baby away.

As Greer's most personal, and probably most readable, book, *Daddy* was well received by critics and the public. Among the many admiring and grateful letters she received after its publication was one that adds a coda to her story. In 1992, an elderly man, Ross Dunham, wrote in a shaky hand to inform her that as a fifteen-year-old bank clerk in Ulverstone, Tasmania, he had known her grandfather, R.R.E. Hamilton ('known as Dicky').

Dunham's memories were of 1940. He was not to know then that Hamilton had a son who was living in a flat in Elwood,

Victoria, with his wife and one-year-old daughter, still making up his mind about whether he should enlist in the armed forces.

The now-retired bank clerk remembered Hamilton, then in his seventies, arriving at the bank every business day at 2.55 pm – five minutes before closing time. After carrying out his banking transactions Hamilton would command, 'Mr Dunham, my [safe deposit] box if you please.' By this time, the bank had closed for the day. The young clerk would fetch the box and Hamilton would shuffle through the papers before calling, 'Mr Dunham, I have finished, would you let me out, please.'

> His manners and demeanour were always impeccable, as was his dress. From memory, he always wore a dark grey or navy suit, a bow tie and homburg hat. He had a small moustache. His face had similarities to yours . . . He had three daughters, lived in a handsome house and drove a smart car – only used on Sundays when he and his wife went for a drive. He was a man of property.[57]

Dunham's was not the only letter Germaine received about Richard Robert Ernest Hamilton. Her archive also contains a copy of an (undated) letter she wrote in reply to one from a woman she addresses as 'Mavourneen'. 'He sounds just like my father . . . Anything else you can remember would be much appreciated.' Mavourneen's letter is not in the file.

8

The Change

I will be calm. I will be mistress of myself.

Jane Austen, *Sense and Sensibility*

Remember Cheryl Davis? She who, on the day Germaine Greer started writing *The Female Eunuch*, was ferrying her four children to and from school in the beat-up Renault 750 while her husband Jim drove off to his business appointments in the Peugeot? Behold her now, twenty-two years later, as she sits on the tram on her way home from work. On her lap is a copy of Germaine Greer's latest book, *The Change*.

Cheryl had gone off Germaine Greer, she told her friend Junie; she now preferred Fay Weldon. She had thought *The Obstacle Race* was unnecessarily highbrow: all those arguments about female artists no one had ever heard of! She had not managed to finish *Sex and Destiny*, and could not see the point of the book, really. She had seen *Daddy, We Hardly Knew You* in a bookshop but the title had put her off. She was enjoying *The Change*, though. In light of her own experience of menopause she believed that, like *The Female Eunuch*, this book would change women's lives. Junie agreed with her.

It was Junie, actually, who had first given Cheryl a copy of *The Female Eunuch* in January 1972. (It was also Junie who had recommended that Cheryl take the pill, even though she feared it had made her, Junie, deaf.) They had read the Australian press coverage of the book and Germaine Greer's promotional tour with some bemusement (why were those journalists being so unpleasant?) and had watched its author on television when she was in Australia. Their husbands had never known a woman like Germaine Greer. Too attractive to be dismissed as a frumpy bluestocking, too raunchy to be a slut, too smart not to be noticed, what could they make of her? Jim and his mates took refuge in derision. Over their evening beers in the pub, they invented a new game: who could make up the funniest nickname for her. Jim won: his contribution 'Wormy Germy' was voted the most hilarious.

At first, Cheryl hid her copy of *The Female Eunuch* from Jim, though she did not think to disguise it in a brown paper cover as, she later found out, many women did. Barbecue discussions on the subject of what middle-class couples were learning to call 'women's lib' had a tendency to turn nasty. The men resented being summoned over to the women's side of the patio to defend themselves against charges of being 'male chauvinist pigs'.

Cheryl had felt as if lights were going on all over her brain when she read *The Female Eunuch*. Then she read Betty Friedan, Simone de Beauvoir, Kate Millett and the rest. Her cousin, who was a schoolteacher, was surprised that Cheryl, with her rudimentary education, could understand these books and comment on them so intelligently. Peeved, Cheryl enrolled in one of the new university degree courses that were now open by special arrangement to women who had not matriculated. She joined the Women's Electoral Lobby and started a new feminist consciousness-raising group in her neighbourhood. All around her she found like-minded women and, at least as long as the Whitlam Labor government remained in office, a degree of public support for women's liberation. Soon after the no-fault divorce laws took effect in 1975, she told Jim she was leaving him. Nice Jim, kind Jim, generous Jim, became abusive: all the way to the Family Court he fought her over custody of the children and her share of the property. Then one day it was all over; Cheryl had salvaged enough money to buy a modest house in an unfashionable suburb, and, after some further study, she got a job teaching English at a local high school. Jim fell into a deep depression, recovered, got himself back on the promotion ladder, went to France on an extended business trip, came home, remarried, bought a new house and had no more children. 'It's all about their dollars and their dicks!' said Junie.

Now, about to get off the tram, Cheryl reflects on her life. It has not been easy over the years. Jim's maintenance payments were irregular and she could not afford to take him back to court. Dealing with teenagers at work all day and returning home each night to more of the same had taken its toll. Stories of Jim's success, his nice house, his attractive younger wife who liked being a homemaker, and their frequent overseas trips made her wince. 'Bastard!' said Junie.

But she regrets nothing. She is now deputy principal of her high school, glad to be relieved of the daily battles of the classroom, earning a good salary, enjoying the company of her colleagues. Her children have left home, finally, she hopes, and she refuses to become too involved in the inevitable dramas and struggles of their lives. She has survived this far and now she is free. Due, in no small part, to reading Germaine Greer's first book, *The Female Eunuch*, she is now firmly her own person. Her own woman.

•

The purpose of *The Change*, according to its author, was 'to demonstrate that women are at least as interesting as men and that aging women are at least as interesting as younger women'.[1] This statement raises the question: interesting to whom? Certainly not to men, for Greer also argued passionately that women who have reached the climacteric have *ceased* to be of interest to men, and that this is a Good Thing.

In *The Female Eunuch*, Greer drew the world's attention to her belief that women had lost control of their sexuality and freedom to enjoy it. They had been turned into castrates whose passive, impotent bodies had become the property and playthings of the men in their lives. Twenty years later, in *The Change*, her arguments were not as inconsistent with those of her first book as some people thought. She identified the same problem – that men controlled women's bodies and most aspects of their lives – but she suggested different solutions. In *The Female Eunuch*, she had advised women to discover their sexuality, enjoy it loudly and freely, and, almost literally, to wallow in it (by tasting their menstrual blood, for example). In *The Change* she argued that younger women had not yet become free because men continued to desire them and to exploit them – find them *interesting* – and the biological and social dice, as she had revealed in *Sex and Destiny*, were still loaded in men's favour. Older women would need to seek other ways to achieve their liberation, and the changes they experienced during menopause would guide them. When no longer interesting to men, women would at last be free to concentrate on becoming interesting to themselves, their sisters and, ultimately, even the world.

The Change begins with middle-aged Germaine and her friend, Sandra, enjoying coffee and croissants in a cafe in Beaubourg, Paris, on a sunny spring day. At a nearby table sit two silver-haired men of about their own age entertaining two 'sleek, expensive, and very much younger women' who appear to be hanging on to every word the men utter. Sandra is depressed and furious. Observing an elderly woman with a plastic shopping bag who is hesitantly making her way through the groups of sex workers and lounging youths on the street, she vows never to become like that – an apologetic old crone living in a bedsit, creeping out each day to buy her bread and cheese. But, she says despairingly, neither will she be able, like the men at the neighbouring table, to command the attention of attractive people of the opposite sex. It's not fair!

Germaine tries to think of some elderly female role models to cheer her friend – women who have defeated the stereotypes to become satisfactory exemplars of successful ageing – but she can't, just at that moment, think of a single one.

The journey inwards towards wisdom and serenity is as long as the headlong rush of our social and sexual career, if not longer, but there are no signposts to show the way. If there are leaders beckoning, most of us have no idea who they might be.[2]

Instead, the only older women who come to mind are like her friend Flora, poor Flora who, at fifty, could not bear to live more than three weeks without a man. Germaine, who occasionally accompanied Flora to bars, despaired of her. Obsessively fishing for new boyfriends, Flora would torture her ageing feet into strappy shoes with impossibly high heels, her peekaboo bra was nearly always visible, her hitched-up slitted skirts were tight and she wore a chain around her ankle. Abandoned again and again, all she could do was wait for the next man. She thought she might kill herself.[3]

In Germaine's view, most of the older women who were rich and famous were no better than Flora. Only consider the magazine images of Elizabeth Taylor (born 1932), with her porcelain teeth, wig and brass earrings, marrying young construction worker Larry Fortensky; airbrushed Joan Collins (born 1933), her crepey arms only just visible, introducing yet another new 'secret' young lover to the press; and Jane Fonda (born 1937), who had made the momentous decision to concentrate on her bum during her fitness workouts 'with rather dire results for her face', and had purchased a mammoplasty to go with her new opal and diamond engagement ring. 'No matter how hard you work out,' commented Greer cattily, 'it seems there is nothing you can do for a bosom but pump it up.'[4]

How had it come to this? Greer's first target was her old enemy, the male medical establishment. For hundreds of years, she argued, male doctors had been torturing menopausal women through various attempts to keep them 'appetizing and responsive to male demand'. Hysterectomy and castration were prescribed as antidotes to midlife despair; Marie Curie had no sooner discovered radium than gentlemen started inserting electrically charged rods into women's vaginas.[5]

All of this and more, till the discovery of hormone replacement therapy (HRT) in the 1960s. Enter more villains, the international drug companies, with their successful efforts to persuade governments all over the world to define menopause as a deficiency disease for which oestrogen should be prescribed. What a bonanza!

Menopausal women themselves were also culpable – and foolish. Rushing, lemming-like, to buy dye for their hair and silicone for their breasts, they forgot, said Greer, that men were only too cruelly able to distinguish between young female bosoms and old. Psychologists convinced women it was all their own fault: the less sexually available, the less generous a woman had been with her friendships during her fertile years, the nastier her menopause was likely to be. Little wonder that she would become depressed and need more medicating still.

Greer did not oppose medical intervention across the board: it was important, she noted, to confront the reality that some women suffered considerable discomfort during and after menopause. She did not oppose the prescription of HRT for such women, recognising that they 'usually do feel better on estrogen, a great deal better, so much better that they realise for the first time just how unwell they felt before estrogen'. But oestrogen therapy was not necessary for all women, and nor was it of any use at all to prevent ageing or to maintain women's attractiveness to men.[6]

The Change is quite different from any of the self-help books about menopause that started to proliferate after the discovery of HRT, largely because it is so exquisitely illuminated by Greer's encyclopaedic knowledge of famous and not-so-famous women in history and literature. Her narrative is populated by a series of fascinating female characters. There is Philippa, daughter of the Count of Holland, who brought her mother's beautifully lettered book of herbal remedies with her when she arrived in England in 1327 to marry Edward III of England. There are the witches, whose long and illustrious history has so much to tell us about older women's power and about cruel male (and female) attempts to neutralise it. There is Vita Sackville-West, distinguished author, lover of Virginia Woolf, whose heroine in *All Passion Spent*, the widow Lady Slane, went off to live in Hampstead with her French maid.

Most poignant of all is Simone de Beauvoir, widely acclaimed as a founder of postwar second-wave feminism, whose intellectual, philosophical and literary capacities were formidable. But, as Greer observes, de Beauvoir believed that the greatest achievement of her life was her relationship with Jean-Paul Sartre, although Sartre never said the same of his association with her. Despite the brilliance of their lifelong intellectual collaboration and 'soul marriage', he controlled her life; they never lived together and his many affairs with other women caused her great pain.

Greer despaired of de Beauvoir's 'repellently male oriented' view of the sexuality of older people, believing that, even in her youth, the Frenchwoman had committed herself to an extreme and irrational fear of old age, based largely on her fear of becoming physically unattractive to men. She faced her future, said Greer, 'as unprovided as any empty-headed beauty queen'.[7]

When she wrote *The Change*, Germaine Greer, as usual, was in the vanguard of new thinking about an important issue for women. She was seven years older than the first baby boomers: much of her influence and marketability lay in her capacity to catch the wave of change in the seconds before it broke, to seize upon her own experiences at critical life stages and generalise from them just as the millions of women lining up behind her were about to seek answers to their own dilemmas. 'But, but, but . . .' they cried upon reading her, 'this is all outrageous, ridiculous, not true . . .' And then they went away and thought about it.

By the 1990s, Germaine Greer was financially secure and more or less settled on her little farm in Essex, with her plants, animals and a moving feast of housemates; she had strengthened her ties with her old college, Newnham, at nearby Cambridge University, where she had become an unofficial fellow and special lecturer.

Her work schedule was extraordinary: as well as her university teaching, she had further established her academic credentials with her continuing research and publications about women writers and with her book *Shakespeare*, published by Oxford University Press in 1986. A collection of non-fiction, *The Madwoman's Underclothes: Essays and occasional writings 1968–1985*, appeared in the same year. In the 1990s she published six books (some of them in collaboration with other writers and editors): *The Change: Women, ageing and the menopause* (1991); *The Collected Works of Katherine Philips, The Matchless Orinda*, Volume II: The Letters (1992) and Volume III: The Translations (1993); *Slip-Shod Sibyls: Recognition, rejection and the woman poet* (1995); *The Surviving Works of Anne Wharton* (1997); and *The Whole Woman* (1999). As if all of this, together with regular appearances on television and radio, lectures and book promotion tours at home and abroad, and an active social life, was not enough, she wrote articles and features for many British newspapers including *The Spectator*, *The Times*, *The Independent*, *The Oldie* and *The Guardian*. Her popular Country Notebook column ran weekly in the *Sunday Times* from 1999 to 2005.

Did all of this hard work have something to do with her professed loss of interest in sex? She claimed to have lived a celibate life after her failed operation to save her fertility in her late thirties: 'I have a bed in there as big as a ball park but nothing ever happens [in it] . . .' she told journalist Christena Appleyard of *The Sun* in 1983. However, in 2017, a female friend, who wishes to remain anonymous, raised her eyebrows in disbelief and laughed when told about this.

Whatever the truth of Greer's personal life, it remains the case that, in middle age, her writing and public comments about sex were very different from those of the days of her involvement with the counterculture and *Oz* magazine. 'I'm beginning to think sex is really disgusting and we should have nothing to do with it,' she said in 1986.[8] She might have added that most articles about sex were no longer the attention-grabbers they had once been. By the 1990s, when images of copulating men and women had become practically de rigueur in every movie with a love story, 'A groupie's vision' and the other pieces Greer wrote to shock a bourgeois society in the 1960s had started to look old hat, their appeal more quaint than scandalous.

•

If her own modified sexual proclivities and the socio-sexual changes she had helped to bring about eventually caused Greer to shift her focus away from the joys and trials of sex, they did not stop her from continuing to enjoy a good fight. Ever the contrarian, she needed to be heard, and she needed to be The Boss. Her personality was such that conflict was all but inevitable.

As the end of the millennium drew closer, she was involved in several headline-grabbing clashes. The first was a court battle with a gynaecologist named Mary Anderson. In *The Change*, Greer had criticised Dr Anderson for suggesting that women's declining interest in sex and failure to make themselves attractive during and after the menopause caused their husbands to become depressed, develop anxiety, even become alcoholic and seek extramarital comfort. Greer wanted to know why this female doctor was taking the husbands' part, why she was refusing to recognise that women needed support at this time in their lives rather than blame for whatever ailed their men. Nowhere, she said, did Anderson suggest that a man should take responsibility for his wife's wellbeing.

The doctor sued Greer, claiming that she had damaged her professional reputation by portraying her as lacking sympathy for women. She won the case and Greer was forced to pay substantial damages. Refusing to capitulate, Greer fought on by attacking the High Court judgment. In November 1998, she attempted to restate her position in an article written for *The Oldie*, a journal edited by her old friend Richard Ingrams. But Ingrams refused to publish it. 'Your article as it stands is very risky,' he faxed her, because '(a) it repeats the libel of Anderson and (b) it could be said to be motivated by malice.' In a clumsy attempt at humour, he ended the fax by pointing out to her the dangers of being seen as a 'mad, malicious rude old bat'.

Germaine's response was swift. 'You should be ashamed of yourself,' she faxed him back. 'Censorship is a way of life, but not of my life . . . I didn't think you would run the piece – I do not have the time to write you another one. Why not ask the lovely rich Mary Anderson to write for you instead?'

Soon afterwards, on 6 December 1998, a report that could only have been instigated by Greer, headed 'Ingrams sacks "Old Bat"', appeared in the *Evening Standard*'s Londoner's Diary. According to this report, Ingrams had sacked her from *The Oldie* and called her 'a mad, malicious, evil, rude old bat'.

Ingrams protested. 'I never said you were sacked,' he faxed, 'I never said you were evil. And you know perfectly well why I refused to print your article. You should be even more ashamed of yourself than before.'[9]

As with so many of Germaine's disagreements with old friends, once the brouhaha had died down, her relationship with Ingrams resumed and they remain amicable to this day. However, this episode provides yet another illustration of why so many people were and are wary of her. Long ago, her schoolmate Margaret O'Keeffe, a gentle, sensitive girl, had recognised the streak of cruelty in Germaine's personality and had chosen to avoid her.

Later, friends who loved her for her many wonderful qualities had to learn how to navigate the shoals of her vitriol and know when it was wise to back off.

In 1995, following the publication of the book *Hippie Hippie Shake* by her old friend Richard Neville, Germaine became involved in another publishing controversy, but this time she was the person threatening to sue. She had refused to co-operate with Neville when he was writing the book, telling him that she was bored with the 1960s. He offered her the opportunity to read the manuscript and amend it if necessary, but she refused to do that too. When she finally read the book, she discovered Neville had misremembered a conversation in which he thought she had told him that the scar on her abdomen was the result of a hysterectomy. She was mightily offended and demanded that the publishers place erratum slips in each copy, under threat of litigation. They didn't and, in the end, she didn't sue either.

The significance of this episode eventually lay more in the resulting publicity than in Neville's actual mistake or Greer's annoyance, which even she must have realised was unreasonable, given that he had offered her the chance to correct the proofs. But in May 1995 she ignited further debate by referring to her friend's faux pas in a *Spectator* column titled 'We shall not be neutered'. Neville's mistake was, she conceded, a bona fide error, 'Richard having only the foggiest notion of what a hysterectomy might be.' But her objections had substance: she had been crusading against unnecessary medical procedures carried out on women for the whole of her life, she wrote, and it would totally discredit her and her arguments if it were thought that she had undergone such a procedure herself.[10]

Sensing a big story, *Guardian* columnist and averred feminist Suzanne Moore weighed in to the discussion. Moore belonged to a younger generation of women who, believing they had discovered newer and better interpretations of feminism for modern times, sought to distance themselves from some of the views of their older sisters. In an article titled 'So why no child for the Female Eunuch?', Moore argued that if Greer had deliberately had her uterus removed all those years ago, it would not only discredit her work but – major statement – 'It would alter the whole history of feminism.' 'A lot of those older feminists did not have children,' she wrote provocatively.

Germaine responded in print with characteristic bile. Belittling Moore as 'the pouting pundit of the *Guardian*'s tabloid section', she remarked on Moore's 'fuck-me shoes' and exposed cleavage. 'So much lipstick must rot the brain,' she opined.

Then, moving away from the personal, she pointed out to Moore and other younger feminists of her ilk that attacks on their own kind, especially attacks on older members of the sisterhood – 'senior feminists' – were destructive. Men, she said, had always known how to support each other, to 'run together behind the Alpha male'. Moore's attack on her was sad proof that younger feminists had failed to learn the important lesson that she, Germaine Greer, had been trying to teach them for years: 'The Running Dog runs for his pack. The Running Bitch runs for his pack too, not quite grasping that she will never be admitted to membership, no matter how many other women she mangles.'[11]

A couple of weeks later, in *The Times Magazine*, Greer told her readers that her sister Jane had faxed her to let her know that the Moore story was all over the Australian press. 'I reckon you can tell she's a disaster by the names of [her] kids . . . "Bliss" and "Scarlett" . . . yeuch!' Jane had commented. The two sisters, Germaine reported, then invented a game of giving names to the children of 'lipstick feminists'. Girls' names were easy – 'Cherry',

'Ruby', 'Poppy'. Boys' presented more difficulty. 'Red' and 'Plum' were allowed, but not 'Raisin' or 'Brandy'.[12]

So much for female solidarity!

A different kind of conflict centred on a novel by the well-known author Salman Rushdie, which the American writer Paul Berman later referred to as 'the most consequential political event in the history of the novel'.[13] Rushdie, an old friend of Germaine, was born in Bombay, in what was then British India, into a Muslim family. He moved to England at the age of eight and was educated at Rugby School and King's College, Cambridge University. The publication of his novel *The Satanic Verses* in 1988 caused an immediate storm in the Muslim world, where it was perceived as mocking Mohammed. This was largely because of its title, which refers to some verses of the Koran that are said to have been dictated to Mohammed by the devil ('Good story,' Rushdie is alleged to have said to himself), but also because of some of the content, not least the writer's choice of giving the names of the Prophet's wives to prostitutes in the scenes in the novel that take place in a brothel.

On Valentine's Day – 14 February – 1989, the theocratic ruler of Iran, Ayatollah Khomeini, issued a fatwa against Rushdie and all who had contributed to the book's publication. Rushdie went into a long period of hiding, protected by Scotland Yard. Violence erupted around the world. Rushdie's Italian translator was stabbed, but survived, his Japanese translator was murdered and his Norwegian publisher was seriously wounded by a terrorist, there were riots in Turkey and Pakistan, bombings in London and in bookstores throughout the United Kingdom. Employees of the publishing house Penguin, the book's original publishers, whom Rushdie's detractors declared to be Jewish, were forced to surround themselves with security agents, bomb-sniffing dogs and bomb detection machines. Peter Mayer, CEO of the Penguin group, received blood-spattered death letters, his daughter was targeted and parents at her school demanded he withdraw her – but the book stayed in print.

In spite of the decision to give Rushdie police protection, many Right-leaning members of the British and American establishments argued against his stance. Robert Runcie, the Archbishop of Canterbury, invoked England's blasphemy laws, and the foreign secretary Geoffrey Howe considered the book to be 'extremely critical [and] rude' about England. Martin Amis, who strongly supported Rushdie, had a mild argument with Prince Charles at a dinner party where, in Amis's words, Charles declared, '"I'm sorry, but if someone insults someone else's deepest convictions, well then," blah blah blah . . .' Former American President Jimmy Carter deplored the 'insult to the sacred beliefs of our Moslem friends'.[14]

Most affiliates of the liberal Left took an opposite view. Members of the British, European and American literary establishments protested angrily in defence of free speech. Many were friends of Rushdie who, to their intense annoyance (because part of their raison d'être was tolerance of difference), were accused of being 'Islamophobic'. Fay Weldon, one of Britain's most powerful female writers, was one of a group of authors, journalists and other supporters of Rushdie who were accused of being guilty of Islamophobia in a 24-page pamphlet published by the Runnymede Trust, a liberal think-tank on race relations and cultural diversity. Weldon retaliated furiously. 'If being an Islamophobe means you express anger when your good friend and colleague is sentenced to death, then I suppose I must qualify,' she declared.[15]

What about Germaine? Forced to choose between her avowed liberalism and her support of 'the sacred beliefs of our Muslim friends', she chose the latter. When asked to sign a petition defending Rushdie, she declined, saying, 'I refuse to sign petitions for this book of his, which was about his own troubles.' She went on to describe him as 'a megalomaniac, an Englishman with dark skin'. Rushdie never forgave her. More than ten years later he said of her lack of support at the height of the fatwa, 'She attacked me in public . . . She may not wish to remember it, but that is what she did. I noticed it and I minded . . . What people don't often say about Germaine Greer is that she is barking mad. She is an idiot . . . She's mad, and her determination to be out of step leads her into batty positions. We just watch her and wonder why.'[16]

In 2012, Rushdie stated his position very clearly. Drawing a distinction between 'multiculturalism' and 'cultural relativism', he argued:

> Cultural relativism is the death of ethical thought, supporting the right of tyrannical priests to tyrannise, of despotic parents to mutilate their daughters, of bigoted individuals to hate homosexuals and Jews, because it is part of their 'culture' to do so. Bigotry, prejudice and violence or the threat of violence are not human 'values'. They are proof of the absence of such values.[17]

Greer did not accept this view. In the years that followed the Rushdie affair, many of her comments on contentious issues like female genital mutilation sprang from her conviction that the West had no right to impose its values upon other cultures, which, she argued, were perfectly capable of making their own rules to suit their own circumstances.

In 1996 the name Germaine Greer again hit the headlines. This time it was about her views on transgender people, a subject that would dog her for many years to come. Her immediate target was a fellow Australian, Rachael (formerly Russell) Padman. In 1977, at the age of 23, Padman had arrived at the all-male St John's College, Cambridge, to complete a PhD in physics. Almost immediately, he started a course of oestrogen and prepared to live as a woman, wearing make-up and women's clothing. After eighteen months, Padman started telling fellow students and college staff of his intention to have gender reassignment surgery. Everyone was very supportive and he discovered that the university actually had a policy of respecting students' choices in this regard, as long as the choice was made on appropriate medical advice. In 1982, after she had changed her name by deed poll to become Rachael, she had the surgery performed in London.

The faculty board approved Rachael's PhD while she was still in hospital, and she subsequently spent two years as a research fellow in the United States. In 1996, having returned to Cambridge, she was elected to a fellowship at Newnham College, where Germaine Greer was also a fellow and a member of the governing board. As Padman tells the story, she had assumed that the all-female governing body knew she was trans (after all, it was no secret in Cambridge), and had agreed it was not an issue before they elected her. When Greer (who later alleged she was among the fellows who did not know that Padman was a trans woman) found out, she spoke publicly about her opposition to Padman's election. 'We have driven a coach and horses through our statutes, and I can't believe we did it,' she told *The Times* and the BBC World Service. 'I like Dr Padman. We all know she is a distinguished physicist, but what is the point of having clear statutes if we just ignore them? . . . We have to be true to the spirit of the original bequest to the college as a women's college for women.'

The national and international press had a field day with the story. The college principal, Dr Onora O'Neill, and most of the fellows supported Padman, and her fellowship proceeded without further incident, but Greer was so angry that she resigned her own fellowship of the college she loved.

On 25 June 1997, journalist Clare Longrigg, writing in *The Guardian*, attacked Greer in an article titled 'A sister with no Fellow feeling'. Longrigg claimed that it was Greer who had outed Padman, and that Greer was an eccentric and unreliable teacher. Greer threatened to sue, and *The Guardian* issued an apology and settled a sum to be paid as damages, which Greer donated to Newnham College. She resumed her fellowship, later describing herself as 'a Fellow of sorts'.[18]

On 26 March 2012, after she had been glitter-bombed by the protest group Queer Avengers in Wellington, New Zealand, Greer issued a statement that gave her side of the events of 1996–97. The accusation levelled at her by the group – that she had 'outed' Padman and that Padman had lost her job as a consequence – she said, was completely false, for Padman had already outed herself 'all over the front page of *The Times*'. Nor had she opposed Padman's election, since no election had been held. If there had been a discussion, she said, she would have argued against it, but if a subsequent vote had gone against her she would have accepted the situation. As it was, Padman was given a fellowship and Greer had resigned hers.

Greer had some legal justification for her stance. Padman's appointment to Newnham pre-dated the *Gender Recognition Act 2004* by nine years, and Greer's argument that the appointment contravened the college's statutes was substantially correct. Padman had no legal status as a woman, yet she was admitted as a fellow of the women's college at a time when the college did not accept men. However, this did not prevent a growing number of people from believing that Germaine Greer was increasingly out of step with progressive thought.[19]

Being out of step was not new to her, but she was more used to being in the vanguard of popular opinion than behind it. Now it was starting to look as if she was stuck in a past age of prejudice and ignorance on a crucial matter of gender. Many bright younger feminists rolled their eyes.

Lest there be any doubt about her opposition to trans women, Greer set out her position on this and other issues in her next major book, *The Whole Woman*, first published in 1999.

The Whole Woman is a grumpy, sour, curmudgeonly tome; iconoclastic one moment, indignant the next. Where *The Female Eunuch*, her most successful book and the child of her youth, offered new insights and hope, and *The Change* promised serenity, this one set out to demonstrate that the tantalising promises of shining new lives for women was yet to be realised: in many ways things were now worse than they had ever been.

Singled out for special, lethal treatment in the book were the 'lifestyle feminists'. For thirty years, said Greer, she had tried to support – even champion – all styles of feminism, from 'lipstick lesbians' to 'the prostitutes' union', believing that all were part of a common struggle, but when these smug lifestyle types tried to assert that the movement had gone just far enough, that women could now have it all – money, sex, fashion – the fire in her belly exploded. She had vowed never to write a book like this, she said, but now, at the turn of the millennium, when some women were starting to believe that old fighting feminists like her were passé and the days of struggle were over, she had to speak.

Matriarch Greer, schoolteacher Greer, had news for young women of the younger generation. In some ways, their lives may have become 'nobler and richer', but if they thought women were now the independent, liberated beings she had once thought they might become, they were deluding themselves. It was never about equality with men: 'I didn't fight to get women out from behind vacuum cleaners to get them on to the board of Hoover.' It was about women becoming the subjects of their own lives rather than the objects of other people's. Who would ever have thought, after the successes of the first liberationists who marched on the Atlantic City Boardwalk in protest at the Miss America contest in 1969, that bigger, brighter, more glitzy pageants of that kind would endure into the twenty-first century? Who could have predicted the rates of sexual abuse suffered by female military recruits and policewomen? What difference had it made that 103 female Labour politicians (lifestyle feminists all) were now 'running around' Parliament in 'little red suits' making the Palace of West-minster look 'like a Butlin's holiday camp', when real power still rested with the men? And women's lives had become so much harder: 'On every side we see women troubled, exhausted, muti-lated, lonely, guilty, mocked by the headlined successes of the few.'

She had vowed never to write this book, but now, in view of what was happening to women, she could not remain silent. It was 'time to get angry again'.[20]

Beginning, like *The Female Eunuch*, with a section on 'Body', *The Whole Woman* recycles all the old arguments about the beauty stereotypes – the Barbies with their improbably long legs and nipple-free bosoms, the Miss America contestants with their impossible-to-emulate textbook body specifications. The old foes are also there in strength: the surgeons who continue to hone their skills in Western versions of female mutilation – hyster-ectomy, mastectomy, episiotomy and the rest; the rapacious multimillion-dollar pharmaceutical and cosmetic companies;

and the newer lifestyle enterprises that have joined in the lucrative sport of exploiting women's vanity. All of these, as discrete industries and as elements of the multinational corporations that devour all before them, are the villains of the book, and a horrified Greer observes how their tentacles are spreading across developing countries.

If it all was bad in 1969, now, in 1999, she writes, it was worse than ever because women everywhere had been outsmarted. Foolish and gullible in their quest for the perfect body, they were racing to avail themselves of every frightening new development in cosmetic surgery, every new 'youth' drug, every new fitness gimmick, as they fell for each latest piece of propaganda put out by the evil empires. And when all their expensive efforts failed, they then turned to the medications that had been cunningly invented by one group of villains to enrich another group – the psychiatrists and psychologists who had created a whole new raft of depressive conditions, just for them.[21] And that is just the 'Body' chapter.

More arch-villains emerge in the sections that follow: 'Mind', 'Love' and 'Power'. There is the economy, which, because it depends on spending before saving, decrees that women must shop. Every time she leaves the house, says Greer, a woman buys something. Men have more important things to do: 'Men don't shop, even for their own underpants.' Shopping exhausts women, as their ever-fruitless quest for that elusive 'something nice' that will make them happy renders them powerless. Shopping is tough work. The supermarkets, especially callous in this regard, make women work so hard and for so long in locating, choosing, loading and paying for their products at the checkout (and she wrote this before self-service checkouts were invented), that there is no longer time (or need) for them to perform traditional household tasks like preserving seasonal food.

Is Greer describing her own experience when she illustrates her point that the supermarket owners dictate what the customer will buy?

> Suppose she is looking for a jar of pimentos. She looks among the tinned vegetables and cannot find it. She looks in the Tex-Mex section. No luck. She looks among the pickles. Foiled again, she asks a man with a company pin in his lapel. 'Never heard of them.' The implications are plain: there is no such thing and the customer is mad.[22]

It will only be when someone higher up works out that the store can buy shipments of pimentos at a price that will permit a huge mark-up, she rages, that bottled pimentos will begin to exist. At that point the advertising will kick in and some TV celebrity chef will be seen 'sticking bottled pimentos in every recipe'.

One imagines a frustrated, 'mad' Germaine at a supermarket somewhere in Essex, searching for a jar of pimentos, shoving her trolley furiously from aisle to aisle, searching shelf after shelf, muttering her usual imprecations and expletives as she goes.

Greer's arguments against transgenderism are set out in a section of the 'Body' chapter pejoratively titled 'Pantomime dames'. Her first and main contention is that male doctors are only prepared to create 'manmade women' because they regard all women as defective men. She distinguishes between trans people who have not 'opted for mutilation' and postoperative transgender people, giving examples of exotic trans prostitutes who are expected to 'bugger' their clients, and a hair-raisingly graphic description of the penectomy operation itself, plus details of all the excruciating things that can go wrong for years after the surgery.

Then she tells us about the 'hitjas', garishly painted individuals in India whose genitalia have been 'bloodily and painfully' removed, sometimes by themselves, and sacrificed to the mother goddess. Her point here seems to be that in India, a third 'intersexual' sex can be acknowledged and created without a man needing to pass himself off as a woman.

Apparently referring to new and forthcoming legislation in Europe and America, Greer notes that people who have undergone male to female (MTF) reconstructive surgery are now being awarded full civil rights (for example, in marriage), according to their chosen gender. In framing these laws, says Greer, no one consulted women as to whether they wanted to accept these male people into their sisterhood, or whether women might think that accepting them could be damaging to their identity and self-esteem. As a variation of her first argument, she claims that people's easy acceptance of male to female gender reassignment might be because females are seen as not possessing a gender at all in their own right, that is, they are simply 'not male'. On this premise, removing a male penis would turn a man into a non-male, thus putting him into the same (assumed) second-rate category as all women. This is objectionable, says Greer, first because it is an insult to all women and second because it gives a man the unwarranted right to claim membership of a proud sisterhood.

Greer has relatively little to say here on the subject of female to male (FTM) transgenderism. She notes that fewer FTM men are prostitutes, that surgery to construct a penis is highly complex, that FTM transitions are much rarer than MTF, and that FTM men do not display themselves as MTF women do. Adding fuel to her argument that 'deficient' males are easily relegated to the female gender because all women are regarded as deficient males anyway, FTM men, she says, find it hard to be accepted into the 'superior' male world by those they wish to join as brothers. In the locker room, the blokes will reject them.

Another contentious section of *The Whole Woman* is 'Mutilation', in which she enlarges on her widely criticised views on female genital mutilation (FGM). Moving seamlessly from describing how, in 1997, the secret women's society Bondo entered the Grafton camp for displaced persons in Sierra Leone and removed the clitorises of 600 women without anaesthetic or antiseptics, she claims that the American Academy of Pediatrics recommends that clitorises of more than three-eighths of an inch should be removed from baby girls before they are fifteen months old, and that five such procedures are performed every day in the United States.[23] The Academy itself presents a different view.[24]

In 'Mutilation', Greer notes that any doctor in the United Kingdom who practises FGM is struck off the medical register, while surgeons routinely perform a variety of gender reassignment and cosmetic surgeries which 'mutilate' both men and women. She suggests that there are two kinds of mutilation: the 'bad' kind comprises practices like cosmetic surgery, hysterectomies, caesarean sections and episiotomies – all legal in Western societies; the 'good' includes genital piercing and clitoridectomies as commonly performed in some Muslim cultures. The basis for the good/bad distinction is that the 'bad' kind of mutilation is done by men to women while the 'good' is about women asserting control over their own bodies.

She also argues that the criminalisation of FGM in most Western countries is culturally offensive.

> Looked at in its full context the criminalization of FGM can be seen to be what African nationalists since Jomo Kenyatta

have been calling it, an attack on cultural identity. Any suggestion that male genital mutilation should be outlawed would be understood to be a frontal attack on the cultural identity of Jews and Muslims.[25]

In the final section of the book, 'Liberation', Greer acknowledges that 'women are acquiring a measure of confidence and beginning to kick free', but she sees even this as problematic. As women have gained more independence, she says, men are backing away from their traditional responsibilities as husbands and fathers. Life for single women is really hard. (Cheryl Davis would agree with her on that one.) She applauds single mothers for their 'loyal, unsparing labour', but she really has it in for those bright young things who stride across the world stage in their high heels and smart suits.[26]

A 'new feminism' that celebrates the right (i.e. duty) to be pretty in an array of floaty dresses and little suits put together for starvation wages by adolescent girls in Asian sweat-shops is no feminism at all.[27]

Recalling the early days of feminism, she remarks that women, like black people, understood themselves to be colonised, but unlike the blacks they did not sing and dance and celebrate their difference. Blacks knew it was futile to pretend to be white, but the new feminists remained unsure of their *identity as women*, and (she implies) probably spent too much time agonising over it. Since those women who seek to ape men's behaviour and aspire to become their equals are rejected by the brotherhood, she argues, it would surely be better not to try. The dignified alternative is for women to stay with their own kind, to keep to their own company, just as men insist on keeping to theirs. If this means segregation, she says grimly, then 'so be it'.[28]

The Whole Woman was not well-received by most critics. (The *New Republic* devoted seven thousand words to rebutting its main arguments.) But she received her usual bag of enthusiastic fan mail from 'ordinary' readers. Young Kiri and Jennie Morley, for example, having decided that the best birthday present for their mother, Valerie, would be a letter from Germaine Greer, wrote to 'Mum's favourite person' asking her to send birthday greetings and to address three questions.

1. How long did it take you to write *The Whole Woman*?
2. Do some of the concepts in the book (as above) come to you in every-day life? Or as you were writing the book?
3. How and why do you believe you got so famous?

Germaine replied:

I don't know the answers to your questions, except that it took me my whole life to write *The Whole Woman*.

Writing is my life, my everyday life. And bugger me if I know why I'm so famous.[29]

9

Coming home

Breathes there the man, with soul so dead,
Who never to himself hath said,
This is my own, my native land!
Sir Walter Scott, 'The Lay of the Last Minstrel', Canto VI[1]

Germaine Greer's public profile has always been much higher in England than Australia, and for some years after her bruising experiences with the Australian media in 1972 she was wary of returning to her homeland. Gradually, however, as the years went by, she came back more often as her ties with her Australian family and friends became closer. In Sydney she generally stays with Margaret Fink and her family, who delight in giving parties for her and all their friends. In Victoria she is always welcome at Ann Polis's house in inner-city Fitzroy, and at her sister Jane's beautiful seaside property in Sorrento.

As a self-employed writer, journalist and performer, she usually manages to ensure that her work contracts include all travel expenses. She insists on business- or first-class airfares and she demands to be well paid, especially for her radio and television appearances. She is not tight-fisted when it comes to spending her money on such items as furniture and pictures for her homes, and jewellery.

Is she English or Australian? By the year 2000, she had spent more of her life in England than Australia. Furious at being made to stand in the 'aliens' queue at British airports after Great Britain joined the European Union in 1973, she eventually decided to take out dual British–Australian citizenship. She has been quoted as saying she will not settle permanently in Australia until the country has a treaty with its Indigenous people.

•

In many of her performances and interviews on British radio and television, Germaine could easily be mistaken for an upper-class Englishwoman, for only the faintest trace of an Australian accent is to be discerned. But the tape recordings now available in her archive reveal the voice of another, private Germaine Greer who, as she records her thoughts while walking her dogs or driving through the countryside, often explodes into pure Australian. On the proposed Identity Card for British residents, for example, she recorded in 1997:

> I managed to be quite funny, thank goodness [in a televised interview] about the bloody Identity Card. Jesus wept! It has to have the Union Jack in the upper corner. I'm not going to carry the Union Jack! I'm Australian. Gimme one with an Australian flag on it. The Australians were good enough to fight the bloody war for these people. I hate the whole idea![2]

With her increasing sense of Australianness came a longing to further repair the rift between herself and her family, which was showing signs of narrowing as the years went by. She had always loved her 'little' brother, Barry, and was growing ever closer to Jane, her sister. Both siblings had families of their own now, nephews and nieces who might be proud to acknowledge Germaine Greer as their aunt. It was not too late for her to become part of the wider family, to experience a sense of real belonging to her own. In 1992, she decided to invite her mother to visit her in England. Her plan was that she and Peg could spend some quiet time at The Mills, do some sightseeing in England and Ireland, and travel to Europe to research the Lafrank side of the family.

The visit was not a success. Peg was not in the best health; at age 73 she had little appetite for rushed, stressful sightseeing. Germaine tried, but she was as impatient as ever with her mother and she made little attempt to adjust her own frantic schedules to accommodate Peg's needs. And, of course, just as Germaine feared but expected, Peg was utterly out of place in England. Eccentric enough on her home turf, the beach at Mentone, in her leotard, she was a complete oddity in the polite academic and literary circles of Cambridge and London. Germaine was not easily embarrassed but she learned to be careful about where to take her mother. She tried to defuse the situation by joking with her friends about Peggy's strange habits and painting a picture of her as a 'character'. 'It's a shame that your mother wasn't able to come,' wrote the organiser of an Eton Literary Society dinner, where Germaine had been the guest speaker:

> I was rather looking forward to seeing her resplendent in her yellow joggers. I hope her chest infection clears up soon and that you yourself will manage to keep your patience with the demands of her egg-sandwich cravings. If you ever did make good on your threat of pushing her off a parapet, you might find the attention you are getting from the tabloids would get worse before it got better.[3]

In 1997, Peggy Greer fell and broke her kneecap. While she was in hospital it became apparent that she was starting to suffer from dementia. Jane, with her brother Barry, was carrying most of the responsibility of caring for her and making decisions about her future. Germaine desperately wanted to be involved in those decisions. 'Jane's in charge. I trust her decisions [but Peggy] must remain free as long as possible, to the last minute. The one thing she's going to want to be is free.'[4]

Eventually, Peggy Greer settled into a retirement home in Hastings, a small seaside town that was close to Jane's property on the Mornington Peninsula. Germaine visited her whenever she was in Australia.

At the same time, her attachment to her English home, The Mills, with its domesticated animals and cultivated vegetation, was waning. Now in her sixties, she was suffering anxiety, and her old depression came back as she realised that, one day, perhaps soon, she would be unable to care properly for her beloved home. Maybe it would be a good idea to sell it. 'It would not be such a terrible trauma because gardening at The Mills has become so desperately hard.'[5]

Germaine had first suffered the 'black dog' of depression as a teenager. 'I thought it was normal,' she told readers of her column in The Oldie in 1992. 'I was the hollow girl, head filled with straw. I won scholarship after scholarship and still I dragged my feet along blank suburban streets. I read books the way other people sniff glue, to get out of my miserable self.'[6] During all the years of her success and adventures, the illness often lay dormant, surfacing mainly after the end of a relationship or in times of financial anxiety, but she always knew it was there, lurking. In the English winter of 1999–2000, she confided to readers of her weekly Daily Telegraph column that she was having a major episode. She would lie awake, night after night, she wrote, staring into the blackness. As each gloomy day dawned, she would find herself trudging miserably through the mud with only her dogs for company. She wondered who would feed her birds and animals if she became too ill to get out of bed. And who, for that matter, would feed her?

The new millennium brought little joy. One of her dogs, Margot, became blind and very ill before dying in 2000. Mollie, the surviving standard poodle, who had always slept outside in her own kennel, took to waiting by the kitchen door, demanding to be allowed to sleep inside. On their regular walks she never let her mistress out of her sight. Her neediness worried Germaine, who had so many other commitments.

Her last cat, Shanghai Jim, had died only a short time before Margot, and the other domestic animals and birds were ailing. 'Life at The Mills has been so muted and sad, with only one dog and no cat, one remaining hen and a goose taken by the fox last week and dragged across the plough, that I could only whinge, and I try not to do that,' she told her *Daily Telegraph* audience.[7]

Shanghai Jim and Christopher had come with her to The Mills in 1985. When Christopher died in 1994, she was bereft. She mourned Jim too, for he had been her faithful companion ever since he was born on the hearthrug of her London flat, but she was grimly aware that his last act had been to kill a bird. She realised now that domestic cats were an ecological disaster: she would never have another one.

She tried to find a logical explanation for her unhappiness. Overwork leading to physical illness? Probably. Spending up to sixteen hours a day in her workshop in front of a computer editing the poetry of Anne Finch, Countess of Winchilsea (1661–1720), might have been damaging to her eyesight. One morning she woke up unable to see out of one eye. She feared blindness, but the problem turned out to be an attack of herpes in the eye, brought on by a weakened immune system. Or could the source of her depression be disappointment? People, perhaps a lover, she declared in one of her columns, had hurt her: by this time in her life she had come to expect that most of them would. But the real problem was the depressive illness itself.

Sympathetic readers wrote letters suggesting various remedies. A female doctor urged her to take antidepressants, but she responded as many a self-disciplined, convent-educated woman would: she could not take the easy way out, she would find redemption through fasting, exertion and self-denial.

She also faced practical problems. Her modus operandi of caring for her labour-intensive property with the aid of assorted students and Non-Paying Guests was still working well enough most of the time. She claimed to be happiest when the bedrooms of her house were all occupied and she was out in the early morning collecting eggs, asparagus and artichokes for lunch, baking bread or driving home from the supermarket, her Mercedes Estate Wagon full of provisions for her household, but she could not rely on her guests to adopt her own standards and level of responsibility for The Mills. Gates would be left open, dogs would attack the geese, and she found it hard to understand why the young people would do annoying things like borrowing and losing her jewellery, leaving lights on and forgetting to lock doors. She was still travelling abroad as a journalist, lecturer and commentator, and her visits to Australia were becoming more frequent, but always she was plagued with anxiety about what might be going on at The Mills in her absence.

Even when she was in residence, she was finding her garden difficult to manage, not least because her enthusiasm was waning.

When a friend, a distinguished poet, inquired one day in an Oxford pub how her garden was faring, she replied, with a colonial bluntness that frightened him into escaping to an alternative hostelry, that it was dying. On reflection, she told this person, she thought the best thing for it would be euthanasia. It was a mess: the herb garden was overgrown, the roses had become impossible to prune, the toughest weeds were gradually taking over. And she hardly cared, because 'these days, the only plants that delight me are those that are naturalising themselves in the wood, sweet violets, narcissi, bluebells, wood anenomae . . .'[8]

Part of her turning away from the ideal of the cultivated English garden was the influence of her sister Jane, who is a well-known Australian botanist. Jane lives with her husband on an attractive property at Sorrento, on the fertile Mornington Peninsula, about one hour's drive from Melbourne. Jane did not go to university upon leaving school, but after she had brought up her two sons she decided to develop her interest in the biodiversity of the Peninsula by studying botany at the University of Melbourne. Before the century's end, she had become a distinguished professional with her own practice, offering expert advice to private and public clients. Her special interests include the preservation and regeneration of indigenous plants and landscapes, and she is an expert on the local coastal vegetation near her home.

Germaine defers to her sister's superior knowledge of plants and botany. As her own passion for gardening, so elegantly expressed in the gardens she created at Pianelli and The Mills, metamorphosed into a love of natural landscapes and a fierce desire to protect them, she at last became fully aware of the extraordinarily fragile and neglected beauty of her native land. She became her sister's pupil, hungry to learn every detail about the identification and cultivation of Australian native species.

Germaine and her sister had not been close in childhood or early adulthood. 'I'm six years older than my little sister,' she told writer Duncan Fallowell in 1994, 'and so I was used by my mother as my sister's nanny. So I hated my sister.' It was not until her 1981 visit to Australia – that same visit on which she had her final lunch in Melbourne with her father – that she began to rediscover her sister. After that, they grew 'closer and closer'. 'We're both foul-mouthed,' she told Fallowell. 'You should hear her playing tennis with her posh friends. She has a huge, passionate heart . . .'[9]

In her book *White Beech: The rainforest years*, published in 2013, Greer describes how she and Jane, on the botanising holidays they had started to take together in the 1990s, developed an intimacy that became precious to both of them. They covered many miles in Jane's off-road vehicle, always on the lookout for 'burny-bits' – tracts of land that had been burned and where new shoots of precious growth could be investigated and photographed. Germaine felt herself to be her happiest, most Australian self on these trips, as she and her sister traversed the country, munching companionably on bags of fruit and aniseed jellies, stopping regularly for a beer and a pie. 'Nothing tastes better,' she commented later, 'than a cold beer and a hot pie at Woollabookankyah or the Black Stump.'[10]

Like many travellers in Australia, the sisters eventually started to feel that they would like to find one part of the vast land that they might buy and call their own. Germaine had created gardens before – in England and in Italy – but never in her home country, and never with another person who was close to her. This new dream was much more than a desire to own property: it was a reaching back to her roots, to home and to a kind of familial intimacy that she had never known, but which she might find with Jane as they worked together to discover, nurture and restore the land.

The other purpose of their travels was to find a suitable resting place for the Germaine Greer Archive, which at that time was stored in a large, purpose-built storage space at The Mills. *White Beech* chronicles this search, telling of the author's pain as she observed the environmental degradation of her country – the decimation of old forests, the gaping quarries, the acres and acres of barren land that had been destroyed by grazing sheep and cattle. As she travelled the continent from Western Australia across the desert heartland to Queensland and New South Wales, she took anguished note of all the evidence of her homeland's rape – the deserted farms, the dying old towns, the forlorn, decaying homesteads of the European settlers whose vain hopes of recreating the verdant farms and pleasant market towns of the old country had been defeated by this stubborn, brooding, timeless landscape.

She considered buying a property at Eden, on the south coast of New South Wales. Once truly a paradise, it was now dominated by a Japanese woodchip mill that had been logging in the old-growth forests of south-eastern New South Wales and the Gippsland region for years. She could never live there, she decided, and she felt she no longer had the stomach to fight the multinational interests that were destroying the place.

What she really wanted, she thought, was a piece of desert. So on her next visit to Australia she flew, alone this time, to Alice Springs and from there to the remote cattle-breeding holding of her friends the Holts, a pioneering family whose ancestors had opened up vast, lonely grazing properties – about one beast per square mile – in the Northern Territory. On the first morning of her visit, Janet and Don Holt took her out to see 'Delny', a remote section of their property where their grandfather had started to build one of the first concrete houses in Australia. Perhaps she would like to buy Delny? The long-unfinished house was still there, baking in the unforgiving sun, surrounded by old farming machinery that was rusting away into the buffel grass. The desert light was clear and fierce. Germaine was intrigued. She could see the house's architectural potential – imagined open colonnades, breezeways, enclosed courtyards – but she sensed that Delny was a sad place.

She understood more when her hosts told her more about Delny's history. The Holt grandparents had abandoned their building project after their youngest child had died of gastro-enteritis, and no family member had ever had the heart to continue. Besides, the house was within earshot of the branding yards. If she lived there she would hear the young animals' screams of pain as they were branded and castrated, and the agonised cries of their mothers, the wet cows who had been separated from their babies.

She could not live at Delny.

Back in the Alice, the real estate agent directed her to a lucerne farm about one hour's drive from the city centre. On the morning of her first sighting of the property she made an impulsive offer of A$360,000, which the owners accepted on the understanding that she would lease back to them that part of the land where the lucerne was being farmed. She would make her home at the back of the property in the foothills of the James Range.

That same afternoon she had to fly back to Sydney and on to England, where she spent the next six months agonising over her hasty decision. In September, she was back in Alice Springs, ostensibly to settle the deal but actually to get out of it. Jane met her at the airport and agreed that there were better ways of spending $360,000.

In 2001, Germaine flew to Logan, Queensland, an unremarkable town situated between Brisbane and the Gold Coast, to speak at a fundraiser for a women's health centre. (The organisers had offered to pay her, but she refused.) After the event, she was telling people about her dream of buying an Australian property where she could store her archive.

'What about Ken's place?' said someone.

'You mean Ken's mother's place?' said someone else.

'Yeah, Ken's really keen to sell that. It might be what you're looking for.'

Ken was Ken Piaggio, a psychotherapist who worked at the centre. He had bought the property to develop it, perhaps as an ecotourism lodge, to provide his mother with some extra income in her retirement, but that plan had failed. It was the old story, thought Germaine, the investment that never came good.

Would she buy it? She thought not. For a start, it was too close to (less than forty kilometres away from) tawdry Surfers Paradise and the ugly suburban spread of the Gold Coast. The next morning, Ken and his wife, Jane-Frances, drove her up through the hills behind the Gold Coast for an inspection of the property. She was mostly silent as she observed the ecological devastation on either side of the road, barely managing to contain her rage at the degradation of a landscape infested with crowded tourist recreation areas, old towns tarted up as 'villages', a prison farm, car parks and public toilets.

They reached Cave Creek, the name of the area where the property was for sale, at noon. Turning left, they entered the Springbrook National Park. Germaine's hosts told her that this section of the park was home to the Natural Arch, a spectacular rock formation in the heart of the forest where water had cut through a ledge to form a deep chasm. The Natural Arch, Ken said, was now a major tourist attraction, reached by a path that led from a busy car park with toilets and an information kiosk. He remarked that busloads of tourists, many of them from Asia, came at night to see the glow-worms around the Natural Arch. 'So much for the tranquillity,' thought Germaine despairingly.

They continued driving for a short distance till they reached the land that was for sale. Entering the property through an open gate, they drove across a concrete causeway through an area where cattle were grazing. Ken stopped the car some distance short of a house with a utility truck parked outside. 'Don't want to disturb the tenant,' he said.

The sun caught them as they got out of the car, but Germaine felt more wet and sticky than hot. The warm day had changed from dry heat to humidity; as they inspected the property, she realised she was in the middle of an ancient rainforest. A poor, abused, exploited rainforest, tortured by grazing cattle and sad attempts to grow fruit; a rainforest with muster yards, a milking parlour and a hay shed; covered in imported weeds, creeping plant life and, in all probability, hordes of hostile animal life – but a rainforest nonetheless.

There was no way she was coming to live here! She would have to tell Ken she was not interested, but in the meantime she would accept his wife's suggestion that they have lunch at 'Angela's'. This turned out to be another tourist trap, a pseudo-farmhouse with a drive bordered by agapanthus, where Angela sold pies, snacks and 'forgetabilia'. 'This is Germaine,' said Ken to Angela.

'I hope you're nothing to do with that bloody Germaine Greer,' she responded.

On the way back to Logan, no one said anything about the property. Embarrassed, Germaine politely told the Piaggios she would be in touch. At her hotel she made a split-second decision to drive rather than fly back to Sydney. The hotel receptionist ordered a hire car for her, which arrived promptly. By now it was late afternoon and she knew the bush would soon be coming alive as the mists rose from the gullies. Had she been fair to Ken's property? Its degradation was not of the forest's making. It was a sad, persecuted, but still most beautiful thing. She had not bargained on a rainforest, but she would need to see it one more time.

Back into the hills she drove, steeling herself to stomach the ugliness along the way. Arriving at the property, she left the car under a stand of jacarandas then fought her way through dense undergrowth down towards the creek. The shadows were lengthening as she found a spot to sit down and contemplate the forest's edge. 'Half a million dollars for a run-down dairy farm. I didn't think so.'

Soon it would be dark. She would need to get back to the hotel, for she must pack her bags and prepare to be on her way to Sydney, then home to her other life in England, her animals, her geese, her wood and garden.

But here and now the forest was brooding, vast and still; the pinkness of the sky was fading to a luminous green; she could just hear a distant thudding, a wallaby, probably. Then, suddenly, something small and alive stepped out from behind a native raspberry bush, directly in front of her, demanding to be noticed. It was a bird.

He was clad in a tabard of a yellow so intense that it seemed to burn, and a cap of the same yellow with a frosting of red on the crown. He walked up to within a few feet of me, fixed me with his round yellow eye and began to move his black rump rhythmically back and forth. There was no doubt about it. He was dancing.[11]

As she walked past the house on her way back to the car, she saw a man standing on the verandah. It was the tenant Ken had told her about. She called to him, 'Hi,' but deep within herself she was thinking, 'Sorry mate, I'm gunna buy your house.'[12]

'You're losing it, girl,' said Jane when Germaine told her. 'Why would you buy something on the Gold Coast? You don't even play golf . . . Let me guess, horsiness, fake villages and avenues of Cocos Palms. The food and wine trail. Bad food and worse wine.'

'No. It's rainforest. Or abandoned dairy farm. It depends which way you look at it.'

'You're the only person I know who would spend two years shopping for desert and come back with rainforest. When am I going to see it?'

On Germaine's next visit to Australia she, Jane and Jane's husband Peter Burke flew to Coolangatta and then drove to the Lamington National Park, where they checked in at an expensive but disappointing 'rainforest retreat'. Next morning, they drove through rain to the Cave Creek property, where they made straight for Germaine's new house, an almost-derelict Queenslander built on columns of cement.[13] Their key did not fit the flimsy door. Germaine was about to kick it down when Peter managed to break in through a rotting window. The house was filthy; decomposing pieces of cheap carpet littered the floor, spider webs obscured every window, internal walls were eaten away by termites and the toilet was unusable because the septic tank had a young Western red cedar growing out of it. But there was water. Jane produced her teapot, cups and fine tea (which accompanied her everywhere), and the three of them sat down to assess the situation. It was raining heavily outside. The tea was good, but everything else looked pretty dire.

Later, they explored the forest, discovering as an added insult that part of it had been cleared to make a quarry. But soon Jane began to see its beauty and its potential. It could be saved, she said, but what a challenge! Rainforests were the most intricate systems on earth, and well-meaning people who tried to 'heal' them often did more damage than good. Her own knowledge of that field of botany was not extensive, and she knew of no 'experts' to advise them. Peter said that it 'could be worse'. It was not his problem.

Before she went back to England this time, Germaine assembled a 'workforce' to commence the task of rehabilitation. The leader was local botanist David Jinks. He put together a tree survey and told her that her land already had some of the highest biodiversity to be found anywhere outside the wet tropics. He also found her two young men, Simon and Will, who were experienced in regeneration work and highly knowledgeable about local plant life. Soon, two 'old-fashioned' botanists, Rob Price and Lui Weber, joined the team.

On her next visit to Cave Creek, Germaine's old friend Ann Polis flew up from Melbourne to keep her company.

'What are you going to do about the cattle?' Ann wanted to know.

Germaine said that she would have to get rid of them. They were fouling the creek and trampling the pythons. But there were two little steers, household pets, who came to her for treats. She felt so sad as she watched them being roughly corralled into a truck with the rest of the herd, to be driven away to a predictable fate.

'You realise that you're steadily reducing the value of this real estate?' said Ann.

'Mm.' replied Germaine.

And then, again, she returned to England, expecting that the work would go on in her absence.

One evening in Cambridge, she was attending a formal college dinner when she got into an argument with a fellow diner, a person who was as opinionated as she was. Unwisely, as it turned out, he was trying to tell her that she should leave her forest alone and allow it to regenerate itself. She couldn't let him get away with that. 'You could be right, but I don't think so.' Then she launched into one of her diatribes about old-growth forests, lawyer and kangaroo vines that would go berserk if not controlled, malignant pioneer species, the proteoid roots of silky oak, *Grevillea robusta* – and more, much more, of the same.

On and on she talked until, looking down at her plate, she realised that the salmon in front of her was stone cold and that her adversary had long given up in boredom. Everyone else was politely waiting for her to finish her course so that the waiter could take her plate and they could get on with their pudding. But, oblivious of the fact that she may have ruined the evening for everyone, she was still locked into thoughts of her forest as she consumed her tarte au citron. All those vines! Morning glory, balloon, white passionfruit, glycine, siratro, and, worst of all, kudzu. They could all be exterminated, but think of the work and the expense!

When the diners moved into the common room to take port, a woman approached Germaine and offered to make a donation to the Cave Creek project. 'You need to set up a charity,' she said. It was a new idea, but one to think about. The rainforest really belonged not to her but to itself, and restoring it was already a task of huge proportions. It was only the knowledge that she was not really alone – that all the organisms of the forest were working together – fungi, bacteria, reptiles, invertebrates, amphibians, birds, trees and a few humans – that kept her going. But how could she keep funding it?

From 2003 onwards, she spent several months each year at Cave Creek. The 'workforce' that cared for the property in her absence were mostly efficient and competent, but they were very expensive. She expected them to look after the property as if it were their own but, similarly to the people who were supposed to care for The Mills in her absence, they did not always live up to those expectations. 'What a strange person he is,' she remarked of one helper, when, arriving at her house alone and exhausted after a long drive, she had to struggle with the faulty garage door lock and found the house wide open with all the lights on. 'Is it against his fucking religion to take care of someone else's property?'[14]

She loved to walk and work at Cave Creek, but her body was ageing and arthritis was taking its annoying toll, especially on her feet and knees. The landscape was unforgiving. While walking in the forest, she recorded her frustration on her tape-recorder as she kept falling over and getting lost in the dense scrub, 'hurting myself beyond bearing'. She was very tired. It was hard to get a foothold and her knees hurt 'disgracefully'. She fell on her hand and it started to turn black. 'This must be the most difficult place on earth to walk . . . Every single step is danger-ous . . . for someone like me who can barely stagger along it's a nightmare.' And characteristically: 'I'm going to have to think of a way of dealing with it because it's my delight.'[15]

The heavy work of restoring the rainforest had to be left to the workforce, but Germaine, as well as directing activities, spent many hours weeding and clearing vines. She developed an encyclopaedic knowledge of rainforest flora and fauna, all of which she documented as meticulously and systematically as she had recorded her studies of art and literature. She noted the work of the great naturalists, especially pioneers of Australian botany like Joseph Banks and Robert Brown, but her main library, she believed, was the forest itself.

At Cave Creek, 'her' animals live in the wild, but she loves them as she has loved her dogs, geese and cats in England. She is particularly fond of the lizards, some of which, like the beautiful lace monitor, can grow up to seven feet in length. And she loves the snakes. Most of them are non-venomous pythons that come in all colours, from greenish-gold to black and red. There are hundreds of pythons at Cave Creek, and some live within feet of Germaine's house or on the verandah. She has seen them hunting in the walls for a way in, following the heat of the marsupial mice who occupy the wall cavities. Once she was woken up by a python who had found his way through the louvres into her bedroom. Drawn to the warmth of her body, he was arching himself, preparing for the strike.[16]

This sort of thing is not everyone's cup of tea, and she is hardly surprised when friends politely decline her invitations to visit. ('Ugh! I won't go there. All those spiders!' says one friend, an urban Sydneysider.)

By the time she had finished writing *White Beech*, Germaine had worked her way through the formalities of handing the rehabilitation project, which was now called the Cave Creek Rainforest Rehabilitation Scheme (CCRRS), over to a UK registered charity called 'Friends of Gondwana Rainforest'. The complicated legal processes of setting up the charity took time and caused much frustration, but, ultimately, she was at peace.

At 74, she realised that she could love and care for the forest, but did not need to own it. She continued to play a powerful advisory role, and she was able to keep her house, but the day she gave away all her cash to the rainforest, she said, was the happiest day of her life.

Germaine's first priority after signing the transfer of land documents for her property over to the charity was to discover the original Aboriginal owners of the land. She even hoped she might find some surviving tribe members to perform a welcoming ceremony for her. In turn, she said, she would be happy for them to use the land as they wished. But very soon she discovered that uncovering the truth about the ancient history of her land would be a much greater challenge than she had first thought. She made many inquiries of local Aboriginal groups and academics, but everything was complicated by competing claims of different clans and intricate land rights politics.

She was fascinated by the spectacular Natural Arch in the Springbrook National Park, adjacent to her property. Because of its striking natural beauty, she wondered whether Aboriginal people of old may have identified it as a place of special significance, a sacred site – maybe a place for women, or for initiation rites, but in any case, a secret site that could not be spoken of – but she could find nothing to corroborate her idea. All of her searches came to dead ends. Her visions of a welcoming ceremony began to fade.

Eventually, however, following the advice of Ann Polis, she discovered what she hoped was an answer in the Australian Institute of Aboriginal and Torres Strait Islander Studies (AIATSIS) library at the National Museum of Australia complex in Canberra.[17] In a PhD thesis written in 1959 by anthropologist Malcolm Calley, she read that the McPherson Range, where Cave

Creek is situated, was the home of *boiun* (ogres) and *derangan* (ogresses). One ogre, Ililarng, was said to have no friends. The area was rugged and inhospitable. No tribe had ever occupied the mountains, and groups who were travelling to feasts and celebrations avoided them in favour of the beaches.

When Ann called from Melbourne, Germaine felt confident enough to tell her that Cave Creek was the home of Ililarng, the friendless ogre who had long brooded over the rainforest. The surrounding Numinbah Valley was a place of demons. There would be no native title claim because no Aboriginal clans had ever lived there. When travelling up the coast and through and around the ancient rainforests, they had carefully avoided the area.[18]

In the 1990s, before she bought Cave Creek and before she had discovered its provenance, Germaine was exploring in her mind an idea – a big idea that reflected the seriousness of her commitment to the Aboriginal people of Australia. So important was this idea to her that when, in November 1999, she received a letter from the British Secretary for Appointments at 10 Downing Street informing her of the Prime Minister's wish to submit her name to the Queen to be awarded the high honour of Commander of the British Empire (CBE) in the New Year Honours of 2000, she 'regretfully' declined the offer. 'In case my refusal should seem ungracious,' she added:

> I should explain that I do all I can to promote the cause
> of aboriginal sovereignty, a cause now recognised in the
> international community as just. Because my acceptance
> of such an award might conceivably alienate me from the
> aboriginal peoples I am trying to help and the Australian
> public whose attitudes I am trying to influence, I have

regretfully decided to forgo the outward sign of a recognition I appreciate greatly and that I would otherwise be proud to accept.[19]

She subsequently expressed her big idea in an essay called *Whitefella Jump Up*. One wonders if she knew, when she started, that she was stirring up another major storm of controversy for herself.

Her idea, put simply, was that Australia is and has always been an Aboriginal nation. 'Try saying that to yourself,' she advised. 'Stand in front of the mirror and say "I live in an Aboriginal country." Then say: "I was born in an Aboriginal country therefore I must be considered Aboriginal."' If the original settlers had done this, she argued, if they had sought to assimilate with the inhabitants instead of assuming their own superiority, rampaging through the country, debasing and destroying all before them, the 'problem' of Aboriginality would never have arisen.

> The ignorant presumed to teach the learned . . . the ignorant set about 'discovering' a country of which the learned carried immensely detailed maps in their heads. The ignorant didn't ask the learned which way to go, or how to survive on the track.[20]

Greer's criticisms of white Australia in *Whitefella Jump Up* are excoriating, though not original. Predictably, she singles out the white males. Drunken, insensitive, emotionally paralysed, spiritually desolated, she says, they attack the land, divert the watercourses, build high-rise buildings on flood plains and, worst of all, 'create an endless nightmare of suburbia from which our kids try to escape by sticking needles in their arms'.[21]

She claims that her intentions in writing the essay are modest. She has no axes to grind, she is simply 'an elderly laywoman who is not in search of a job or a promotion'.[22] She sincerely believes she has discovered a way out of the impasse and she wants to share her insights. People will say she has lost her marbles, but what's new? Her friends will simply see this, her latest preposterous suggestion, as yet another example of her 'ratbaggery'. Yet she will persevere, for she believes she is right.

She asks herself if she is qualified to write this book. What right has she, as a person who has spent more time away from Australia than in it, to offer such a simple solution to an immensely complex set of problems? (A good question.) As a child and young adult, she, like most Australians of her generation, had never seen an Aboriginal person. She recalled that when she first 'came up' to Melbourne University, she sat on a committee for Aboriginal scholarships, only to discover that there was not one eligible Aboriginal matriculand. (An interesting aside here: her use of the phrase 'came up' in this context betrays her expatriate orientation. Australians do not say 'came up' to university. To their ears it sounds pretentious.)[23]

Greer's answer to her own question is that distance provided her with an international perspective. In the years between 1964 and 1971, when the thought of returning to Australia was, for personal reasons, painful to her, she had followed developments in other postcolonial countries, including South Africa. It was only when she was half a world away, she wrote, that she started to realise that Australia was also guilty of apartheid. How absurd was it for Australians to demonstrate against the Springbok tour of 1971 when they could not see what was happening in their own backyard?

Indigenous issues had been in Greer's mind as long ago as 1972, when she had flown to Alice Springs with Aboriginal rights activist and poet Roberta 'Bobbi' Sykes.[24] To her friend Louise Ferrier, who was living with Richard Neville in London at the time, she had written:

> Tomorrow I go to Alice Springs with Bobby Stykes [sic]. We are going to live on a creek bed with about 800 abos, in order to find out what it's really like to be black and Australian. Me and my ulcer. What I shall eat I have no idea. There won't even be any fresh milk, let alone yoghurt, and the bland things I need to ease my pain.

She concluded: 'I'd better stop writing and prepare for a rollicking week in the humpies of Alice Springs.'[25]

This letter shows that, like most Australians at that time and later, Germaine Greer had a lot to learn about the First Peoples of Australia, but unlike most of them she was attempting to find out. Choosing to sleep at an Aboriginal camp on the dry bed of the Todd River, she and Sykes sat down every day with a group of Aboriginal people who became her friends. On her mattress, on the warm sand under the river gums, she listened to the stories they had to tell, realising that they had far more to teach her than she was then capable of learning. On the Saturday night of her necessarily brief visit, she was drinking with a group of these new friends in the beer garden of the Alice Springs hotel when the pub was raided by police. All of the Aboriginal people were arrested, and pleaded guilty to the charge of drunk and disorderly. Some received long custodial sentences. They had broken no law, she said.

In *Whitefella Jump Up* she goes on to describe how, on subsequent visits to Australia, she made a point of spending time with Aboriginal groups – the Yolngu people at Yirrkala, the Anmatyerre people at Utopia and Yuendumu, and urban

Aboriginal people in Sydney and Melbourne. Over time, she said, she had spent more time with blackfellas than with her own family. In the 1980s, Kulin women from the Melbourne suburb of Fitzroy had offered to adopt her. She was taken aback. Would she be expected to isolate herself in some remote spot for a month or more and be 'painted, smoked or cut about?' she asked herself. But her fears were groundless. 'That's it,' said the Kulin women. 'It's done, we've adopted you!'[26]

Then Germaine asked herself another very good question. She was able to spend no more than four months in Australia each year: her visits were taken up with a myriad of activities – managing her rainforest enterprise, catching up with friends and family, interacting with the curious media. Could her relatively brief encounters with people like the Kulin women and the friends she had made in Alice Springs be typical of the superficial relationships many white people – nurses, teachers, missionaries – had with Aboriginal people? It is a familiar scenario: these well-meaning people fly in, stay for a while and must then return to their own white lives and social institutions. Quoting anthropologist Gillian Cowlishaw, Greer recognised the 'shallowness' of such people's incorporation into the Aboriginal kinship systems: 'they would suddenly depart, often never to be heard of again. "Must have gone back to 'im own country," people would say with a sense of betrayal or disappointment'.[27]

It is partly because of this – what many people, including Aboriginal people themselves, saw as her necessarily underdeveloped relationships with Indigenous people – that the publication of Germaine Greer's *Whitefella Jump Up* attracted so much criticism. This is particularly true of the response of the non-Indigenous writer Mary Ellen Jordan, who understood the complexities of white engagement with black cultures, having spent fourteen months living and working in Maningrida, an Aboriginal community in Arnhem Land. The main problem with Greer's essay, she believed (and there were many who agreed with her), was that it had very little to say about what taking on Aboriginality might mean in practice. The very concept of Aboriginality, as Greer herself acknowledged, had not even existed in the time before colonisation, when distinct Aboriginal groups did not think of themselves as a single collective society: even today, said Jordan, many Aboriginal people's identities were grounded not in 'Aboriginality', but in their own tribe or language group. Of what, exactly, were white people expected to think when they declared themselves to be 'Aboriginal'?

Jordan also believed that Greer had failed to fully understand the vast differences between white and black cultures. In Maningrida, she had learned that any coming together of black and white must involve changing cultures – an immensely difficult and confronting prospect. In the area of health care, for example, the urgency of saving lives, treating diseases, and preventing high rates of infant mortality surely had to be placed above considerations about the impact that white medicine was having on native culture.[28]

Predictably, Germaine Greer's harsh criticisms of the early white settlers infuriated some of their descendants, including and especially Patsy Millett – the daughter of Dame Mary Durack, whose classic history of her pastoralist forbears, *Kings in Grass Castles*, chronicled the life and work of her grandfather, nineteenth-century Western Australian pastoral landowner and pioneer Patrick Durack. 'Mary Durack,' Greer wrote sneeringly in her essay, 'was descended from landless and illiterate peasants who attempted to improve their wretched situation by brewing poteen . . .' Patrick Durack, she opined, may have been less murderous of blacks than many of his ilk, but it had been written of him that he had once stamped a cattle brand on the rump of a slow-moving young Aboriginal male.[29]

It is hardly surprising that the present-day Duracks were incensed. After reading the essay, Millett launched into an ad hominem attack that Greer was hardly in a position to object to (because she often used the same tactic herself). Millett ridiculed Greer's proposition, that all Australians should embrace 'their' Aboriginality, as 'whimsical', claiming that it was an attention-grabbing 'stunt'.

> The key to her long career as a hit and run artist upon our shores has been to ride in upon a white horse of indignation and/or outrage at some aspect of Australian failure – pronounce upon it loudly and prominently via the media – and depart.[30]

P.A. Durack Clancy, daughter of Dame Mary's sister Elizabeth Durack, added to her cousin's criticism.

> It is possible to ignore the main thrust of Greer's essay – her admonition to whitefellas to become jumped-up born-again blackfellas. Let those who will, 'sit on the ground with [Greer] and think'. Others will give her nought out of ten for workable shortcuts; ten out of ten for media coverage.[31]

Greer took this kind of vilification in her stride, although she protested that, far from seeking attention, she spent four months of every year in Australia trying to be so inconspicuous that nobody knew she was there. Far more important to her were the reactions of Aboriginal people. These were less censorious than the Duracks', but, on the whole, disappointingly lukewarm if not outright critical. She was saddened by the 'vein of nastiness' in the response of Professor Marcia Langton, long-time campaigner for Aboriginal rights and justice, claiming to be puzzled as to why Langton, a former friend, had referred to her as 'Dr Greer' when 'I am as much a professor as she is, and she knows it.'[32]

Langton's essay in response to *Whitefella Jump Up* was well-considered and scholarly. Like Patsy Millett, she used the word 'whimsical' to describe Greer's big idea and, again like Millett, she expressed reservations – 'a niggling doubt' – about the depth of expatriate Greer's engagement with her subject.[33]

Langton also criticised Greer for her apparent ignorance of the enormous body of fictional and non-fictional writing, cinema and art on Indigenous topics over the past thirty years. 'Greer's heavy reliance on "classical" Australian literary fiction,' she said, 'is redolent of the late 1960s and the sense of protest at the colonial legacy of Australian literature.' Germaine was wounded at this attack on her scholarship, but she could not entirely refute it.

The greatest weakness of Greer's essay, according to Langton, was its 'zany disconnectedness'. She dismissed the notion that the Australian accent may have been formed from such influences as Aboriginal nannies teaching white children to speak as fanciful and eccentric, noting that Greer's ideas on the subject were unsupported by evidence and research.

In response to these and the many other criticisms, Greer pointed out that while her proposal was a necessary condition for Australia to achieve a new kind of 'cultural coherence' (aka nationhood), it was not sufficient.

In case I didn't make myself unmistakeably clear (and the title of the essay could mislead), let me restate it. Australia will never achieve political maturity unless and until it recognises its ineradicable Aboriginality.[34]

Even Professor Langton, or so Professor Greer believed, was prepared to move into that 'imaginative space'.[35]

All gloves were off, however, when Langton wrote her response to Greer's 2008 essay *On Rage*.

The political context of *On Rage* was the introduction of the Australian federal government policy that is commonly called 'the Intervention'. This policy was developed in 2007 in response to mounting evidence of serious and mostly unreported physical and sexual abuse of women and children by men in some Aboriginal communities. The series of measures included the quarantining of a proportion of welfare benefits to Aboriginal people who were judged to be neglecting their children, changes to law enforcement and land tenure, and restrictions on alcohol. Many people, white and black, opposed the Intervention, and many others supported it. Controversy raged over its implementation, which was initially carried out by six hundred soldiers and detachments from the Australian Defence Force.

The essence of Greer's *On Rage* is that Aboriginal men are suffering from a kind of 'disabling rage' that is driving them to self- and socially destructive behaviour. They have lost their land, their women, their language. Alcohol abuse and violence are symptoms of the problem that is male rage engendered by centuries of white abuse, especially the rape and prostitution of Aboriginal women.

Marcia Langton was one of several influential Aboriginal activists (Bess Price and Noel Pearson were others) who gave their qualified support to the Intervention. In an angry article that appeared in *The Australian* on 19 August 2008, Langton wrote that Greer should stop her attention-grabbing behaviour and cease 'baiting' Aboriginal people like herself. They were all much too busy working for the wellbeing of Indigenous people, she said, to be bothered by such 'distractions'.

Langton then launched a personal attack on Greer, accusing her of racism, attention-seeking and poor scholarship. Greer's 'little treatise', she said, ignored the growing body of critical literature on the real causes of Indigenous disadvantage. She agreed with Noel Pearson and Dr Hannah McGlade (a Nyungar human rights lawyer and academic) that the perpetrators of abuse should take responsibility for their own behaviour: 'We are not in the mood for failed leftist excuses for the rising levels of homicide, femicide, and suicide.' Germaine Greer was 'just plain wrong'. Aboriginal people of the future who had been victims of unchecked violence against women and children would wonder why a feminist of Greer's stature would defend the men who had destroyed their innocence.[36]

Germaine Greer's personal commitment to the welfare and advancement of Indigenous Australians is beyond question. Her archive presents much evidence of this, but it also includes revelations about her frustration with some Aboriginal groups that, albeit with excellent reasons, have not been willing to work with her. For example: in July 2007, she received an email from Scottish filmmaker Roy Colquhoun, who proposed making a video that would 'put the case for the Aborigine [sic] peoples to a wider audience'. He hoped that Greer would lend her support. She replied:

When I have been involved in projects such as you suggest, the most difficult part has been the attitude of the aboriginal people themselves. They don't want their situation exposed or publicised. These are peoples with a culture of reticence and avoidance.

More to the point, perhaps, is that there is a self-elected caste of official spokespersons who claim the sole right to funding and support. Even when I have been making programs about wildflowers I've had to deal with these people disrupting what I was doing and claiming that I had co-opted the Aboriginals' story, culture, whatever. Subsidised koori quisling 'koori' media exist and nothing much can be accomplished without their active participation, which means, in effect, that nothing can be accomplished.

You will not be helped by my giving public support, I'm afraid.[37]

•

For one who claimed to avoid public attention, Germaine Greer managed to grab a disproportionate amount of it in the first decade and a half of the twenty-first century. Increasingly, she upset the LGBTIQ community with her unpopular views on transgender issues. As well as upsetting black and white people with her views on Aboriginality, she got herself accused of paedophilia; she insulted prominent public individuals like Catherine, Duchess of Cambridge (too thin), Mother Teresa (why did she travel first-class?), First Lady Michelle Obama (big head and poor dress sense at her husband's inauguration) and the late Steve Irwin (he had it coming to him). She professed to be unconcerned (and probably was) when, shortly after Steve Irwin's death, his portrait replaced hers in the Australian National Portrait Gallery.

In 2005, she made what was arguably the worst and certainly the most embarrassing mistake of her public life when she appeared on *Celebrity Big Brother* series three.

Until Sylvester Stallone's mother Jackie (born 1921) joined the 'housemates' in the Big Brother house on the fifth day, Germaine and John McCririck, a racing commentator who became known in the house for his uncouth behaviour and attitudes, were the oldest of the nine participants by at least twenty years, and the age gap showed. The younger people were totally under-whelmed by Professor Greer, who was simply 'Germaine'. They tolerated her as one politely tolerates an out-of-touch old aunt, but kept her low in the pecking order and complained about her habit of 'going on and on'. In a challenge styled around a medieval court, in which everyone appeared in costume and all decisions were made by Lisa l'Anson, who played the part of 'queen', Germaine was allotted the demeaning role of cook. In her serving-wench costume – long white full-skirted dress with dark jerkin, apron and cap – she looked old and dumpy. Grumpy, as well, especially when her housemates would not let her have her own way.

She stood it until the sixth day, when she demanded to leave the Big Brother house. Subsequently, writing in the *News Review* of 16 January 2005, she said that she had tried to make a stand against the bullying culture that had developed in the house, but the other housemates had not gone along with her. She had expected 'Big Brother' to be a bully, she wrote, but what she did not expect was that the show's producers would deliberately create appalling conditions – lack of palatable food, a filthy kitchen and refrigerator, dirty, shared towels and bathrobes – that would reduce the housemates to such a state of abjection that they would turn upon each other.

Why did she do it? In an article for the *Daily Telegraph*, she claimed that she wanted to experience something of the life her mother was leading in her nursing home in Australia. One angry reader responded, 'Perhaps some of the "lump of cash" you have been paid for your few days in the Big Brother house could go towards a better home for your mother.'

Greer replied, 'As an Australian war-widow, my mother has the best accommodation and health care that money can buy as of right . . . my mother has a great deal more money than I do . . .'[38]

She was certainly stretching the truth in making this claim, but she was probably referring only to her own disposable income. At this time her Australian rainforest was turning into a money pit: she had to purchase expensive equipment and pay the salaries of five staff. The £40,000 she had been offered to appear in *Celebrity Big Brother* would be a big help.

Germaine's supporters praised her for exposing the reality show as not just tasteless, but culturally and morally disgraceful. Other people thought she had simply embarrassed herself, and to some, this gaffe was just another indication that she and her opinions were becoming passé.

In 2003, she was labelled a paedophile following the publication of her book *The Beautiful Boy*. By then she had turned 64, and women of that age are not expected to enjoy looking at the bodies of young boys.

The Beautiful Boy (in some editions simply *The Boy*) is a history of boys in art. Its more than two hundred sumptuously presented photos and discussions depict boys from ancient Greek times to the present – Eros, Cupid, Elvis Presley, Boy George, Kurt Cobain. Unsurprisingly (or perhaps intentionally?) the book was controversial, but Greer took accusations of paedophilia in her stride. *The Boy* was full of pictures of 'ravishing' pubescent boys with hairless chests, wide-apart legs and slim waists, she declared in the *Daily Telegraph*. The blurb on the back cover proclaimed that she wanted to reclaim for women the right to appreciate the short-lived beauty of boys. Asked on Canadian television to explain the attraction, she replied, 'Sperm that runs like tap-water will do.'[39]

She laughed when the Australian television interviewer Andrew Denton put it to her that what she had written in *The Boy* was 'creepy – no different to an old man staring after a young girl and lusting after them'. What was wrong about that, she wanted to know: 'Of course the old men leaning on their sticks would appreciate the figure of a beautiful young woman walking down the street. How, and why, would anyone want to stop the old bastards? Part of the joy of life is admiring beautiful things.'[40]

Greer was used to receiving hate mail, but she received some particularly unpleasant letters after *The Boy* was published. She was accused of being a paedophile, a dirty old woman, a sexual deviant. As usual, there were demands for her to go back to where she came from. 'What is it with all you whining Aussies?' – 'Piss off!' – 'Join the Luftwaffe, you are ugly enough.' – 'Have you thought about euthanasia?' – 'You are a vitriolic, bitter and twisted being.' One woman warned her to check her computer files before the police could get to them. 'Did you ever stop to consider the boy's mother?' she railed. 'You have a serious problem and should seek help,' advised another correspondent. Many people sent her poems and articles, most of them racist, pornographic, misogynist, anti-migration, some containing various interpretations of religious tracts. 'No reply whatsoever,' she directed her assistant, Carol Horne, who filtered the correspondence.[41]

More sophisticated readers castigated Greer for the sloppiness of her arguments. No sooner had the reader managed to swallow one outrageous assertion in *The Boy*, complained writer and historian Ian Britain, than they became aware of the extent to which it contradicted the claims that preceded it. Never mind that her case studies in 'boyhood' included a picture of a Frank Sinatra, who was well into his twenties at the time, and of Kurt Cobain with a five o'clock shadow: her definition of 'boyhood' was of a male who was old enough to be capable of sexual response, but not old enough to shave. But then again, she stated elsewhere in the book, the reader must understand that boyhood actually starts as soon as a baby is weaned.

'Silly reader,' says Britain, 'for daring to crave consistency.'[42]

Some of the apparent inconsistency in Greer's writing can be put down to sloppy thinking, as in the examples above, but more often it stems from her old libertarian roots, her refusal to align her views with any set of fixed beliefs or principles, and her preparedness to change her mind if she thinks a new idea is an improvement on its predecessors. Inconsistent she may well be, but no one can accuse her of being politically correct for the sake of it.

Examples of her unwillingness to conform to any credo – even feminism – abound: they include her criticisms of Michelle Obama and Australian Prime Minister Julia Gillard, both of whom she castigated for their appearance and fashion sense. The dress Michelle wore on her husband's election night, she said, was 'a travesty', 'a lava-lamp look'. Just as well her low-heeled shoes disguised the fact that her head was bigger than her husband's. But as for that black cardigan . . .![43]

Was Michelle's cardigan a bigger fashion gaffe than Julia Gillard's jackets? Probably not, for Greer's dressmaking eye picked up that the jackets were cut too narrow, causing a horizontal crease to appear across the Prime Minister's backside. 'What I want her to do is get rid of those bloody jackets,' she protested. 'You've got a big arse, Julia, just get on with it!'[44]

Insensitive as remarks like these were, she was generally able to laugh them off so that most people did not take her too seriously, but her insulting comments about transgender people were another matter. 'Just because you lop off your penis and then wear a dress doesn't make you a fucking woman,' she proclaimed in her interview with the comedic actor Rebecca Root, who is a trans woman, in October 2015. 'I've asked my doctor to give me long ears and liver spots and I'm going to wear a brown coat but that won't turn me into a fucking cocker spaniel.' She understood, she said, that some people were born intersex and that they deserved support, but that was not the same thing as a man deciding to become a woman. She particularly objected to post-operative transsexuals: 'A man who gets his dick chopped off is actually inflicting an extraordinary act of violence on himself.'

Ms Root said she was 'beeping gobsmacked' by Greer's comments. 'This is something that I would equate with the worst of the gutter press,' she said, 'not from somebody of such academic standing; a woman who should know better . . . her comments are grossly offensive, quite ludicrous and very, very out of date and out of line with the current way that the trans community is progressing . . . She is a negative force. She's like the worst baddie in your classic panto.'[45]

By 2015 the age of social media had well and truly dawned, and some who agreed with Root used it to express their outrage. 'Christ, Germaine Greer does just come across as a rancid old bigot on trans comments,' pretty well summed up the popular view.[46]

If the opinions of the twittersphere were mostly not on her side, she could take comfort from the fact that some people of her own generation agreed with her: 'the far Left is so conservative, paradoxically, inflexible, doctrinaire and humourless,' commented her old friend Barry Humphries.

> You can't describe the world as it is any more . . . I agree with Germaine! You're a mutilated man, that's all . . . Self-mutilation, what's all this carry on? Caitlyn Jenner – what

a publicity-seeking ratbag. It's all given the stamp – not of respectability, but authenticity or something. If you criticise anything you're racist or sexist or homophobic.[47]

Humphries was referring to the immediate cause of the 2015 controversy – Greer's accusation that television personality Caitlyn (formerly Bruce) Jenner had stolen the limelight from other female members of her family, the Kardashians, by being prepared to accept *Glamour* magazine's decision to give Jenner its Woman of the Year award. 'I think misogyny plays a really big part in this,' said Greer, in an interview with the BBC's *Newsnight*, 'that a man who goes to these lengths to become a woman will be a better woman than someone who is just born a woman.' When the interviewer suggested that she was being hurtful to transgender women she rolled her eyes. 'People are being hurtful to me all the time,' she exclaimed.

> Try being an old woman. For goodness sake, people get hurt all the time. I'm not about to walk on eggshells . . . I'm not saying that people should not be allowed to go through that procedure. What I'm saying is it doesn't make them a woman. It happens to be an opinion. It's not a prohibition.[48]

Greer had been scheduled to speak at Cardiff University on 18 November 2015, in a lecture titled 'Women and Power: The lessons of the 20th century', but in mid-October, Rachael Melhuish, women's officer at the university's students' union, circulated an online petition for the lecture to be cancelled. 'While debate in a University should be encouraged,' it stated, 'hosting a speaker with such problematic and hateful views towards marginalised and vulnerable groups is dangerous.'[49]

Greer's memories of being 'glitter-bombed' for her views on transgender people in Wellington, New Zealand, in 2012 were still fresh. 'I've had things thrown at me, I've been accused of things I have never done or said, people seem to have no concern about evidence or, indeed, even about libel,' she told BBC News.

Despite the petition attracting more than a thousand signatures, Cardiff University refused to cancel the lecture. She appreciated the university's adherence to principles of free speech and academic freedom, but she baulked at exposing herself to violent abuse. 'I'm getting a bit old for all this. I'm 76. I don't want to go down there and be screamed at and have things thrown at me,' she said. 'Bugger it, it's not all that interesting or rewarding.'[50]

10

Full circle

The wheel is come full circle . . .

William Shakespeare, *King Lear*

Tuesday, 10 January 2017

Who is that sitting at the L'Oréal cosmetics counter in the David Jones store? Yes, it's Cheryl – Cheryl Davis. She has come to buy a new moisturiser advertised by film star Helen Mirren, the elderly but still beautiful 'face of L'Oréal'. It is now forty-five years since Cheryl first read *The Female Eunuch*, the book that changed her life. She is 78, the same age as Germaine Greer, and now more happily single than ever. Her arthritis, like Germaine's, sometimes keeps her awake at night, but she is generally healthy and, again like Germaine, she enjoys her garden and has many friends.

The L'Oréal 'beauty consultant', Mary-Jane, is an attractive, professionally made-up 55-year-old. She's talking to Cheryl about Germaine Greer.

'I just love her!' she says. 'I first read her book when I was twelve. I was a boarder in a convent in Sydney. I decided to take "Germaine" as my confirmation name. The nuns thought it was after a saint, but it wasn't, it was after Germaine Greer.'

'But I was disappointed,' she continues, 'when I heard what she said the other day about Princess Diana.'

'What was that?' asks Cheryl. 'I must have missed it.'

Mary-Jane giggles; she doesn't want to shock the old lady.

'Go on!' says Cheryl impatiently.

'Well – she said Princess Diana would be 56 now and no one would be interested in her. She also . . . um . . . said that Diana was the worst fuck in the country. I thought it wasn't very nice of her to say that.'

'She does tend to say rather outrageous things sometimes,' says Cheryl carefully.

'Maybe she's just trying to get attention. You know – make everyone sit up and listen to her. In case they forget who she is.'

At that moment, a trim, young beauty consultant comes across from the Dior counter.

'Hi, Li. We're just talking about Germaine Greer.'

Li Chen looks nonplussed.

'Who is he?' she asks politely.

Wednesday, 8 March 2017

Germaine Greer has come to the University of Melbourne for an International Women's Day event called 'Germaine Greer meets the archivists'.

She is to speak to an audience of five hundred people in the Kathleen Fitzpatrick Theatre. Four hundred people have had to be turned away for lack of space in the theatre.

I, the teller of Germaine Greer's story, am sitting about five rows from the front, where she is seated next to the University Librarian, Philip Kent. I have seen her walk into the theatre – not as tall as I expected, broader, but quite stylishly dressed in black and white. She limps a bit, but carries herself well, exuding a kind of bored but wary confidence.

Julie Willis, Professor and Dean of the Faculty of Architecture, is the first speaker. After the acknowledgement of country, she draws the audience's attention to the person after whom the theatre is named – Kathleen Fitzpatrick, Associate Professor of History at the university in the 1950s and 1960s – noting that, like Germaine Greer, Fitzpatrick is an alumna of the University of Melbourne and that she was a prominent feminist of her time. Rachel then beams up onto the big screen at the front of the theatre the old student record cards of the two women; the audience laughs.

The similarities between the two women are striking, but I reflect on some significant differences: Fitzpatrick was acquainted with the student Germaine but, like her close friend and neighbour Professor Keith Macartney, she would have found the undergraduate's behaviour 'most ir-reg-ular'. Like Germaine, Fitzpatrick was a star performer in a lecture theatre, but unlike her she was 'ladylike' almost to the point of caricature.

In *The Female Eunuch*, Greer targeted the shortcomings of the first wave of feminism, chief of which was women's failure to recognise that external factors alone were not responsible for their plight, for they themselves had been conditioned ('castrated') into subservience. Seen in this light, Kathleen Fitzpatrick, staunch feminist of the first wave, is a sad example of Greer's argument. She excelled in her field and she fought tirelessly for women's rights, but she did not think she was good enough to be a full professor when she was offered it, and she constantly deferred to men, most notably, and sometimes pathetically, to her male superior, Professor Max Crawford. Throughout her life, though she would surely have read *The Female Eunuch*, she remained deaf to Greer's credo that women should seek the causes of their oppression within themselves, and should reassess their own feelings, attitudes and beliefs before they tried to change the world.

Soon it is Germaine Greer's turn to speak. She surveys her audience with a practised eye: 'Well,' she says, when the long round of applause finally stops, 'I'm feeling a bit breathless, really. I had no idea I was so interesting.'

She speaks without notes. The archive is not about her, she insists, and she dislikes the kinds of images that have been created of her, especially by the Australian media. Recalling how, in 1971, she was presented to the public as 'a kind of mythical beast that was returning from abroad', she tells her audience that she does not see herself as a celebrity; she has never had a dress made for a celebrity event and she has never appeared on a red carpet. (Has she forgotten *Celebrity Big Brother*? I wonder. Better to not go there.)

Nor has she ever, ever, ever had a celebrity lifestyle. 'My life was work and teaching and gardening and animals and all those things.'

She hammers her point: 'I'm not interested . . . I'm bored. I don't want to explain myself . . . I don't know why I am the way I am . . . I don't think it's interesting.'

She has enjoyed acting, especially at Cambridge in the Footlights years, she tells her audience, because this gave her access to 'a different kind of life from academe, for which I do not have enormous respect'. Similarly, her appearances on *Nice Time* were 'about being very, very silly and having fun'.

She has been angered by 'fictionalised' accounts of her life (Christine Wallace scores a mention), but not especially offended (not quite true, I think, remembering her fury at the Wallace biography), because she is used to being offended – she is offended every day. As an 'old-fashioned libertarian' she is opposed to censorship. She is resigned to the fact that people will want to write about her. 'I want to hear your reality. I'll fight it, if I must, but I won't ban it, and I won't silence you . . .' (Well, that's reassuring, but she won't hear my reality because she has vowed never to read anything about herself.)

She goes on to make the point that Australian people do not know her as well as the English who read her newspaper columns 'every week' and watch her on television. However, she acknowledges that she could only have achieved as much as she has by being an Australian: 'it's one reason for my thinking in my own way . . . and to follow what I would have thought of as common sense'.

Then she turns to the many letters, now preserved in her archive, that are from ordinary people. Admitting that she herself is quite 'glib', she says she has been deeply touched by the sincerity and lack of glibness in these people. (I think of the letter from the French girl and of the pages-long letters from desperate women, trapped in dreadful marriages, who tell her of their deepest fears and terrors. And I recall her genuine attempts to offer them useful advice. And her frustration as she realises that they will probably not take it. She is right when she says that, in this respect, the archive is 'a portrait of a moment, of a time'.)

Now it is Christopher's turn. Referring to an image displayed on the screen of the ginger cat settled comfortably on Germaine's shoulder, she says, 'He travelled on my shoulder nearly all the time . . . When I had visitors in the house, he hated it . . . He would sit in a cupboard . . .'

Then back to the archive. It is a 'big lump of hard evidence about the years when I have been on earth . . .' She doesn't know everything there is to know about those years, she declares modestly, and those who might cast her in the drama would present her as a celebrity, or a self-promoter or a self-publicist – or something. (No, I wouldn't. Or at least not as only those things.) Again, she asserts people's right to do so. She doesn't care, or so she says.

And then some advice to the people who will access her archive – 'just keep on plugging, on doing what it is that you do, and just hanging on to your own rag of self-belief . . . Use [the archive] for whatever journey of discovery you're on . . . be somebody who is earnest in your search for truth . . . be hard on yourself.' Shades of the convent. This could be Sister Bernadine, my old history teacher, speaking. I feel quite inspired.

Finally, it is time for questions. The first is about her views on LGBTIQ issues and policies. She responds that this has been a problem for her ever since she wrote about it in *The Whole Woman*. But she asserts that she does not 'buy' the notions of gender that are being supported by, among others, academe. 'If four-year-old children are telling their parents that they are in need of gender reassignment, something has gone completely crazily wrong,' she continues. And those members of the medical establishment who destroy perfectly healthy tissue and force people into a lifetime of corrective surgical interventions need to examine their ethics. Then she offers her example of the fifty-year-old truck driver with four children who 'thinks he was a girl' but is probably mistaken. We have met him before.

In her reply to the next question, which asks her to consider her 'favourite' and 'least favourite' things that she has included in the archive, she slides into a discussion of domestic violence and starts talking about her mother. '[W]hen I used to talk about domestic violence, I had no idea that my mother was abusing my father . . . she kicked him downstairs and beat him with the broomstick and shut him out of his house and starved him.'

The audience is looking uncomfortable but she goes on to say that her mother had 'high-level Asperger's' and was 'demented'. She, Germaine, should be able to forgive her mother but she can never forgive her, not because of what she did to her but because of the way her father was made to suffer. Her own experiences were dreadful: 'I was only little when my father wasn't there, in the war, and there was nothing to protect me from her wild paroxysms of rage . . .'

The next questioner asks Germaine for her views on what it means to be human and to have a spiritual relationship with religion. I am thinking that this is all getting very heavy. Germaine must think so too, because she decides to lighten up.

'If God exists, I am against him. I do not want to go to heaven, I do not want to live with God. I have lived with people who thought they were God, and I definitely don't want to be anywhere near the real McCoy.'

Laughter: the mood relaxes. The scene is set for her to deliver the most serious message of the night. She is asked what she thinks has changed and not changed for women in the forty-seven years since she wrote *The Female Eunuch*.

'What everybody has accepted is the idea of equality feminism,' she begins. 'As far as I'm concerned, equality is a profoundly conservative aim. It will change nothing.'

She goes on to consider the state of the world today in which, she believes, women and children have become casualties in places like Syria where the rich make war on the poor. 'Women are drawing level with men in this profoundly destructive world,' she declares, but as far as she is concerned, they are doing it the wrong way. 'We are getting nowhere.'

'If we're going to change things, I think we're going to have to start creating a women's polity that is strong, that has its own ways of operating, that makes contact with civilians in places like Syria, that actually begins to show a network that challenges the right of destructive nations to bomb the crap out of people they don't agree with . . . If what happens when women join the army is that they discover that the army is no place for a sane human being, then they've learned something.'

For some reason at this point I am reminded of groups of women I have met in the Catholic Church – modern-day nuns, some of them – who are standing up to the bishops and the hierarchy, attempting in their own ways to shift the values of that obdurate monolith towards compassion and tolerance. A women's polity. This is a big idea, a good idea, and an impossible idea – just like the idea of liberating 'castrated' women was perceived to be in 1970.

Question time is finished and the bouquets are being presented. Too late to ask the question I want to ask. 'Why don't you write a book about the power of women's polity to change the world, Germaine?'

Friday, 15 September 2017

I am seated at my usual desk in the Reading Room of the Baillieu Library, third floor, at the University of Melbourne, where I have been working for the past five months on the massive Germaine Greer Archive. Greer herself has said that mastering it all would take at least five years, and I cannot claim to have done that. However, with the help of the University of Melbourne Archives' impressive online 'finding aids', and supportive UMA staff, I am confident of having discovered most of the information that is relevant to my project. Others will delve deeper into her contributions to the fields of Shakespearean scholarship, feminist studies, women's literature and the rest. Almost every aspect of her work deserves a book, or at the very least a PhD thesis, in its own right.

The weather is grey and dismal. When I look outside, I can see, through intermittent rain, the clock tower of the Old Arts building. I reflect on Germaine Greer's love of libraries, a love that I share, and of the many hours we both spent in this library five decades ago. Trees now partly obscure the view of the lawns below, where a few students scurry in search of shelter, but this view of her alma mater and mine would still be as familiar to her as it is to me.

Today, I am working on Box 7 of the Print series, which, in separate acid-free manila folders, contains what seem to be hundreds of drafts, proofs and published copies of Germaine Greer's opinion pieces and other contributions to various newspapers and magazines. Attached to some drafts is her correspondence with editors, publishers and her agent.

Her subjects range from Shakespeare to First Ladies to footballers who refuse to share the joys of childbirth with their wives. Some pieces are obviously well-researched and informative. Others are sketchy. Some simply recycle views she has expressed many times before. She is paid around £1 a word for each article. 'No fee no work', she writes at the bottom of some requests for gratis contributions. Her assistant will translate this into a polite refusal: 'Professor Greer regrets . . .'

Maybe it's the weather, but I am finding myself irritated by much of Greer's correspondence with editors. She is incredibly rude: 'In view of the fact that you had CLEAN copy in three forms, fax, hard copy and diskette,' she writes to Peter Forbes, editor of *Poetry Review* (undated), 'the sloppiness of this setting is a DISGRACE.'[1] And to Georgina Goodman at *Elle* magazine: 'This is ON CONDITION that I see what you propose to print.

One of the first laws of journalism is that free copy is treated like garbage, which is why I do my best not to supply it. SEND THE PROOFS TO ME FOR CORRECTION, PLEASE. YOU MAY SHORTEN BUT NOT REWRITE.'[2]

Does she really have to be so ill-mannered? So arrogant?

I move on to the several drafts of a feature article she wrote for the *New Yorker*, provisionally titled 'Singin' in the Rain', about The Three Tenors, in which she describes her experience of seeing and hearing them in rehearsal and actual performance at Wembley Stadium in July 1996. Senior editor Bill Buford, who is a good friend of Germaine, comments on an early draft: 'It's wonderful to read about the tenors and their muted bitchiness, and their antics on stage and only slowly, bit by bit, discover that the thing is sordid,' he writes tactfully, before advising her to make some alterations and cuts. Drafts then returned to her contain editorial changes and some rewriting. She is furious. 'You want a completely different piece and then you will cut it to a third of its length. Fuck off!' And later, when rewritten sections include some grammar mistakes of which she herself would never be guilty: 'Look at the mess you made of the paragraph beginning . . . Don't you know that such tinkering is vandalism?' And 'I will not allow rubbish written by you to appear with my by-line. Already paragraphs have been rewritten as gibberish which I have to waste time trying to restore . . . You fuck the whole thing up with blind abandon . . .'

In the end, she will not allow this piece to be published. 'I have saved it from your arrogance and carelessness . . .' The reluctance to go to print was mutual, for the *New Yorker* editors were also concerned about possible libel implications.[3]

I am feeling a certain empathy with her, however, as I return to the article itself. It is a good read and she wins me over in the final section in which she describes her impressions of the Three Tenors concert and her efforts to get to Wembley from Essex. She tells of how she decided to share one of the two free tickets she was given with Charlie, her 75-year-old gardener, who was on his fifth hip and third knee replacement. The weather was vile and she feared that the show might be cancelled, but nothing would deter the shining-eyed Charlie. They drove off in the rain to take up their £350 seats – better ones, she noted with some satisfaction, than those occupied by Prime Minister and Mrs Major and the Duchess of Kent. She found it all quite excruciating: the stadium was more suited to a football game than an operatic concert, there were acoustic difficulties, the rain clouds lowered and the tenors sang – badly – the hackneyed songs her father used to sing in his bath. But dear Charlie sat through it all entranced, motionless on his orange cushion, his lips parted. At the end, he was so cold she could hardly lift him out of his seat to get him back to Stump Cross. 'That was a wonderful experience,' was all he had to say.[4]

My irritation has dissipated before I come to the end of this story. Rude, arrogant, insensitive as some of her correspondence with publishers shows her to be, Germaine Greer has her priorities right. This time, anyway.

Tuesday, 9 January 2018

Germaine Greer is in town to be part of the Sydney Festival, and so am I. On a wonderfully balmy summer evening, my husband and I stroll along the promenade to the Drama Theatre at the Sydney Opera House to watch a performance of *The Town Hall Affair*, a play performed by New York experimental theatre company the Wooster Group. Two days earlier, on Sunday, 7 January 2018, Germaine was present at the opening performance of the play.

The Town Hall Affair is a recreation of the original 'Town Bloody Hall' debate of 1971. The actors in the play, as in the film, are seated at a long table. At stage right is a lectern, and behind the actors is a screen on which grainy episodes of D.A. Pennebaker's film are shown.

The play is technically brilliant, as the actors speak the words of their on-screen characters in perfect sync with the characters in the film, but I, who am familiar with *Town Bloody Hall* and its origins, am disappointed to find the production unnecessarily complicated and even confusing. Some people I speak with during the interval who know nothing of the play's provenance comment that they 'can't make it out'. Better to just watch the original again, I think. (I hear later that Germaine has made a similar comment.)

The Town Hall Affair is timely in that it gives cause for reflection about current developments in the circumstances of women's lives. As reporter Joyce Morgan commented in her lukewarm review of the play in the *Sydney Morning Herald*, the 'obnoxious' Mailer would not now get away with his gross comments. But how much, she added, have things really changed?

> Now crass and demeaning comments are uttered by a pussy-grabbing President. As writer Susan Faludi recently noted, the patriarchy is bigger than the patriarch.[5]

In October 2017, just three months before the start of the Sydney Festival, movie producer Harvey Weinstein became the first of many men charged and humiliated for their crimes of predatory sexual behaviour against women. The arrival of the #MeToo movement launched a new wave of feminist protest across the world.

'For too long,' proclaimed Oprah Winfrey, speaking out for #MeToo at the glittering 2018 Golden Globes Awards ceremony, 'women have not been heard or believed if they dare speak their truth to the power of those men. But their time is up. Their time is up.'

In Sydney, on 9 January, the day after the Golden Globes, Germaine Greer spoke at the Opera House. Her audience was excited. Was she about to follow Oprah's rallying call? Everyone was looking to her, one of the most renowned elders of the feminist movement, to guide them through what was shaping up to be a major shift in the history of feminism. But Germaine is rarely inclined to follow the rallying calls of others. Disappointingly for her audience, she made no reference to the #MeToo movement in her speech. Her performance was something of a fizzer. She even had a seniors moment in which she forgot the name of Emily Pankhurst.

Sunday, 21 January 2018

Less than two weeks after her appearances at the Sydney Festival, Germaine Greer is back in London. On the evening of 21 January, she attends a gala event that is being held in her honour at Australia House. She has been declared UK Australian of the Year. 'I'm thinking of myself as representative of all the old ladies who've never been given anything,' she says, after graciously accepting the medal from High Commissioner Alexander Downer.

Later in the evening, she clarifies her opinion of #MeToo in an interview with Fairfax media. Acknowledging that the issue is complex, she reminds her interviewer that she has always denounced men in positions of power who sexually harass relatively powerless women. 'What makes it different is when the man has economic power, as Harvey Weinstein has. But if you spread your legs because he said "be nice to me and I'll give you a job in a movie" then I'm afraid that's tantamount to consent, and it's too late now to start whingeing about that.'[6]

She has done it again – infuriated the sisterhood and perhaps even more disturbingly, been hailed by conservative commentators like Rita Panahi of the Melbourne tabloid the *Herald Sun*, who accused feminists of conducting a 'witchhunt' against her. 'We have become so accustomed to such demented histrionics from some of the soundest members of the sisterhood that Greer, by comparison, seems sane and measured.'[7]

Germaine would probably not mind being described as a witch, but 'sane and measured'? I don't think so. Not even at 79.

February 2018

I have almost come to the end of my three-year project to research and tell the story of the life of Germaine Greer. It is time to answer the two questions I asked at the beginning: How significant was Germaine Greer's contribution to second-wave feminism?, and Who is she, really?

I have formed my impressions of Greer's contributions to second-wave feminism in light of feminist literature and on the basis of her life story as it emerges from her archive, her own writing and journalism, her theatre, television and radio performances, and the verbal and written impressions of people who have known her and her work. I have been highly cognisant of the context – the history of her time, which has also been my own time, on this earth.

Indubitably, life has changed for women in the half century since the thirty-year-old Germaine Greer wrote *The Female Eunuch*. The changes began before Greer's book with the advent of second-wave feminism in the early 1960s. In 1962, Betty Friedan's book *The Feminine Mystique* identified the pain and frustration of women, especially middle-class, college-educated women, who were feeling trapped inside their homes, their lives reduced to servitude – cleaning, cooking, nappy-changing and submitting to the sexual and other demands of their men. *The Feminine Mystique* sold three million copies in its first three years of publication. Other books followed, women began to organise, the pill was developed and the rest, as they say, is history.

But what of Germaine Greer's contribution?

I believe that Greer's contributions to second-wave feminism have been significant in three main ways. First, she has consistently challenged not only the accepted beliefs of her time and place in the world, she has also challenged their challengers. Back in the days of the Royal George, she learned how to subject every idea and argument to the most rigorous, energetic, critical scrutiny, and she has never forgotten those lessons or abandoned their principles. She is fearless in asserting what she sees to be the truth about women and their lives, even if every feminist in the world should want to disagree with her.

Her second major contribution has been to encourage women to look hard within themselves, as individuals and as half of the human race, to discover their essential femaleness, to assert their own values and order their own lives. It is not helpful, she suggests, to blame men or their institutions for the female condition, and pointless for them to try to join the brotherhood, for the brotherhood will never accept them. Firmly, she steers women away from the illusion that by becoming like men they will be their 'equals'. Male values, she argues, are already destroying not only women, but people all over the world. Surely women should be opposing those values and asserting their own?

Her third major contribution to second-wave feminism is more about the 'how' than the 'what'. Thousands of feminist tracts are now in circulation, and some may well be more erudite than hers, but many will be read only by professional academics or students in the field of women's studies. They are none the less influential for that but the work of Germaine Greer is different in that, as her many letters from 'ordinary' people attest, she has managed to reach out and personally touch the lives of women, and some men, everywhere. She is a performer, a superb communicator, and highly skilled in promoting herself and her ideas. As a writer, she is raunchy, engaging and amusing. Almost alone among feminist writers, she has the capacity to illumine her books with the products of her scholarship that include individual, often fascinating stories about women's struggles, disasters and achievements over hundreds of years. Her knowledge of classical European literature, especially of women's writing and Shakespeare, has given her a wonderful understanding of how and why human beings behave as they do (who better than Shakespeare in this respect?).

And so to the second question: 'Who is Germaine Greer, really?' In the early stages of writing, I gave my book the provisional title 'Behind the Mask', as I was working on an assumption that behind the public face of Germaine Greer was a 'real' woman whose personal history, once uncovered, would shed light on her massive contribution to second-wave feminism. However, as I read what she had written at different stages of her life, watched her many 'performances' in film clips of various kinds, listened to her speaking in video and audio recordings, discovered what others had said and written about her and, finally, delved into her archive, I arrived at the conclusion that the public Germaine Greer is also, pretty much, herself. There is no mask. What you see is what you get.

In 1989, the psychologist Anthony Clare put it to Germaine in a radio interview that, more than anyone he had ever interviewed, she had already discussed in public almost everything about herself – things that people, in England at least, would describe as 'personal intimacies'. He knew about her abortions, her miscarriages, her infertility, how she lost her virginity. (Greer, interrupting: 'He married one of my greatest friends.') She seemed surprised at Clare's observations, but replied that she didn't believe people are like onions – that if you keep peeling back layers you will eventually find a tiny 'real' person at the core. There was no frightened little Germaine Greer hiding at her core, waiting to be discovered, she declared – she was all of the layers, and forming a picture of her, the person, would be more about piecing the layers together than digging into the onion.[8]

This book has attempted to do just that – piece the layers of Greer's life together, from her early childhood and years at school and university; through her unconventional years as a groupie and hippie in the counterculture of 1960s London; her dramatic success as an international celebrity after the publication of *The Female Eunuch*; and her enduring fame as a writer, performer, journalist and public intellectual. Then, finally, how she came to terms with some of the painful memories of her childhood and learned to understand and bond with the land of her birth.

•

At every stage of her life, Germaine Greer, large in stature, huge in intellect, personality and soul, has towered over her contemporaries. Her capacity for physical as well as intellectual work is amazing.

Yet, there is something in her or not in her that sets her apart. Her behaviour can be as puzzling as it is annoying. Despite her singular intelligence, she can be as inconsistent and irrational as she is insulting. Her apparent lack of emotional empathy is strangely at odds with her literary sensibility. It is amazing to see how a bruising clumsiness in personal relations sits beside the almost pitch-perfect refinement of the best of her writing. A complete contradiction.

Feminist publisher Carmen Callil and writer Fay Weldon, among others, believe that she is a genius, and I tend to agree. She exhibits the hallmarks of genius: unique, prescient, transformative intuitions; formidable intellect; tremendous energy; and the capacity to produce new knowledge that changes the lives of millions.

Germaine Greer, a genius? Many will scoff at the idea, but it does suggest an explanation, if not an excuse, for the worst of her behaviour: geniuses think and behave differently from the rest of us, their conduct may seem odd and they can be difficult – sometimes impossible – to understand and get along with. In entertaining the proposition that Greer may be a genius, we can discover a reason for the contradictions in her behaviour, an answer to the perplexing question as to why this brilliant woman has felt driven, publicly and privately, to unleash such floods of irrationality and vituperation on so many well-intentioned people.

Christine Wallace concluded that Greer's angry response to *Untamed Shrew* was fuelled by intellectual insecurity – fear that her body of work would not stand up to scrutiny. Justified or not, such fears could bring about a kind of 'insanity' that would block out her critical faculties. Madness. Not uncommon in a genius. Like Virginia Woolf and Vincent van Gogh, Germaine

Greer is often accused of being at least batty, if not actually barking mad. She evens admits to it herself.

Carmen Callil suspects that the price Germaine Greer pays for her genius is her essential aloneness. This may well be true in the sense that she does not have time for the minutiae upon which close friendships are formed. David Plante speculated that she kept busy to avoid loneliness, but it could be the other way around – her compulsion to work, to create, to produce, whether it is about Shakespeare, femaleness or a new garden, is stronger and more important to her than human contact. Like an eagle, she flies high and free, not so much avoiding the kinds of intimate relationships that might bring her down as being incapable of bending herself to them.

Yet all kinds of people seek her companionship and her archive is full of 'thank you' letters from grateful guests who have driven away from dinners and lunches at her homes replete with memories of her excellent food, wine and company. She enjoys nothing more than a good 'knees-up' with Margaret Fink and their friends, who love her as much for her eccentricity as for her capacity to enjoy herself. Like her school companions of long ago, people are bewildered and hurt when she turns on them in spite, they fear her ire, but they forgive her, for they believe that spitefulness is not her intention, however much her words and actions may suggest otherwise. 'Oh Ger*maine*!' they sigh, resignedly.

Germaine makes no apologies. She says that she is used to being offended – people offend her every day – and she jokes about all the hate mail she has consigned to her 'nutters' drawer'. Her implication is that if crazy people who have never read or understood her choose to judge her on the basis of a few shocking comments and the caricatures the press like to make of her, that is their problem, not hers. 'I don't care,' she says.

But she does care. How could she not? Does she forget that in other accounts she has told us different stories – stories of sleepless nights, depression, anguish at lost opportunities and lost loves? She is not insensitive – quite the contrary – although she does avoid introspection. Like her father, she knows how to push concerned people away from her with a glib remark, defuse awkward situations with humour and stay on the surface where it is safe.

None of her environments has been able to contain her – not Mentone, not academe, not Australia, not even the English and European centres of Western culture that are her lodestar. Now, as she approaches her eightieth birthday, she who has been described as 'a force of nature' has chosen to live much of her life in the most elemental of all environments, a primeval rainforest. She will not attempt to control the forest and it will never contain her.

And so, for now, I leave her at Cave Creek, a lone figure as always, struggling through the undergrowth, tearing out the alien weeds and vines or resting by the creek at dusk, listening to the sounds of the forest, watching her dancing 'birdie'.

Has she found peace? Has she stopped fighting? I cannot ask her these questions, but I can imagine her answer: 'Not bloody likely!'

Acknowledgements

In acknowledging the people who have supported me over the four years I have been engaged in writing this book, I would like to begin with Teresa Pitt and Professor Stuart Macintyre, who have patiently read each chapter, draft by draft, and given valuable, professional advice. I also wish to acknowledge the support of my agent, Sheila Drummond, and Penguin Random House publisher Meredith Curnow, for their encouragement and friendship. Thank you also to editor Kathryn Knight for her patience, helpful suggestions and professional skill in editing the manuscript, and to proofreader Bronwyn Sweeney.

One of the pleasures of writing biography is meeting people who have been associated with the subject. This has been more difficult for this biography than for most. Greer's friends, family and acquaintances are aware of her unwillingness to contribute to anything that is written about her. In deference to her feelings, many of them, understandably, do not wish to make public comments about their association with her. However, I thank the following people for sharing some memories and experiences: Kerry Doquile, Star of the Sea archivist; Jan Coleman, Theo Kinnaird and Marian Shanahan, who were close friends of Greer at Star of the Sea convent; Sister Felicity Cordner and Sister Diana Gabel, nuns of the Presentation Order who knew Germaine at school and were friends of the nuns who taught her;

Jenny Wilkinson and June O'Keeffe, who remember Germaine from those days; Phillip Frazer, publisher, who shared his house with Greer in Paddington, Sydney; Professor Stephen Knight, who worked with her at the University of Sydney; Richard Walsh, publisher and a founding editor of *Oz* magazine and of *Nation Review* in Australia, who knew her in Sydney and London; Fay Weldon, well-known feminist author, who describes herself as Greer's colleague; Dame Carmen Callil, publisher and founding editor of Virago Press; and historian and writer John Thompson. I also wish to thank Christine Wallace and Ian Britain, who shared with me their experiences and recollections of writing about her.

Thank you, too, to Sue Fairbanks, archivist, Jane Beattie, assistant archivist, and Dr Rachel Buchanan, curator of the Germaine Greer Archive at the University of Melbourne, who have been most generous in giving their support and professional assistance to the project, together with members of the 'Greer team' Sarah Brown, Lachlan Glanville and Kate Hodgetts. In particular, I want to thank Chen Chen, Leanne McCredden and Carl Temple, staff of the Baillieu Library Reading Room, for their unfailingly cheerful professional assistance on a day-to-day basis.

Notes

Introduction

1 Germaine Greer has disagreed with women when they attempted to tell her that she had changed their lives. People changed their own lives, she said. She had only helped them along.

2 University of Melbourne Archives, Germaine Greer Collection, Audio recordings produced and received by Greer 1971–2010, 2014.0040.00032, Unit 1, Germaine Greer interviewed by Dr Anthony Clare for the BBC Radio 4 program *In the Psychiatrist's Chair*, 23 August 1989

1 Who does she think she is?

1 The dirty and dilapidated Spencer Street station, the construction of which began in 1859, had many modifications over the years and was totally rebuilt in 2006, when it was renamed Southern Cross station.

2 Greer, Germaine, *Daddy, We Hardly Knew You*, Ballantine Books, a division of Random House, New York, 1989 (originally published in Great Britain by Hamish Hamilton Ltd, London, 1989), p. 8

3 Wallace, Christine, *Untamed Shrew*, Richard Cohen Books, London, 2000, p. 7

4 'Turn' was an expression in common use at this time. The Catholic Church strongly discouraged marriage between Catholics and non-Catholics, and intending non-Catholic spouses were persuaded to become Catholic – to 'turn' – before the wedding ceremony. If they refused, the ceremony would have to be conducted in a vestry, out of sight of the congregation, rather than in front of the main altar. A condition of the marriage, imposed by the Church, was that any children of the union should be brought up as Catholics.

5 Greer, *Daddy, We Hardly Knew You*, p. 10

6   ibid., p. 298

7   Wallace, *Untamed Shrew*, p. 3

8   Sir Frederick Lloyd Dumas (1891–1973) was the managing editor of the *Adelaide Advertiser*, a conservative newspaper that was taken over in 1929 by a syndicate headed by (Sir) Keith Murdoch, who was at that time managing director of the *Melbourne Herald*. Dumas, who claimed Huguenot ancestry, was a prominent and widely respected leader in the newspaper industry. His papers are in the National Library of Australia Archives. From the *Australian Dictionary of Biography*, Volume 14, Melbourne University Publishing, 1996

9   Wallace, *Untamed Shrew*, p. 233

10   Long, Gavin, *The Six Years War: A concise history of Australia in the 1939–45 war*, Australian War Memorial and the Australian Government Publishing Service, Canberra, 1973, pp. 29–30

11   At the outbreak of war, to overcome Britain's shortage of trained air personnel, it was decided that fifty thousand men from the dominions would be trained annually as aircrew under the Empire Air Training Scheme. Each dominion conducted its own initial training and further training took place in Canada and Rhodesia.

12   Greer, *Daddy, We Hardly Knew You*, p. 145

13   Wallace, *Untamed Shrew*, p. 6

14   ibid., pp. 10–11

15   University of Melbourne Archives, Germaine Greer Collection, Audio recordings produced and received by Greer 1971–2010, 2014.0040.00032, Unit 1, Germaine Greer interviewed by Dr Anthony Clare for the BBC Radio 4 program *In the Psychiatrist's Chair*, 23 August 1989

16   Greer, *Daddy, We Hardly Knew You*, p. 8

17   ibid., p. 310. Kilbreda is a Catholic college in the suburb of Mentone, Melbourne. When Jane Greer attended the school, it was staffed by nuns of the Mercy Order. It is now staffed mainly by lay teachers.

18   ibid., p. 303

19   Greer, Germaine, in *The Pleasure of Reading*, Antonia Fraser (ed.), Bloomsbury, London, 1992, pp. 55–8

20   ibid.

21   Greer, Germaine, 'Lessons in the convent', *Music*, November (special edition, guest editor Simon Callow), vol. 5, no. 6, Warner Music, London, 1996

22   This information and a copy of a school report which listed the subjects taught at Holy Redeemer Diocesan School, Ripponlea,

were provided by Jenny Wilkinson (nee McLeod), a former pupil, in Melbourne, 2016.

23 Conversation between Elizabeth Kleinhenz and Jenny Wilkinson, Ballarat, December 2016

24 Greer, Germaine, 'My convent career', *Reader's Digest*, March 1985, pp. 33–6

25 Bartholomew Augustine Santamaria, known as 'B.A. Santamaria' or 'Santa', was a prominent Australian Catholic political activist. A close friend of the Catholic Archbishop of Melbourne Daniel Mannix, he was a powerful intellectual influence in the formation of the anti-communist Democratic Labor Party.

26 Greer, 'My convent career'

27 Wallace, *Untamed Shrew*, p. 20

28 Dabbs, Jennifer, *Beyond Redemption*, McPhee Gribble, Ringwood, 1989, p. 139

29 Wallace, *Untamed Shrew*, p. 22

30 ibid., p. 20

31 University of Melbourne Archives, Germaine Greer Collection, General correspondence 1958–2014, 2014.0042.00183, Unit 23, Interview with Susan Coffey, mature age student studying at Queen Mary & Westfield College, for her final year English project 'Thirty Years of Feminism via Germaine Greer', 13 April 2000

32 Dreifus, Claudia, 'The life and loves of Germaine Greer', *Forum: The international journal of human relations*, vol. 7, no. 5, January 1975, p. 14. Copy of article held in University of Melbourne Archives, Germaine Greer Collection, Early years academic, performance, writing and personal papers 1957–2005, 2014.001.00235, Unit 17

33 Greer, Germaine, 'Star girl', *Sunday Times*, 3 April 1983, p. 34

34 ibid.

35 ibid.

36 ibid.

37 Waby, Heather, 'The class of 54', *Sunday Sun-Herald Magazine*, 6 December 1998, pp. 16–19

38 ibid.

39 University of Melbourne Archives, Germaine Greer Collection, General correspondence 1958–2014, 2014.0042.0244, Unit 30, McCarthy (Easton), Michaela, letter to Germaine Greer, 15 January 1975

40 Recollections of June O'Keeffe, younger sister of Margaret, as told to Elizabeth Kleinhenz. June later became a Head Prefect of Star of the Sea.

41 Fallowell, Duncan, *20th Century Characters*, Vintage, London, 1994, p. 13

42 Greer, Germaine, in *There's Something About a Convent Girl*, Jackie Bennett and Rosemary Forgan (eds), Virago Press, London, 1991, p. 87

43 Greer, 'My Convent Career'

44 Fallowell, *20th Century Characters*, p. 14

45 Wright, Claudia, 'The young Germaine: An incredible girl, says the nun who taught her', *The Herald*, Melbourne, 3 June 1971, p. 21. Claudia Wright (1934–2005) was a colourful Australian print journalist, radio and television presenter, and controversial talkback host in the 1960s, 1970s and early 1980s. A feisty, committed feminist and fighter for social justice, she was tragically affected by early-onset Alzheimer's disease and suffered a slow decline over more than twenty years until her death. Germaine Greer was a lifelong friend, and godmother to one of her children. She gave the eulogy at Wright's memorial service in February 2005.

46 University of Melbourne Archives, Germaine Greer Collection, Early years academic, performance, writing and personal papers 1957–2005, 2014.0044.00013, Unit 2, Sister Eymard of the Presentation Order, letter to Germaine Greer

47 Greer, *Daddy, We Hardly Knew You*, p. 288

48 ibid., p. 234

49 ibid., p. 235

50 ibid., p. 234

51 ibid., p. 193

52 ibid., p. 141

53 ibid., p. 192

54 ibid., p. 9

2   A difficult girl

1 Wallace, Christine, *Untamed Shrew*, Richard Cohen Books, London, 2000, p. 29

2 ibid., p. 30

3 ibid.

4 At the time it was more usual for future teachers to be given a studentship for the three-year Pass degree. Only the highest achievers were financed to take the four-year Honours degree. The University of Melbourne was the only university in the state of Victoria at this time.

5   As told to the author by the mother of a student at Melbourne University circa 1960.

6   Studentships had long been available for 'pre-service' primary school teachers who were trained in the Education Department–owned and controlled Primary Teachers Training Colleges, where students wore blazers and were trained to 'serve'. Secondary studentships became available when the growing numbers of high schools being built in the 1950s led to a shortage of trained secondary teachers.

7   Wallace, *Untamed Shrew*, p. 29

8   *Farrago*, 8 May 1956, p. 9; 5 June 1956, p. 3; and 25 September 1956, p. 2

9   Recollections of Jan Coleman, who was a friend and classmate of Germaine at Star of the Sea and at the University of Melbourne.

10 The 'Caf' is the student cafeteria in the union building at the University of Melbourne. Today there are many other eating venues on campus, but in 1956 it was a centre of student social life.

11 Greer, Germaine, *Daddy, We Hardly Knew You*, Ballantine Books, New York, 1989

12 Packer, Clyde, *No Return Ticket: Clyde Packer interviews nine famous Australian expatriates*, Angus & Robertson, Sydney, 1984, pp. 89–90

13 ibid., p. 38

14 Watson, Don, *Brian Fitzpatrick: A radical life*, Hale & Iremonger, Sydney, 1979, p. 32

15 Humphries, Barry, *More Please*, Penguin, Ringwood, 1992, p. 149

16 Koval, Ramona, Interview with Germaine Greer, *One to One*, ABC Enterprises, Sydney, 1992

17 Greer, *Daddy, We Hardly Knew You*, p. 198

18 Dreifus, Claudia, 'The life and loves of Germaine Greer', *Forum: The international journal of human relations*, January 1975, pp. 12–19. Copy of article held in University of Melbourne Archives, Germaine Greer Collection, Early years academic, performance, writing and personal papers 1957–2005, 2014.001.00235, Unit 17

19 University of Melbourne Archives, Germaine Greer Collection, Audio recordings produced and received by Greer 1971–2010, 2014.0040.00032, Unit 1, Germaine Greer interviewed by Dr Anthony Clare for the BBC Radio 4 program *In the Psychiatrist's Chair*, 23 August 1989

20 Greer, Germaine, in Packer, *No Return Ticket*, pp. 90–3

21 Wallace, *Untamed Shrew*, p. 46

22 ibid., p. 47

23 *Q&A*, ABC Television, broadcast 16 April 2016

24 Rickard, John, 'Macartney, Keith Lamont (1903–1971)', *Australian Dictionary of Biography*, National Centre of Biography, Australian National University, 2000, http://adb.anu.edu.au/biography/macartney-keith-lamont-10894/text19343, accessed 20 July 2018

25 Review of Peter Blazey's autobiography *Screw Loose*, *The Age*, 9 August 1997

26 Jacobson, Howard, 'Howard Jacobson on being taught by FR Leavis', *The Telegraph*, www.telegraph.co.uk/culture/books/8466388/Howard-Jacobson-on-being-taught-by-FRLeavis.html, accessed 19 June 2018

27 Wallace, *Untamed Shrew*, p. 53

28 Greer, Germaine, 'Why the young need their freedom', in Rusbridger, Alan (ed.), *The Guardian Year 1994*, Fourth Estate, London, 1994, pp. 204–6

29 Greer, Germaine, 'Why the young need their single ticket to freedom', *The Guardian*, 24 January 1994, copy held in University of Melbourne Archives, Germaine Greer Collection, Print Journalism, 2014.0046.00364, Unit 6

30 Packer, *No Return Ticket*, pp. 94–5

31 'Greer on revolution; Germaine on love: A discussion between Germaine Greer, Ian Turner and Chris Hector recorded in Melbourne, February 1972. Published in *Overland* 50/51, Autumn 1972', 25 January 2002, www.takver.com/history/sydney/greer1972.htm, accessed 20 July 2018

32 Recollection of Jan Coleman, schoolfriend of Germaine Greer at Star of the Sea, whose family were friends and neighbours of the Greer family. Germaine felt bad about leaving her father to pay her bond. As soon as she could, using some of her earnings from *Nice Time*, she sent Reg a cheque in repayment of the debt.

33 Humphries, *More Please*, p. 169

34 James, Clive, *Unreliable Memoirs*, WW Norton and Company, New York, 2009, pp. 176–7

35 ibid.

36 Coombs, Anne, *Sex and Anarchy: The life and death of the Sydney Push*, Penguin Books, Ringwood, Victoria, 1996, p. 38

37 University of Melbourne Archives, Germaine Greer Collection, Early years academic, performance, writing and personal papers 1957–2005, 2014.0044.00236, Unit 17, Germaine Greer, 'Notes for a presentation on BBC Radio 4', May 1975

38 University of Melbourne Archives, Germaine Greer Collection, Audio recordings produced and received by Greer 1971–2010, 2014.0040.00067, Unit 2, Roelof Smilde interviewed for *The Coming Out Show*. *The Coming Out Show* was a radio program broadcast by the Australian Broadcasting Corporation, first broadcast on ABC Radio 2 in 1975, the United Nations–designated International Women's Year.

39 University of Melbourne Archives, Germaine Greer Collection, Audio recordings produced and received by Greer 1971–2010, 2014.0040.00100, Unit 3, Diary 1997, audio diary recorded while walking her dogs on the fields near her home

40 Franklin, James, 'The Push and critical drinkers', in *Corrupting the Youth: A history of Australian philosophy*, Macleay Press, Sydney, 2003, pp. 157–78

41 ibid.

42 Coombs, *Sex and Anarchy*, pp. 135–6

43 Franklin, 'The Push and critical drinkers'

44 Conversation between Elizabeth Kleinhenz and a former Push member and friend of Germaine's who wishes to remain anonymous, 2017

45 Wallace, *Untamed Shrew*, p. 72

46 Coombs, *Sex and Anarchy*, p. 213

47 University of Melbourne Archives, Germaine Greer Collection, Audio recordings produced and received by Greer 1971–2010, 2014.0040.00100, Unit 3, Diary 1997, audio diary recorded while walking her dogs on the fields near her home. Reflecting on Coombs's book, she said dismissively that Coombs's claim was 'wildly inaccurate'. Like some other ideas in *Sex and Anarchy*, she thought it was probably traceable to Darcy Waters. She decided that she would annotate her copy of the book and place it in her archive, which she did.

48 Greer, Germaine, 'Germaine Greer's Sydney', in McGreevey, John (ed.), *Cities*, Lester & Orpen Dennys, Toronto, 1981, p. 158

49 ibid., p. 153

50 Coombs, *Sex and Anarchy*, p. 203

51 Greer, 'Germaine Greer's Sydney', p. 165

52 Wallace, *Untamed Shrew*, p. 58

53 Leser, David, 'Her wild ways', *Australian Women's Weekly*, January 2007, pp. 64–70

54 Conversation between Richard Walsh and Elizabeth Kleinhenz, Sydney, 14 February 2017

55 Cooper, Jilly, article in *Sunday Times*, 7 September 1980, copy held in University of Melbourne Archives, Germaine Greer Collection, General correspondence 1958–2014, 2014.0042.01065, Unit 119, correspondence between Germaine Greer and Claudia Wright

56 University of Melbourne Archives, Germaine Greer Collection, Early years academic, performance, writing and personal papers 1957–2005, 2014.0044.00236, Unit 17, Germaine Greer, 'Notes for a presentation on BBC Radio 4', May 1975

57 From *Manfred*, a dramatic poem by Lord Byron written in 1816–1817

58 Byron, George Gordon, *Don Juan*, Canto 61

59 Conversation between Elizabeth Kleinhenz, Professor Stephen Knight and Professor Stuart Macintyre, May 2016

3 Changing skies

1 Greer, Germaine, 'On the end of the Commonwealth', *The Independent* magazine, July 1989, p. 14

2 Britain, Ian, *Once an Australian: Journeys with Barry Humphries, Clive James, Germaine Greer and Robert Hughes*, Oxford University Press, Melbourne, 1997, p. 128

3 Packer, Clyde, *No Return Ticket: Clyde Packer interviews nine famous Australian expatriates*, Angus & Robertson, Sydney, 1984, p. 95

4 University of Melbourne Archives, Germaine Greer Collection, General correspondence 1958–2014, 2014.0042.00183, Unit 23, Interview with Susan Coffey, mature age student studying at Queen Mary & Westfield College, for her final year English project 'Thirty Years of Feminism via Germaine Greer', 13 April 2000

5 Nicolson, Nigel, *Long Life*, Weidenfeld & Nicolson, London, 1997, p. 66

6 University of Melbourne Archives, Germaine Greer Collection, digitised collections, *The Female Eunuch* first draft, 'Summary', http://hdl.handle.net/11343/42290, accessed 31 August 2018

7 University of Melbourne Archives, Germaine Greer Collection, digitised collections, *The Female Eunuch* first draft, 'Dedication', http://hdl.handle.net/11343/42290, accessed 31 August 2018

8 ibid.

9 James, Clive, *May Week Was in June*, Picador, London, 2008, p. 18

10 ibid., p. 15

11 ibid., p. 18

12   ibid., p. 145

13   ibid.

14   Buchanan, Rachel, 'Friday essay: How Shakespeare helped shape Germaine Greer's feminist masterpiece', *The Conversation*, 27 May 2016, https://theconversation.com/friday-essay-how-shakespeare-helped-shape-germaine-greers-feminist-masterpiece-59880, accessed 20 June 2018

15   ibid.

16   ibid.

17   Wallace, Christine, *Untamed Shrew*, Richard Cohen Books, London, 2000, p. 166

18   Shakespeare, William, *The Taming of the Shrew*, Act 3, Scene 2

19   ibid., Act 5, Scene 2

20   The letter is reproduced in full in Henderson, Archibald, *George Bernard Shaw, His Life and Works: A critical biography*, Steward & Kidd, Cincinnati, 1911, p. 196

21   Detmer, Emily, 'Civilizing subordination: Domestic violence and *The Taming of the Shrew*', *Shakespeare Quarterly*, vol. 48, no. 3 (Autumn 1997), pp. 273–294

22   ibid.

23   University of Melbourne Archives, Germaine Greer Collection, Early years academic, performance, writing and personal papers 1957–2005, 2014.0044.00129, Unit 10, Greer, Germaine, 'The Ethic of Love and Marriage in Shakespeare's Early Comedies', pp. 191–2

24   Wallace, *Untamed Shrew*, pp. 121–2

25   Greer, Germaine, *The Female Eunuch*, Harper Perennial Modern Classics, New York, 2008, p. 234

26   Wallace, *Untamed Shrew*, p. 122

27   Greer, Germane, *The Madwoman's Underclothes: Essays and occasional writings 1968–1985*, Pan Books, London, 1986, p. xiii

28   Greer, Germaine, *Daddy, We Hardly Knew You*, Ballantine Books, New York, 1989, p. 152

29   University of Melbourne Archives, Germaine Greer Collection, digitised collections, *The Female Eunuch* first draft, 'Dedication', http://hdl.handle.net/11343/42290, accessed 31 August 2018

30   University of Melbourne Archives, Germaine Greer Collection, General correspondence 1958–2014, 2014.0042.00154, Unit 19, Address given by Germaine Greer at the Thanksgiving Service for Gay Clifford at Holy Trinity Church, Minchinhampton, Gloucestershire, 6 August 1998

31   University of Melbourne Archives, Germaine Greer Collection, General correspondence 1958–2014, 2014.0042.00154, Unit 19, Correspondence from and relating to Gay Clifford

32   University of Melbourne Archives, Germaine Greer Collection, General correspondence 1958–2014, 2014.0042.00154, Unit 19, draft of introduction by Greer to a book of poetry by Gay Clifford

33   University of Melbourne Archives, Germaine Greer Collection, Audio-visual recordings featuring Greer's television and radio appearances, 2014.0041.0001, 'Milk – Nice Time: Outtakes, featuring Germaine Greer and Kenny Everett, 1969', https://vimeo.com/201973004, accessed 20 June 2016

34   Grant, Linda, 'In defence of the 1970s: Germaine Greer was there as well as Stuart Hall', *The Guardian*, 6 May 2013, www.theguardian.com/commentisfree/2013/may/06/in-defence-of-the-1970s, accessed 20 June 2018

35   ibid.

36   Thea Porter (1927–2000) was a designer of expensive bohemian-chic fashion in 1970s London. Her clients included Pink Floyd, the Beatles, Elizabeth Taylor and Princess Margaret.

37   Farren, Mick, *Give the Anarchist a Cigarette*, Jonathan Cape, London, 2001, pp. 218–21

38   'Philippe Mora', Milesago, www.milesago.com/people/mora-philippe.htm, accessed 20 June 2018

39   Trinca, Helen, 'The sum of OZ magazine', *The Australian*, 23 March 2013, www.theaustralian.com.au/arts/review/the-sum-of-oz-magazine/news-story/1c5c6d21a634174619f30afb1167591b, accessed 31 August 2018

40   Neville, Richard, *Hippie Hippie Shake*, Duckworth Overlook, London, 2009, p. 71

41   ibid., p. 151

42   ibid., p. 121

43   Greer, Germaine, 'In bed with the English', *Oz*, no. 1, January 1967, pp. 16, 18

44   Neville, *Hippie Hippie Shake*, pp. 145–7

45   Greer, Germaine, 'The Universal Tonguebath', *Oz*, no. 19, March 1969, pp. 31–3, 47

46   Greer in *POL* magazine, quoted in Wallace, *Untamed Shrew*, p. 145

47   Du Feu, Paul, *Let's Hear It for the Long-Legged Women*, Angus & Robertson, London, 1973, p. 118ff.

48 University of Melbourne Archives, Germaine Greer Collection, Early years academic, performance, writing and personal papers 1957–2005, 2014.0044.00148, Unit 10, Diary 1968

49 Du Feu, *Let's Hear It for the Long-Legged Women*, p. 118

50 Greer, Germaine, Country Notebook, 'Drunken ex-husband', *The Telegraph*, 29 May 2004, www.telegraph.co.uk/gardening/3320728/Country-notebook-drunken-ex-husband.html, accessed 20 June 2018

51 University of Melbourne Archives, Germaine Greer Collection, digitised collections, *The Female Eunuch* first draft, http://hdl.handle.net/11343/42290, accessed 31 August 2018

52 University of Melbourne Archives, Germaine Greer Collection, General correspondence 1958–2014, 2014.0042.00309, Unit 38, letter from Germaine Greer to Kate Garrett, 18 January 1973

53 University of Melbourne Archives, Germaine Greer Collection, General correspondence 1958–2014, 2014.0042.00374, Unit 46, letter from Jim Haynes to Germaine Greer, 31 January 1973

54 University of Melbourne Archives, Germaine Greer Collection, Early years academic, performance, writing and personal papers 1957–2005, 2014.0044.00173, Unit 13, Greer, Germaine, writing as 'Earth Rose' in *Suck*, no. 1, August 1970

55 Greer, *The Madwoman's Underclothes*, p. 74

56 Wolfe, Tom, 'The "Me" decade and the third great awakening', *New York*, 23 August 1976, http://nymag.com/news/features/45938/index10.html, accessed 20 June 2018

57 ibid.

58 Neville, *Hippie Hippie Shake*, p. 239

59 ibid., p. 241

60 Bacon, Wendy, 'Sex and censorship', Anarchism in Australia, first published in *Lot's Wife*, 18 March 1971, www.takver.com/history/aia/aia00033.htm, accessed 20 June 2018

4   *The Female Eunuch*

1 University of Melbourne Archives, Germaine Greer Collection, digitised collections, *The Female Eunuch* editorial, 'TFE Editorial', handwritten notes dated 21 April 1969, http://hdl.handle.net/11343/42289, accessed 31 August 2018

2 Friedan, Betty, *The Feminine Mystique*, W.W. Norton & Company, New York, 1963

3   Pearson, Richard, 'Segregationist governor Ross Barnett dies at 89', *Washington Post*, 8 November 1987, www.washingtonpost.com/archive/local/1987/11/08/segregationist-governor-ross-barnett-dies-at-89/7760cd0c-8272-440f-a980-79383300d7a8, accessed 31 August 2018

4   Friedan, Betty, 'Statement of Purpose', National Organization for Women, https://now.org/about/history/statement-of-purpose, accessed 21 June 2018

5   Milliken, Robert, 'Lillian and Germaine in New York', *Inside Story*, 20 January 2011, http://insidestory.org.au/lillian-and-germaine-in-new-york, accessed 22 May 2018

6   *Rock Encyclopedia* is dedicated to Leon and Margaret Fink.

7   Milliken, 'Lillian and Germaine in New York'

8   ibid.

9   Roxon, Lillian, 'Germaine Greer, that female phenomenon', *Woman's Day*, 24 May 1971, p. 5

10   Milliken, Robert, *Mother of Rock*, Black Inc., Melbourne, 2010, p. 290

11   Sewall-Ruskin, Yvonne, *High on Rebellion: Inside the underground at Max's Kansas City*, Thunder's Mouth Press, New York, 1998, digital edition

12   Milliken, 'Lillian and Germaine in New York'

13   University of Melbourne Archives, Germaine Greer Collection, digitised collections, *The Female Eunuch* first draft, 'Dedication', http://hdl.handle.net/11343/42290, accessed 31 August 2018

14   Greer, Germaine, *The Female Eunuch*, Harper Perennial Modern Classics, New York, 2008, p. v

15   Milliken, 'Lillian and Germaine in New York'

16   University of Melbourne Archives, Germaine Greer Collection, digitised collections, *The Female Eunuch* editorial, 'TFE Editorial', handwritten notes dated 21 April 1969, http://hdl.handle.net/11343/42289, accessed 31 August 2018

17   University of Melbourne Archives, Germaine Greer Collection, digitised collections, *The Female Eunuch* editorial, typewritten notes, http://hdl.handle.net/11343/42289, accessed 31 August 2018

18   ibid.

19   University of Melbourne Archives, Germaine Greer Collection, digitised collections, *The Female Eunuch* editorial, draft 'Synopsis, http://hdl.handle.net/11343/42289, accessed 31 August 2018. Jerry Rubin and Abbie Hoffman were flamboyant American social activists and icons of the counterculture in the 1960s and 1970s. Together they

founded the Youth International Party, which made extensive use of the media to spread their ideas. Both were charged with 'un-American' crimes and both had voluminous FBI files that ran to thousands of pages.

20 University of Melbourne Archives, Germaine Greer Collection, digitised collections, *The Female Eunuch* first draft, 'Dedication', p. 2, http://hdl.handle.net/11343/42290, accessed 31 August 2018

21 ibid., pp. 1–2

22 ibid.

23 ibid., pp. 12–13

24 University of Melbourne Archives, Germaine Greer Collection, General correspondence 1958–2014, 2014.0042.00492, Unit 60, letter from Germaine Greer to Gershon Legman, fan and author, May 1972

25 Weinraub, Judith, 'Germaine Greer – Opinions that may shock the faithful', *New York Times*, 22 March 1971, www.nytimes.com/1971/03/22/archives/germaine-greer-opinions-that-may-shock-the-faithful.html, accessed 31 August 2018

26 Greer, Germaine, 'Summary', *The Female Eunuch*, Harper Perennial, New York, 2008, pp. 13–26

27 ibid.

28 Greer, *The Female Eunuch*, p. 57

29 ibid., p. 63

30 ibid., p. 69

31 ibid., p. 166

32 ibid., pp. 198–9

33 ibid., p. 203

34 Mailer, Norman, *An American Dream*, Dial Press, London, 1966, p. 25. Quoted in Greer, *The Female Eunuch*, p. 215

35 Greer, *The Female Eunuch*, p. 241

36 ibid., p. 264

37 ibid., p. 289

38 ibid., p. 335

39 University of Melbourne Archives, Germaine Greer Collection, digitised collections, *The Female Eunuch* editorial, draft 'Summary', http://hdl.handle.net/11343/42289, accessed 31 August 2018

40 University of Melbourne Archives, Germaine Greer Collection, General correspondence 1958–2014, 2014.0042.00686, Unit 83, copy of letter from Angela Phillips, Sheila Rowbotham, Liz Heron, Hilary Wainwright, Reva Klein, Kate Falcon, Gail Lewis and Judith Hunt published in the *Sunday Times*, 8 February 1984

41 University of Melbourne Archives, Germaine Greer Collection, General correspondence 1958–2014, 2014.0042.00308, Unit 38, letter from Helen Garner to Germaine Greer, 30 June 1971, reproduced with the kind permission of the author. Helen Garner (b. 1942) is an Australian novelist, short story writer and journalist whose first novel, *Monkey Grip*, established her as one of Australia's most accomplished writers. In 1972, she was sacked from the Victorian Education Department for giving an unscheduled sex-education lesson to her thirteen-year-old students. Her case became notorious as a watershed moment in the history of the department.

42 University of Melbourne Archives, Germaine Greer Collection, General correspondence 1958–2014, 2014.0042.00435, Unit 53, letter from Clive James to Germaine Greer, 23 July 1970

43 Greenfield, Robert, 'A groupie in women's lib', *Rolling Stone*, 7 January 1971

44 University of Melbourne Archives, Germaine Greer Collection, General correspondence 1958–2014, 2014.0042.00374, Unit 46, letter from Germaine Greer to Jim Haynes, 25 October 1972

45 University of Melbourne Archives, Germaine Greer Collection, General correspondence 1958–2014, 2014.0042.00374, Unit 46, letter from Jim Haynes to Germaine Greer, 20 March 1973

46 University of Melbourne Archives, Germaine Greer Collection, General correspondence 1958–2014, 2014.0042.00374, Unit 46, letter from Jim Haynes to Germaine Greer, 12 February 1974

47 University of Melbourne Archives, Germaine Greer Collection, General correspondence 1958–2014, 2014.0042.00374, Unit 46, letter from Jim Haynes to Germaine Greer, 28 February 1973

48 University of Melbourne Archives, Germaine Greer Collection, General correspondence 1958–2014, 2014.0042.00374, Unit 46, letter from Jim Haynes to Germaine Greer, 25 January 1991

49 University of Melbourne Archives, Germaine Greer Collection, General correspondence 1958–2014, 2014.0042.00374, Unit 46, letter from Germaine Greer to Sarah Hardie, Faber & Faber publishers, London, 17 February 1983

50 University of Melbourne Archives, Germaine Greer Collection, General correspondence 1958–2014, 2014.0042.00374, Unit 46, letter from Germaine Greer to Jim Haynes

51 *Melody Maker* was a respected British pop/rock/electronic music weekly newspaper. It was founded in 1926 and continued until 2000.

52 University of Melbourne Archives, Germaine Greer Collection, digitised collections, *The Female Eunuch* editorial, http://hdl.handle.net/11343/42289, accessed 31 August 2018

53 University of Melbourne Archives, Germaine Greer Collection, General correspondence 1958–2014, 2014.0042.00326, Unit 40, Germaine Greer and Tony Gourvish correspondence 1971–76

54 ibid.

55 ibid.

56 ibid.

57 ibid.

5 The commercialisation of Germaine Greer

1 Buchwald, Art, 'The bra burners', *New York Post*, 12 September 1968, https://library.duke.edu/digitalcollections/wlmpc_maddc02018, accessed 20 July 2018

2 Mailer, Norman, 'The prisoner of sex', *Harper's Magazine*, March 1971, pp. 41–92

3 Crawford, Leslie, 'Kate Millett, the ambivalent feminist', *Salon*, 5 June 1999, www.salon.com/1999/06/05/millet, accessed 24 May 2018

4 Greer, Germaine, 'The slag heap erupts', *Oz*, no. 26, February 1970, pp. 18–19. Reprinted in *The Madwoman's Underclothes: Essays and occasional writings 1968–1985*, Pan Books, London, 1986, p. 27

5 ibid.

6 Zito, Tom, 'The Greer career', *Washington Post*, 22 April 1971. Quoted in Wallace, Christine, *Untamed Shrew*, Richard Cohen Books, London, 2000, p. 179

7 Quoted in Mosmann, Petra, 'A feminist fashion icon: Germaine Greer's paisley coat', *Australian Feminist Studies*, vol. 31, no. 87, 2016, pp. 78–94

8 Dreifus, Claudia, 'The selling of a feminist', in Koedt, Anne, Levine, Ellen, and Rapone, Anita (eds), *Radical Feminism*, Quadrangle Books, New York, 1973, pp. 100–1

9 Pacifica Radio Archives, 'FTV 411 Germaine Greer at the National Press Club, 1971', From the Vault, posted 31 March 2014, http://fromthevaultradio.org/home/2014/03/31/ftv-411-germaine-greer-at-the-national-press-club-1971, accessed 21 June 2018

10 Johnston, Jill, *Lesbian Nation: The feminist solution*, Simon & Schuster, New York, p. 25

11 Greer, Germaine, 'My Mailer problem', *Esquire*, 7 September 1971, p. 80

12 Mailer, Norman, *The Prisoner of Sex*, Little Brown & Co., New York, 1971

13 Pennebaker, D.A., et al., *Town Bloody Hall*, documentary film, recorded 30 April 1971, distributed by Pennebaker Hedegus Films

14 Greer, 'My Mailer Problem', p. 80

15 Greer, *The Madwoman's Underclothes*

16 Mailer, Norman, *The Spooky Art: Some thoughts on writing*, Random House, New York, 2003, p. 282

17 Johnston, *Lesbian Nation*, p. 18

18 ibid., p. 19

19 ibid., p. 24

20 Pennebaker et al., *Town Bloody Hall*. There are also some clips of the debate available on YouTube.

21 Greer, 'My Mailer problem', p. 85

22 ibid., p. 88

23 University of Melbourne Archives, Germaine Greer Collection, Early years academic, performance, writing and personal papers 1957–2005, 2014.0044.00013, Unit 2, letter from Christopher Hitchens to Germaine Greer, 14 April 1979

24 Sheehan, Rebecca J., '"If we had more like her we would no longer be the unheard majority": Germaine Greer's reception in the United States', *Australian Feminist Studies*, vol. 31, no. 87, 2016, p. 10

25 ibid., pp. 25–6

26 The Women's Organization of Iran (WOI), created in 1966, was run mostly run by volunteers. Its committees worked on various issues of interest and importance to women. By 1975, the United Nations International Women's Year, the WOI had established 349 branches, 120 women's centres, a training centre and a centre for research. It was dismantled after the Islamic revolution in 1978.

27 Greer, Germaine, 'The Betty I knew', *The Guardian*, 8 February 2006, www.theguardian.com/world/2006/feb/07/gender.bookscomment, accessed 21 June 2018

28 ibid.

29 ibid.

30 Greer acknowledged that she had experienced lesbian relationships, but asserted that she was 'not homosexual'. 'I could have a strong and enduring relationship with a woman but it's never happened. What has happened is that on several occasions women have made strong

advances to me and I've been compelled to respond.' See Dreifus, Claudia, 'The life and loves of Germaine Greer', *Forum: The international journal of human relations*, vol. 7, no. 5, January 1975, pp. 12–19

31 Johnston, Jill, 'Germaine and Guillaume in Baltimore', *Village Voice*, New York, 22 April 1971, pp. 31–2

32 University of Melbourne Archives, Germaine Greer Collection, General correspondence 1958–2014, 2014.0042.00737, Unit 89, letter from Lillian Roxon to Germaine Greer, 1971

33 ibid.

34 University of Melbourne Archives, Germaine Greer Collection, General correspondence 1958–2014, 2014.0042.00737, Unit 89, letter from Germaine Greer to Lillian Roxon, 1971

35 University of Melbourne Archives, Germaine Greer Collection, General correspondence 1958–2014, 2014.0042.00737, Unit 89, letter from Lillian Roxon to Germaine Greer, 1971

36 University of Melbourne Archives, Germaine Greer Collection, General correspondence 1958–2014, 2014.0042.00267, Unit 33, letter from Germaine Greer to Louise Ferrier, 1 March 1972

37 University of Melbourne Archives, Germaine Greer Collection, General correspondence 1958–2014, 2014.0042.00267, Unit 33, letter from Louise Ferrier to Germaine Greer

38 University of Melbourne Archives, Germaine Greer Collection, General Correspondence, 2014.0042.00737, Unit 89, letter from Germaine Greer to Nika Hazelton, 30 September 1973

39 University of Melbourne Archives, Germaine Greer Collection, General correspondence 1958–2014, 2014.0042.00737, Unit 89, letter from Germaine Greer to 'Dearest Lonni', 30 September (no year)

40 University of Melbourne Archives, Germaine Greer Collection, General correspondence 1958–2014, 2014.0042.00737, Unit 89, letter from Germaine Greer to Nika Hazelton

41 Cook, Andrew, 'Hinch hits back at Greer's Roxon death claims', *Crikey*, 11 August 2010, www.crikey.com.au/2010/08/11/hinch-hits-back-at-greers-roxon-death-claims, accessed 21 June 2018

42 University of Melbourne Archives, Germaine Greer Collection, General correspondence 1958–2014, 2014.0042.00737, Unit 44, Lillian Roxon to David Harcourt, 1971

43 Hancock, Ian, 'Events and issues that made the news in 1972', National Archives of Australia, www.naa.gov.au/collection/explore/cabinet/by-year/1972-events-issues.aspx, accessed 21 June 2018.

Graham Freudenberg was Australian Prime Minister Gough Whitlam's one-time speechwriter.

44 'That girl Germaine flies out in silence', *The Age*, 12 January 1972, p. 1

45 Keavney, Kay, 'The liberating of Germaine Greer', *Australian Women's Weekly*, 2 February 1972, pp. 4–5

46 Australian Broadcasting Commission, 'Germaine Greer and women's liberation, 1972', clip from *This Day Tonight*, first broadcast 22 March 1972, ABC Education, http://splash.abc.net.au/home#!/media/1245334/germaine-greer-and-women-s-liberation-1972, accessed 21 June 2018

47 ibid.

48 Forshaw, Thelma, 'Feminist yen for a grizzle and a bit of rough', *The Age*, 15 January 1972, p. 10

49 Fry, Elsie, Letter to the Editor, 'A book that is unhealthy', *The Age*, 20 January 1972, p. 9

50 Faust, Beatrice, 'The Germaine question', *Australian Humanist*, no. 21, 1972, p. 2

51 Conversation between Elizabeth Kleinhenz and Phillip Frazer, Byron Bay, 27 July 2017

52 University of Melbourne Archives, Germaine Greer Collection, General correspondence 1958–2014, 2014.0042.00267, Unit 33, letter from Germaine Greer to Louise Ferrier

53 ibid.

54 Conversation between Elizabeth Kleinhenz and Richard Walsh, Sydney, 14 February 2017

55 Sue Kedgley is a New Zealand politician and author. She worked for the United Nations for eight years and was also a television presenter, director and producer. She represented the Green Party in the New Zealand parliament from 1999 to 2011.

56 Kedgley, Sue, 'Caught in the crossfire: Women's liberation in the seventies', speech given to the Green Party of Aotearoa New Zealand, 4 December 2014

57 University of Melbourne Archives, Germaine Greer Collection, General correspondence 1958–2014, 2014.0042.00491, Unit 60, photocopy of court transcript 'Police v. Germaine Greer – a charge of indecent language', Magistrate's Court, Auckland, New Zealand, date of hearing 10 March 1972

58 Greer, Germaine, 'Bye-bye bull-shit', *The Review*, 18–24 March 1972, p. 621

59 Australian Broadcasting Commission, 'Germaine Greer and women's liberation, 1972'

6 Wind of Tizoula

1   Anonymous Berber woman's song, quoted in Warnock Fernea, Elizabeth, and Bezirgan, Basima Qattan, *Middle Eastern Muslim Women Speak*, University of Texas Press, Austin and London, 1977, p. 134. The song was quoted by Germaine Greer as part of the chapter heading for Chapter 3 of *Sex and Destiny: The politics of human fertility*, Harper & Row, New York, 1984, p. 59

2   Greer, Germaine, 'Taking the Queen out of the picture', *Financial Times*, 7–8 February 1998, p. 4, copy held in University of Melbourne Archives, Germaine Greer Collection, Print journalism 1959–2010, 2014.0046.00476, Unit 8

3   Greer, Germaine, Country Notebook, 'Memories', *The Telegraph*, 16 February 2002, www.telegraph.co.uk/gardening/3297630/Country-notebook-memories.html, accessed 19 June 2018

4   ibid.

5   University of Melbourne Archives, Germaine Greer Collection, Early years academic, performance, writing and personal papers 1957–2005, 2014.0044.00168, Unit 12, correspondence between Germaine Greer and David Brooke, July and August 1971

6   University of Melbourne Archives, Germaine Greer Collection, Early years academic, performance, writing and personal papers 1957–2005, 2014.0044.00168, Unit 12, letter from Germaine Greer to Clive Bush, 29 August 1971

7   University of Melbourne Archives, Germaine Greer Collection, General correspondence 1958–2014, 2014.0042.00688, Unit 83, letter from Nat Lehrman, *Playboy* editor, to Diana Crawfurd, 8 July 1971

8   Lehrman, Nat, Germaine Greer Interview, *Playboy*, January 1972, p. 27

9   Dunstan, Keith, *Ratbags*, Golden Press Limited, Sydney, 1979, pp. 259–64

10 Greer, Germaine, 'Blame the English, blame the frost, but Tuscany is so over', *The Independent*, 28 March 2004, www.independent.co.uk/voices/commentators/germaine-greer-blame-the-english-blame-the-frost-but-tuscany-is-so-over-567881.html, accessed 21 June 2018

11   University of Melbourne Archives, Germaine Greer Collection, Early years academic, performance, writing and personal papers 1957–2005, 2014.0044.00168, Unit 12, letter from Germaine Greer to Clive Bush, 29 August 1971

12   University of Melbourne Archives, Germaine Greer Collection, General correspondence 1958–2014, 2014.0042.00154, Unit 19, draft of introduction by Greer to a book of poetry by Gay Clifford

13   University of Melbourne Archives, Germaine Greer Collection, General correspondence 1958–2014, 2014.0042.00739, Unit 89, letter from Germaine Greer to Franki Roberts, 1971

14   Smart, Jeffrey, *Not Quite Straight: A memoir*, William Heinemann, Melbourne, 1996, p. 420. Quoted in Drakard, Jane, 'Elusive landscapes: Australians and "the Italian garden"', in Kent, Bill, Pesman, Ros and Troup, Cynthia (eds), *Australians in Italy: Contemporary lives and impressions*, Monash University Publishing, http://books.publishing.monash.edu/apps/bookworm/view/Australians+in+Italy%3A+Contemporary+Lives+and+Impressions/52/Ch18_AI.html, accessed 30 August 2018

15   Zeroni, Tiziana, 'Germaine Greer: Her heart is in Tuscany', *Northern Territory News*, 3 April 1982. Quoted in Drakard, 'Elusive landscapes'

16   Greer, Germaine, 'Federico Fellini wanted to cast me in Casanova. We ended up in bed together', *The Guardian*, 12 April 2010, www.theguardian.com/culture/2010/apr/11/germaine-greer-federico-fellini, accessed 22 June 2018

17   University of Melbourne Archives, Germaine Greer Collection, General correspondence 1958–2014, 2014.0042.00739, Unit 89, letter from Franki Roberts to Germaine Greer, 3 September 1973

18   'A drift on Germaine Greer: One telling incident, feminism, modern day shameless Ranterism, wreckage and total loss', Revolt Against Plenty, September 2007, www.revoltagainstplenty.com/index.php/archive-local/49-a-drift-on-germaine-greer-feminism-and-modern-day-shameless-ranterism.html, accessed 22 June 2018

19   Greer, Germaine, 'My most gracious and beautiful dwelling', *The Guardian*, 22 October 2007, www.theguardian.com/artanddesign/2007/oct/22/architecture, accessed 22 June 2018

20   The Women's Electoral Lobby is a political lobby group that was founded by Beatrice Faust in 1972. It surveys state and federal political candidates on their policies regarding women.

21   Germaine Greer quoted in *Sunday Times*, London, 7 December 1975

22   Roots, Hilary, 'Germaine Greer: Why I want a baby . . .', *Australian Women's Weekly*, 14 January 1976, pp. 2–5, https://trove.nla.gov. au/aww/read/224700?q=Germaine+Greer&s=0&resultId=num4# page/4/mode/1up, accessed 22 June 2018

23   ibid.

24   Wallace, Christine, *Untamed Shrew*, Pan Macmillan Australia, Sydney, 1977, p. 221

25   Roots, 'Germaine Greer: Why I want a baby . . .', p. 3

26   The Gräfenberg ring, an early IUD contraceptive device, was developed by Ernst Gräfenberg in 1929. In *Sex and Destiny*, Germaine Greer notes: 'The Grafenberg ring was still being fitted by discreet doctors in a handpicked clientele as far afield as Victoria, Australia, in the 1950s.'

27   Greer, Germaine, 'The truth is, says Germaine Greer, I was desperate for a baby and I have the medical bills to prove it', *Aura*, March 2000, pp. 23–6

28   Grizzuti-Harrison, Barbara, 'Germaine Greer: After the change', *Mirabella*, September 1992, p. 90. Quoted in Wallace, *Untamed Shrew*, p. 221

29   Hughes-Onslow, James, 'My doomed love for Ms Greer', *Daily Mail*, 20 February 1999, p. 20

30   ibid.

31   ibid.

32   Simons, Margaret, '"The long letter to a short love, or . . .": In her love letter novella to Martin Amis, Germaine Greer bared her fragile heart and complex soul', *Meanjin*, vol. 74, no. 4, Summer 2015, pp. 28–44

33   ibid.

34   ibid.

35   Nochlin, Linda, 'Women painters and Germaine Greer', *New York Times*, 28 October 1979, www.nytimes.com/1979/10/28/archives/ women-painters-and-germaine-greer-artists-greer.html, accessed 22 June 2018

36   Brophy, Brigid, 'The one-eyed world of Germaine Greer', *London Review of Books*, 22 November 1979, www.lrb.co.uk/v01/n03/ brigid-brophy/the-one-eyed-world-of-germaine-greer, accessed 20 July 2018

37   Fell, Liz, Interview with Germaine Greer for ABC Radio *The Coming Out Show*, 25 January 1979, quoted in Wallace, *Untamed Shrew*, pp. 223–4

38 University of Melbourne Archives, Germaine Greer Collection, Early years academic, performance, writing and personal papers 1957–2005, 2014.0044.0014, Unit 2, correspondence relating to Greer's taxation problems, March 1978 – September 1979: Felton, Anton; Felton & Partners, accountants; Collector of Taxes, London; Controller of Inland Revenue, London; Inland Revenue Enforcement Office, London; Peter Grose, London

39 ibid.

40 Chambers, Andrea, 'Witty, raunchy and nobody's eunuch, Germaine Greer is teaching Tulsa a thing or two', *People*, 17 December 1979, https://people.com/archive/witty-raunchy-and-nobodys-eunuch-germaine-greer-is-teaching-tulsa-a-thing-or-two-vol-12-no-25, accessed 20 June 2018

41 Boeth, Richard, 'Naugahyde mouth meets the Sooner aesthetic', *Westward: Dallas Times Herald*, 21 February 1981

42 ibid.

43 Chambers, 'Witty, raunchy and nobody's eunuch, Germaine Greer is teaching Tulsa a thing or two'

44 ibid.

45 University of Melbourne Archives, Germaine Greer Collection, General correspondence 1958–2014, 2014.0042.0131, Unit 16, correspondence between Germaine Greer and a young girl, 24 April 1980, 22 May 1980

46 University of Melbourne Archives, Germaine Greer Collection, General correspondence 1958–2014, 2104.0042.00041, Unit 5, photograph of John

47 Boeth, 'Naugahyde mouth meets the Sooner aesthetic'

48 University of Melbourne Archives, Germaine Greer Collection, General correspondence 1958–2014, 2014.0042.00041, Unit 5, correspondence between John Attwood and Germaine Greer. Most letters are undated.

49 ibid.

50 University of Melbourne Archives, Germaine Greer Collection, Early years academic, performance, writing and personal papers 1957–2005, 2014.0044.00014, Unit 2, letter from Felton & Partners, accountants, to Germaine Greer, 3 April 1981

51 University of Melbourne Archives, Germaine Greer Collection, years academic, performance, writing and personal papers 1957–2005, 2014.0044.00016, Unit 3, letter from Harbottle & Lewis, London, solicitors, to Germaine Greer, 25 September 1981

52 Plante, David, *Difficult Women*, E.P. Dutton, New York, 1983, p. 120

53 University of Melbourne Archives, Germaine Greer Collection, General correspondence 1958–2014, 2014.0042.00041, Unit 5, correspondence between John Attwood and Germaine Greer

54 Plante, *Difficult Women*, p. 126

55 ibid., p. 128

56 ibid., p. 126

57 University of Melbourne Archives, Germaine Greer Collection, General correspondence 1958–2014, 2014.0042.00041, Unit 5, correspondence between John Attwood and Germaine Greer

58 Greer, Germaine, 'Reality can bite back', *The Guardian*, 5 August 2006, www.theguardian.com/commentisfree/2006/aug/05/bookscomment, accessed 22 June 2018

7 Recalibration

1 Greer later declared that she had never suffered from an STD. 'Despite a lifetime of service to the cause of sexual liberation,' she wrote in an article for the *Sunday Times*, 'I have never caught a venereal disease, which makes me feel rather like an arctic explorer who has never had frostbite. I have several times had occasion to verify the fact beyond any doubt and have not always fared well. My NHS doctor in the Midlands fixed me with a terrible stare and asked me what else I expected, given the life I led.' Greer, Germaine, 'It's time that VD was socially accepted', *Sunday Times*, 25 February 1973, copy held in University of Melbourne Archives, Germaine Greer Collection, Print Journalism, 2014.0046.00078, Unit 2

2 Greer, Germaine, *Sex and Destiny: The politics of human fertility*, Harper & Row, New York, 1984

3 ibid., pp. 70–1

4 James, Clive, 'A question of quality', *The Observer*, 3 February 1980, quoted in Greer, *Sex and Destiny*, p. 44

5 Greer, *Sex and Destiny*, p. 43

6 Mason, Michael, 'Thought control', *London Review of Books*, vol. 6, no. 5, 15 March 1984, pp. 3–4

7 Greer, *Sex and Destiny*, p. 257

8 University of Melbourne Archives, Germaine Greer Collection, General correspondence 1958–2014, 2014.0042.00358, Unit 44, 'WH' to Germaine Greer

9   Singer, Peter, 'Sex & superstition', *New York Review of Books*, 31 May 1984, www.nybooks.com/articles/1984/05/31/sex-superstition, accessed 22 June 2018

10 Plante, David, *Becoming a Londoner: A diary*, Bloomsbury, New York, 2013, p. 440

11 ibid., p. 441

12 ibid., p. 442

13 ibid., p. 444

14 The iconic Reading Room of the British Museum, officially opened on 2 May 1857, was used by many famous writers, including Rudyard Kipling, Karl Marx, H.G. Wells and Vladimir Lenin. In 1973, the British Library Trust detached the library department from the Museum. In 1997, the British Library moved to its own specially constructed building near St Pancras station. All books and shelving were removed from the Reading Room. From 2000 it was used for exhibitions, but the building is now closed to visitors and its future remains uncertain. The Reading Room of the Melbourne Public Library (now the State Library of Victoria), where Germaine Greer spent much time in her student days, was modelled on the old Reading Room at the British Museum.

15 University of Melbourne Archives, Germaine Greer Collection, General Correspondence, 2014.0042.00065, Unit 8, letter from Germaine Greer to Anne Barton, 9 January 1985

16 Hughes-Onslow, James, 'My doomed love for Ms Greer', *Daily Mail*, 20 February 1999, p. 20. Hughes-Onslow contacted Greer before he wrote this article to ask for her approval. She responded, 'By all means write the piece.' But it would not be with her approval. After the article was published, he sent her a copy that is now housed in University of Melbourne Archives, Germaine Greer Collection, General correspondence 1958–2014, 2014.0042.00413, Unit 50

17 Polly Toynbee and Jill Tweedie were best known for their columns in *The Guardian*. The purpose of this visit was to assist in the promotion of Germaine Greer's latest book, *Kissing the Rod*. Both women are commemorated in a group portrait in the British National Gallery that also includes *Guardian* Women's Page contributors, Mary Stott, Posy Simmons and Liz Forgan.

18 Toynbee, Polly, 'Behind the lines: Ironing in the soul', in Cochrane, Kira (ed.), *Women of the Revolution: Forty years of feminism*, Guardian Books, London, 2010, pp. 123–33

19   Fallowell, Duncan, *20th Century Characters*, Vintage, London, 1994, p. 18

20   Greer, Germaine, 'Where the chill wind blows', *The Observer Magazine*, 13 April 1986

21   University of Melbourne Archives, Germaine Greer Collection, Print journalism 1959–2010, 2014.0046.00500, Unit 8, Greer, Germaine, typed copy faxed and emailed to Tiffany Daneff, *Daily Telegraph* (not published), 17 July 1999

22   University of Melbourne Archives, Germaine Greer Collection, General correspondence 1958–2014, 2014.0042.00072, Unit 9, Correspondence between Germaine Greer and a house guest, May 1986

23   University of Melbourne Archives, Germaine Greer Collection, General correspondence 1958–2014, 2014.0042.00543, Unit 66, letter from Paul McHugh to Germaine Greer, 26 January 1992

24   Greer, Germaine, 'Translating for Tynan and Canada versus New York', in Craven, Peter (ed.), *The Best Australian Essays: 1999*, Bookman Press, Melbourne, 1999, pp. 11–20

25   Fitzpatrick, Kate, *Airmail: Three women, letters from five continents*, John Wiley & Sons Australia, Milton, Queensland, 2005

26   Fitzpatrick, Kate, *Name Dropping: An incomplete memoir*, Harper-Collins, Pymble, New South Wales, 2010, pp. 391

27   Greer, Germaine, 'The false gods of poetry', *Sunday Times*, 3 June 1990

28   University of Melbourne Archives, Germaine Greer Collection, General correspondence 1958–2014, 2014.0042.00154, Unit 19, letter from Germaine Greer to Pam Clifford

29   University of Melbourne Archives, Germaine Greer Collection, General correspondence 1958–2014, 2014.0042.00154, Unit 19, letter from Germaine Greer to Pam Clifford, 16 March 1986

30   University of Melbourne Archives, Germaine Greer Collection, General correspondence 1958–2014, 2014.0042.00154, Unit 19, letter from Germaine Greer to Pam and Freddie Clifford, 11 August 1986

31   University of Melbourne Archives, Germaine Greer Collection, General correspondence 1958–2014, 2014.0042.00154, Unit 19, draft of introduction by Greer to a book of poetry by Gay Clifford

32   University of Melbourne Archives, Germaine Greer Collection, General correspondence 1958–2014, 2014.0042.00154, Unit 19, Address given by Germaine Greer at the Thanksgiving Service for Gay

Clifford at Holy Trinity Church, Minchinhampton, Gloucestershire, 6 August 1998

33 Virago Press was founded by Carmen Callil in 1973 and was the first mass-market publisher of books for and by women.

34 Email correspondence between Elizabeth Kleinhenz and Carmen Callil, 2017

35 University of Melbourne Archives, Germaine Greer Collection, Print journalism 1959–2010, 2014.0046.00180, Unit 4, draft titled 'Callil interviewed by Greer', sent to Gail Heathwood of *Vogue* magazine

36 Hoggart, Simon in *The Guardian*, 8 February 1994, copy held in University of Melbourne Archives, Germaine Greer Collection, Print journalism 1959–2010, 2014.0046.00400, Unit 6

37 University of Melbourne Archives, Germaine Greer Collection, Print journalism 1959–2010, 2014.0046.00400, Unit 6

38 Greer, Germaine, Country Notebook, 'Home truths about John Peel', *Daily Telegraph*, 13 June 2006, copy held in University of Melbourne Archives, Germaine Greer Collection, Print journalism 1959–2010, 2014.0046.00577, Unit 10

39 University of Melbourne Archives, Germaine Greer Collection, General correspondence 1958–2014, 2014.0042.00027, Unit 4, letter to Germaine Greer. (Greer notes that this letter is from an 'anon maniac'.)

40 ibid.

41 University of Melbourne Archives, Germaine Greer Collection, General correspondence 1958–2014, 2014.0042.00638, Unit 78, correspondence between Germaine Greer and Peter O'Shaughnessy

42 University of Melbourne Archives, Germaine Greer Collection, General correspondence 1958–2014, 2014.0042.00027, Unit 4, letter from Germaine Greer to Cambridgeshire Constabulary, 26 May 1988, and their reply, 10 June 1988

43 Sapsted, David, 'Stalker jumped on Greer crying "Mummy, Mummy"', *The Telegraph*, 5 July 2000, www.telegraph.co.uk/news/uknews/1346664/Stalker-jumped-on-Greer-crying-Mummy-Mummy.html, accessed 19 July 2018

44 Clout, Laura, 'West End play "The Female of the Species" angers Germaine Greer', *The Telegraph*, London, 13 July 2008, www.telegraph.co.uk/news/uknews/2403697/West-End-play-The-Female-of-the-Species-angers-Germaine-Greer.html, accessed 19 July 2018

45 University of Melbourne Archives, Germaine Greer Collection, General correspondence 1958–2014, 2014.0042.00299, Unit 37, piece for *Front Row* BBC Radio 4 about *The Female of the Species*

46 Conversation between Elizabeth Kleinhenz and Christine Wallace, Melbourne, 23 February 2018

47 University of Melbourne Archives, Germaine Greer Collection, General correspondence 1958–2014, 2014.0042.00974, Unit 113, letter from Germaine Greer to her solicitor, addressed to 'Geoffrey', with copy of letter sent to Pan Macmillan, 4 November 1999

48 Wallace, Christine, 'Metaphors from a compost heap', *The Guardian*, 2 November 1994, copy held in University of Melbourne Archives, Germaine Greer Collection, General correspondence 1958–2014, 2014.0042.00974, Unit 113

49 Email correspondence between Elizabeth Kleinhenz and Christine Wallace, January 2018

50 Brown, Tina, *Sydney Morning Herald* article quoted in Wallace, Christine, *Untamed Shrew*, Richard Cohen Books, London, 2000, p. 246

51 Greer, Germaine, *Daddy, We Hardly Knew You*, Ballantine Books, New York, 1989, pp. 3–4

52 ibid.

53 Fallowell, *20th Century Characters*, p. 18

54 Greer, *Daddy, We Hardly Knew You*, p. 17

55 ibid., p. 281

56 ibid., pp. 246–7

57 University of Melbourne Archives, Germaine Greer Collection, General correspondence 1958–2014, 2014.0042.00236, Unit 29, letter from Ross Dunham, Launceston, to Germaine Greer, 1992

8   *The Change*

1 Greer, Germaine, *The Change: Women, aging and the menopause*, Ballantine Books, New York, 1991, p. 31

2 ibid., p. 12

3 ibid., pp. 297–8

4 ibid., p. 338

5 ibid., p. 86

6 ibid., p. 174. In 1994, two years into her own menopause, Greer confided to writer Duncan Fallowell that she had experienced severe menopausal symptoms that included sleeplessness and teeth-grinding. She had 'given in' to having HRT. See Fallowell, Duncan, *20th Century Characters*, Vintage, London, 1994, p. 22

7 Greer, *The Change*, p. 246

8   Greer, Germaine, 'A life in the day of Germaine Greer', *Sunday Times*, 3 August 1986

9   University of Melbourne Archives, Germaine Greer Collection, General correspondence 1958–2014, 2014.0042.00640, Unit 78, faxed correspondence between Germaine Greer and Richard Ingrams

10 Greer, Germaine, 'We shall not be neutered', *The Spectator*, 20 May 1995, p. 54, copy held in University of Melbourne Archives, Germaine Greer Collection, Print journalism 1959–2010, 2014.0046.00425, Unit 7

11 Moore, Suzanne, and Greer, Germaine, articles in *The Guardian*, copies held in University of Melbourne Archives, Germaine Greer Collection, Print journalism 1959–2010, 2014.0046.00431, Unit 7

12 University of Melbourne Archives, Germaine Greer Collection, Print journalism 1959–2010, 2014.0046.00431, Unit 7, copy faxed to Nicholas Wapshott for *The Times Magazine*, 5 June 1995

13 Berman, Paul, 'The Rushdie affair and the struggle against Islamism', *New Republic*, 7 December 2012, https://newrepublic.com/article/110804/who-are-the-real-blasphemers, accessed 20 June 2018

14 Elie, Paul, 'A fundamental fight', *Vanity Fair*, May 2014, www.vanityfair.com/culture/2014/05/salman-rushdie-ian-mcwean-martin-amis-satanic-verses-fatwa, accessed 12 June 2018

15 Ball, Graham, 'Fay Weldon hits back at the Islamically correct', *The Independent*, 2 March 1997, www.independent.co.uk/news/uk/home-news/fay-weldon-hits-back-at-the-islamically-correct-1270602.html, accessed 22 June 2018

16 Moir, Jan, '"We're all living under a fatwa: you just have to get on"', *The Telegraph*, 18 August 2006, www.telegraph.co.uk/culture/books/3654603/Were-all-living-under-a-fatwa-you-just-have-to-get-on.html, accessed 20 July 2018

17 Rushdie, Salman, *Joseph Anton: A memoir*, Random House, New York, 2012, p. 187

18 Rae, Fiona, 'Germaine Greer: Glitter-bomb neither here nor there', *The Listener*, 26 March 2012, www.noted.co.nz/archive/listener-nz-2012/germaine-greer-glitter-bomb-neither-here-nor-there, accessed 22 June 2018

19 The UK *Gender Recognition Act 2004* gives people with gender dysphoria legal recognition as members of the sex appropriate to their gender (masculine or feminine), allowing them to acquire a Gender Recognition Certificate that affords recognition of their sex in law, including for the purposes of marriage. The two main exceptions are

a right of conscience for Church of England clergy (who are normally obliged to marry any two eligible people by law), and that the descent of peerages will remain unchanged. Additionally, sports organisations are allowed to exclude trans people if it is necessary for 'fair competition or the safety of the competitors'.

20 Greer, Germaine, *The Whole Woman*, Anchor Books, New York, 2000, p. 5

21 ibid., pp. 23–4

22 ibid., p. 149

23 ibid., p. 101

24 American Academy of Pediatrics Committee on Bioethics, 'Female genital mutilation', *Pediatrics*, vol. 102, no. 1, July 1998, https://pediatrics.aappublications.org/content/102/1/153, accessed 22 June 2018

25 Greer, *The Whole Woman*, p. 102

26 ibid., p. 332

27 ibid., p. 334

28 ibid., p. 142

29 University of Melbourne Archives, Germaine Greer Collection, General correspondence 1958–2014, 2014.0042.00584, Unit 71, correspondence between Germaine Greer and Kiri and Jennie Morley, December 1999

9 Coming home

1 'The Lay of the Last Minstrel' is a long narrative poem in six cantos by Walter Scott, published in 1805.

2 University of Melbourne Archives, Germaine Greer Collection, Audio recordings produced and received by Greer 1971–2010, 2014.0040.00100, Unit 3, Diary 1997, audio diary recorded while walking her dogs on the fields near her home. In this quote she is reflecting on her performance on a BBC breakfast television show.

3 University of Melbourne Archives, Germaine Greer Collection, General correspondence 1958–2014, 2014.0042.00492, Unit 60, letter to Germaine Greer from Sam Leith, Eton, 20 June 1992

4 University of Melbourne Archives, Germaine Greer Collection, Audio recordings produced and received by Greer 1971–2010, 2014.0040.00100, Unit 3, Diary 1997, audio diary recorded while walking her dogs on the fields near her home

5 ibid.

6   Greer, Germaine, Stump Cross Roundabout, *The Oldie*, no. 16, 18 September 1992, copy held in University of Melbourne Archives, Germaine Greer Collection, Print journalism 1959–2010, 2014.0046.00275, Unit 5. The 'hollow girl' is a reference to T.S. Eliot's poem 'The Hollow Men'.

7   Greer, Germaine, Country Notebook, 'Housewives in Strasbourg', *Daily Telegraph*, 25 November 2000, copy held in University of Melbourne Archives, Germaine Greer Collection, Print journalism 1959–2010, 2014.0046.00601, Unit 10

8   Greer, Germaine, Country Notebook, 'These days, I prefer nature, not nurture', *Daily Telegraph*, 22 April 2000, p. 11, copy held in University of Melbourne Archives, Germaine Greer Collection, Print journalism 1959–2010, 2014.0046.00570, Unit 10

9   Fallowell, Duncan, *20th Century Characters*, Vintage, London, 1994, p. 13

10 Greer, Germaine, *White Beech: The rainforest years*, Bloomsbury, London, 2013, p. 38

11 ibid., p. 93

12 ibid.

13 'Queenslanders' are houses built on high stumps so that the living areas are raised off the ground. This allows for good ventilation in the hot, humid climate and also protects the house from termite infestation. Most Queenslanders have wide verandahs. The space under the house is used for storage, drying washing, or for extra cool living space in the hot months.

14 University of Melbourne Archives, Germaine Greer Collection, Audio recordings produced and received by Greer 1971–2010, 2014.0040.00116, Unit 3, audio diary recorded by Germaine Greer at Cave Creek, 2003

15 ibid.

16 Greer, *White Beech*, p. 295

17 The Australian Institute of Aboriginal and Torres Strait Islander Studies (AIATSIS), established in 1961, is devoted to the study of Indigenous culture and history. It incorporates disciplines such as anthropology, archaeology, art, health, education, linguistics and ethnomusicology.

18 Greer, *White Beech*, p. 140

19 University of Melbourne Archives, Germaine Greer Collection, Honoris causa and recognition 1963–2014, 2017.0028.00004, Unit 1, letter from Germaine Greer to W.E. Chapman, Secretary for

Appointments, Prime Minister's Department, 10 Downing Street, London, 28 November 1999

20 Greer, Germaine, *Whitefella Jump Up: The shortest way to nationhood*, Profile Books, London, 2004, p. 23

21 ibid., p. 3

22 ibid., p. 2

23 ibid., p. 35

24 Bobbi Sykes (1943–2010) was an Australian poet and author. She was a lifelong campaigner for the rights of Indigenous people, although she was not herself of Aboriginal descent.

25 University of Melbourne Archives, Germaine Greer Collection, General correspondence 1958–2014, 2014.0042.00267, Unit 33, letter from Germaine Greer to Louise Ferrier, 1 March 1972

26 Greer, *Whitefella Jump Up*, p. 37

27 Cowlishaw, Gillian, *Rednecks, Eggheads and Blackfellas: A study of racial power and intimacy in Australia*, Allen & Unwin, St Leonards, New South Wales, 1999, quoted in Greer, *Whitefella Jump Up*, p. 38

28 Jordan, Mary Ellen, 'Response', in Greer, *Whitefella Jump Up*, p. 187

29 Greer, *Whitefella Jump Up*, p. 52

30 Millett, Patsy, 'Response', in Greer, *Whitefella Jump Up*, p. 204

31 Durack Clancy, P.A., 'Response', in Greer, *Whitefella Jump Up*, p. 146

32 Greer, *Whitefella Jump Up*, p. 226

33 Langton, Marcia, 'Response', in Greer, *Whitefella Jump Up*, pp. 158–70

34 Greer, *Whitefella Jump Up*, p. 222

35 ibid., pp. 226–7

36 Langton, Marcia, 'Greer maintains rage of racists', *The Australian*, 19 August 2008, www.theaustralian.com.au/opinion/greer-maintains-rage-of-racists/news-story/2a157d5b9029135ae6ac609a047a0769?sv=8bc403754767577667e3e26b0649c551, accessed 22 June 2018

37 University of Melbourne Archives, Germaine Greer Collection, General correspondence 1958–2014, 2014.0042.00185, Unit 23, Correspondence between Germaine Greer and Roy Colquhoun, July 2007

38 University of Melbourne Archives, Germaine Greer Collection, Print journalism 1959–2010, 2014.0046.00983, Unit 18

39 Devine, Miranda, 'Generation of taboo breakers are a selfish lot', *Sydney Morning Herald*, 10 July 2003, www.smh.com.au/articles/2003/07/09/1057430278896.html, accessed 22 June 2018

40 *Enough Rope with Andrew Denton*, ABC TV, 15 September 2003, transcript, www.abc.net.au/tv/enoughrope/transcripts/s946782.htm, accessed 6 June 2017

41 University of Melbourne Archives, Germaine Greer Collection, 2014.0042.00024, Unit 3, Correspondence (mostly anon)

42 Britain, Ian, 'Mad about The Boy', *Australian Book Review*, December 2003/January 2004, pp. 11–12

43 Greer, Germaine, 'If Michelle Obama's such a great dresser, what was she doing in this red butcher's apron?' *The Guardian*, 17 November 2008, www.theguardian.com/world/2008/nov/17/michelleobama-fashion, accessed 20 July 2018

44 'Politics and porn in a post-feminist world', *Q&A*, ABC TV, 19 March 2012, transcript, www.abc.net.au/tv/qanda/txt/s3451584.htm, accessed 22 June 2018

45 Clarke-Billings, Lucy, 'Germaine Greer in transgender rant: "Just because you lop off your penis . . . it doesn't make you a woman"', *The Telegraph*, 26 October 2015, www.telegraph.co.uk/news/health/news/11955891/Germaine-Greer-in-transgender-rant-Just-because-you-lop-off-your-penis...it-doesnt-make-you-a-woman.html, accessed 22 June 2018

46 Twitter user @FameForNothing, 26 October 2015, quoted in Clarke-Billings, 'Germaine Greer in transgender rant'

47 Llewellyn Smith, Julia, 'Barry Humphries: "Caitlyn Jenner is a publicity-seeking ratbag", *The Telegraph*, 5 January 2016, www.telegraph.co.uk/comedy/comedians/barry-humphries-caitlyn-jenner-is-a-publicity-seeking-ratbag, accessed 22 June 2018

48 Gayle, Damien, 'Caitlyn Jenner "wanted limelight of female Kardashians" – Germaine Greer', *The Guardian*, 25 October 2015, www.theguardian.com/books/2015/oct/24/caitlyn-jenner-wanted-limelight-of-female-kardashians-germaine-greer, accessed 22 June 2018

49 Quinn, Ben, 'Petition urges Cardiff University to cancel Germaine Greer lecture', *The Guardian*, 24 October 2015, www.theguardian.com/education/2015/oct/23/petition-urges-cardiff-university-to-cancel--germain-greer-lecture, accessed 20 July 2018

50 McMahon, Alle, 'Germaine Greer defends views on transgender issues amid calls for cancellation of feminism lecture', 25 October 2015, www.abc.net.au/news/2015-10-25/germaine-greer-defends-views-on-transgender-issues/6883132, accessed 13 June 2018

10 Full circle

1   University of Melbourne Archives, Germaine Greer Collection, Print journalism 1959–2010, 2014.0046.00437, Unit 7, Germaine Greer to Peter Forbes, editor, *Poetry Review*

2   University of Melbourne Archives, Germaine Greer Collection, Print journalism 1959–2010, 2014.0046.00438, Unit 7, Germaine Greer to Georgina Goodman, editor, *Elle*, 23 August 1995

3   University of Melbourne Archives, Germaine Greer Collection, Print journalism 1959–2010, 2014.0046.00453, Unit 7, correspondence between Germaine Greer and Bill Buford, senior editor, *New Yorker* magazine, July 1996

4   University of Melbourne Archives, Germaine Greer Collection, Print journalism 1959–2010, Unit 7, 2014.0046.00453, Draft copy of article 'Singin' in the Rain' by Germaine Greer (not published), in correspondence between Germaine Greer and Bill Buford, senior editor, *New Yorker* magazine, July 1996

5   Morgan, Joyce, 'Sydney Festival review: Mailer and Greer trade hammerblows in early feminist fracas', *Sydney Morning Herald*, 8 January 2018, www.smh.com.au/entertainment/sydney-festival-review-mailer-and-greer-trade-hammerblows-in-early-feminist-fracas-20180108-h0eyu7.html, accessed 22 June 2018. The reviewer gave *The Town Hall Affair* 2.5 stars out of 5.

6   Miller, Nick, 'Germaine Greer challenges #MeToo campaign', *Sydney Morning Herald*, 21 January 2018, www.smh.com.au/world/germaine-greer-challenges-metoo-campaign-20180121-h0lpra, accessed 22 June 2018

7   Panahi, Rita, 'The #MeToo sisterhood is on a witch hunt', *Herald Sun*, 14 January 2018, www.heraldsun.com.au/news/opinion/rita-panahi/rita-panahi-the-metoo-sisterhood-is-on-a-witch-hunt/news-story/4472c7fdc58608b7d3bcf556bdc701f5, accessed 22 June 2018

8   University of Melbourne Archives, Germaine Greer Collection, Audio recordings produced and received by Greer 1971–2010, 2014.0040.00032, Unit 1, Germaine Greer interviewed by Dr Anthony Clare for the BBC Radio 4 program *In the Psychiatrist's Chair*, 23 August 1989

Index